BIG GUN
BATTLES

1. All the American battleships at Surigao Strait were supplied with flashless propellent for their main battery guns. As this image of *West Virginia* (BB48) firing a half-salvo from her after turrets attests, 'flashless' was a relative term. Flashless powder burned more quickly (and less completely) than the more conventional 'smokeless' powder developed for daylight engagements, meaning that more smoke and less flame emerged from the barrel behind the shell. It is easy to see how the gunfire of Oldendorf's battleships and cruisers produced enough light to silhouette the destroyers of Smoot's DesRon56. (*NARA*)

BIG GUN BATTLES

Warship Duels of the Second World War

ROBERT C STERN

Seaforth
PUBLISHING

First published in Great Britain in 2015 by
Seaforth Publishing,
Pen & Sword Books Ltd,
47 Church Street,
Barnsley S70 2AS

www.seaforthpublishing.com

British Library Cataloguing in Publication Data
A catalogue record for this book is available from the British Library

ISBN 978 1 84832 153 3

Typeset and designed by JCS Publishing Services Ltd,
www.jcs-publishing.co.uk
Printed and bound in China by 1010 Printing International Ltd

CONTENTS

Acknowledgements   ix
Introduction   xi

1   The Curtain Rises (August 1939–June 1940)   1
2   Light in the Darkness (June 1940–March 1941)   36
3   Pyrrhic Victory (October 1940–May 1941)   65
4   A Clean Sweep (February–March 1942)   96
5   An Old-Fashioned Gunfight (March 1943)   130
6   An Unfair Fight I (March 1942–December 1943)   152
7   An Unfair Fight II (October 1944)   184

Afterword   229

Notes   231
Sources   251
Index   259

To my brother, Dick, for setting the bar high
before I was old enough to appreciate it
and for continuing to raise it higher now that I am.

ACKNOWLEDGEMENTS

ANY WRITER OF HISTORY LIVES SURROUNDED by a support system of friends and colleagues without whose assistance no work such as this could be written. This work is no exception. Many people have helped, in ways small and large, whose contributions I failed to note. To them I offer my sincerest apologies and gratitude. Those whose help I made the effort to record are listed here: Vincent O'Hara for his unfailing generosity and patience in the face of my many requests for assistance; Enrico Cernuschi for his gracious help with photographs and information on the Mediterranean theatre, particularly the Regia Marina; Randy Stone for his willingness to share his encyclopedic knowledge of US Navy actions in the Pacific and to fact-check my write-ups at several points; Rick E. Davis, who helped with photo identification and generally useful information; and Dave McComb, who ran the Destroyer History Foundation and its indispensable website – www.destroyerhistory. org. Sadly, Dave passed away in July 2014 at far too young an age. His contribution to the community of naval historians will be sorely missed, as will his unfailing willingness to share his knowledge. More anonymously, but no less importantly, I wish to thank the staffs at the US National Archives, College Park, MD and The National Archives, at Kew, Surrey in England.

The help of all these fine people was invaluable, but, as always, any mistakes of omission or commission are mine alone.

Photo Credits

Most of the photographs come from the US National Archives, which contains the US Navy's photographic assets for the time period covered by this book. Others have been sent to me by friends and colleagues over the years and, if I was wise enough to record the source, are credited as such. If I happened to note the original source, that is credited as well. One source in particular needs special mention. Enrico Cernuschi generously made available to me a collection of photographs of Italian ships engaged in the Battle of Punta Stilo, which was given to him by Admiral Giovanni Vignati, editor of *Marinai d'Italia* magazine. The full credit for these images is 'Associazione Nazionale Marinai d'Italia. Fondo ANMI, collezione Castegnaro', which I have shortened in the captions to 'ANMI via Cernuschi'. I also wish to thank Toni Munday of the HMAS Cerberus Museum. Other photo sources are abbreviated as follows:

NARA US National Archives and Records Administration
NHHC US Naval History and Heritage Command
NRL US Naval Research Laboratory
NZOH New Zealand Official History
USAF US Air Force

I would also like to thank Ken MacPherson, Bob Cressman and David Doyle, who have made photographs from their collections available to me over the years.

INTRODUCTION

THE PREMISE OF THIS BOOK IS quite simple – to recount some of the most interesting and important naval gun battles of the Second World War. Possibly the most difficult part came at the very beginning, deciding which of the many naval engagements to describe, which to exclude and how much background was necessary to place them in context. As this author has always had a strong interest in the technology of naval warfare, one criterion was that, taken in sequence, the chosen engagements should trace the evolution of naval gunfighting from the beginning to the end of the war, showing how changes in technology helped (or hindered) the process of destroying enemy warships by gunfire. The author's intent has also been to include those engagements that are of the greatest interest because of their influence on the course of the war or because they involved the most intriguing ships and men.

To be considered for inclusion in this study, a battle must have been primarily decided by naval gunfire. This deliberately excludes not only the famous carrier air battles such as the Coral Sea and Midway, but also some very interesting engagements in the Solomons Campaign that were primarily exchanges of torpedoes. It also excludes engagements which, while not considered carrier air battles, were nonetheless primarily decided by air attack, such as the dramatic Battle off Samar. Finally, the author has chosen to exclude actions already described in detail in others of his books, such as the battles of Narvik or the naval battle of Casablanca.[1]

This still leaves a large number of engagements from which to choose. Therefore, in making the final selection, the author opted when possible to favour lesser-known engagements over more famous ones, to include engagements from all periods of the war and as many theatres and nationalities as possible and to include engagements involving both large and small warships. Ultimately, it is the author's hope that the result is a book that meets all these criteria, that is a coherent and interesting depiction of the ebb and flow of the Second World War at sea and at the same time pays proper tribute to the ships that carried the guns and to the men who manned them.

The single greatest driver of change in the practice of naval gunnery during the Second World War was the rapid development of more-capable sensor systems. In order to understand how the advent of vastly improved sensors, primarily radar, and the genesis of the necessary shipboard command facilities,

2. When the first of the all-big-gun battleships – HMS *Dreadnought* – was under construction in 1905, all that was thought necessary for fire control was a spotting top aloft on a tripod foremast, never mind that it was placed abaft her fore funnel, where it would often be shrouded in smoke. With four main battery turrets on each broadside, the need for more than spotting from the foretop became obvious to Royal Navy's gunnery experts, such as Captain John Jellicoe. (*NHHC*)

it is necessary to look briefly backwards at the revolution in warship design that took place in the century preceding these events. By the end of the 1850s, most warships being built for major navies were steam-powered and the first armoured ships were entering service. Admiral Nelson would have known how to fight these ships because, despite their steam propulsion and armoured sides, their guns were muzzle-loaders and were carried in individual mounts along the broadside, so the tactics of Trafalgar would have sufficed fifty years later. Fire control would also have looked the same, with ship's officers telling the guns when to start and stop firing and, in only the most general terms, where to aim. Everything else was left up to individual gunners.

A new tactical element was introduced in the American Civil War, with the invention of the ironclad ram. While armed with cannons and armoured against opposing cannon fire, the primary weapon of the CSS *Virginia* was a massive cast-iron ram, which she was able to use effectively only once.[2] During her first sortie in Hampton Roads on 8 March 1862, she rammed one of the Union Navy's blockading ships, USS *Cumberland*, leaving her sinking, but also leaving her ram embedded in *Cumberland*'s side. That night, USS *Monitor* arrived from New York, and the next day the two ironclads fought to a draw, but the impact of *Virginia*'s single successful sortie would be felt for many years, as larger warships were commonly designed with ram bows well into the 1880s. The ram also affected tactical thinking: at the Battle of Lissa in 1866, and as late as the Battle of the Yalu in 1894, one of the opposing fleets adopted a line-abreast formation, which would make ramming easier and being rammed less likely.

It was, however, another lesson from the Battle of Hampton Roads that had much greater and longer-lasting impact – the fact that neither ship had been able to seriously damage the other. In what was to be a constant struggle between hitting power and protection, armour showed itself in this instance to be superior. This naturally led to the mounting of bigger and much heavier guns, which in turn meant that fewer guns could be mounted in a single hull. By the time the First World War broke out in 1914, the 'standard' battleship design, epitomised by the Royal Navy's *Iron Duke*-class, was a ship of 25,000t, mounting ten 13.5in naval long rifles with a range of over 20,000yd and protected by up to 12in of belt armour. While this ship was vastly more powerful than anything Nelson could have imagined, it was built by the main combatants in numbers he would have understood how to command. When the Royal Navy's Grand Fleet met Imperial Germany's High Seas Fleet off the Danish coast in 1916, the two sides mustered a total of fifty-eight similar behemoths – forty-four battleships and fourteen battlecruisers – plus scores of armoured cruisers, light cruisers and smaller craft. It is safe to say that never before and never since have so many ships and so many men been brought together expressly to fire guns at each other. As had happened at Hampton Roads, despite all the effort and staggering cost required to enable the Battle of Jutland to be fought, the result was tactically a draw.

Jutland was tactically indecisive for many reasons, not the least of which was poor visibility when the main fleets engaged late in the afternoon. (Visibility had been better earlier in the day, at least for the Germans, when the battlecruiser forces of the two sides met, which allows an examination of the still rudimentary state of fire control.) The British had a fire control system that employed a director position in the foretop and a Dreyer Table in the transmitting station below decks.[3] The director acted as a 'master gun'; it had a pair of telescopes used to designate the ship's target and estimate that target's course and speed. The ship's multiple rangefinders would follow the director. The ranges and the estimates of enemy course and speed they generated were supplied to the Dreyer Table. This was a hybrid instrument marrying a Dumaresq, a Vickers Clock and moving paper plotters for range and bearing.[4] The transmitting station would pass its adjusted range and bearing 'solution' to the guns, where the individual gunners would elevate their guns based on the known muzzle velocity of each barrel to achieve the desired range.[5] The guns were fired by a master key located at the director, thus allowing salvo fire.

The British fire control system proved to be slow in practice, both because of its complexity and because British gunners had come to depend on the generation of plots on the Dreyer Table, which required a large enough set of data points (rangefinder readings) for a 'smooth' rate to emerge, a process that could take several minutes. As a result, when Beatty's Battlecruiser Fleet encountered Hipper's 1st Scouting Group (six battlecruisers supported by four fast battleships versus five battlecruisers), the Germans opened fire first and, throughout the first phase of the encounter, maintained faster and more accurate gunfire.[6] This was only partly due to better visibility from the German side; the Germans also benefitted from significantly better rangefinders and a doctrine that emphasised firing a 'ladder' of ranging shots to find the range, rather than attempting to plot the range before opening fire.[7]

When the Americans entered the First World War in 1917, they brought with them a quite different approach to fire control. The American battleships that joined the Grand Fleet late in that year were equipped with various marks of the Ford Range-keeper. Designed by Hannibal Choate Ford – no relation to the automobile maker – the Ford was similar in concept to the Argo Clock developed by Arthur Pollen for the Royal Navy.[8] Both were 'synthetic' systems, meaning that they started calculating a firing solution based on initial data, assuming that this solution would be refined over time as more data became available; the Dreyer Table represented the alternative 'analytic' approach, which did not generate a firing solution until sufficient data had been plotted and 'smoothed', a process that was not only slower to arrive at an initial solution but was also less well-suited to handling rapid changes in enemy course and speed.

Even before Jutland, the Royal Navy began to appreciate the inherent problems with the Dreyer Table and the 'analytic' approach to fire control, and began to implement an approach that in many ways resembled the German system.[9] At the end of the war, a complete reassessment of fire control procedures was undertaken, resulting in a vastly improved Admiralty Fire Control Table (AFCT), which, in conjunction with an improved fire-control director called the Director Control Tower (DCT), incorporated the 'synthetic' solution found in Pollen's and Ford's computers. The first AFCT/DCT installations were in the new battleships HMS *Nelson* (28) and *Rodney* (29) commissioned in 1927. This proved to be an excellent and robust gunfire control system, later marks being installed in cruisers

3. In 1920, HMS *Renown* (72) was modified to give her a high-angle control position at her foretop, including a 12ft rangefinder on the roof, acknowledging the growing threat represented by aircraft. Immediately below was a fully glassed-in spotting position that provided information to the main battery director position (located in the cylindrical 'office' one platform below the spotting top). Note the multiple communications tubes running from the spotting top to the main battery director position and to the legs of the tripod foremast where they were routed to the armoured main battery rangefinder mounted atop the conning tower in the lower right in this photograph and to the transmitting station below decks where the Dreyer Table was located. (*NHHC*)

4. HMS *Nelson* (28), seen soon after her completion in 1927, shows off the fully evolved Royal Navy capital ship fire control system that remained in use through the end of the big-gun-ship era, lacking only the radar antennas that multiplied along ships' upperworks beginning in the late 1930s. *Nelson* has an armoured main battery control position (minus the rangefinder) atop her conning tower, just forward of her massive tower foremast. There are four control towers atop the foremast: two secondary battery control towers to either side, a high-angle control tower on the tall pedestal and the first-generation fully evolved DCT in front. This can be seen more clearly to the right in this image, as there was an identical DCT mounted abaft her mainmast as an auxiliary control position. (*USAF*)

and in war-construction battleships. For smaller ships, the Royal Navy adopted a Vickers-built system called the Admiralty Fire Control Clock. The Americans continued developing the Ford Range-keeper; their larger warships in the Second World War being equipped with various 'Mods' of the Mk8 Range-keeper.

All of these fire control computers were analogue devices, clockwork mechanisms that calculated rates and ranges with gears and ratchets similar to the mechanical calculators used in financial businesses at the time. The versions in ships in 1939 differed from those in 1918 mainly in that much of the data, such as own-ship course and speed, wind data, etc., was entered by mechanical linkages rather than by human operators. The most significant difference between the fire control systems at the end of the First World War and at the beginning of the second was the emergence of radar as a rangefinding instrument.

The idea of radar was literally in the air in the 1930s. From the beginning of regular radio broadcasts in the previous decade, it was noticed that certain objects interfered with reception of radio signals. Once it was realised that any object of sufficient size and solidity, including ships and aircraft, could cause this interference by reflecting radio waves, the idea of radar followed logically.[10] The development of usable radar systems proceeded in fits and starts due to the need to conceive of and develop the electronic hardware necessary to co-ordinate (and eventually co-locate) the transmitting and receiving antennas.[11] In the US, development had reached the point where an experimental installation was made in April 1937 of a 1.5m-wavelength radar on the destroyer *Leary* (DD158) which proved reliable and capable of detecting an aircraft at 18nm. An improved version of this radar, complete with rotating and tilting 17ft[7] mattress antenna, designated

XAF, was installed on the battleship *New York* (BB34) in December 1938. So successful were the tests that a production run of six sets, redesignated CXAM, was ordered in October 1939 from the Radio Corporation of America (RCA).

The British started experimenting with radar in the same time frame as the Americans, but pushed the idea forward faster in response to the ominous rise of Fascist Italy, Spain and Germany on the continent. The first experimental installation of the land-based Chain Home air-search radar dates to July 1935. The first naval radar installation was the Type 79X on HMS *Saltburn* (N58) in October 1936. The first production Type 79 was installed on HMS *Sheffield* (24) in September 1938. Like CXAM, the Type 79 was an air-search radar.

Also in 1936, the Germans began sea testing of a naval radar operating at 50cm wavelength. This was found to have inadequate range, leading to the decision to lengthen the wavelength to 60cm in order to gain power.[12] It was this still-experimental set, designated 'DeTe-Gerät' or 'Seetakt', that was installed in *Admiral Graf Spee* in January 1938. Later production sets operated at 80cm. Unlike the contemporary American and British radars, the Seetakt was intended from the beginning as a surface-search set for use in fire control. The first British and American production fire control radar installations came in June 1940 and June 1941 respectively.

Five other nations are known to have worked on radar development before the outbreak of the Second World War: Japan, Italy, France, the Netherlands and the Soviet Union.[13] For various reasons, none of these nations had an operational naval radar prior to their entry into the war.

At the beginning of the war, these technological developments actually had little impact on the outcome of engagements. It would take time and hard experience to learn how to use the increasingly sophisticated fire control computers and radars available to some of the participants in these battles. They would have profound impact well before the end of the war, particularly as many of the engagements described in this book were between naval forces with far different access and ability to exploit these technologies. This is part of the story to be told here, but by no means all of it. Ultimately this is a book about men and ships which sought each other out in snow squalls or dank tropical nights to fight for control of patches of water that would otherwise mean little to most.

As this is a study of naval gun battles, it is only appropriate that particular attention should be paid in the following narratives to the physical act of projectiles striking the hull structure. Most ships of this era were made of steel, for the most part 'mild' steel, meaning low-carbon steel without hardening admixtures (such as nickel or chromium). Only the United States Navy made extensive structural use of armour steel, the so-called 'special treatment steel', a homogeneous high-tensile steel used for bulkheads, armoured decks and lower armour belts, as well as splinter protection for command spaces and gun houses. Generally, warships larger than destroyers were given some amount of armour protecting magazines, machinery spaces, gun turrets, barbettes and conning towers. This armour was often face-hardened, meaning it was cooled more slowly on one side than the other, leaving one side harder, but more brittle and the other side somewhat softer, but more ductile. The combination of a harder outer surface and a more flexible inner surface made for an armour plate that optimally combined resistance to penetration and reduced likelihood of spalling.

The rounds fired from naval guns during the Second World War generally looked much alike, differing in how large a bursting charge it contained, whether the shell had a hardened cap to assist it to penetrate armour plate and where the fuse for the bursting charge was located. Smaller main-battery guns, generally up to 5in calibre, were not expected to defeat armoured opponents, so guns of this size generally fired a 'common' round (often called high-explosive (HE) or high capacity (HC)). These would have a relatively large bursting charge, often greater than 10 per cent of the weight of the shell. They might have a base fuse or a nose fuse (or both), depending on the 'softness' of the intended target. As guns of this size were sometimes 'dual-purpose' weapons, used against aircraft as well as surface targets, shells might be fitted with a timed fuse, in which case they would be referred to in the US Navy as 'AA common' rounds. Medium-calibre guns, the size used as the main battery for cruisers, generally were supplied with both a common shell and an armour-piercing (AP) shell, the latter having a bursting charge between 25 per cent and 10 per cent of that in a common round. Because it was considered unlikely that cruisers would very often find themselves fighting armoured opponents, the Royal Navy (RN) supplied their medium-calibre guns with a hybrid shell with a bursting charge midway between that of a common and an AP round and then provided this round with a hardened cap, coming up with a common pointed ballistic capped (CPBC, sometimes called a semi-armour-piercing capped (SAPC)) round that was carried by RN cruisers almost to the exclusion of any other type. The Germans differed in providing two types of HC shells – a base fuse round and a nose fuse round, the latter having between 50 per cent and 100 per cent greater bursting charge. The ideal shape for an AP shell in terms of armour penetration was blunt-nosed, but this made for poor aerodynamics; therefore many nations developed an AP shell with a pointed cap, resulting in an armour-piercing capped (APC) round.

The impact of a shell hitting a ship varied depending on a huge number of factors, including (but not limited to) the shell's mass and type, its velocity at impact, the angle at which it hit, the nature of the structure hit (armour plate versus 'softer' surface) and whether the shell's fuse functioned properly. The initial damage was the result of the kinetic energy of the fast-moving shell striking a static structure; depending on the type of structure, the physical deformation could be considerable. Thin shell plating or other 'soft' structures could be torn apart, with pieces of the destroyed structure themselves fragmenting, adding to the damage. If the shell struck armour plate, the energy was often dissipated in distorting or fracturing the plate, reducing the damage in the area behind the plate.

Either way, the kinetic energy was soon spent. The rest of the damage caused by a shell came after the bursting charge exploded. As the name indicates, the primary function of a bursting charge is to break a shell into smaller pieces, thereby increasing the area of potential damage before the shell's energy was spent. An HE/HC shell, with a larger bursting charge and thinner shell wall, would break into a large number of smaller fragments (splinters) that, along with the explosion of the charge, could start fires and cause casualties, while the smaller charge and thicker wall of an AP shell made for fewer, heavier fragments which would do more structural damage deep inside a target ship.

To the extent possible, the narratives in this book will describe the impact of individual shells that affected the outcome of the chosen engagements. That this is possible at all is the result of the small percentage of hits obtained in many of these battles, meaning that the damage caused by individual hits can in some cases be determined. Despite improved fire control compared to the First World War, especially after fire control radars became common in the US and Royal navies, these battles so often took place at extreme range, in poor visibility or at night, that the percentage of hits was often 2 per cent or less. Even in those cases when individual hits cannot be isolated, the cumulative effect of gunfire on ship's structure and personnel will be documented to the extent possible.

A Note on Nomenclature and Units

Distances over water are given in feet (12in/304.8mm/abbreviated 'ft'), yards (3ft/0.91m/abbreviated 'yd') and nautical miles (2025.37yd/1.85km/abbreviated 'nm'). Distances over land are given in statute miles (1760yd/1.61km/abbreviated 'mi'). These are the units used by Allied seamen in the 1940s and remain in use in America and, to a lesser extent, Great Britain. Gun calibres are given in the system used by the nation to which a ship belonged. Radar wavelengths are given in metric units. Place names are those that would have been used by an educated English-speaker in the 1940s. Where those differ from the current name or spelling of a place, I give that current version when first mentioned. Ranks and rates for men of navies other than the US Navy, excepting only the

Royal Navy, are translated to the closest USN equivalent. Royal Navy ranks and rates were similar to, but by no means identical to, the US Navy's.

When first referenced, US Navy ships are identified by their hull number (e.g., *South Dakota* (BB57)) in which the letters designate hull type (BB – battleship) and the number is a one-up counter of hulls of that type ordered. Royal Navy ship pennant numbers are given when they are first mentioned (e.g., HMS *Nelson* (28)). Warship prefix designators, when appropriate, are also used only the first time a ship is mentioned. Some nations, such as Nazi Germany and Imperial Japan, used no such designator and none is used in this book.

List of Abbreviations/Acronyms

AA	Anti-Aircraft
AMC	Armed Merchant Cruiser (a merchant ship outfitted with guns to act as a commerce raider, scout cruiser or convoy escort)
AP	armour piercing
APC	armour piercing capped
AR	action report
B-Dienst	Beobachtungsdienst (reconnaissance service) German naval codebreaking organisation
CIC	In American usage: Combat Information Center (an evolving concept of shipboard tactical control by organising radars and inter-ship radio into a single command space, probably first attempted in the Solomons in late 1942; see http://destroyerhistory.org/fletcherclass/ussfletcher)_ In Royal Navy usage: Commander-in-Chief
CinC	In American usage: Commander-in-Chief
CO	commanding officer
CPBC	common pointed ballistic cap
CNO	US Navy Chief of Naval Operations
CPO	Chief Petty Officer
DCT	Director Control Tower
DesDiv	Destroyer Division (USN destroyer unit, generally four ships) – besides DesDivs, the USN has CruDivs and BatDivs for cruisers and battleships
DesRon	Destroyer Squadron (USN destroyer unit, generally eight ships)
DP	dual purpose (referring to guns that could be fired at aircraft and surface targets)
ESM	electronic support measures (In the Second World War, this comprised detectors to identify enemy radios and radars, and transmitters to jam them)
FAA	Fleet Air Arm (The afloat component of the RAF)
FuMB	*Funkmessbeobachter* (German word for radar detector)
FuMO	*Funkmessortung* (German word for radar device)
GC&CS	Government Code & Cypher School (the British codebreaking establishment eventually located at Bletchley Park; the source of ULTRA decrypts)

GFCS	gunfire control system (US Navy term for a system combining optical and electronic target detection and tracking with automatic gun pointing)
GRT	gross register tons (a measure of the volume of cargo a merchant ship can carry)
HA	high-angle (often used in Royal Navy parlance in the place of AA)
HC	high capacity (used interchangeably with HE)
HE	high explosive (used interchangeably with HC)
HMAS	His Majesty's Australian Ship (Royal Australian Navy warship designator)
HMS	His Majesty's Ship (Royal Navy warship designator)
HNOMS	His Majesty's Ship (used by the Royal Navy to designate Norwegian vessels)
HrMs	His Majesty's Ship (Royal Netherlands Navy warship designator)
IJA	Imperial Japanese Army
IJN	Imperial Japanese Navy
KM	Kriegsmarine (the German navy)
MV	motor vessel
RA	Regia Aeronautica (Royal Italian Air Force)
RAF	Royal Air Force
RAN	Royal Australian Navy
RFA	Royal Fleet Auxiliary
RM	Regia Marina (Royal Italian Navy)
RN	Regia Nave (Royal Italian Navy warship designator)
RN	Royal Navy
SAPC	semi-armour piercing capped (later name for CPBC)
SKL	Seekriegsleitung (High Command of the Kreigsmarine)
TBS	Talk-Between-Ships (A high-frequency, low-power, line-of-sight voice telephony radio system)
TF	task force (USN designation for a large *ad hoc* force given a specific task)
TG	task group (USN designation for a subdivision of a TF)
TU	task unit (USN designation for a subdivision of a TG)
UK	United Kingdom
USA	United States Army
USN	United States Navy
USS	United States Ship (USN warship designator)
W/T	wireless telegraphy (Royal Navy term for radio, particularly Morse as opposed to voice communication)
XO	executive officer

Note: In USN parlance, it was common to refer to the commander of a unit, such as DesDiv14 as ComDesDiv14, with the exception of task designations, in which case the commander of TF14 would most often be referred to as CTF14.

THE CURTAIN RISES

ROYAL NAVY VS KRIEGSMARINE IN THE ATLANTIC
AUGUST 1939–JUNE 1940

JUST OVER TWENTY YEARS EARLIER, A dominant Royal Navy had watched the German High Seas Fleet steam into captivity in the Firth of Forth. Except for five American battleships forming the 6th Battle Squadron, and a smattering of ships representing France and the other Allies, the vast majority of the warships present to witness the German surrender on 21 November 1918 were British. The Royal Navy's Grand Fleet was one of the most powerful military forces of any kind assembled to date.[1]

However, this appearance of power was more than a little illusory. Many of the Grand Fleet's largest ships – battleships and battlecruisers – had been built early in the naval arms race with Imperial Germany and were obsolescent (and worn-out) by 1918. Gun calibre had increased from 12in in the earliest Dreadnoughts to 13.5in starting with the *Orion*-class in 1909, but even the ships of this interim generation were overshadowed by the 15in main batteries of the war-construction *Queen Elizabeth*- and *Revenge*-class battleships and *Renown*-class battlecruisers, and would be of questionable value in battle against any future opponent.

The Grand Fleet had been horribly expensive to create and maintain, and it was inevitable that this massive fleet would be dismembered soon after its great victory. The defeat of Germany and the fact that the nations possessing the next four largest navies (United States, France, Italy and Japan) were now nominally allies, removed a great deal of the impetus to maintain such a large fleet. Politically and economically, it would be hard to convince voters in Great Britain that the dozens of great ships sent to the breakers in the immediate post-war period would need to be replaced.

Despite the general euphoria at the war's end, it was obvious that the alliances forged against Imperial Germany would be unlikely to survive long in the years to come. In particular, the US and Japan had continued to build fast, modern capital ships during the war and, with economies unaffected by the conflict, were planning continued naval expansion. The Royal Navy drew up plans for a class of large, fast battlecruisers armed with 16in guns and another of battleships armed with an 18in main battery, but neither was ever started. With massive debt accrued from the war, politicians in Great Britain, supported by many in the US, opted in favour of a naval arms limitation process that started with the convening of the Washington Naval Conference in November 1921. Dragging along Japan, France and Italy, all reluctant to accept lesser status, the resulting

Five Power Treaty set fleet sizes for the five nations, set tonnage and gun calibre limits for various ship types and declared a ten-year 'holiday' on the construction of new battleships. To compensate Great Britain for the capital ships not ordered in 1921, the Royal Navy was allowed to design and build two battleships that conformed to the treaty's 35,000t displacement and 16in main-battery limits.

The Royal Navy of 1939

While a dramatic reduction in the size of the Royal Navy may have been inevitable following the end of the First World War, it was in no way inevitable that when Britain found itself at war with Germany again on 3 September 1939, the Royal Navy would be inadequate to meet the demands it would face. This sad state of affairs came about because the British had put too much faith in the arms limitation process and because, at the point in the early to mid-1930s when the newest of the First World War era warships still in service were in need of rebuilding or replacement, the political will did not exist to spend the necessary funds. The only major warships added to the Royal Navy between the wars were the two less than completely satisfactory battleships of the *Nelson*-class (*Nelson* and *Rodney*), three aircraft carriers constructed on light battlecruiser hulls (HMS *Furious* (47), *Courageous* (50) and *Glorious* (77)), one purpose-built aircraft carrier (HMS *Ark Royal* (91)) and forty cruisers of varying quality. Of the First World War vintage warships still in commission (ten battleships, three battlecruisers, five aircraft carriers and several dozen cruisers), the quality also varied considerably. Some, such as HMS *Warspite* (03), had been fully modernised with a new powerplant, upgraded armour, increased main-battery range and a rebuilt superstructure, but most of these older ships had received few, if any, similar upgrades. Simply put, the Royal Navy that went to war in September 1939 had too few of all types of ships to both protect the worldwide trade network on which the nation's survival depended and dominate the waters around Great Britain. This problem remained even if the excellent, but small, French Marine Nationale was added in on the British side, and Japan and Italy remained neutral, but within the first nine months of the war France had been defeated and Italy had come in on the German side, stretching the Royal Navy even thinner.

The British had a number of new warships under construction when war broke out, including a class of five new battleships, five large and one smaller aircraft carriers, and a score of light cruisers, though it would be mid-1940 before the first of these was commissioned, much less reached operational status.[2]

Problematical *Panzerschiffe*

To make matters worse, the British knew full well that by 1939 the Germans had rebuilt their Kriegsmarine – with British acquiescence – with several classes of large powerful ships for which they had no good answer. The ships that probably most alarmed the British were the large armoured ships (*Panzerschiffe*) of the *Deutschland*-class. At least nominally in conformance with the Versailles and Washington treaties when they were built, these were publicly declared to displace 10,000t and were armed with six 28cm/54 guns in two triple turrets.[3] This was an extremely heavy main battery for a ship the size of a heavy cruiser.

Their propulsion was equally as revolutionary. They were powered by four sets of MAN nine-cylinder, double-acting, two-stroke diesel motors producing 54,000shp for a designed speed of 26kt.[4] The decision to power these ships with diesel motors was made because the resulting powerplant was far smaller than a steam turbine installation generating similar power. It was hoped that it would also be lighter in weight, saving displacement, but this proved not to be the case.

So unique was the *Deutschlands*' combination of speed and armament at the time they were built that the British seemed to be at a loss as how to classify them and eventually came up with the term 'pocket battleship'. They truly embodied Sir Jacky Fisher's concept for the original battlecruisers, in that they were, when built, faster than anything stronger and stronger than anything faster.[5] By 1939, this was no longer the case, as several nations had built warships that were both stronger and faster. These included the French *Dunkerque*-class and German *Scharnhorst*-class battlecruisers.[6]

What made the *Deutschland*-class *Panzerschiffe* such a great concern at the outbreak of the war, even after they had been eclipsed by larger and faster German designs – not only the recently completed *Scharnhorst*-class, but also the two massive *Bismarck*-class battleships near completion – was their extraordinary endurance combined with high cruising speed due to their diesel propulsion. They could cruise at least 15,000nm at 13kt and between 8,900nm and 10,000nm at 20kt. (Contemporary Royal Navy cruisers had at least one-third less endurance.) With this range and speed, they would make ideal commerce raiders, exactly the type of vessel most feared by an understrength Royal Navy tasked with protecting distant trade routes.

Panzerschiffe into the Atlantic

The German naval leadership (Seekriegsleitung – SKL) was well-aware of the relative weakness of the Kriegsmarine compared to the Royal Navy, both in terms of numbers of ships and geographical position. (The British Isles were perfectly located astride the routes from Germany to the Atlantic. Any German warship would have to use the English Channel or one of sevcral passages between Scotland, Norway, Iceland and Greenland to reach open water.) Early in 1939, Hitler had committed to the construction of a large and powerful navy to be completed by 1945, but when war broke out in September, none of the hundreds of promised ships had even been started. With the navy Germany possessed at the outbreak of hostilities, the best strategy available to Admiral Erich Raeder, head of the Kriegsmarine, was to maintain a 'fleet in being' while beginning an aggressive campaign against Allied commerce with the few U-boats then in service and his fast and long-legged *Panzerschiffe*.[7] With this in mind, as tensions rose in Europe over the 'Polish Crisis', the Kriegsmarine was put on a war footing. In April, the Kriegsmarine held a training exercise in the North Atlantic with the three *Panzerschiffe* and the battlecruiser *Gneisenau* and, afterwards, the newest of the *Panzerschiffe*, *Admiral Graf Spee*, had ostentatiously returned to Germany through the English Channel, attracting a great deal of attention.[8] She then operated as normal out of her home port of Wilhelmshaven, often leaving port for a day or two to exercise her weapons.

6. In April 1939, having completed a major fleet exercise in the North Atlantic, the newest of Nazi Germany's three *Panzerschiffe* (pocket battleships), *Admiral Graf Spee*, made a highly visible daylight passage up the English Channel, as if taunting the British. This view from off her starboard beam shows two of the type's most easily identifiable characteristics: the two massive turrets, each mounting three 28cm guns, and the long, uninterrupted row of scuttles from her quarterdeck to her bow, indicating that her armour belt did not extend very far above her waterline. (*via Bob Cressman*)

The approach of war triggered a carefully orchestrated plan, the first move of which was the departure from Germany on 5 August of *Altmark*, a modern motor oiler/supply ship purpose-built for the Kriegsmarine.[9] Designed to carry almost 10,000t of fuel oil and 2,000t of ammunition, stores and spare parts at a cruising speed of 15kt and a maximum speed of 21kt, she left Germany with her storage tanks nearly empty.[10] Taking the shortest possible route, she passed down the English Channel and then headed west across the Atlantic, making for Port Arthur, Texas.[11] After taking on 9,400 tons of diesel, she sailed out into the Gulf of Mexico and effectively disappeared. Her destination was the northern of two predetermined waiting areas, a large rectangle of rarely traversed ocean bisected by the Tropic of Cancer midway between Africa and the West Indies, where, appropriately enough, she was to wait.

She was waiting for *Graf Spee*, which departed Wilhelmshaven at dusk on 21 August. She slipped unnoticed up the Norwegian coast, avoiding all contact with passing ships, and passed into the Atlantic between the Faroes and Iceland three days later, heading southwest and then due south until she met the waiting *Altmark* on 1 September. *Graf Spee* was commanded by Hans Langsdorff, a young-looking forty-five-year-old captain with only limited command experience. Langsdorff was given considerable flexibility in choosing the area where he wanted to operate; in conjunction with Lieutenant Commander Jürgen Wattenberg, his navigator, he chose an area west of Freetown and north of the equator, in the middle of the narrowest part of the Central Atlantic between Brazil and Sierra Leone. After refuelling, the two ships sailed slowly south in loose company.

A similar pair of ships was assigned a waiting area just south of Greenland. The supply ship *Westerwald* – sister to *Altmark* – sailed from Wilhelmshaven before dawn on 22 August.[12] Like *Graf Spee*, she moved well inshore up the Norwegian coast until north of Bergen, where, at the point that the coast turns towards the northeast, *Westerwald* turned northwest and increased speed, heading for the Denmark Strait, between Iceland and Greenland. *Westerwald* was followed two days later by the *Panzerschiff Deutschland*, the two meeting on 30 August at a point southeast of Cape Farewell (Kap Farvel/Nunap Isua), the southernmost tip of Greenland. The orders to the two *Panzerschiffe* were to remain undetected and to resupply regularly so they would be ready when ordered into action.

'Commence Hostilities against British Merchant Shipping'

That order came on 3 September, but it allowed the *Panzerschiffe* only to attack British shipping; all neutral shipping was still off limits, as was French shipping – despite the fact that France declared war on Germany only six hours after the British. This put the two captains in an awkward position. As long as they had to stop and identify a ship before sinking it, then a stopped French ship would be free to report the raider's location without fear of reprisal. This situation did not last long: four days later, before either *Panzerschiff* had even sighted a potential target, they were again ordered to avoid all contact and await further orders.[13] Apparently, Hitler hoped that, with the rapid defeat of Poland and the apparent reluctance of Britain and France to take aggressive action on Germany's western border, perhaps the Allies might be amenable to another negotiated capitulation. It was only on 26 September, after a reportedly tumultuous Allied meeting with Hitler, that the *Panzerschiffe* again 'were ordered to leave their waiting areas and commence hostilities against British merchant shipping'.[14]

The Royal Navy Stretched Thin

During the last month of peace, the British knew that the Germans were moving ships around, even that some were heading for the Atlantic, but the state of the Royal Navy's intelligence branches was still primitive. Making matters worse was the Royal Navy's shortage of cruisers, exactly the type of vessel most needed to protect far-flung trade routes. The Admiralty had consistently stated, based on First World War experience, that a minimum of seventy cruisers was needed to meet these needs, but, when war broke out in September 1939, the Royal Navy could dispose only fifty-eight cruisers, counting those contributed by Dominion navies.[15] Many of this already small number were 'C', 'D' and 'E'-class light cruisers dating back to the previous war, best suited for escort duties. Indeed, a number of the oldest light cruisers had been converted into anti-aircraft (AA) escorts by replacing their original single-6in mounts with twin-4in DP mounts. Because they were intended as escorts, it was mostly these older cruisers which were dispersed to the distant stations maintained by the Royal Navy at the beginning of the war. Two were based at Gibraltar as part of the North Atlantic command, four more were at Freetown, along with one newer light cruiser, constituting the South Atlantic command, while a separate South Atlantic Division under Commodore Henry H Harwood operated along the South American coast, nominally based in the Falklands, but effectively provisioning at any friendly port.[16] At the beginning of the war, this squadron comprised two heavy cruisers (HMS *Exeter* (68) and *Cumberland* (57)) and one light cruiser, HMS *Ajax* (22). Four cruisers (two heavy and two light) were assigned to the America and West Indies Station, based mainly at Bermuda and Trinidad, and there was a similar number of ships assigned to the China Station. By far the largest of the fleet's detachments, other than the Home Fleet, was the Mediterranean Fleet based at Alexandria. While this force will play a major role in later chapters, it has no part to play in the opening moves of the Royal Navy and the Kriegsmarine.

All of these dispositions would be called into question on 30 September when *Graf Spee*, having steered west-northwest towards Pernambuco (Recife) since parting from *Altmark* three days earlier, stopped SS *Clement*, a British steamer carrying a cargo of kerosene to Salvador (Bahia). Her master, chief engineer and an injured crewman were taken aboard *Graf Spee*; the rest of the crew was allowed to board lifeboats and given directions to Maceió, the nearest landfall. Once the crew was clear, *Clement* was sunk by gunfire. Her radio operator had manged to send a raider signal before she was stopped, which was picked up by a passing ship and forwarded to the Admiralty, but even if that message had not been passed along, *Graf Spee* herself signalled the Olinda radio station near Pernambuco about the location of the lifeboats of the crew of *Clement*, signing the message with the peacetime callsign of sistership *Admiral Scheer* in an attempt to confuse any pursuit. A few hours later, *Graf Spee* stopped the neutral Greek steamer *Papalemos* further south along the coast. She was released after the three prisoners were transferred and after extracting from her master the promise that he would not report the encounter until she reached the Cape Verde Islands. Certain that the British were now well aware of his location, Langsdorff turned his ship away from the Brazilian coast and headed east towards Africa and the busy trade route between Cape Town, Freetown and points north.

History Repeating Itself?

In many ways, this situation was eerily familiar to the British. The First World War had started with a German force – in that case, the five cruisers of the German Pacific Squadron, commanded ironically enough by Admiral Graf Maximilian von Spee, namesake of the *Panzerschiff* – loose in the southern hemisphere. At the time, the Royal Navy was able to detach two battlecruisers from the Grand Fleet and send them south to reinforce a South Atlantic squadron already comprising five cruisers. Arriving at the Falkland Islands just the day before von Spee approached, the British squadron surprised and overwhelmed the German force. Only the light cruiser SMS *Dresden* escaped.

Almost exactly twenty-five years later, the situation seemed to be repeating itself, except that Langsdorff had advantages von Spee never had. With *Graf Spee*'s far greater endurance and support from *Altmark*, Langsdorff was effectively free of the need to find fuel for several more months, while von Spee's movements would have been constrained to a much greater extent by the need to find fuel. Knowing *Graf Spee* had many more options than her namesake, the Royal Navy was forced to disperse its search into numerous small groups, rather than concentrating its forces. Besides the ships already stationed in the West Indies, at Freetown and Gibraltar, the Royal Navy established eight 'lettered' hunting groups (including Harwood's South Atlantic Division, now called Force 'G') drawn from the Home Fleet, the China Station and the Mediterranean. They even went so far as to order HMS *Achilles* (70), one of the two cruisers in the New Zealand Division (which did not officially become the Royal New Zealand Navy until two years later) to the Atlantic.

One Hunter Home; the Other Far Afield

The two *Panzerschiffe* loose in the Atlantic continued their depredations despite the best efforts of the Royal Navy. *Deutschland* moved slowly north, capturing the US steamer *City of Flint* on 9 October east of the Grand Banks, for allegedly carrying contraband to Great Britain, and beginning a saga with serious diplomatic repercussions that only ended over a month later at Bergen, Norway.[17] Five days later, she sank a small Norwegian steamer and then started a slow, looping route that took her north of Iceland again and finally down the Norwegian coast, through the Skagerrak and on to Gotenhafen (Gdynia), arriving safely on 16 November.

Graf Spee would have much greater success during this period and cover many more miles. Between the end of September, when she turned away from the Brazilian coast, and mid-November, she had found good hunting along the Cape Town–Freetown trade route, finding and sinking four merchantmen in October. Deciding that the Royal Navy was likely closing in, Langsdorff replenished again from *Altmark*, turned over the prisoners taken in October and headed his ship south, intending to round the Cape of Good Hope and try his luck off the east coast of Africa. At first, he found no traffic, defeating his purpose of drawing the pursuit away from the South Atlantic. It was not until he pushed north into the Mozambique Channel that he found a victim, sinking a small coaster on 15 November just a few miles offshore. The coaster's crew was put in lifeboats and, certain that they would shortly report the raider's presence, the *Panzerschiff* turned south and began to retrace her steps back into the South Atlantic.

An Unfair Fight in the Far North

In an attempt to draw attention away from *Graf Spee* and attack the Royal Navy's Northern Patrol, SKL ordered a sweep through the North Sea as far west as the Iceland–Faroes Passage by the battlecruisers *Scharnhorst* and *Gneisenau*, starting 21 November. The Northern Patrol was an essential part of the system of blockade of Germany set up at the outbreak of war. By denying passage to merchant ships heading for Germany, the enemy would be denied access to essential raw materials unavailable except by overseas trade. Controlling the southern route to Germany through the English Channel was relatively simple for the Royal Navy, but blocking the northern route, coming through the Denmark Strait or one of the gaps between Iceland, the Faroes and the Shetlands was much more difficult, especially given the Royal Navy's shortage of cruisers, which were the ideal craft to patrol these wide passages. Initially, this patrol was carried out by old cruisers recently reactivated from reserve, but these proved to be poorly suited to handle the rough weather and long distances involved in this work and they were largely replaced by armed merchant cruisers (AMCs), former passenger liners hastily armed with ancient 6in guns. For the purpose of stopping merchant shipping, these AMCs were more than adequate, but with primitive fire control and no armour, they were under standing instructions to avoid any engagement with enemy warships of any size. The Northern Patrol was at full strength at this time, as the British still believed *Deutschland* to be making her way homewards.

For this reason, and because from many angles all major German warships looked much the same, it is understandable that Captain Edward C Kennedy of the AMC *Rawalpindi* identified the warship seen coming over the southeastern horizon at high speed in the dusk of 23 November as *Deutschland* when in fact it was *Scharnhorst*.[18] A sighting report from *Rawalpindi* was received by Home Fleet at 1531 and Admiral Forbes immediately ordered all warships supporting the Northern Patrol to make best speed to the AMC's position and ordered the battleships *Nelson* and *Rodney*, then at the Clyde, to put to sea as soon as possible.[19]

Kennedy ordered full speed and a sharp turn away from the approaching warship and towards a fog bank, but it soon became clear that *Scharnhorst* was closing too fast and it was already too late for this manoeuvre to succeed.[20] *Scharnhorst* signalled twice for the AMC to heave to, but Kennedy had no intention of allowing his ship to be taken so easily. After several more signals and a warning shot off her bow, *Rawalpindi* responded with a broadside of four 6in shells, leaving *Scharnhorst*'s Captain Kurt Hoffmann no choice but to return fire. At 1545, the two battlecruisers – *Gneisenau* having meanwhile approached – opened fire and disabled the former liner with surgical precision. Their first salvo destroyed the bridge, but Kennedy was unharmed; the second demolished the gun control station and one of the eight single-6in mounts; the third exploded in her engine room and cut power to the shell hoists serving the remaining guns. *Rawalpindi* was dead in the water and the crew was beginning to abandon ship when her forward magazine detonated at 1600 and the ship broke in two and rapidly sank. The explosion and sinking prevented the launching of most of *Rawalpindi*'s lifeboats and the close passage of *Scharnhorst* at high

7. A prewar image shows *Rawalpindi* before she was pressed into service as an AMC covering the escape routes from Germany north of the British Isles. Other than a coat of dark grey paint, she would not have looked much different when she encountered *Scharnhorst* at dusk on 23 November 1939. Armed with the same calibre weapons as *Graf Spee*, only more of them, the German battlecruiser made quick work of the converted liner, which was lost with most of her officers and men. (*via Bob Cressman*)

speed swamped those already in the water, but the German battlecruiser rapidly slowed and returned to the site of the sinking and began picking up survivors.

Scharnhorst had rescued twenty-seven men (out of a complement of 265) when HMS *Newcastle* (76) was seen approaching from the west. *Newcastle* veered away, not wanting to take on two much stronger adversaries, but hoping to shadow them until *Warspite*, approaching from the west, or *Nelson* and *Rodney*, coming up from the south, could intercept. Luck, however, was not on the side of the Royal Navy that evening. A rain squall intervened and, by the time *Newcastle*, came out of the other side, the Germans had disappeared into the deepening gloom. The two battlecruisers escaped to the northeast, waiting in the Norwegian Sea until a period of poor visibility after 26 November allowed them to slip south through the North Sea, arriving at Wilhelmshaven the next day. Both had suffered damage to their foremost turret due to heavy seas breaking over their bows.

A Few More Before Heading Home

Back in the South Atlantic, *Graf Spee* replenished from *Altmark* and then returned to the profitable Cape Town–Freetown route, finding two more victims at the beginning of December. But, by this time there were considerations other than enemy hunting groups on Langsdorff's mind. *Graf Spee* had now been at sea and operating continuously in mostly tropical waters for three and a half months. Marine growth and corrosion had cut her top speed by several knots and her engines were showing signs of wear. *Graf Spee* was in need of a good scraping and a major overhaul and that could only be done in Germany. Additionally, *Altmark*, after replenishing the raider again on 6 December, now had only enough fuel for her own return to Germany.[21] The *Panzerschiffe* would have to reach home with the fuel she now had on board, but, given her endurance, this was enough to keep her going at economical speed well into March. Thus, fuel was not a limiting factor in Langsdorff's mind. His plan was now to head west towards a point along the Brazilian coast south of Rio, find some targets there to attract the attention of the enemy, then head south to the mouth of the River Plate (Rio Plata), make additional noise there and, most importantly, be seen heading further south. The idea was to convince the British that he was heading for the Falklands or even planning on rounding Cape Horn and trying out the Chilean coast. His real intent was then to turn north and begin his homeward journey.

An unexpected encounter with a solitary steamer on 7 December convinced Langsdorff that he had happened on a trade route between Montevideo and Freetown. He changed course to the southwest, heading directly towards the Plate estuary, hoping to find more targets on this unexpected trade route.

Harwood's Hunch

The Royal Navy seemed always to be one step behind Langsdorff; for example, setting up a patrol line south of Cape Town with an aircraft carrier, a battlecruiser and two heavy cruisers days after *Graf Spee* had already doubled back into the Atlantic. Once news arrived of the sinking of SS *Doric Star* – the

8. The main reason why *Rawalpindi* had been pressed into service in the Northern Patrol was because the Royal Navy simply had too few ships like HMS *Achilles* (70), a light cruiser ideally suited for patrolling long stretches of open ocean. *Achilles* became part of the New Zealand Division in 1936 and was in the South Pacific when she was photographed on 26 February 1938. With *Graf Spee* loose in the South Atlantic and the situation in the Pacific appearing calm, *Achilles* was ordered to join Commodore Henry Harwood's Force 'G' in the South Atlantic in October 1939. (*Allan C. Green Collection – State Library of Victoria*)

9. On 19 October 1939, *Achilles* passed through the Straits of Magellan in calm spring weather, unusual for that notoriously tempestuous passage. In this view looking forward from her fantail, her upperworks are still uncluttered by the multiple anti-aircraft guns and electronics antennas that would soon come to dominate the profiles of warships. The two pipes rising on either side of her after superstructure are galley exhaust vents. (*NZOH*)

first ship *Graf Spee* sank after returning to the South Atlantic – those ships were ordered to refuel at Cape Town and head north towards Freetown, exactly the area Langsdorff had just vacated.

The force best placed to intercept *Graf Spee* was Harwood's Force 'G', though its ships were widely dispersed at the beginning of December. *Cumberland* and *Exeter* were at Port Stanley to protect against any move towards the Falklands as the anniversary of von Spee's defeat there on 8 December 1914 approached. *Achilles*, which joined Force 'G' in October, was off Rio and *Ajax* was on patrol alone off the River Plate. Commodore Harwood, on 3 December, looked over his charts and, based on Langsdorff's previous pattern of movement, deduced that it was likely that he would again try his luck off the South American coast.[22] Because Harwood had only four cruisers – two heavy and two light – and because at any one time one of them would be replenishing at Port Stanley, he knew he had to concentrate his remaining force in order to have any chance of success against the *Panzerschiffe*. He also knew that, although Rio de Janeiro was closer to Langsdorff's last reported position, the shipping traffic in and out of the Plate was a more tempting target. By logic and luck, Harwood came to the correct conclusion and acted decisively. Reasoning that *Graf Spee* would most likely arrive off the Plate estuary on 13 December, he ordered *Achilles* down from Rio and *Exeter* up from the Falklands, to rendezvous on 12 December, with *Cumberland* to continue her 'self-refit' at Port Stanley, ready to steam at short notice.[23] Rarely would a hunch pay off as well as Harwood's.

The Commodore's plan for tackling a *Panzerschiffe* with three smaller cruisers was equally logical and decisive:

> My policy with three cruisers in company versus one pocket battleship – attack at once by day or night. By day act as two units. First Division and *Exeter* diverged to permit flank-marking. First Division will concentrate gunfire. . . My object . . . is to avoid torpedoes and take the enemy by surprise and cross his stern.[24]

Harwood's squadron formed line ahead with *Ajax*, his flagship, in the lead, followed by *Achilles* and then *Exeter*. The evening of 12 December they practised this manoeuvre, in which *Exeter* detached from the other two and crossed to the other side of the hypothetical enemy. The idea was to force the *Panzerschiffe* to divide her fire between the two forces, while they would be able to 'flank-mark' for each other, meaning they could report each other's fall of shot.

The First Real Test: Harwood's Cruisers vs *Graf Spee* off the Plate Estuary

In what must be an almost unique occurrence in military history, *Graf Spee* showed up the next morning 240nm east of Cabo Santa Maria on the Uruguayan coast, precisely where and when Harwood predicted she would. The battle that ensued is not easy to explain. *Graf Spee* was significantly larger and better armed than any of the British cruisers individually; a full salvo from either of her turrets outweighed a full broadside from *Exeter* or one from the two light cruisers combined. Although *Graf Spee*'s armour was no thicker than

10. HMS *Exeter* (68) was a veteran of duty at distant stations. The heavy cruiser is seen here at Coco Solo, at the northern (Atlantic) end of the Panama Canal on 27 February 1939. At the beginning of October, she was also assigned to Force 'G', hunting for *Graf Spee*. Having been in commission continuously since her last refit in 1936, she was in need of repairs and general maintenance, but the war situation forced a planned refit at Simon's Town to be cancelled. She was at Port Stanley at the end of November for a period of 'self-refit', but that was cut short when she was summoned to the Plate estuary on 9 December. (*NARA via David Doyle*)

the cruisers', it was more extensive and she had an armoured deck, which the cruisers lacked. The British, however, had the advantage of speed; all three cruisers had a designed best speed of 32kt versus *Graf Spee*'s designed maximum of 26kt, but it had been a while since any of these ships had been docked and their actual best speed was several knots slower than the theoretical maximum. Despite the fact that *Graf Spee*'s 28cm main battery outranged *Exeter* by 9,000yd and the two light cruisers by 14,000yd, this speed advantage would allow the British to determine the range at which a battle would be fought, when and if it was joined, and would have made any attempt by *Graf Spee* to break off the action likely to fail. However, this advantage was partially offset by the ability of *Graf Spee* to increase rapidly from cruising to maximum speed, while the British ships, with conventional steam turbine propulsion, would take much longer to increase speed.

The most interesting and important question is, therefore, why was this battle fought? When *Graf Spee*'s lookouts identified the shapes of warships above the southeastern horizon at 0600, just after sunrise on 13 December 1939, Langsdorff had the opportunity to turn away, increase speed and disappear over the horizon to the north. Their masts had been first sighted eight minutes earlier and Langsdorff began a cautious approach, hoping he had happened upon a convoy full of fat targets. The fact that these warships were identified as a cruiser and two destroyers should have given Langsdorff pause. As important as his mission to sink enemy shipping and disrupt maritime traffic was, it could only be achieved by avoiding any engagement that might damage his ship. At sunrise on 13 December, *Graf Spee* was 6,500nm from the nearest friendly dockyard, more than twenty days away at economical speed. The question Langsdorff should have been asking himself that morning was whether, in fighting through an escort comprising at least three warships, he might in the process sustain damage that would make reaching Germany problematic. Damage sufficient to endanger his ability to return home need not be serious enough to threaten the ship's survival: any damage that reduced *Graf Spee*'s speed or endurance would suffice. Even if he avoided such damage, there would be no chance that his attack on these ships would go unreported. Langsdorff was well aware that his activities had caused the assembly of multiple hunting forces to the north, east and south. With his position accurately pinpointed, there could be no doubt that these forces would converge on any route he might choose after the engagement.

Given all this, it is necessary to ask why, at 0600, having identified three warships that could only be enemies, he did not immediately turn away, but instead turned towards the enemy and increased speed to 24kt. The explanation he gave at the time to the officers on *Graf Spee*'s bridge was that he intended to engage the cruiser – correctly identified as *Exeter* – and destroyers, which he stated would be easily disposed of, and then fall upon the now-unprotected convoy which he assumed lay over the horizon.[25] This explains what he intended to do, but not why. Many believe that, knowing this would be *Graf Spee*'s last action before heading home, he wanted his cruise to end with a spectacular victory. Some even speculate that he thought *Graf Spee*'s destruction of twelve merchantmen had been too easy and that he longed for a real fight before returning home.[26]

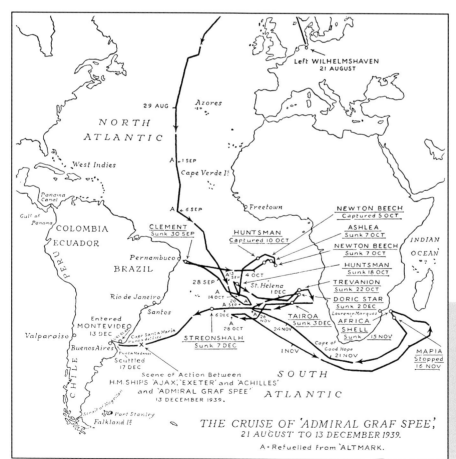

11. This excellent chart shows *Graf Spee*'s track from her departure from Wilhelmshaven on 21 August 1939 up to her encounter with Force 'G' on 13 December. Each of the twelve ships stopped, captured or sunk by the German is noted. (*NZOH*)

12. Harwood's uncanny prescience in predicting where *Graf Spee* would be on the morning of 13 December 1939, and Captain Langsdorff's blunder at falling into Harwood's trap when he had a chance to escape to the north, are both clearly laid out in this track chart of the Battle of the River Plate.

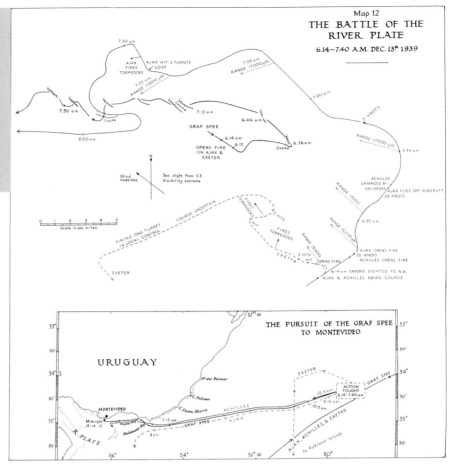

Map 12
THE BATTLE OF THE RIVER PLATE
6.14–7.40 A.M. DEC. 13ᵗʰ 1939

In this author's opinion, another possibility needs to be considered, namely that Langsdorff believed that he was already trapped and had no choice but to fight his way out, and, given this situation and his exaggerated sense of duty, he felt that to fight through the enemy was better than a probably futile attempt to run away. At 0600, with the enemy plainly visible, it appears that he believed *Graf Spee* had been spotted by the British. The only evidence for this is a mention in his report of the action stating that he decided to attack rather than retire 'in order to close to effective range before the enemy could work up to maximum speed, since it appeared to be out of the question that three shadowers could be shaken off'.[27] Having identified *Exeter*, he knew she carried two aircraft and thus was capable of finding and tracking him if he headed north. Given the superior speed of the British cruiser, it would only be a matter of time before she would again be within visual range and able to track him from a safe distance, especially given that this was just the beginning of a long late-spring day with clear skies and calm seas. The fact that *Exeter* had significantly shorter endurance would have been understood to be irrelevant, as other hunting groups would likely be able to close long before fuel became an issue for the British cruiser.

If this was in fact what Langsdorff was thinking, then immediately engaging *Exeter* and her escorting destroyers made sense, because the sooner they were destroyed, the sooner he could disappear again into the vast South Atlantic and regain freedom of action. Long before Langsdorff was able to correctly identify the two smaller adversaries as light cruisers, he was committed to an engagement from which he had little chance of winning free. If this speculation is correct, and much in *Graf Spee*'s behaviour as the battle progressed that day argues that it is, then it is the greatest of ironies that, at 0600, *Graf Spee* had not been sighted by the British. In fact, it was not until 0610 that lookouts on *Ajax* first noted smoke on the northwestern horizon and Harwood ordered all ships to come to full speed and *Exeter* to investigate.[28] The three cruisers, which were steaming in line-ahead northeast-by-east at 14kt, thus split into two groups exactly as Harwood had planned, with *Exeter* turning to the west-northwest at 0614 towards the rapidly approaching *Graf Spee*, and the other two cruisers, led by *Ajax*, continuing northeast-by-east for another six minutes.

On *Exeter*, events happened in rapid succession. By 0616, the superstructure of the enemy ship, approaching on a nearly reciprocal course and at a closing rate of more than 40kt, resolved itself into the unmistakeable tower structure of a German *Panzerschiffe* and that information was passed to Harwood on the

13. Almost no photographs exist of the actual Battle of the River Plate that show more than shell splashes or distant puffs of smoke. This image taken from *Achilles* showing HMS *Ajax* (22) late in the battle as the two light cruisers chased *Graf Spee* towards the west is an exception. It is interesting because it shows the blistered paint on the 6in barrels of *Achilles*' 'X' turret, rotated as far forward to port as possible. It also shows the collapsed main topmast on *Ajax*, which allows the time of this image to be established as sometime after 0748, when the two cruisers turned to the west again to trail *Graf Spee*. (*NZOH*)

14. The paint has entirely burnt off the barrels of *Achilles*' forward main battery turrets as she chases *Graf Spee* towards Montevideo. Her forward turrets had fired far more rounds than her after battery, accounting for the greater damage to the paintwork. *Achilles* had received only splinter damage during the battle, mainly to her bridge and DCT, not discernible in this image. (*NZOH*)

flagship. If any doubt lingered in Harwood's mind, it was cleared up when at 0617 *Graf Spee* turned 90° to port to allow both turrets to bear and opened fire at 22,500yd, her after turret firing at *Exeter* and the forward at *Ajax*. Her first salvo fell 300yd short of *Ajax*. *Exeter* opened fire two minutes later. The First Division turned 45° towards the enemy and *Achilles* opened fire at 0621 and *Ajax* two minutes after that. Harwood ordered his division to fire in concentration, meaning that *Achilles* would take target range and bearing from *Ajax*.[29]

It is clear from *Graf Spee*'s behaviour that *Exeter*'s gunfire was of greater concern than that of the light cruisers because immediately after completing her turn to port, she began a slow turn back to starboard to allow both main-battery turrets to bear on the heavy cruiser, while firing at the light cruisers with her 15cm secondary battery. At 0623, one shell from *Graf Spee*'s third main-battery salvo burst just short of *Exeter* and caused serious damage amidships, killing or injuring most of the men manning her starboard torpedo tubes. This was followed a minute later by a direct hit that passed through her hull beneath her forward superstructure without exploding and another that burst on the face of 'B' turret, putting one-third of her main battery out of action.[30] The shell exploded on striking the 1in armour between the gun barrels, destroying the armour plate and killing eight men in the gun crew, and, just as seriously, spraying the bridge with shell fragments, killing or seriously wounding all bridge personnel except the captain and two others, and destroying all communications between the bridge and the rest of the ship. For several minutes, before Captain F S Bell was able to resume command at the after conning station, the ship began a

BIG GUN BATTLES

slow turn to starboard. During that brief interval, *Exeter* was hit twice more and near-missed several more times. One hit her starboard bower anchor right forward, leaving a large gash and numerous splinter holes in her shell plating, starting a fire in her paint locker; the second hit the forecastle deck forward of 'A' turret, starting fires and adding more splinter holes forward. The cumulative effect of these multiple small holes in *Exeter*'s shell plating forward was a steady accumulation of water in her bow compartments.

Though suffering from very good initial shooting on the part of *Graf Spee*, *Exeter* was able to exact some measure of revenge. One 8in shell from an early salvo hit *Graf Spee*'s starboard 10.5cm anti-aircraft mount at approximately 0623, killing most of the gun crew and continuing through two decks before exploding in her auxiliary engineering space. The detonation damaged the boiler that generated steam for both her fresh water distillation unit and fuel cleaner.[31] While this damage did not have immediate impact, it would explain decisions made over the next several days.

While *Graf Spee* continued duelling with *Exeter* off to starboard as the range between them narrowed, it was the rapid gunfire from the two light cruisers directly ahead – sixteen 6in shells four times a minute – that began to concern Langsdorff. Worried about their gunfire and the danger of a torpedo attack, he ordered 'Anton' turret switched to firing at the light cruisers, and at 0637 decided to haul about nearly 180° towards the northwest and at the same time make smoke. By doing so, Langsdorff tacitly admitted that his hope for a rapid victory over the British had vanished and that the best he could hope for was a brief respite from threat of the light cruisers while he attempted to knock *Exeter* out of the fight.

Ironically, the torpedo attack Langsdorff feared came not from the light cruisers, but from *Exeter*, which fired her starboard torpedoes at 0632 and then, turning to the northeast, fired her port tubes at 0643. All six torpedoes missed. Just as *Graf Spee* was turning, *Exeter* managed one more hit; an 8in shell penetrated the upper strake of her armour belt on her port side directly below her conning tower, exploding on her armoured deck, demolishing her galley and causing minor flooding. At the time, this was considered the most serious hit she received in the battle.

As *Exeter* was turning to port and *Graf Spee* was momentarily hidden from the light cruisers by her smokescreen, Langsdorff ordered both main turrets back onto the heavy cruiser and again hit *Exeter* hard. At 0638, a 28cm shell hit the right-hand gun of 'A' turret, disabling that turret. A short time later, two more 28cm shells hit *Exeter*. One passed through her forward superstructure, exploding on the foremost starboard 4in AA mount; the other penetrated her deck just aft of the bridge and exploded in the CPO's flat, starting fires and punching numerous holes in her shell plating on the starboard side near the waterline. On fire forward and amidships, *Exeter* turned towards the west-southwest wreathed in smoke. Observers on *Graf Spee* thought *Exeter* was now out of action, though she continued to fire her 'Y' turret under local control, and both of *Graf Spee*'s main-battery turrets swung back towards Harwood's division, which was well behind on her port quarter.

15. A closer look at the front of *Achilles'* DCT shows two large holes where shell splinters penetrated the lower part of the tower structure. These metal fragments, along with four more that entered the DCT's starboard side, killed three men outright and wounded most of the rest of the DCT crew and several more on the bridge, including the ship's captain. (*NZOH*)

16. *Exeter* was hit hard by *Graf Spee* at the Battle of the River Plate. Looking aft from her forecastle, the damage is apparent in this photograph taken at Port Stanley after the battle. The right-hand gun of 'A' turret, on the left in the foreground in this image, took a direct hit near the turret face at 0638, putting the turret out of action. 'B' turret was hit between the gun barrels at 0624, demolishing the armour there and disabling that turret. The face of the bridge has been hit by multiple shell fragments from these hits and numerous near-misses.

17. The view inside *Exeter*'s bridge looking forward shows some of the holes punched through the thin steel upper face and overhead by shell splinters from the hits on her forward main battery turrets. Note the recognition silhouettes painted on the upper bulkhead; each column of three shows the same ship from three different angles – broadside on, aft of the starboard beam and from the starboard quarter. The column on the right appears to show *Admiral Scheer*, near-sister to *Graf Spee*.

18. Looking forward from *Exeter*'s bridge, this image was taken during the passage to Port Stanley, before her 'A' turret had been rotated back to facing forward. Note the large black letters 'EX' painted on the roofs of both forward turrets as a recognition feature and that the letters on 'A' turret faced the ship's starboard side while those on 'B' turret faced aft.

Her first full broadside at the light cruisers, fired at 0640, drew blood. At least one shell fell just short, exploding in line with *Achilles'* bridge, spraying her bridge and the DCT above with shell splinters. Her gunnery officer, Lieutenant R E Washbourne, described an all-too-typical scene as seen from his position in the DCT:

> I was only conscious of a hellish noise and a thump on the head which half stunned me . . . Six heavy splinters had entered the DCT. The right-hand side of the upper compartment was a shambles. Both W/T ratings were down with multiple injuries . . . A.B. Sherley had dropped off his platform, bleeding copiously from a gash in his face and wounds in both thighs. Sergeant Trimble, Royal Marines, the spotting observer, was also severely wounded . . . A.B. Shaw slumped forward onto his instrument, dead, with multiple wounds in his chest . . . The rate officer, Mr. Watts, quickly passed me a yard or so of bandage, enabling me to effect running repairs to my slight scalp wounds which were bleeding fairly freely. I then redirected my attention to the business in hand, while Mr. Watts clambered round behind me to do what he could for the wounded.[32]

Three men died in *Achilles'* DCT and most of the remaining crew were injured to varying degrees. One man was seriously injured on the bridge and Captain W E Parry took a splinter in his right shin, but remained in command. More importantly, the splinters damaged her radios, leaving *Achilles* unable to receive range and bearing data from *Ajax*, causing her to revert to local control. At almost the same time, *Ajax* flew off her spotting aircraft, but the spotter initially used the wrong frequency and, even after that was corrected, was unaware that *Achilles'* gunfire was no longer conforming to that of *Ajax*, causing invalid correction data to be passed back to the ship. The combined impact of these two errors was that the gunfire from Harwood's light cruisers was ineffective for more than twenty minutes, starting at 0646.[33]

It is again necessary to ask at this point why Langsdorff did not take advantage of this situation, with *Exeter* obviously seriously damaged, and the two light cruisers well aft, to either double back in an attempt to complete the destruction of the First Division or turn north to escape. Neither manoeuvre was guaranteed success, but to try neither and simply continue to the west was to concede the initiative and reduce his tactical options with each passing minute. There has never been a simple explanation for why Langsdorff failed to take the initiative at this point. He was wounded on two occasions by 6in shells hitting *Graf Spee's* tower mast, once at 0717 and again a few minutes later. None of his wounds was serious, although the second left him unconscious for a few minutes. However, by this time, Harwood's cruisers, now making 31kt, were catching up to *Graf Spee* and his best opportunity to take decisive action had already passed. His ship had at some point received one more serious hit, a 6in shell that entered her forecastle from the starboard side and exploded against her port side, blowing several holes in her bow plating just above the waterline. It is unlikely that Langsdorff was even aware of this damage or the damage to the auxiliary boiler at this time. Whatever the reason, *Graf Spee* continued towards the west.

At approximately 0715, Langsdorff again ordered smoke and a turn to port. This manoeuvre was seen by Harwood, who ordered a matching turn to close the enemy and, if possible, to distract him from following *Exeter*. The manoeuvre worked: *Graf Spee* came around to starboard and again engaged the light cruisers with both main-battery turrets. Still quite capable of accurate gunfire, *Ajax* was quickly straddled and, at 0725, was hit aft by a single 28cm shell that destroyed the rotating machinery of 'X' turret and then jammed 'Y' turret in place, effectively reducing Harwood's gunfire by 25 per cent. Uncomfortable with *Graf Spee*'s accurate shooting, the light cruisers turned away 45° to open the range and, perhaps, throw off the German's rangefinding. Langsdorff did not turn to follow. At 0729, flooding put *Exeter*'s 'Y' turret out of action and, with no operational main-battery guns, she turned away to the southeast, towards the Falklands. Langsdorff did not follow this turn either.

Ajax fired torpedoes soon after her turn to starboard, but they broached and were seen from *Graf Spee*, which turned to port to avoid them and fired a single torpedo at *Ajax*, which also missed. As Langsdorff brought *Graf Spee* back to a northwest and then a due west heading, Harwood received a report that *Ajax* only had 20 per cent of her main-battery rounds remaining. It transpired that this report was accurate only for 'A' turret – in fact, there was significantly more ordnance available, but before this was cleared up, Harwood had decided to break off the engagement, turning east at 0740. Just as she was turning away, a shot from *Graf Spee* severed *Ajax*'s main topmast, bringing down all her radio aerials. At 0748, the two light cruisers turned back to trail *Graf Spee* to the west.

It is not clear when Langsdorff decided to find refuge at Montevideo. He did not receive a full report on his ship's damage until after Harwood broke off the action, and he concluded, after consulting his officers, that *Graf Spee* was in no condition to undertake the passage home without significant repairs and that he had no chance of escaping Harwood's pursuit. However, it is likely that he had reached this conclusion much earlier, given *Graf Spee*'s generally westerly course since well before 0700 and his failure to attempt any manoeuvre that would have allowed him other choices.

Langsdorff composed a report to SKL, informing them of his intentions. They had little choice but to approve his decision. *Graf Spee* continued at a steady 23kt, maintaining a course just south of due west, heading for the dredged channel north of English Bank that led into the Uruguayan port. At 1010, she fired off three salvos at *Achilles*, which had come a bit too close, but did not hit her. She fired at the British cruisers several more times, the last time at 2145. At 2350, *Graf Spee* entered Montevideo.

Who Shot Well?

Assuming that, as postulated, Langsdorff believed he had already been sighted at 0600 and therefore was committed to fight Harwood, the question remaining to be answered is, seen purely as a gunnery duel, how well did each side fight that

19. *Graf Spee* coming to anchor in Montevideo, Uruguay, 14 December 1939. The German supply ship *Tacoma*, which had been interned at the beginning of the war, is at the left in this view. One of her motor whaleboats is to the left, carrying crew members ashore. Very little of the damage done to the *Panzerschiff* could be seen from any distance, leading to a great deal of speculation as to why Captain Langsdorff had brought his ship into this neutral harbour, where international law limited the repairs that could be done to only those necessary to make the ship seaworthy. The only damage obvious in this view is the large shell hole forward, directly aft of her anchor. (*NHHC*)

day? *Graf Spee* opened fire at 22,500yd, half her theoretical maximum range, a range at which, in the good visibility then prevailing, accurate shooting should have been expected.[34] Her DeTe-Gerät radar set was operating normally but played no role in fire control during this battle.[35] Rangefinding was done with her excellent 10.5m (34ft) Zeiss stereoscopic rangefinders, one mounted high on her tower foremast and a second on her after superstructure. (The British cruisers were equipped with rangefinders that were both smaller in base length and were coincidence type, which, while theoretically as accurate as stereoscopic rangefinders, were more prone to error in battle conditions.)

Initially, both *Graf Spee* and *Exeter* shot very well. *Exeter* was straddled on *Graf Spee*'s third salvo and hit twice within the next two minutes. *Exeter* shot just as well, likewise straddling *Graf Spee* on her third salvo and hitting her hard on her fifth or sixth. As seen by Commander F W Rasenack, a gunnery officer in *Graf Spee*, describing *Exeter*'s initial shooting in general, and this first hit in particular: '. . . its marksmanship is astonishing and the rapidity with which the salvos follow each other surprising. An 8-in. shell goes through the armour plate of one of our anti-aircraft guns of 10.5cm on the starboard side. It kills half the gun crew, goes through two decks and finally explodes in the apparatus for producing fresh water.'[36]

Graf Spee began the battle with her full complement of 100 rounds per main-battery gun (two-thirds HE (half base fuse and half nose fuse) and only one-third APC). Her first ranging shots were HE base fuse because they would not immediately explode upon hitting water, making them better for gauging fall of shot. The shell which passed through *Exeter*'s forecastle without exploding was probably a base fuse round. The shell that exploded on the face of 'B' turret might have been either type of HE shell. She continued firing primarily HE shells, eventually expending all the nose fuse rounds, all but

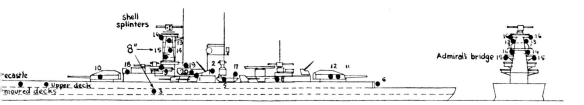

shell splinters

8"

recastle

moured decks

upper deck

Admiral's bridge

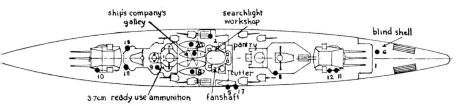

ships company's galley

searchlight workshop

pantry

blind shell

cutter

37cm ready use ammunition

fanshaft

Admiral Graf Spee

Diagram showing hits

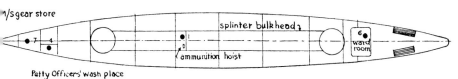

M/s gear store

splinter bulkhead

ward room

ammunition hoist

Petty Officers' wash place

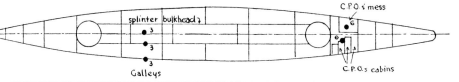

C.P.O.'s mess

splinter bulkhead

C.P.O.'s cabins

Galleys

N°s 3 & 15 are 8" hits
The remainder are 6"

20. This chart shows one set of estimates of the hits obtained on *Graf Spee* by Harwood's Force 'G' on 13 December 1939. The narrative offered by the author differs in some significant ways from this chart, particularly in that hit #2 was also an 8in shell and that after damaging the starboard 10.5cm mount, it went down through both armoured decks to cause significant internal damage not shown in this chart in the general area where the damage from hit #1 is shown.

21. The large exit hole in *Graf Spee*'s forecastle shell plating recorded as hit #4 in the preceding chart can be seen in this image, as can the white false bow wave painted on to confuse enemy attempts to estimate her speed. Judging from the size of this hole, it is tempting to presume it was caused by an 8in rather than a 6in shell. (NHHC)

22. More of the damage sustained by *Graf Spee* at the Battle of the River Plate, 13 December 1939. Her Ar-196A-1 is now a burnt-out shell and there is splinter damage visible along her hull shell plating and 15cm secondary battery mounts. There is even a neat hole punched through her aircraft-handling crane. (*NHHC*)

23. Late in the afternoon on 17 December 1939, *Graf Spee* ran out of time. International law required her to leave Montevideo. Rather than face what he believed to be an overwhelmingly powerful British squadron waiting out to sea, Langsdorff turned his ship towards the shallow water west of the port and set off scuttling charges, bringing about the only end possible for his ship once he decided to engage Harwood's squadron. (*NHHC*)

24. Captain Hans Langsdorff (left) had perhaps too romantic a notion of naval warfare, growing up idolising the German naval hero Graf von Spee, after whom his command was named. It is speculated that he found the commerce warfare he conducted so successfully in *Graf Spee* to be unsuited to a true warrior and craved the 'real' battle he found against Force 'G'. After scuttling his ship, he committed suicide in a naval hostel in Buenos Aires, Argentina, wrapped in his ship's ensign, on 20 December 1939. (*NHHC*)

25. On 15 February 1940, *Exeter* arrived at Plymouth after a long, slow passage north from Port Stanley, to be met by a cheering crowd of dockyard workers. Considerable effort had been put into patching up her forward turrets and forward bridgework with sheet metal and paint, but, as can be seen from the plated-over turret faces, the repairs were entirely cosmetic. Only 'Y' turret could have functioned had she been forced to fight on her way home. She would be under repair and refit for a full year. (*NHIIC*)

sixteen of the base fuse and 30 of the APC rounds, leaving 186 rounds (or 31 per barrel) at the end of the day.[37] For this expenditure of munitions, she achieved eight hits on *Exeter* and two on *Ajax* for a hit percentage of 2.7 per cent. To this must be be added some number of near-misses for damage, but on the negative side *Graf Spee*'s secondary batteries fired 377 15cm and 80 10.5cm rounds for no recorded hits.

While an exact record of the hits obtained on *Graf Spee* by Harwood's squadron is impossible to obtain, the best estimate is that twenty rounds struck the *Panzerschiff*, three 8in shells from *Exeter* and seventeen 6in rounds from the light cruisers. *Exeter* fired approximately two hundred 8in rounds, meaning she recorded a hit rate of 1.5 per cent, though it must be remembered that most of the shells she fired were from 'Y' turret, which primarily fired under local control. *Ajax* fired 823 6in rounds and *Achilles* fired 1,241, obtaining between them seventeen hits, for a hit percentage of 0.8 per cent, making *Graf Spee*'s shooting look excellent in comparison. Regardless, the shooting of Harwood's squadron was good enough to damage *Graf Spee* to the extent that an immediate attempt to head for home was out of the question, and that was enough to doom the *Panzerschiff*.

An Anti-Climactic Ending

The remaining days of *Graf Spee*'s life were anti-climactic, taken up mainly with diplomatic negotiations over how long she would be allowed to stay at Montevideo. In the end, the British were able to apply more pressure than the Germans and after seventy-two hours, she was required to leave port without having repaired the most serious damage. Convinced that a strong British squadron had now assembled off the La Plata estuary, Langsdorff sought and received permission from Germany to scuttle his ship if he decided he had no chance of 'fighting her through' to Buenos Aires. After most of her crew had been landed, *Graf Spee* left port at 1700 on 17 December, turned west and, after the last of her crew was taken off by tugs, blew herself up as the sun was setting.

The human cost needs to be reckoned. *Exeter* took the greatest damage and paid the greatest price. Sixty-three of her officers and men died that day or of wounds in the next few days.[38] Seven from *Ajax* and four from *Achilles* also were killed. Thirty-seven of *Graf Spee*'s men were killed in the battle, to which total must be added Hans Langsdorff, who committed suicide two days later, shooting himself on a bed covered with his ship's battle ensign.

'The Navy's Here!'

Graf Spee's supply ship, *Altmark*, was now on its own and headed back towards Germany, carrying 299 prisoners taken off ships sunk by the raider. By mid-February 1940, she had reached the coast of Norway and entered the Inner Leads, hoping to reach the Skagerrak without interference by the Royal Navy. However, her presence was soon noted by the still-neutral Norwegians, who stopped and boarded her three times on 15 February. Each time she was given a cursory inspection which failed to discover the presence of the prisoners and each time was allowed to proceed further south. The next day, she was stopped

26. The next day, 16 February 1940, the *Graf Spee* story came to an end when her supply ship *Altmark*, carrying 299 captured British merchant seamen, was stopped and boarded by HMS *Cossack* (F03) in Jøssingfjord on the Norwegian coast. (*NHHC*)

27. The winter of 1939–40 was one of the coldest on record in northern Europe, causing icing in North Sea estuaries that are normally ice-free all year round. The ice hindered naval operations, delaying the start of Operation Nordmark, a plan by the Kriegsmarine to sweep from Wilhelmshaven towards the Shetlands looking for suspected British convoy traffic headed for Norway. On 18 February 1940, *Scharnhorst* is seen attempting to lead a destroyer and her sister *Gneisenau* through the ice towards open water. The operation failed to find any enemy ships. (*NARA*)

and boarded in Jøssingfjord southeast of Egersund by sailors from HMS *Cossack* (F03) under the command of Captain Philip Vian (later Admiral of the Fleet Sir Philip Vian) and the prisoners were rescued in an incident that drew protests from the Norwegian government. More importantly, the incident fed Hitler's fears that the British were planning to occupy Norway, thus cutting the traffic in Swedish iron ore vital to the German war economy, causing Hitler to intensify planning for a 'pre-emptive' German occupation of the country.

Move and Countermove into Norway

The German invasion of Norway, Operation Weserübung, was the largest and most ambitious naval operation of the war by the Kriegsmarine. In no sense an amphibious operation like the various Allied invasions in North Africa, Europe and the Pacific, it required the movement of large numbers of troops and their equipment by naval vessels. Most of the landings on 9 April, at ports along the Norwegian coast between Oslo and Bergen met little opposition, but the Germans lost a heavy cruiser and light cruiser operating in narrow waters. Troops intended for landings at two ports further north, Trondheim and Narvik, were dispatched earlier than the more southerly groups because they had farther to travel, leaving Wilhelmshaven in the early hours of 7 April. These troops were carried in two groups under the command of Vice-Admiral Günther Lütjens. Group 1, heading for Narvik, comprised ten destroyers carrying troops, screened by the battlecruisers *Scharnhorst* and *Gneisenau*; Group 2, heading for Trondheim, comprised the heavy cruiser *Admiral Hipper* and four destroyers.

28. At the beginning of April 1940, both the Kriegsmarine and Royal Navy launched operations designed to occupy part or all of Norway. The German operation, Weserübung, was larger, better prepared and much more successful. At several points, the rival forces intersected, with violent results. In terrible weather, the destroyer HMS *Glowworm* (H92) ran into the German heavy cruiser *Admiral Hipper* northwest of Trondheim soon after dawn on 8 April and lost a brief, very unequal fight, but not before damaging the cruiser. This image is from early in the fight, when *Glowworm*, laying a smokescreen, cut across *Hipper*'s bow before turning sharply and ramming the cruiser. (*NHHC*)

BIG GUN BATTLES

29. *Renown* was the flagship of Vice-Admiral Whitworth, leading a force of destroyers tasked with laying mines at the entrance to Vestfjord. Compared to how she appeared in 1920, she has had a major reconstruction that replaced her tripod foremast with a massive forward superstructure topped by a large main battery DCT and, above that, two high-angle directors. Whitworth arrived off Vestfjord on 8 April 1940 with orders to prevent any German ships entering the fjord, but, concerned about the weather and U-boats, he turned west at dusk, opening the way for ten German destroyers to proceed on towards Narvik. (*NHHC*)

The Allies also had a complicated two-stage plan for occupying several Norwegian ports. The first stage, called Operation Wilfred, was to involve mining the Inner Leads at several points. This was supposed to provoke a German response, to which the Allies would respond by occupying Narvik, Trondheim and Bergen, which was covered under Plan R4. Wilfred was supposed to be carried out on 5 April, but was delayed until 8 April. A force comprising the battlecruiser HMS *Renown* (72) and four destroyers left Scapa Flow on 5 April, tasked with screening eight more destroyers which were to lay a minefield at the entrance to Vestfjord, the waterway leading to Narvik.[39]

Given the timing of the departures and the speed of the respective forces, it seemed possible that they would meet somewhere off the Norwegian coast. Bad luck and bad weather guaranteed that it would happen. A day out of Scapa, with the weather steadily building into a full-strength North Sea gale, one of *Renown*'s escorts, HMS *Glowworm* (H92) turned back to recover a man lost overboard. By the time the recovery was effected, *Glowworm* had lost touch with *Renown* and had turned back towards Scapa, but was told to reverse course again and attempt to rejoin the battlecruiser as she headed towards the entry to Vestfjord. Following alone through heavy seas, *Glowworm* spotted a destroyer-sized ship at dawn two days later, 8 April, northwest of Trondheim. Not immediately able to identify the other ship, Lieutenant Commander B G Roope ordered the challenge flashed, to which the other ship replied that she was the Swedish destroyer *Göteborg*. Not believing this, Roope opened fire on the other ship, which was in fact *Z18* (*Hans Lüdemann*), one of the Group 1

30. When *Renown* approached Vestfjord again the next morning, she was greeted by *Scharnhorst* and *Gneisenau*. The German commander, Vice-Admiral Günther Lütjens, followed his orders, which were to avoid contact with enemy capital ships. Accordingly, he turned away and made smoke, as *Gneisenau* is doing in this image taken from *Scharnhorst* that morning. Heavy seas and engine trouble allowed *Renown* to maintain contact for more than three hours and hit *Gneisenau* once in her foretop. (*NHHC*)

destroyers bound for Narvik, but after just two salvos the German disappeared in the mist and *Glowworm* ceased fire.

Only moments later, *Glowworm* sighted another German destroyer, *Z11* (*Bernd von Arnim*), and the two ships exchanged gunfire starting at 0802, neither scoring a hit due to the rough seas. The gunfire continued sporadically for almost an hour as *Glowworm*, which was handling the heavy weather marginally better than the larger German destroyer, was gradually overtaking the German. She was nearing a position to launch torpedoes when, at 0850, *Hipper* emerged from the gloom and, nine minutes later, opened fire. Much larger and more stable than a destroyer in these conditions, *Hipper* soon scored multiple hits, despite *Glowworm* laying an effective smokescreen. Wishing to finish off the destroyer, *Hipper* plunged into the smokescreen and emerged on the other side to find *Glowworm* on course to ram her starboard bow. The collision proved unavoidable and *Glowworm*'s prow scraped along *Hipper*'s starboard side, opening a gash from her bow to just under her bridge. Now dead in the water, afire and listing heavily, the destroyer capsized at 0924. Thirty-nine of her crew were rescued from the frigid water; 111, including Roope, were not. *Hipper* took on over 500t of water, but was not seriously damaged. She was able to deliver her troops to Trondheim and then steam at speed back to Germany where she was under repair until the beginning of June.

Scharnhorst and *Gneisenau* continued north as escort for the ten destroyers carrying troops to Narvik. *Renown*, now accompanied by nine destroyers, arrived off the entrance to Vestfjord during the day on 8 April with orders to prevent any German ships entering the fjord. The British commander in *Renown*,

Vice-Admiral W J Whitworth, decided that, given the foul weather, a close blockade of the fjord entrance overnight was dangerous and unnecessary and withdrew to the west at dusk. The German invasion force arrived at the entrance to Vestfjord barely two hours after Whitworth withdrew; the destroyers entered the fjord and the two battlecruisers turned northwest, unknowingly following Whitworth's wake. At 0240 the next morning, 9 April, *Renown* turned back towards Vestfjord and, almost exactly an hour later, sighted the two Germans to the east. Despite poor visibility, the action quickly developed into a stern chase, with the Germans in the lead. *Scharnhorst* and *Gneisenau* were handling the rough seas somewhat better and began to pull away, but mechanical problems in the former reduced her speed and allowed *Renown* to maintain intermittent contact until 0615.[40] During the long chase, *Gneisenau* took one hit in her foretop that destroyed her primary gun control and killed six crewmen. *Renown* was hit twice, for minor damage.[41]

An Inglorious Ending

The ten German destroyers which entered Vestfjord on 8 April were destined never to leave. Two battles were fought in the fjord on 10 April and 13 April, in the course of which two Royal Navy destroyers and all of the Germans were sunk.[42] The Allies followed this advantage up very slowly, but, by 29 May, Allied forces had occupied Narvik. However, this was a classic case of 'too little, too late'. Even before the town itself was taken, the decision had been made to evacuate the Allied troops because of events elsewhere, particularly the collapse of the Allied armies in Belgium and northern France that led to the evacuations from Dunkirk.

Before this became known in Germany, the Kriegsmarine planned a sortie codenamed Operation Juno by the two battlecruisers, *Hipper* and four destroyers against Harstad, the main Allied base supporting the Narvik operation. Departing Kiel on 4 June, the plan was to arrive off Harstad during the night of 8–9 June. The German squadron, under Vice-Admiral Wilhelm Marschall, replenished on 6–7 June from the supply ship *Ditmarschen*, a sister of *Altmark*. As this was completing, Marschall received word that the Allied evacuation of Narvik was underway and that there were two groups of transports crossing the North Sea towards England. On the morning of 8 June, the German squadron sighted the trawler HMS *Juniper* (T123) escorting the tanker *Oil Pioneer* and quickly dispatched both. A little more hunting turned up the empty troopship *Orama* and hospital ship *Atlantis*. The latter was spared. While *Hipper* and the destroyers were left to finish off the troopship and hunt for other stragglers, the two battlecruisers were ordered to hunt bigger game closer to Harstad.

Earlier that same morning, further east, near the Lofoten Islands, two Royal Navy aircraft carriers (HMS *Ark Royal* (91) and *Glorious* (77)) waited for an evacuation convoy from Harstad.[43] Two RAF squadrons based near Harstad had been ordered to fly out to *Glorious* and land on her short flight deck, a feat of considerable skill and daring, especially considering that none of the pilots had previously made a carrier landing. To allow room for these aircraft to be struck below into her hangar, *Glorious* had sailed with a reduced air group of Sea

31. Operation Juno was another attempt by the Kriegsmarine to influence the Norwegian campaign. At the beginning of June, the two battlecruisers and *Hipper* were dispatched to the latitude of Narvik in an attempt to interrupt the Allied traffic to and from Harstad. On 8 June 1940, *Hipper* and two destroyers came across the troop transport *Orama*, fortuitously empty (except for 100 German POWs), and dispatched her speedily with gunfire and torpedoes.

Gladiator fighters and Swordfish torpedo-bombers.[44] By all accounts, *Glorious* was not a happy ship, with serious dissension between her CO, Captain Guy D'Oyly-Hughes, and her air staff, particularly her air officer, Commander J B Heath, who had been left ashore at Scapa Flow to await discipline before she sailed on 3 June. The official story given at the time was that, after flying on the RAF aircraft, D'Oyly-Hughes requested and received permission to proceed immediately to Scapa, without waiting for the convoy, due to fuel shortage. It is now known that *Glorious* was ordered home by Admiral Forbes in order to resolve the issues between D'Oyly-Hughes and Heath. *Glorious* and two destroyers, HMS *Acasta* (H09) and *Ardent* (H41), parted company with *Ark Royal* at 0253 on 8 June and set course west-southwest at 22kt.

The dissension may have distracted D'Oyly-Hughes from his responsibilities as captain of a major warship and commander of a group of three ships in a war zone. While there had been no specific warnings of enemy activity passed to *Glorious*, these were contested waters known to be prowled by enemy submarines and periodically traversed by surface units. (The attacks on *Juniper*, *Oil Pioneer* and *Orama* had not yet occurred when *Glorious* started for Scapa and there is no evidence D'Oyly-Hughes was ever informed of them.) Regardless of the reason, it is difficult to understand D'Oyly-Hughes' actions, or, more specifically, lack of actions, as the day wore on. By 1600, *Glorious* was zigzagging around a base course of 205° at 17kt, at cruising stations, with only two-thirds of her boilers lit, no lookouts at her masthead, no aircraft aloft and none ready on deck. In other words, she was in no way prepared to give battle should an enemy appear, which, at approximately 1620, was exactly what happened. Two ships were sighted coming bow-on over the western horizon. They might have been spotted sooner but none of the British ships had radar. *Ardent* was ordered to investigate. At the same time, 'action stations' was ordered and word was passed for the available Swordfish torpedo-bombers to be armed and brought up to the flight deck.[45] (*Glorious* reportedly had one Swordfish at ten minutes' readiness and two more at twenty minutes' notice.)

It probably would have made little difference had there been more aircraft at a higher state of readiness. Lookouts on *Scharnhorst*, which was steaming towards the northwest at 19kt, east of and somewhat abaft her sister, sighted smoke on the eastern horizon at 1546. They maintained course and speed for another twenty minutes as the mast of a warship gradually appeared over the horizon, not increasing speed and turning towards the enemy until 1606. Within minutes after that, the Germans could see that they were approaching an aircraft carrier and two destroyers, on a nearly reciprocal course. *Scharnhorst* opened fire at 1632 at a range of 28,600yd. Once again, German shooting was extremely good. On her third salvo, a 28cm shell penetrated *Glorious*' flight deck, exploded in her upper hangar, disabling the aircraft being readied there, starting multiple fires and damaging two boilers, temporarily reducing her speed. *Glorious* maintained a steady course until 1647. (This hit, at a range of slightly greater than 26,000yds, is a candidate for the longest recorded gunfire hit; the only competition is a hit by HMS *Warspite* at the Battle of Punta Stilo described in the next chapter.)[46]

32. That same day, the two German battlecruisers found a target for their 28cm main battery guns. *Gneisenau* is firing a three-gun salvo from 'Bruno' turret while the guns of 'Anton' appear to have been lowered to the loading angle for this mount (Drh LC/34), which was 2°. Judging from the grey tones in this image, in particular the field surrounding the white disk painted on her foredeck, a field known to be red – and given that there is ample documentary evidence that the turret tops of the ships involved in Operation Juno were painted dark grey, and further noting the similarity in value of the turret tops with the red field on the foredeck, there appears to be reason to doubt the common attribution of this photograph as showing *Gneisenau* firing at HMS *Glorious* (77) on 8 June 40. (*NHHC*)

Ardent approached to within 16,000yd, under fire from the secondary battery of both battlecruisers, fired torpedoes which missed and then withdrew to join *Acasta* in laying a smokescreen around *Glorious*. This smokescreen was sufficient to obscure the carrier to the extent that the Germans ceased fire at 1658. But just before that, at 1656, a hit by *Gneisenau* on *Glorious'* homing beacon destroyed her flying bridge and killed D'Oyly-Hughes. This did not bring the action to an end. *Ardent* emerged from the smoke to fire torpedoes again and was again engaged by the battlecruisers' secondary batteries. She was hit hard at 1704 and was now afire, listing to port and had slowed to 15kt. *Ardent* received such a steady rain of gunfire from both ships' 15cm and 10.5cm batteries that the order was passed from *Scharnhorst* not to waste ammunition. At 1722, *Ardent's* mast was seen to collapse, after which she rapidly rolled over and sank.

Meanwhile, without *Ardent's* contribution to the smokescreen, *Glorious* was under fire again at 1718. Two minutes later, she was hit by a 28cm shell from *Gneisenau* that detonated in her centre engine room, after which her speed dropped, she took on a starboard list and began circling to port. From that point, it was only a matter of time before she was destroyed. By 1740, the Germans ceased firing as she was now dead in the water and ablaze along her whole length. *Glorious* sank at approximately 1810.

Acasta, which had been on *Glorious'* far side, crossed over to her port side at about 1705 to do a better job of screening the carrier, and she continued this until *Glorious* was obviously doomed. At that point, her CO, Commander Charles Glasfurd, his ship undamaged, made the rash decision to attack the battlecruisers, emerging from the smokescreen and looping ahead of *Scharnhorst*, firing two salvos of four torpedoes, one of which hit *Scharnhorst* near her after

33. Regardless of whether the preceding photograph shows *Gneisenau* on 8 June 1940, there can be no doubt that this image shows *Glorious* on that date, sometime after the hit in her centre engine room by *Gneisenau* at 1720 that started a major fire, caused a serious list to starboard and started her circling to port. (*NHHC*)

main-battery turret on the starboard side, blowing a hole 45ft long in her shell plating, flooding thirty compartments with 2,500t of water, damaging two of her three shafts and killing forty-eight officers and men. *Acasta* was overwhelmed by the battlecruisers' secondary batteries and was seen to sink at 1820.

Because of the damage to *Scharnhorst*, the Germans departed the scene immediately, heading for Trondheim. This meant they would not be in position to intercept the second evacuation convoy loaded with troops, following just hours behind *Glorious*. More importantly for the crews of the three British warships, it meant the Germans made no effort to rescue survivors, which they might have otherwise done. The closest British ship was heavy cruiser HMS *Devonshire* (39), which was carrying the Norwegian royal family from Tromsø. She picked up a garbled version of the only sighting report sent by *Glorious*, but never considered coming to her aid, given the importance of her passengers. Wreckage and bodies in the water were sighted the next day by ships in the evacuation convoy, but no effort was made to recover the bodies or look for survivors. A Norwegian steamer en route from Tromsø to Tórshavn (in the Faroes) found twenty-one rafts and thirty-five survivors on 10–11 June and took them to Tórshavn, where they boarded the destroyer HMS *Veteran* (D72) for passage to Rosyth. Another four were rescued by a Norwegian ship that returned them to Norway, and one was picked up by a German reconnaissance seaplane. Thus forty men survived out of the combined crews of three ships, their air complements and the RAF pilots who had the misfortune to fly on to *Glorious*. The best estimate is that 1,519 officers and men died in the three ships.

Mutual Exhaustion

This ended the Norwegian campaign and the war at sea in the north entered a lull. With the Germans soon in possession of a coastline stretching from above the Arctic Circle to the Spanish border and a seemingly invincible army across the Dover Strait, the Royal Navy was very much on the defensive in home waters, tasked with protecting against a potential invasion from the continent. Meanwhile, the Kriegsmarine had to assess the damage sustained since the beginning of the war. Besides losing *Graf Spee* early on, they had now lost a heavy cruiser and two light cruisers during the Norwegian campaign and the remaining large combatants were either under repair or refit.[47] It would be months before the Germans would be in a position to resume any surface-ship activity in the Atlantic.

While this temporary encumbrance of Germany's major warships should have offered a respite to the Royal Navy, with its own wounds to lick, the reality facing the British instead had got much darker as the summer of 1940 approached.[48] Not only had they lost the support of the French fleet, which in Allied planning was responsible for controlling the western Mediterranean, but, as of 10 June, the Italians had declared war and now the fifth largest fleet in the world was arrayed against them in the very waters where the French were now noticeably absent. The focus of the Admiralty's attention would shift very quickly to the Middle Sea.

2

LIGHT IN THE DARKNESS
ROYAL NAVY VS REGIA MARINA IN THE
MEDITERRANEAN, JUNE 1940–MARCH 1941

THE WAR IN THE MEDITERRANEAN BEGAN with a 'stab in the back'.[1] Regardless of the treachery with which Italy's entry into the war was viewed by FDR, and no doubt by the British and French, in the end, after France's surrender on 25 June, it left Great Britain with a strategic headache of massive proportions. As a nation utterly dependent on the import of nearly all strategic resources, the prospect of losing the use of the Mediterranean to bring oil from the Middle East and food and raw materials from India and the Far East was devastating. Routing shipping around the Cape of Good Hope rather than through the Suez Canal added weeks to the passage each way, leading to an immediate and significant reduction in the level of imports.

Notwithstanding the issue of imports, two more pressing problems arose from the defeat of France and the hostility of Italy. Although the French fleet, the fourth largest in the world, was now technically neutral, the British were uncomfortably aware of the possibility of some or all of it falling into German hands, which would dramatically shift the balance of naval power. While a few French warships had been based at English ports in June 1940, including the old battleships *Courbet* and *Paris* and several destroyers and submarines, and another eight ships, including the old battleship *Lorraine*, were based at Alexandria, most of the modern French warships were at Vichy-controlled African ports, mainly at Oran (Mers-el-Kébir) or Algiers (Alger/al-Jazaër), but also at Casablanca and Dakar. Churchill pressed hard for the neutralisation (through internment, surrender or demilitarisation) or destruction of all warships not actually at metropolitan French ports. For reasons both professional and personal, many of the Royal Navy's highest officers were reluctant to carry out the prime minister's desires, but he persuaded the War Cabinet to issue the necessary directives and these were quickly turned into orders for Operation Catapult, carried out at the beginning of July, which included the capture of French ships in British harbours, the negotiated demilitarisation of the squadron at Alexandria and an air attack on the almost-complete battleship *Richelieu* at Dakar by aircraft off HMS *Hermes* (D95) which obtained one hit by aerial torpedo, partially immobilising the battleship. The biggest consequence of Catapult, in terms of damage, casualties and political repercussions, was the attack on Mers-el-Kébir – where the French based the old battleships *Bretagne* and *Provence*, the new battlecruisers *Dunkerque* and *Strasbourg*, plus six destroyers – by the newly formed, Gibraltar-based Force 'H', comprising *Ark*

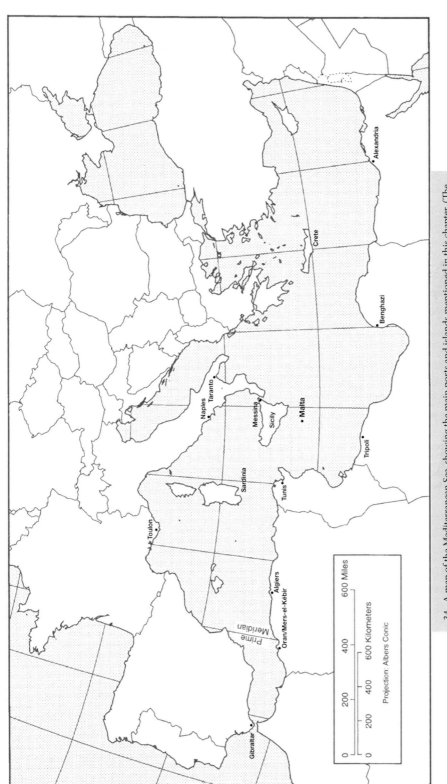

34. A map of the Mediterranean Sea, showing the main ports and islands mentioned in this chapter. (The political boundaries shown are modern, not those of the Second World War era.)

Royal, *Hood*, the old battleships *Resolution* (09) and *Valiant* (02) and supporting cruisers and destroyers. When the French refused the British demands, Force 'H' opened fire on the French ships, still moored at their quays. *Bretagne* was sunk, and *Dunkerque* and *Provence* were damaged along with one of the destroyers; *Strasbourg* and the remaining destroyers got underway, much to the surprise of the British, and escaped to Toulon along with the cruisers from Algiers. The French suffered 1,147 dead along with a massive blow to their *amour-propre*, which would colour their relations with the British for years to come.

Of equal consequence was the belligerence of the Italian Fleet, centrally positioned to divide the main British bases at Gibraltar and Alexandria, isolate the island bastion of Malta and support the expected Italian moves from Albania against Greece and from Libya against Egypt. The build up of Force 'H' at Gibraltar, where previously there had been only a small squadron of escort vessels, was an inevitable consequence of the changed strategic picture. That this force and the Mediterranean Fleet based at Alexandria would clash with the Regia Marina (RM), the Italian navy, was now predictable. Just as the Royal Navy needed to move transports, tankers and cargo ships east and west between its main bases and Malta if that island was to survive, the Italians needed to move the same kinds of ships north and south between Italy and North Africa if they were to attack the British position in Egypt.

The Italian Fleet had a number of old battleships that had been extensively modernised and two brand-new battleships (RN *Littorio* and *Vittorio Veneto*) just working up, along with a large fleet of fast, modern cruisers and destroyers. It should have been more than a match for the Royal Navy units on either flank separately or combined, but for some weaknesses that would plague it throughout the war. The Italians lagged far behind the Royal Navy in the acquisition of modern electronics of most types, particularly radars and sonars.[2] This would cost them dearly as the war progressed. From the beginning, naval leadership, both in Rome and at sea, was often overly cautious, well-aware that Italian industry had little ability to replace lost ships and that all resources, particularly fuel oil, were always in short supply. Perhaps the most serious problem facing the Regia Marina, similar to that faced by the Kriegsmarine, was the lack of an organic land-based naval aviation branch.[3] Lacking aircraft carriers, the RM depended on land-based aircraft for reconnaissance and air support, both offensive and defensive. Given the geography of the central basin of the Mediterranean, where no point is more than a few hundred miles from land, aircraft carriers should not have been necessary, but, in practice, the Regia Aeronautica (RA), the Italian air force, repeatedly failed to provide timely or adequate support for the Italian Fleet, while the Royal Navy, lacking the many land bases available to the Italians, but possessing a small number of vulnerable and undersized aircraft carriers, was able to effectively apply air power at critical points over the coming years.

An Expensive Victory

The war in the Mediterranean was barely two weeks old when the first of a seemingly endless series of skirmishes occurred between the two navies. Three Italian destroyers carrying an army anti-tank unit bound from Taranto to Tobruk

(Tubruq, Libya) were sighted by an RAF reconnaissance aircraft early on 28 June west of the Ionian Islands. The Mediterranean Fleet was at sea, escorting three convoys returning to Alexandria from Malta and Greece, and a squadron of five light cruisers was detached to intercept the Italians. The catch was made at 1830 west of Cape Matapan, with the destroyers silhouetted against the westering sun. The lead destroyer, *Espero*, developed a machinery defect that limited her to a maximum of 25kt; the Italian commander, Captain Enrico Baroni, ordered the two other destroyers to make good their escape while he made smoke and returned fire. The result was predictable but nonetheless instructive. *Espero* proved hard to hit, chasing shell splashes, dodging in and out of an effective smoke screen to fire off an occasional 120mm round at her pursuers.[4] The British cruisers, at this stage of the war not yet fitted with fire control radar, displayed far more enthusiasm than skill in gunnery. It took the British cruisers almost an hour and a half to sink *Espero*, by which time the other two destroyers had disappeared in the deepening gloom. The five cruisers had fired off nearly five thousand 6in rounds, approximately 85 per cent of their stock of that calibre munition in the theatre, requiring the temporary postponement of two Malta convoys.

Indecision off Calabria

The first major engagement between the British and Italian fleets would come just over a week later, again the result of convoy movements. Both sides had plans to run convoys through the central Mediterranean, the Italians moving five fast ships carrying reinforcements and supplies to Benghazi (Banghazi, Libya), the British wanting to run the convoys postponed after the *Espero* action. The

36. (*Left*) The man who commanded the Mediterranean Fleet at Punta Stilo, Admiral Sir Andrew B Cunningham, is seen here a little more than two years after that event, standing next to American General Dwight D Eisenhower. This photograph was taken on 16 October 1943 at the change of command ceremony at which Cunningham relinquished command of the Mediterranean Fleet to take up the post of First Sea Lord of the Admiralty. (*NARA*)

37. (*Right*) Commanding the Italian 1st Fleet was Admiral Inigo Campioni, seen here on the flag bridge of battleship *Conte di Cavour* at the Battle of Punta Stilo, 9 July 1940. (*ANMI via Cernuschi*)

Italian convoy left Naples on 6 July, joined by an escort eventually comprising two battleships, six heavy cruisers, eight light cruisers plus destroyers, and safely reached its destination late on the 8th. At this point, the Italian battle fleet, under the overall command of Vice-Admiral Inigo Campioni, turned for home.

Campioni knew that the Mediterranean Fleet, under Admiral Sir Andrew B Cunningham, then made up of three battleships, an aircraft carrier, five light cruisers and their escorts, had moved into position to his north, hoping to bar his return to Taranto. (The Italians had intercepted and decoded Cunningham's orders, which included his plan to sweep off the Sicilian coast during the afternoon of the 9th.)[5] Italian air attacks during the 8th had hit one cruiser and near-missed a battleship, though both remained with the fleet. Cunningham pressed on to the west, setting up an encounter off the coast of Calabria in the afternoon of 9 July 1940, an engagement the Italians would call the Battle of Punta Stilo.[6] The Mediterranean Fleet was strung out in three separate groupings, led by the five cruisers, commanded by Vice-Admiral John Tovey. Cunningham, in his flagship, HMS *Warspite*, escorted by five destroyers, trailed Tovey by about 10nm. Another 10nm back were his two slower battleships with another flotilla of destroyers. A fourth group was formed at 1446, a minute after smoke was sighted on the western horizon by Tovey's cruisers. The damaged cruiser, along with the old aircraft carrier HMS *Eagle* (94) and two destroyers, was detached with orders to operate independently. Cunningham ordered the two slower battleships to increase to their best speed to close the gap to *Warspite*, while reducing his flagship's speed by 2kt.

The smoke was coming from a pair of Italian light cruisers, deployed on Campioni's starboard wing as his fleet steered northwards. Fire was opened by light cruisers *Giuseppe Garibaldi* and *Luigi di Savoia Duca degli Abruzzi* at 1520 as Tovey's cruisers came around to a northerly heading at a range of 23,600yd. The British responded two minutes later. Two more Italian light cruisers came within range and opened fire at 1527. This long-range exchange continued for approximately ten minutes while the British cruisers increased speed and pulled away to the north-northeast, attempting to draw the Italians towards *Warspite*. Neither side achieved any hits, although the Italian gunfire came too close for Tovey's liking. One 152mm shell from *Garibaldi* landed close enough to HMS *Neptune* (20) at 1524 to damage her catapult and put her Seafox floatplane out of action.

At 1508, HMAS *Sydney* (D48) sighted the second pair of Italian light cruisers, but misidentified them as the two Italian battleships *Conte di Cavour* and *Giulio Cesare*. Like *Warspite*, they were of First World War vintage, and also had been extensively modernised between the wars. Their main-battery guns had been rebored to 320mm and given greater elevation, giving them a range of 31,000yd, compared to *Warspite*'s 15in main battery, which had been modified to achieve a range of 32,000yd with increased elevation and a redesigned APC MkXXIIb (6crh) shell with a streamlined ballistic cap. (The other two British battleships present that day, HMS *Malaya* (01) and *Royal Sovereign* (05), had not been as extensively modernised and, although fitted with the same 15in main battery, fired an older model APC shell to a maximum range of 23,700yd.)[7] At 1526, *Warspite* opened fire on the Italian light cruisers, firing eighteen salvos before they pulled out of range, seeking their assigned battle position on the far side of their approaching battleships.

Over the next few minutes, the major units on both sides manoeuvred to gain advantage. *Warspite* reduced speed again, by stages to 17kt and then 15kt, and steamed a 360° circle to allow the two older battleships to close the gap to the flagship. The Italian heavy cruisers, which had been farthest from the enemy, steamed hard to pull ahead of *Cesare*. For quarter of an hour neither side fired, the silence only being broken at 1552 by *Cesare* firing at *Warspite*, which

38. The scene that Campioni could see from *Cavour* shortly after 1553 on 9 July 1940 looked like this. The other Italian battleship present that day, *Giulio Cesare*, was on *Cavour*'s starboard bow, and was firing at *Warspite* at extreme range (approximately 26,000yd) and Cunningham's flagship was responding, causing the large shell splashes at the left. Note that the left gun of both after turrets has just fired. During ranging fire at the beginning of an engagement, it was common practice to fire half-salvos to save munitions and prevent unnecessary barrel wear. (*via Cernuschi*)

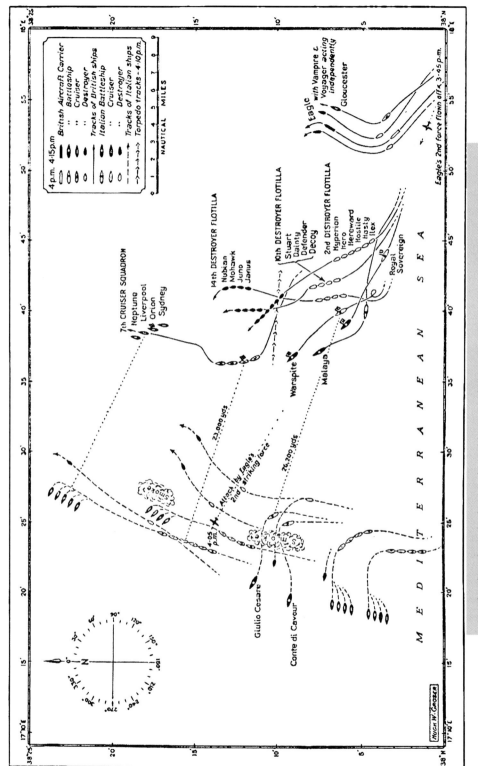

39. This chart shows the decisive phase of the Battle of Punta Stilo, between approximately 1530 and 1615.

replied a minute later. *Cavour* opened fire on *Royal Sovereign*, which had pulled to within 3,000yd of *Warspite*. After this, *Royal Sovereign*, which could steam no faster than 19kt, was left behind by the somewhat faster *Malaya* and played no further role in the battle.

Both sides shot well, regularly straddling each other, but, at 1600, *Warspite* scored the decisive hit of the engagement. At a range of slightly more than 26,000yd, making it one of the longest gunfire hits ever recorded, a 15in round hit *Cesare*'s after funnel and detonated there, well above her upper deck, blasting a 20ft hole in the funnel. This was a failure in the designed functioning of the APC shell, which should not have burst until it hit a more solid structure, but it turned out to be a fortunate failure for the British.[8] The forward half of the shell body continued down through an anti-aircraft magazine and a mess space before being stopped at a bulkhead, starting fires as it went, killing twenty men and wounding more. Forced air ventilation fans sucked the smoke into the fire rooms, causing the temporary shutting down of four of the eight boilers, reducing *Cesare*'s speed over the next seven minutes from 25kt to 20kt. Trailing thick smoke, *Cesare* continued towards the north, firing steady broadsides once a minute at *Warspite* until 1606, when she turned away from the enemy, followed by *Cavour*, effectively bringing the main engagement to an end.

Warspite fired her last salvo at 1603; the last shots from the Italian battleships came five minutes later. Even before the Italian battleships turned away, Cunningham had obviously decided to disengage; at 1602 he ordered *Warspite* to increase speed to 20kt and turned from west northwest to almost due north.

41. Taken at approximately 1605, this image shows smoke pouring from *Cesare* after she was hit in her after funnel by a single 15in round from *Warspite*, causing this massive plume of smoke and reducing her speed by 5kt. Due to this damage, Campioni ordered his fleet to turn away. (*ANMI via Cernuschi*)

42. Looking aft from *Cesare*'s bridge a few minutes after being hit by *Warspite*'s single long-range shot. The dense smoke is starting to clear away and *Cesare* would shortly regain the speed she had lost. (*ANMI via Cernuschi*)

Curiously, *Malaya*, which had been under fire from *Cavour*, chose this moment to open fire despite being hopelessly out of range. She checked fire after four two-gun salvos, all of which fell well short. The last gunfire from the Italian battleships came at 1608 from their after turrets just before they disappeared into a well-placed smokescreen laid by the destroyers *Freccia* and *Saetta*.

At 1605, as the heavy cruisers at the head of the Italian formation duelled with Tovey's light cruisers, *Neptune* managed to hit heavy cruiser *Bolzano* with three 6in rounds in rapid succession. The first hit her starboard side right aft below the waterline, jamming her starboard rudder to port, causing her to turn through 180° before it could be freed, and flooding compartments aft with 300t of seawater. The second hit the starboard torpedo flat, killing two men and causing six of her eight torpedoes to be accidentally launched. The third hit near turret II, damaging the starboard gun. As bad as this may have looked, the damage to *Bolzano* was in fact minor. She completed her circle to port and rapidly resumed her position in line. Not a moment too soon, because, at 1606, Campioni ordered the heavy cruisers to follow his battleships to the west, away from the British. The last gunfire between large ships that afternoon was a salvo from *Bolzano* aimed at Tovey's cruisers at 1620.

The aircraft carrier *Eagle* had been busy, sending out a small raid of nine Swordfish torpedo-bombers at 1545, which found the heavy cruisers *Bolzano* and *Trento* at 1610. (This was in fact her second attack of the day: an earlier attack, also by nine Swordfish, at 1330 had yielded no results.) The British fliers claimed a crippling hit on one of the cruisers and the Italian anti-aircraft gunners claimed to have downed several of the attackers. Both were wrong; no success was obtained by either side.

To cover the withdrawal of the larger Italian warships, Campioni ordered his destroyers to attack, which they did with courage and enthusiasm, and a similar lack of success. At least thirty-two torpedoes were launched in six separate attacks, the last at 1645, after which the Italians headed towards Messina. Cunningham continued probing to the west, hoping to find the cruiser the Swordfish pilots claimed to have crippled, until he called it quits at 1737 and turned south towards Malta. The Regia Aeronautica rewarded his efforts with attacks by seventy-six bombers before dark, which managed to do some minor damage to *Eagle*. To show their impartiality, fifty Italian bombers attacked Campioni's fleet, fortunately missing their targets.

There is no question that both sides shot equally well (or poorly) this day. Of the battleships, *Warspite* obtained the only hit, but the Italians straddled their targets regularly. One of their 'overs' did minor splinter damage to the destroyers HMS *Hereward* (H93) and *Decoy* (H75). To achieve this result the Italian battleships fired 105 rounds (64 by *Cesare* and 31 by *Cavour*). *Warspite*'s single hit came from thirty-three four-gun salvos, for a hit rate of less than 1 per cent. The cruisers on both sides shot carefully and accurately, though the only hits registered were the three by *Neptune*. For the Italians, shooting carefully conformed to a gunfire doctrine that called for marking each fall-of-shot and correcting accordingly. For the British cruisers, the slower, more careful shooting was uncharacteristic, forced on them by the fact that, due to the profligate expenditure of 6in rounds

used to sink *Espero* less than two weeks earlier, there were no immediately available reserves beyond the rounds carried in their magazines.

Better Shooting Brings Victory off Crete

The next encounter, a fairly minor engagement involving only a few cruisers and destroyers of the Italian and Royal navies, was one of the few 'pure' gun battles this war would witness. This was the Battle of Cape Spada, which occurred on 19 July 1940. Neither side had a particularly clear idea of the other's location or intentions. Acting on intelligence that a small convoy of British tankers had departed Romania heading south through the Dardanelles, on 17 July the Italians dispatched a division of two light cruisers from Tripoli without destroyer escort. *Giovanni delle Bande Nere* and *Bartolomeo Colleoni* under Rear-Admiral Ferdinando Casardi were instructed to make for Leros, an Italian-held island in the eastern Aegean Sea, by a route that would take them through the Antikithera Strait just north of Cape Spada (Akra Spatha - the northernmost tip of Crete) soon after dawn on the 19th. The British had no advance warning of this movement, as the Italians had sent the orders to Casardi by cable and also had just changed operational cyphers.[9]

Unbeknownst to the Italians, the British were simultaneously mounting a high speed anti-submarine sweep by a division of four destroyers from east to west along the north coast of Crete, supported at a distance by an anti-shipping sweep into the Gulf of Athens by *Sydney* and another destroyer under Captain J A Collins, RAN, in advance of a planned convoy from Egypt to Greece.[10] The

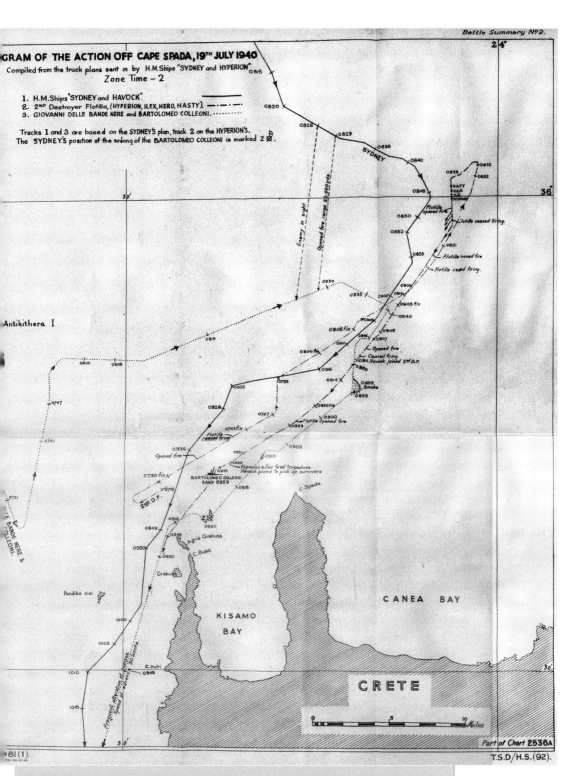

44. This chart, reproduced from Admiralty *Battle Summaries, No. 2*, shows the tracks of the participants in the Battle of Cape Spada, 19 July 1940. (Note that the times on this chart are an hour later than the times given in the accompanying narrative.)

Italian cruisers had been sighted the day before by RAF reconnaissance aircraft, but word of this sighting had apparently not been passed to Collins.[11] As four destroyers of the 3rd Division, 2nd Flotilla (Commander (D) H St L Nicolson) approached the Antikithera Strait from the northeast at 0600 on 19 July, they maintained their sweep formation and speed – line abreast at 18kt.[12] Casardi had been promised air reconnaissance, but attempts to launch floatplanes earlier that morning from Italian Aegean bases had failed and Casardi considered the seas too rough to launch aircraft from either of his cruisers, so the Italians were as surprised as the British when enemy warships came into view in the bright early-morning haze at approximately 0622.

The Italian cruisers had been designed with just this situation in mind, the chasing down and destruction of enemy destroyers. They had a designed speed of 36.5kt and eight 152mm main-battery guns with a calculated maximum range of 31,060yd, but shell weight and muzzle velocity had been incrementally reduced in an attempt to improve accuracy, so that by the time of this engagement, their maximum range was 26,900yd firing an HE shell. Even at this reduced range, they far out-ranged the 4.7in main battery of the 'H'- and 'I'-class destroyers they encountered that morning.

The four RN destroyers – HMS *Hyperion* (H97) leading *Ilex* (I61), *Hero* (H99) and *Hasty* (H24) – led around to the northeast and gradually increased speed to 31kt. Nicolson knew only that *Sydney* was generally north of his location, as Collins had been maintaining radio silence, but his report of the contact was received by Collins at 0633. *Sydney* was in fact approximately 40nm due north of the destroyers and immediately turned south and increased speed.

Casardi likewise ordered his cruisers to increase speed and come about, with *Bande Nere* leading. The two Italian cruisers had only recently been added back into the battlefleet; they were the oldest Italian postwar light cruisers, very lightly built and armoured, notoriously poor gun platforms prone to roll excessively in any seaway, and, on this day, they were encountering significantly rougher water than the enemy destroyers closer to shore. There had been plans to rebuild them as anti-aircraft cruisers, but the work was not carried out due to lack of funds. Attempts were made to sell *Colleoni* to Japan in 1939 and two others of the class to Sweden in 1940, but neither sale was completed. With some reluctance, they were reassigned to the battlefleet on 30 April, just two and a half months before this engagement, with time neither for adequate training nor a full refit. They were considered expendable units, best suited for escort or minelaying duty.[13] Given the state of their engineering plant and the sea state they were encountering, they were barely gaining on the British destroyers.

Concerned that the destroyers might be screening a larger force, Casardi turned towards the north-northeast so that range gradually opened between 0626, when the Italians opened fire, and 0645 when they ceased, having failed to achieve any hits. For those nineteen minutes, the Italians maintained a slow, deliberate fire that was correct for range, but frequently off in azimuth. This was neither the first nor the last time this phenomenon would be encountered. It can be explained in part by the fact that the Italians were aiming towards the rising sun at small elusive targets obscured by patchy mist and funnel smoke, but it also seems to have been a function of the tendency of these ships to roll, which can cause angular dispersion of gunfire.[14] All the Italians achieved for this effort was to provide the destroyermen with a show, 'His salvos . . . throwing up red, yellow and green splashes' – this despite the fact that the Italians did not use dye packets to mark fall of shot.[15] The British destroyers returned fire sporadically, but to no effect.

By 0647, both forces were steaming due north, the Italians southeast of Antikithera Island, the British north of Cape Spada. Collins was still over the horizon to the north, steaming due south. At 0650, Casardi turned first northeast and then, seven minutes later, due east. He was wary of the destroyers' torpedoes and still unsure that no larger ships lurked to the southeast, but his orders required him to head well to the east before turning north towards Leros and he had no choice but to take the risk. Nicolson saw Casardi's turn, but, hoping to continue closing the gap to *Sydney*, turned northeast at 0653 and did not match Casardi's turn to the east four minutes later. The range decreased steadily for another ten minutes, until the Italians turned left to a course that nearly matched Nicolson's.

Despite a slightly converging course and a small advantage in speed, the Italians did not get a clear enough view of the British destroyers to open fire again until 0725 and were still chasing them to the northeast, firing erratically, when, at 0729, *Sydney* finally came within range and opened fire at 20,000yd. The visibility was such that the Italians were unaware of *Sydney* before then: 'several salvos fell near the *Bande Nere*, coming from our port side where a thick bank of low fog could be seen. It was only possible to distinguish the flashes of guns and not the hulls of the ships, nor their numbers.'[16] It took Casardi three minutes to establish *Sydney*'s course, bring his cruisers around to the southeast on a parallel course, obtain a firing solution and open fire on what was initially believed to be two cruisers, when it was actually *Sydney* and her accompanying destroyer – HMS *Havock* (H43). Of greater concern was the fact that his new course would rapidly squeeze him against the coast of Crete. He had no choice but to turn away towards the south-southwest at 0840, making smoke, hoping to clear Cape Spada and reach open water.

Even before Casardi turned away, *Sydney* had scored, hitting *Bande Nere* at 0735 with a single 6in CPBC shell that passed through her forward funnel and detonated on the port side of her upper deck, killing four crewmen and wounding the same number. Throughout the remainder of this battle, *Sydney*'s shooting remained better than the Italians'. *Sydney* was a superior gun platform, far more stable than the Italian cruisers, and had more modern and capable fire control. Discounting all other factors, this would allow *Sydney*'s gunfire to be more effective.

Seeing the Italians turn away, Collins followed, turning first southeast and then south-southwest to parallel their course. After some violent manoeuvres, the Italians finally settled again on a course of 230°, all the while attempting to cover these manoeuvres with smoke. These may have been an attempt to throw off *Sydney*'s pursuit, though some Italian survivors claimed they were simply due to a signalling error.[17] The engagement then settled into a stern chase, with neither side gaining advantage, *Sydney* shifting fire between the two Italian cruisers as first one and then the other became more visible. At 0815, Collins decided to open *Sydney*'s 'A' arcs (allowing all four turrets to bear) by turning 35° to starboard. At 0820, Italian lookouts sighted an island, Agria Grabusa, straight ahead. This meant that although they had cleared Cape Spada, they were too far south to round Cape Busa, the northwestern tip of Crete, and needed to bear off briefly to starboard to reach open water.

Ironically, this jog to the north, which allowed the range to close to 17,500yd, seemed to make *Sydney* more visible to the Italians and, at 0821, she was hit by a 152mm shell that blew a hole 3ft square in the casing of her forward funnel, the only hit she received, causing one minor injury. This was to be of no benefit to the Italians. At 0824, *Colleoni* suffered a steering casualty, jamming her rudder, leaving her unable to manoeuvre.[18] This became irrelevant moments later when she was hit three times. One hit was in her bow and caused only minor damage, but the other two fell in rapid succession, probably from the same salvo, and disabled the ship. The first hit her bridge, causing multiple casualties, including her captain, Umberto Novaro, who was seriously wounded. The other struck amidships, penetrating her outer deck by way of her torpedo tubes and detonating in the starboard shaft tunnel, disabling both boilers in her after fire room and the steam lines to her forward engine room. The same hit also disabled her electric power system, leaving her both dead in the water and unable to serve her main and secondary battery, as her shell hoists were electrically operated.

45. At approximately 0825 on 19 July 1940, the old Italian light cruiser *Bartolomeo Colleoni*, having suffered a steering casualty, was hit three times in rapid succession by 6in shells fired by HMAS *Sydney* (D48), one of which disabled her after fire room and sent this plume of black smoke into the sky. Without power to her turbines or guns, *Colleoni* was doomed. (*via Cernuschi*)

46. and 47. Soon after 0830, *Colleoni* was hit by a torpedo from an unidentified source that took off her forepeak. Then a second torpedo took off most of what remained of her forecastle forward of turret 'I'. (*via Cernuschi*)

48. A third torpedo caused *Colleoni* to capsize at 0859. (*via Cernuschi*)

Casardi saw *Colleoni* falling behind and turned *Bande Nere* back to see if any assistance could be rendered, but it quickly became obvious that *Colleoni* was beyond assistance, with the British rapidly closing from the northeast, and equally obvious that *Bande Nere*'s only chance for survival was to resume her flight to open water. So, at 0830, Casardi turned *Bande Nere* to the west and then around to the west-southwest and finally to the south-southwest as he cleared Agria Grabusa. *Sydney*, with *Hero* and *Hasty*, continued in pursuit. The Italian had a small speed advantage over *Sydney*, and gradually pulled away while steering an evasive course generally in the direction of Tobruk. Running low on CPBC rounds for her forward turrets, *Sydney* ceased fire at 0845, but opened fire again thirteen minutes later and obtained another hit at 0858 that penetrated *Bande Nere*'s quarterdeck and killed four men, wounding twelve more, but did not affect her speed. *Bande Nere* continued firing, but most of her shots 'fell consistently 300 yards away on the "Sydney's" quarter'.[19] *Sydney* turned towards Alexandria at 0937, down to four rounds of CPBC per gun for 'A' turret and one round per gun for 'B' turret.[20] The Italians firmly believed *Sydney* turned away because she was hit again, but Royal Navy records indicate no second hit on the Australian cruiser.

At 0830, Captain Novaro – his ship without power and able to serve only 37mm and rifle-calibre machine guns, with no prospect of improving either condition in time to fight off the approaching British – ordered *Colleoni* scuttled (by opening seacocks in the magazines) and the crew to abandon ship. Almost immediately after this, *Colleoni* was hit by a torpedo well forward that caused about three or four feet of her forepeak to collapse. British records do not report this hit, nor do they record which destroyer might have fired the torpedo.[21] At 0835, *Hyperion* fired four torpedoes and *Ilex* two. Of these six torpedoes, only one from *Ilex* hit, immediately forward of Turret I, severing most of what

49. *Sydney*, seen immediately after the Battle of Cape Spada, shows the hole high up in her forward funnel caused by the one hit she received in that engagement, a 152mm shell fired by one of the Italian light cruisers. (*HMAS Cerberus Museum*)

remained of her forecastle.[22] *Hyperion* approached within a few hundred yards of *Colleoni*, which, despite missing most of her bow, seemed to be stable and in no immediate danger of sinking. Thought was given to attempting to board the cruiser, but at 0854 a large fire was seen to break out in her bridge structure and the decision was made to fire another torpedo at point-blank range.[23] This one hit amidships, and *Colleoni* immediately turned turtle and sank, disappearing at 0859, 4.6nm from the Agria Grabusa Light.[24]

Hyperion and *Ilex* immediately began rescuing survivors, soon joined by *Havock*, which was left to continue the work alone when the other two destroyers were ordered to rejoin *Sydney* at 0924. Between the three destroyers, 545 survivors were rescued out of a complement of approximately 650; the survivors included Novaro, although he would succumb to his wounds in the hospital ship RFA *Maine* in Alexandria harbour four days later. Seven further survivors were picked up the next day by a Greek freighter. No lifeboats or rafts had been launched, but the crew was amply supplied with lifebelts, which allowed a high percentage to survive. Including those who died after being rescued from the water, 121 of *Colleoni*'s crew perished.

More would have been rescued, but *Havock* was interrupted in her rescue work by an air attack by two waves of three Savoia bombers each. While this attack did no damage, it did force *Havock* to abandon the rescue effort and head towards Alexandria at high speed. Another air attack later in the day damaged *Havock*, flooding a boiler room and putting her out of action for more than a month. This was ironic on multiple levels. Casardi had requested air support multiple times the day before and the day of the battle, yet, sadly, it only appeared after *Colleoni* had been lost and *Bande Nere* forced to exit the scene. Worse, the fact that *Havock* was attacked while rescuing Italian survivors led directly to the issuance of a memorandum on 22 July by Cunningham, warning his captains – particularly destroyer captains – of the dangers of stopping to rescue survivors:

> 5. Difficult and distasteful as it is to leave survivors to their fate, Commanding Officers must be prepared to harden their hearts, for, after all, the operations in hand and the security of their ships and ships' companies must take precedence in war.[25]

Between them, the Italian cruisers fired approximately five hundred rounds, but for their efforts they achieved only one hit on *Sydney* and none on the destroyers, reinforcing their reputation as poor gunnery platforms. *Sydney* fired 935 rounds of CPBC and 21 of HE, achieving five hits, for an accuracy of 0.5 per cent. For a ship that was purportedly a far superior gunnery platform, that was marginal shooting at best.

Ajax Rules the Night

Malta proved to be the cause of many of the naval engagements between the British and the Italians. Actually a pair of small islands held by the British, it is located almost exactly in the middle of the Mediterranean – slightly more than 50nm southwest of Cape Passero, the southeastern tip of Sicily, less than

50. East of Malta and south-southeast of Cape Passero, the southeastern tip of Sicily, the Italians attempted to intercept a convoy of empty transports departing Malta late on 11 October 1940. A sweep line of Italian torpedo boats and destroyers was sighted by HMS *Ajax* (22) – veteran of the River Plate action – part of the Mediterranean Fleet waiting for the transports. Though equipped with a Type 279 air-search radar, *Ajax* was seen by the Italian torpedo boats long before her lookouts detected them in the dark, but the British cruiser got much the better of the resulting mêlée, sinking two torpedo boats and damaging two destroyers that came up in support. One of those destroyers was *Artigliere*, seen here adrift the following morning, smoke still rising from a fire in her forward munitions-storage space. Not visible is more serious damage that destroyed her bridge and fire room.

51. The Italians had attempted to tow *Artigliere* clear, but three Royal Navy cruisers caught up with her shortly after dawn on 12 October 1940, forcing her to be left behind. HMS *York* (90) had the honour of finishing off the destroyer with a torpedo to her after magazine.

200nm east of Cape Bon, the northeastern tip of Tunisia, and about the same distance from Tripoli. It was a major irritant to the Italians, as it lay directly across their convoy route to North Africa. To the British, it was an invaluable asset, providing an excellent harbour and strategically placed airfields, and it was, at the same time, a constant liability, as all supplies had to be brought in, not just the expected military items for the defenders, but all the basic necessities for a civilian population of approximately 250,000. The movement of convoys of transports, tankers and cargo ships to Malta from either Gibraltar

BIG GUN BATTLES

or Alexandria became major battles, contested not only by Italian surface forces and submarines, but also by aircraft based in Libya, Sicily and Sardinia.

In early October, the British had run in a small convoy of four cargo ships from Alexandria, which had arrived safely on 11 October, aided by overcast weather. The full Mediterranean Fleet – four battleships, two aircraft carriers, six cruisers and sixteen destroyers – was deployed in support. The main body of this fleet waited south of Malta for three returning merchantmen, while the 7th Cruiser Squadron scouted north and east of the fleet. The northernmost of these, HMS *Ajax*, the same ship last seen off Montevideo, was sighted by a patrol line of three Italian torpedo boats backed up by four destroyers soon after midnight on 12 October. Despite *Ajax* being equipped with radar, the Italian torpedo boats surprised the cruiser and launched torpedoes before being sighted, but the attacks were poorly organised and executed and *Ajax* reacted quickly and effectively.[26] Before withdrawing to seek support from her squadron mates, *Ajax* sank one of the torpedo boats and damaged another and one of the destroyers to the extent that both later sank, while receiving relatively minor damage in return. This action off Cape Passero firmly establish the ascendency of the Royal Navy over the Regia Marina in night actions.

Stringbags over Taranto

On 11 November 1940, the Royal Navy used its most potent capability, the naval air power represented at the time by the aircraft carrier HMS *Illustrious* (87), which had just joined the fleet in September, to dramatically alter the balance of naval power in the Mediterranean. After escorting convoy MW.3 (five merchantmen) to Malta, *Illustrious* detached and, making a high-speed run to the north, launched two waves, totalling twenty-one Swordfish bombers – twelve of which carried torpedoes, the rest bombs. Of the eleven torpedo-bombers that actually attacked the harbour at Taranto, five scored hits on three of the six battleships moored in the outer harbour. One, the old *Conte di Cavour*, sank to the bottom in deep water after being hit by one torpedo. Two, the old *Caio Duilio* (one torpedo) and the new *Littorio* (three torpedoes), were beached to prevent the same fate. *Duilio* and *Littorio* would be under repair for four and six months respectively; *Cavour* would not return to service before Italy surrendered in September 1943.

Punching Holes in the Sea near Sardinia

This shift in power emboldened the British to plan some long-delayed ship movements between Gibraltar and Alexandria, including the direct passage from west to east of two cruisers carrying RAF and army personnel and three fast cargo ships loaded with mechanical transport (two intended for Malta and one for Alexandria). The complex plan that resulted, Operations Collar and MB 9, called for nearly all of Force 'H' (for some reason renamed Force 'B' for the duration of this operation), commanded by Vice-Admiral Sir James F Somerville, to provide support for Force 'F', the transport force comprising the two cruisers – each encumbered by approximately seven hundred supernumeraries, the three merchantmen, a destroyer unable to steam faster than 20kt and four 'Flower'-

class corvettes that could hope to see 14kt on a good day, slower by 2kt than the three cargo ships.[27] Force 'D', comprising the old battleship HMS *Ramillies* (07), cruisers *Newcastle* (76), *Coventry* (D43) and *Berwick* (65), plus five destroyers of the Mediterranean Fleet based at Alexandria, was to meet Force 'F' and Force 'B' south of Sardinia at noon on 27 November and all three forces would continue together east as far as the entrance to the Sicilian Narrows, where Force 'B' would turn back, joined by *Ramillies*, *Newcastle* and *Berwick*, each of which was in need of yard work unavailable at Alexandria. (The two cruisers in Force 'F' – HMS *Manchester* (15), flagship of Vice-Admiral Lancelot E Holland, and *Southampton* (83) – were intended to replace the two cruisers passing to the west.) The remainder of the Mediterranean Fleet would meet Force 'F', minus the ships heading for Malta, to the east of the Narrows.

In fact, the attack on Taranto in no way deterred the Italians – if anything, it made them more aggressive in responding to Royal Navy activity, particularly in the western Mediterranean. Operation White in mid-November, one of the regular sorties carrying Hurricanes to Malta, caused the Italians, alerted by agents at Gibraltar, to send out two battleships and six heavy cruisers from Naples and led directly to the loss of most of the aircraft.[28] Alerted to the next set of movements from Alexandria and Gibraltar, the Italians sortied from Naples on 26 November, again under the overall command of Vice-Admiral Campioni, with two battleships (*Vittorio Veneto* and *Giulio Cesare*), a division of three heavy cruisers (*Pola*, *Fiume* and *Gorizia*, commanded by Rear-Admiral Pellegrino Matteucci) and three destroyer squadrons comprising eleven escorts. An additional heavy cruiser division (*Trieste*, *Trento* and *Bolzano*, commanded by Rear-Admiral Luigi Sansonetti) escorted by three destroyers soon followed from Messina and met the main force north of Sicily heading east on a course to intercept Force 'B' and the western convoy south of Sardinia the next day.

The situation just before dawn on 27 November was far from clear for either side. The Italians were in three groups: Matteucci's cruiser division with four destroyers 19nm southeast of Cape Spartivento, the more easterly of two capes at the southern tip of Sardinia, heading west-southwest; Sansonetti's cruiser division on the same course 5nm south of Matteucci; and the two battleships and seven destroyers directly under Campioni's command, trailing 14nm behind the cruisers. Campioni was aware that Force 'B' was somewhere relatively close. Reconnaissance aircraft had left Sardinian bases at first light, but he was understandably sceptical of their utility and launched a pair of his own floatplanes to augment the search. He did know the approximate location of Force 'D': it had been spotted by the torpedo boat *Sirio* during the previous night heading west near Cape Bon. He correctly assumed it intended to rendezvous with the British units known to be approaching from the west, of whose exact location he was, at 0800, still unsure.

At that hour, Somerville was even more in the dark. The force under his immediate command – Force 'B', comprising HMS *Renown*, *Ark Royal*, *Sheffield* and four destroyers – was 95nm southwest of Cape Teulada, the western cape at the southern end of Sardinia, putting him approximately 110nm west-southwest

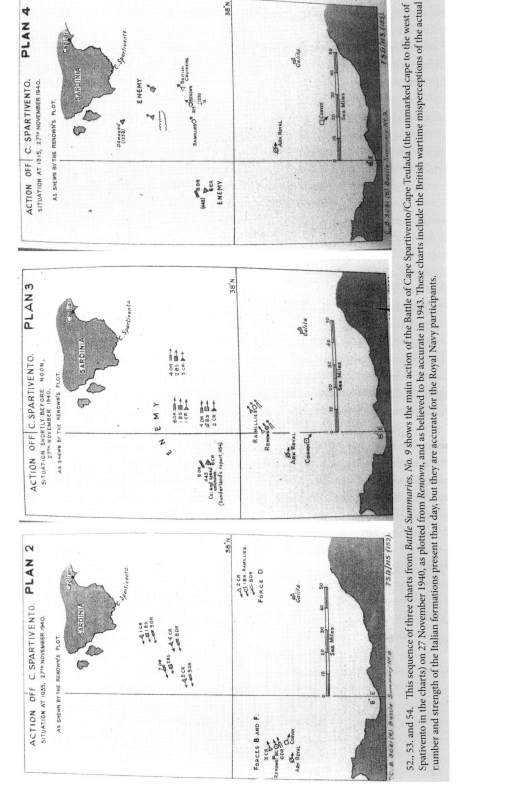

PLAN 2

ACTION OFF C. SPARTIVENTO.

SITUATION AT 1035, 27TH NOVEMBER 1940.

AS SHEWN BY THE RENOWN'S PLOT.

SARDINIA

Cagliari

C. Spartivento.

FORCES B AND F.

Galita

38°N

FORCE D

Sea Miles

8°E

C. B. 3041 (6) Battle Summary N° 9.

TSD/HS (152).

PLAN 3

ACTION OFF C. SPARTIVENTO.

SITUATION SHORTLY BEFORE NOON, 27TH NOVEMBER 1940.

AS SHEWN BY THE RENOWN'S PLOT.

SARDINIA

Cagliari

C. Spartivento

ENEMY

Co. and speed unknown.
(Sunderland's report 1154)

RAMILLIES

RENOWN

ARK ROYAL

CONVOY

Galita

38°N

Sea Miles

8°E

PLAN 4

ACTION OFF C. SPARTIVENTO.

SITUATION AT 1315, 27TH NOVEMBER 1940.

AS SHEWN BYTHE RENOWN'S PLOT.

SARDINIA

Cagliari

C. Spartivento.

Damaged (1350)

ENEMY

ENEMY

RAMILLIES

RENOWN

ARK ROYAL

BRITISH CRUISERS.

Galita

Convoy

Sea Miles

38°N

8°E

C. B. 3041 (6) Battle Summary N° 9.

TSD/HS (155).

52., 53. and 54. This sequence of three charts from *Battle Summaries, No. 9* shows the main action of the Battle of Cape Spartivento/Cape Teulada (the unmarked cape to the west of Spativento in the charts) on 27 November 1940, as plotted from *Renown*, and as believed to be accurate in 1943. These charts include the British wartime misperceptions of the actual number and strength of the Italian formations present that day, but they are accurate for the Royal Navy participants.

of the nearest of the Italian formation, the two sides heading towards each other at a combined 32kt. (The ensuing engagement would be known to the British as the Battle of Cape Spartivento and to the Italians as the Battle of Cape Teulada.) Force 'F' was together 25nm west-southwest of Somerville except for the four corvettes that were unable to keep up and were trailing about 10nm behind. *Ark Royal* flew off seven reconnaissance aircraft at 0800 to sweep the area ahead and north of Force 'B' between Sardinia and North Africa, as far as Force 'D', which was still approximately 125nm to the east. An hour later, Somerville had received no sighting reports and, concerned that air attacks on the convoy from Sardinia could materialise at any time, turned Force 'B' to the southwest to take station on the convoy's port quarter. It was not until 0956 that Somerville received word from *Ark Royal* that ships, reported as five cruisers and five destroyers, had been sighted nearly forty minutes earlier 65nm to the northeast. Although it was uncertain whether this sighting was of enemy ships or Force 'D', Somerville decided to take no chances: he immediately detached a pair of destroyers each to guard *Ark Royal* and the convoy, and ordered *Southampton* and *Manchester*, despite their encumbrance, to join *Sheffield* ahead of *Renown*, which turned to east-northeast and increased speed to 28kt.[29] *Ark Royal* was ordered to operate independently to the southwest of the convoy. It was Somerville's intent to meet Force 'D' as soon as possible and then aggressively confront whatever Italian forces were in the vicinity.

As Campioni has anticipated, even though a shore-based floatplane spotted Somerville at 0930, its report took hours to be delivered. He was much better served by the shipboard aircraft launched before dawn. At 0945, *Bolzano*'s aircraft reported a battleship and accompanying cruisers not far over the horizon to the southwest, heading east at 16kt. Campioni received this report at 1015. The composition of this force was similar to that reported by *Sirio* the night before, raising the possibility that it was the same force, but its position and course made this unlikely, though not entirely impossible. The uncertainty whether he was facing one British force with one battleship or two forces, each with a battleship, added to the contradictory nature of his orders – to 'be animated by a highly aggressive spirit' and, at the same time, to remember the 'material difficulty of replacing our warship losses' – and caused Campioni to delay almost half an hour before turning his three groups to the southeast and increasing speed to 18kt.[30]

Campioni now believed that there were two British units of roughly equal size to the south of him, and that, by heading southeast, he might be able to intercept one or the other and defeat it before the second group could intervene. It was a sound strategy, based on the very limited information at his disposal, but it was already too late for this manoeuvre. By 1045, Force 'B' and Force 'D' were both southwest of his position and rapidly approaching each other. The two British forces sighted each other at 1128; Somerville, aware of Force 'D's speed limitations, ordered *Ramillies*, with her accompanying destroyers, to come about to the northeast, putting them temporarily ahead of Force 'B'. *Newcastle* and *Berwick* were ordered to take station with Holland's cruisers on *Renown*'s port bow. *Coventry* was detached to join the convoy. With the Italians

now coming down from the northwest, the only question was who would sight the other first and would any tactical advantage be gained.

At 1154, a Sunderland flying boat reported Italian ships – six cruisers and eight destroyers – 30nm to the north-northwest of *Renown*, but flew off before giving the enemy's course or speed.[31] Realising he was already to the east of this force and heading further eastward, and fearing the Italians might slip behind him and attack the convoy, Somerville changed course to due north. At almost exactly the same time, Campioni received his first report of the presence of a well-escorted convoy, as well as the presence of *Ark Royal*, to the south of the already-identified British forces. Now believing himself outnumbered by the nearby enemy forces and in receipt of orders from Rome to return to base, he ordered his two cruiser divisions to close on his flagship, preparatory to reversing course away.

Finally, at 1207, the British cruisers, in a ragged line of roughly east-northeast to west-southwest bearing, sighted smoke on the northern horizon, followed within minutes by more smoke and then masts between 006° and 346°. These quickly resolved themselves into two groups of ships, a 'Western Group' – Sansonetti's cruiser division – bearing 340–350° at a range of 11nm from Holland's cruisers, and an 'Eastern Group' – Matteucci's cruiser division – bearing 003–013°, somewhat further away and steaming just south of east. The British cruisers were sighted by the Italian destroyer *Alfieri*, escorting Matteucci's division, at 1215. Campioni, over the horizon 13nm further to the north, ordered his cruisers to refrain from engaging the British, but this did not stop the impulsive Mantteucci from opening fire at 1220 at 24,000yd. *Fiume* was the first to fire. As had already been noted at Cape Spada, Italian gunnery was inaccurate in a characteristic manner. 'The enemy's first salvo fell close to the *Manchester*, exact for range but 100 yards out for deflection.'[32] (In fact, it is likely that *Fiume*'s target was not *Manchester* at all, but rather was *Berwick*, next east in the line of cruisers, as subsequent events would demonstrate. Italian gunfire doctrine called for three initial salvos in a range 'ladder' with the foremost turret aimed 7° ahead of the azimuth determined by the director and the aftermost 7° behind. If the process worked as designed, the correct range and deflection would be determined in three salvos, but poor visibility or radical course change by the target might force the process to be repeated multiple times. When the British on the receiving end saw shell splashes correct for range but off for azimuth at the beginning of engagements, they assumed this indicated a flaw in Italian gunnery.) *Pola* joined in the firing at *Berwick* and *Gorizia* at *Southampton*, followed almost immediately by Sansonetti's division. It took the Italians just two minutes to draw first blood; at 1222, *Berwick* was hit by either *Fiume* or *Pola*:

> This shell entered 'Y' gun barbette about 15 in. above the quarter deck, and traveling down through the training pump space, burst on the starboard side of the barbette above the main deck, and expending itself in the cabin flat, killing Surgeon-Lieut. W. W. Wildman, R.N.V.R., and six ratings, and wounding nine others. A considerable fire was started inside the turret training space, which spread to the gunhouse and was not subdued for over an hour.[33]

Manchester, burdened with 35 officers and 623 men of the army and RAF, was straddled multiple times. Holland noted: 'To carry a shipload of passengers into battle is an unenviable lot, but their presence had perforce to be dismissed from my mind. They themselves were exhilarated at having been in a sea battle.'[34]

Holland turned his bearing line due north with the intent of pushing between the two groups of Italian cruisers, but neither side was making best speed at this stage of the battle. The destroyer *Lanciere* escorting Sansonetti had suffered an engine casualty and was dropping behind the rest of the 'Western Group'. Neither *Berwick* and *Newcastle*, with pre-existing powerplant defects – the reason they were being replaced at Alexandria – could maintain the speed of Holland's three other cruisers and also dropped slowly behind.[35] (This was particularly serious in the case of *Berwick*, which was the only 8in cruiser among the five Royal Navy cruisers present, the rest mounting 6in main-battery guns. During much of this engagement, the return fire of the British cruisers fell short.) *Renown* opened fire at the extreme range of her 15in guns – 26,500yd – on the 'Western

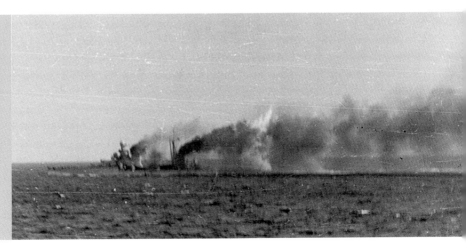

56. Shell splashes from near-misses fired by *Renown* fall around *Bolzano*, another of the heavy cruisers in Sansonetti's division at Cape Teulada on 27 November 1940. She would appear to be just starting to generate smoke, as it is coming mainly from only one funnel and is not yet very dense. (*via Cernuschi*)

57. The third of
Sansonetti's heavy
cruisers, *Trento*, is seen
laying smoke while
shells fall well off her
starboard quarter at
Cape Teulada on 27
November 1940. This
image gives an idea of
the density of the smoke
screen that could be laid
by these large ships. (*via
Cernuschi*)

Group' at 1224 but was never able to gain on them as she had developed a hot
bearing on one of her propeller shafts at 1207 that limited her speed to 27.5kt.
Despite this limit, she passed *Ramillies* and left her behind as that old battleship
could do no better than 20.7kt and never came within range of the Italians.

Under orders to concentrate on Campioni's battleships and following
tactical doctrine which called for engaging enemy cruisers at extreme range,
both groups of Italian cruisers turned to the northeast and made smoke. After
this, the engagement was sporadic on both sides as the smoke limited visibility
to occasional glimpses of the enemy that would bring a brief flurry of salvos.
Berwick was hit again at 1235 by a 203mm round from *Fiume*: this one hit
aft and, while it caused no reported casualties, it destroyed the after electrical
distribution panel, knocking out power to both after main-battery turrets. The
British obtained a small measure of revenge when they sighted *Lanciere* in the
clear behind the 'Western Group' at 1240. The destroyer had managed to restore
engine function to the extent that she was now making 23kt, but a shift in the
wind exposed her to the chasing cruisers and *Southampton* put a 6in shell into
her engine room and, five minutes later, one more shell right through her hull
that failed to explode. The British had bigger game in mind and left *Lanciere*
alone after that, but the damage had been done and, by 1300, she was drifting
without power to the southwest of both squadrons.

Sansonetti's 'Western Group' came around more to the north and gradually
pulled away from the other Italians and the British. The 'Eastern Group' headed

58. One of the major participants in the Battle of Cape Teulada, the battleship *Vittorio Veneto*, is seen in the background in this image taken later in the war at La Spezia, 20 March 1943. This port on the Ligurian Sea was also used by the Germans as a base for U-boats. *U380* is moored in the foreground; *U617* is on her way out of the harbour in the middleground. (*NARA*)

more towards the northeast, closing Campioni, who had steered his battleships in a circle to help the cruisers catch up. Just as they were coming out of this loop, eleven Swordfish torpedo-bombers off *Ark Royal* attacked. The slow biplanes came in unobserved until they were only 1,500ft from *Vittorio Veneto*, but, despite being dropped less than 800ft from their targets, all eleven torpedoes missed. The lack of success in this and later attacks was not surprising, given that 'the *Ark Royal* had a number of inexperienced pilots and observers, and the efficiency of her torpedo striking force was low, owing to the lack of opportunities for exercise.'[36] Italian anti-aircraft fire was equally inaccurate and all eleven aircraft were safely recovered, erroneously reporting a definite hit.[37]

At some point during this, *Trieste* received minor shell splinter damage, quite possibly at 1240:

> On losing her first target the *Renown* altered course to starboard to close these supposed battleships and to bring the cruisers of the western group broader on the bow.[38] She had hardly done so when the centre ship of the latter group [probably *Trieste*] appeared momentarily through the smoke and was given two salvos.[39]

The ship was straddled and was hit by shell splinters aft. According to one sailor in *Trieste*, a shell splinter holed the ship's ensign right aft.[40]

Besides the two hits on *Berwick*, the only other damage to a British warship that day came when, after the Italian battleships settled once more on a northeasterly heading, spotters on *Vittorio Veneto* caught sight of *Manchester*, the leading British cruiser at that point, through a gap in the smoke and loosed a ranging salvo at 1300 at 32,000yd that straddled the target, shells falling less than

BIG GUN BATTLES

100yd off the cruiser's bow and stern, piercing *Manchester*'s upperworks with a few splinter holes, but causing no casualties. It took Holland only a few moments of this bombardment to be convinced that engaging enemy battleships was not a wise use for light cruisers, and, at 1305, he ordered his squadron to make smoke and turn away to close *Renown*. This effectively brought the engagement to an end, as Somerville concluded that he had strayed far too close to Sardinia and its numerous airfields and too far from the convoy he was charged with protecting, so, at 1312, he ordered a general retirement towards the southeast.

All ships involved in the engagement off Cape Teulada reached port safely. Even *Lanciere*, last seen drifting without power, was taken under tow and would be repaired. From the British point of view, the most important result was the safe arrival of all of the merchantmen and the two laden cruisers at Malta and Alexandria.

The presence of *Ark Royal* had no direct impact on this engagement, as the first attack by her aircraft shortly after noon, and two attacks on the Italian cruisers later in the day, caused no damage, but her proximity had been on Campioni's mind and had influenced his decision to avoid closer contact with the British squadron. Italian aircraft became involved offensively only later in the day, an attack by land-based bombers on Force 'B' at around 1410 and two smaller attacks on *Ark Royal* at 1645. No hits were obtained in these attacks, although *Ark Royal* was missed by less than 10yd by two bombs.

Interestingly, both sides claimed to have won the battle, but both commanding admirals came under pressure after the event for not having achieved more. (Holland, too, was criticised for lack of aggression, which may have had an influence on events recounted in the next chapter.[41] The British believed they had hit *Vittorio Veneto* with a torpedo and, besides damaging *Lanciere*, incorrectly reported as a cruiser, thought they had damaged two other cruisers and two destroyers. In fact, the only direct hits scored by the British were two 6in rounds in *Lanciere*, one of which failed to explode. *Renown* fired eighty-six 15in rounds,

59. The most seriously damaged of the Royal Navy ships that participated in the engagement off Cape Teulada was HMS *Berwick* (65), seen here in 1942. She was hit twice by 203mm shells fired by Italian heavy cruisers. Already hobbled by a balky powerplant, she was not further slowed by either hit, nor would they prevent her from returning to action almost immediately.

achieving several near-misses; *Berwick* fired forty-seven 8in salvos for no hits; the four light cruisers, with the sole exception of the two hits by *Southampton* on *Lanciere*, fired off most of their magazine capacity, almost entirely at targets beyond the range of their 6in guns. *Vittorio Veneto* fired nineteen salvos of three 381mm shells from her after turret, straddling her target on the initial salvos; the six cruisers fired 673 rounds, achieving two hits and numerous near-misses.

The Italians noted again how tightly grouped the British salvos were, but how frequently they were off for range. This was the opposite of the British observation of Italian shooting, which suffered from excessive dispersion within salvos, caused in part because the 203mm guns in the twin turrets of the Italian heavy cruisers, like the 152mm guns of the light cruisers at Cape Spada, were mounted too close to each other, causing unavoidable interference, despite efforts to correct the problem by reducing muzzle velocity and introducing a small interval between firing the two barrels. Both British admirals, in their post-action reports, stressed the superior initial rangefinding of the Italians, crediting their use of stereoscopic rangefinders, as opposed to the older, coincidence rangefinders still used by the Royal Navy.

This argument was already being rendered moot by the introduction of the Type 284 surface fire control radar just coming into service, which would give the Royal Navy an undisputed technical advantage, particularly in poor visibility or at night. This and the now regular presence of aircraft carriers with British battle groups meant that the action off Cape Teulada was the last in which radar or aircraft played very little, if any, role in the outcome. It is in no way ironic that this battle proved inconclusive, because the two sides were, after the defeat of France and before electronics and air power came to overshadow naval activity in the confined waters of the Mediterranean, fairly evenly matched.

Pyrrhic Victory
Royal Navy vs Kriegsmarine in the Atlantic
October 1940–May 1941

3

THE LOSS OF *GRAF SPEE* BY scuttling at Montevideo did nothing to dissuade the Kriegsmarine from planning more commerce raiding by major surface fleet units. It must be remembered that, at the same time that *Graf Spee* was being cornered off the Plate Estuary after a long and successful cruise, her sister *Deutschland* (soon renamed *Lützow*) safely completed a raid into the North Atlantic, albeit much shorter and with many fewer successes. Still, the lesson SKL appeared to draw from the experience was that, with luck and caution, surface raiders could wreak havoc among the enemies' shipping lanes far out of proportion to the risks incurred.

Independent of any decision to again send large warships on commerce raids, SKL sent out a first wave of auxiliary cruisers – *Hilfskreuzer*, armed merchant vessels – starting in April 1940, which caused great dislocation of Allied merchant traffic and naval dispositions for very little cost to the Germans. But, as the summer passed and plans to invade the British Isles were repeatedly postponed, interest in sending major warships out commerce raiding was gradually revived. Early on 24 September, *Hipper* departed Kiel, intending to make for the North Atlantic and future basing on the French Atlantic coast, but she suffered a series of engine problems that caused the mission to be cancelled. The sole class of modern German heavy cruisers, of which *Hipper* was the lead ship, was equipped with a high-pressure steam turbine propulsion system that proved to be poorly designed and unreliable. A cooling-pump-shaft failure caused her to put into Kristiansand the night of the 24th. Setting out from there four days later, she suffered a complete engine failure within hours west of Stavanger, barely 125nm further around the Norwegian coast. A leak in an oil-feed line to one of her boilers caused a fire that burned out of control for over an hour. By the time the fire was controlled and the damage repaired to the point that she could make way again, *Hipper* had been adrift without power for four hours. Fortunately for the Germans, *Hipper*'s plight went undetected by the Royal Navy and she was able to creep slowly to Bergen late on the 28th. Even her arrival there was exciting, as a balky steam valve caused her central turbine to race as she approached the dock, being unstuck barely in time to prevent a serious collision. As it was, she limped back to Kiel, arriving there on 30 September.

If she was undetected by the British, it was not for lack of trying. The cryptographers at GC&CS had not yet achieved the great success they would later enjoy reading German naval machine cyphers, but they had penetrated German Luftwaffe and army Enigma cyphers and had determined by the 28th that *Hipper* was attempting a breakout into the Atlantic, and Home Fleet units were deployed to the north and west of the British Isles.[1] They had no way of knowing *Hipper* would fail to reach their blocking positions.

Scheer on the Loose

The next attempts by the Germans would be more successful. The 'pocket battleship' *Scheer*, which, having completed a lengthy refit in September, departed Brunsbüttel at the western end of the Kiel Canal on 27 October, on what was to be a long and spectacularly successful cruise. In every possible way better suited than *Hipper* for the task of commerce raiding, not the least due to her more reliable and economical powerplant, *Scheer* stopped briefly at Stavanger to top up her fuel bunkers and then headed for the Denmark Strait, which she transited undetected on the night of 31 October. On this occasion, British naval intelligence failed to pick up any hints of *Scheer*'s breakout – not even at 1227 on 5 November, when, almost exactly halfway between Halifax and Londonderry, *Scheer* stopped the SS *Mopan*, a fast reefer carrying bananas independently from Port Antonio, Jamaica. *Scheer* approached *Mopan* rapidly, and had her stopped and her crew in boats before they could radio a raider report, which proved to be fortuitous, because, no sooner had she dispatched the freighter, than convoy HX.84 – thirty-seven merchantmen escorted by a single armed merchant cruiser, HMS *Jervis Bay* (F40) – came slowly over the southwestern horizon. The convoy had started from Halifax with thirty-eight ships and three escorts, but two of the escorts were newly transferred ex-American flush-deckers assigned local escort duties and turned around barely two days into the voyage, and one of the merchantmen was too slow to keep up with the 9kt average speed of an HX convoy and had fallen far behind. *Jervis Bay* was a passenger-cargo steamer completed in 1922 for the Britain-to-Australia route; taken over by the Admiralty at the outbreak of war, armed with seven old 6in guns, she 'had had her holds filled with timber and empty oil drums for a bit of added buoyancy should she be torpedoed, the fate that seemed most likely to await her as she worked the North Atlantic convoy routes. Nothing, not her antique guns nor the buoyant cargo, would help against *Scheer*'s 28cm main battery when the *Panzerschiff* opened fire at 1442.

The auxiliary cruiser's captain, Captain Edward S F Fegen, reacted with a decision and courage that truly deserved the Victoria Cross he was awarded posthumously. *Jervis Bay* was located in the middle of the convoy when a single large warship was first sighted coming over the northern horizon. Knowing that this was unlikely to be friendly, he immediately ordered full speed and turned toward the unidentified ship, at the same time ordering the convoy to turn away towards the southeast. Despite the fact that *Scheer* was approaching head-on, it took only a few minutes to identify the *Panzerschiff*. *Jervis Bay* began sending up red signal rockets, the sign for the convoy to scatter. The action that followed against the convoy lasted until dark, which on that day at that latitude came at 1708. The battle between *Scheer* and *Jervis Bay* was mercifully much shorter, lasting just twenty-four minutes. The two ships turned to parallel each other heading east, separated by approximately 16,000yd, at which point the *Panzerschiff* opened fire. *Scheer's* second salvo fell close enough that shell splinters caused casualties among the AMC's gun crews. At least one shell from her third salvo hit *Jervis Bay's* bridge, severely wounding Fegen and destroying what little she had in the way of fire control. From that point on, the destruction of *Jervis Bay* was methodical. Only one shell she fired fell close enough to even splash water on *Scheer*. Besides Captain Fegen, all but 65 of her crew of 255 officers and men perished. In the two hours that remained before full dark, *Scheer* went on to catch and sink five more ships and damage a sixth.

Scheer's cruise was far from over. She turned south and headed for a refuelling rendezvous with the tanker *Eurofeld* and supply ship *Nordmark* in the Sargasso Sea, correctly assuming the Royal Navy would react strongly in the North Atlantic to her attack on HX.84.[2] She sank another merchantman northeast of Puerto Rico on 24 November and then, heading east, another on 1 December west-southwest of the Canary Islands. After briefly searching without success further to the north, *Scheer* turned south towards another meeting with *Nordmark* near the equator. On 18 December, she captured the British refrigerator ship SS *Duquesa* near the Peter and Paul Rocks midway between the westernmost bulge of Africa and the easternmost point of Brazil. The *Panzerschiff's* captain, Theodor Krancke, deliberately made no effort to jam the radio report made by *Duquesa* before she was boarded.

Hipper, too

Krancke allowed *Duquesa's* raider report to be broadcast because he wanted the Royal Navy's attention directly on him and not on the North Atlantic, where he knew *Hipper* had ten days earlier finally succeeded in passing unobserved through the Denmark Strait into the open ocean at the start of Operation Nordseetour. Being of much shorter range and far less durable than *Scheer*, the plans for *Hipper* were that she should make a sweep south and then east across the North Atlantic convoy routes and then head for France. Her search for Halifax convoys failed because she was looking too far south, but with her engines again acting up as she headed east across the north–south Freetown route, she got lucky. Late on Christmas Eve she sighted a large southbound convoy approximately 700nm west of Finisterre (Cabo Fisterra). Thinking it was a standard mercantile convoy and concerned about the danger of torpedo-armed escorts, *Hipper* trailed the convoy throughout the night beyond visual range using its FuMO 27 radar.[3] Only once during the long night did Captain Wilhelm Meisel close the convoy, when around 0200 he came close enough to fire torpedoes, all of which missed, after which he dropped back again.[4]

Despite intermittent rain squalls, Meisel approached again soon after 0630 Christmas Day, as soon as it was light enough to make out targets. He was dismayed to discover that the nearest escort was not a sloop or corvette or even a destroyer, but the heavy cruiser *Berwick*, last seen a month earlier at Cape Teulada. This could only mean that the convoy was not a normal one, returning south in ballast, but rather was a much more important and valuable target.

It was in fact WS.5A, carrying troops, transport and munitions to the Middle East. It comprised twenty-five transports carrying forty thousand troops, two aircraft carriers (HMS *Argus* (D49) and *Furious*) loaded with crated aircraft for delivery to Egypt via Takoradi. (Between the two carriers, they had only five usable aircraft; in an almost comical case of poor planning, these were divided such that *Furious* had three Skua dive bombers, but no bombs, while *Argus* had two Swordfish, but no torpedoes.) Besides *Berwick*, the escort included two light cruisers and four corvettes.

Hipper opened fire, taking on *Berwick* with her main battery of eight 20.3cm guns, while her port-side secondary battery of six 10.5cm guns fired at the nearest transports, a pair of stragglers from the main body of the convoy. *Berwick*, although at dawn action stations, was taken by surprise, but recovered almost immediately. During this initial phase of the engagement, with *Berwick* and *Hipper* on parallel courses, neither side scored. As the two light cruisers (HMS *Dunedin* (D93) and *Bonaventure* (31)) closed, Meisel mistook them for destroyers, and, fearing a torpedo attack, he turned away, breaking contact. While not hitting *Berwick* during this phase, which lasted less than ten minutes, *Hipper*'s secondary battery put one round into the cargo ship SS *Arabistan* (5,874GRT) for minor damage, narrowly missing a hold full of munitions, and another 10.5cm shell into SS *Empire Trooper* (14,106GRT) below the waterline for more serious damage.[5] This exploded in a berthing space, killing sixteen of the troopers she was transporting and causing a serious list.

Hipper turned towards the convoy again and sighted *Berwick* once more at approximately 0700. Again they exchanged fire, with *Bonaventure* joining in with its fast-firing, dual-purpose 5.25in main battery.[6] Over the next fifteen minutes, *Hipper* fought the two British cruisers, hitting *Berwick* four times with 20.3cm shells. Two hit at or below the waterline and penetrated her armour belt, but failed to explode. The third likewise hit below the waterline in way of 'B' turret and exploded there, causing serious flooding. The fourth penetrated 'X' turret and exploded, killing seven of its Royal Marine gun crew and disabling the turret. The best the British could achieve in return was to rattle a few shell splinters off *Hipper*'s shell plating. Despite his better shooting, Meisel was not happy to be facing two British cruisers with a third coming into range, and, when a rain squall intervened at approximately 0715, he took advantage of the reduced visibility to turn away to the northeast, ending the engagement.

By this point, the convoy had scattered and the British cruisers busied themselves attempting to reassemble the dispersed transports. The two aircraft carriers, however, with more energy than intelligence, set dutifully to clearing their flight decks sufficiently such that they could operate their aircraft. *Furious*' Skuas were launched unarmed to search for the German raider; the two Swordfish were cross-decked to *Furious* and armed with torpedoes, and were awaiting word from the air search when orders came from the Admiralty for them to stand down.

No ships were sunk that Christmas Day. *Berwick* limped into Gibraltar to land her wounded and effect temporary repairs. She would not return to active service until July 1941. The two damaged transports both survived. *Hipper* found

and sank an independently routed merchantman, the 6,078GRT SS *Jumna*, while en route to Brest, where she was subsequently docked for a month. *Hipper* had fired 185 main-battery rounds and 113 secondary battery rounds to achieve four and two hits respectively. *Bonaventure*, with characteristic profligacy, fired 438 rounds for no hits.

Scheer in the South

At the beginning of 1941, the Royal Navy had much to look back on with satisfaction, but certainly no reason to feel confident that the worst had been overcome. Only one major enemy surface unit, *Scheer*, was still at large, but others, old and new, were poised to join her. *Scheer* was loose in the South Atlantic, where there were few Royal Navy assets to chase her, though also far fewer targets. Nevertheless, she maintained a slow but steady rate of successes. On 18 January, she captured the Norwegian motor tanker SS *Sandefjord* off Gabon and then sank two large merchantmen in quick succession over the next two days off Luanda, Angola. At a large rendezvous in the middle of the South Atlantic starting 24 January, *Scheer* met *Sandefjord*, as well as *Duquesa*, *Nordmark*, *Eurofeld* and the auxiliary merchant cruiser *Thor*. *Scheer* and *Sandefjord* remained at the rendezvous for four days before the tanker headed north for Bordeaux, carrying over two hundred captured seamen, and Krancke, deciding the Atlantic was getting too crowded and following *Graf Spee*'s precedent, headed southeast to round the Cape of Good Hope.[7]

The Atlantic Gets Crowded

The reason why Krancke thought the Atlantic was getting too crowded included not only the presence of *Thor* in the South Atlantic, but also *Kormoran* and

61. Sailors work chipping ice off the forward turrets on *Gneisenau* during Operation Berlin, January 1941. Generally, an inch or so of ice covering the upperworks of a ship the size of a battlecruiser is no problem, but it can cause some essential moving parts, such as the doors covering the turret's rangefinder optics, to freeze shut, which would be a serious issue if an enemy were encountered. (*NARA*)

Pinguin approaching the area from the north and south. Adding to the congestion was the entry into the North Atlantic in early February of no less than three major German warships. The two battlecruisers *Scharnhorst* and *Gneisenau*, both damaged in June 1940 during operations off Norway, were now ready for action again. They left Kiel on 23 January on Operation Berlin and made their way slowly to a point east-northeast of Iceland before turning southwest on the 27th and making a high-speed dash for the Iceland–Faroes Gap. With only the barest of intelligence to act on, the Royal Navy's Home Fleet deployed to block the gap with a patrol line of cruisers backed up by two battleships and a battlecruiser. On this occasion, German FuMO 22 radar outperformed the Type 279 carried by the British cruisers; Admiral Lütjens (he had been promoted to full admiral rank in September 1940), commanding the two battlecruisers, had six minutes warning before HMS *Naiad* (93) made first contact in the pre-dawn gloom on 28 January, and he was able to reverse course and work up to full speed rapidly enough to lose contact again. So brief and nebulous was *Naiad*'s contact that Admiral Tovey (promoted to command the Home Fleet in November with the acting rank of admiral) wrote it off as false.[8]

Lütjens backtracked to a position east-northeast of Iceland where he refuelled and then, taking a long loop north of that island, broke into the Atlantic through the Denmark Strait on 4 February. He began sweeping the Halifax convoy route and almost immediately had success, spotting eastbound HX.106 southeast of Cape Farewell early morning on the 8th. Lütjens split his two ships, sending

BIG GUN BATTLES

Scharnhorst around to the south and himself approaching from the north, hoping to trap the convoy between them. However, when lookouts on *Scharnhorst* sighted the upperworks of a battleship coming into view, Lütjens ordered an immediate high-speed withdrawal to the northwest. His orders, reinforced by common sense, forbade him engaging enemy capital ships. The battleship, the post-refit *Ramillies*, far too slow to keep up with the retreating Germans, was no doubt equally happy to see *Scharnhorst* (misidentified as *Hipper*) disappear over the horizon.

Hipper's Big Success

The misidentification was understandable, given that *Ramillies* was escorting HX.106 in great part due to Royal Navy concern about *Hipper*'s threat, poised as she was at Brest, a day's steaming from the Sierra Leone convoy route and two days at the most from the critical Halifax route. Aerial reconnaissance on 4 February revealed that *Hipper* had sailed, so *Ramillies* had every reason to expect her to show up in the middle of the North Atlantic four days later.

In fact, *Hipper* had sailed late on 1 February, but headed west-southwest towards a refuelling rendezvous west of Finisterre. She remained in company with the tanker for four days, until 10 February. Two days earlier, *U37* (Lieutenant Commander Nicolai Clausen) had made contact with convoy HG.53: twenty-two merchantmen escorted by a sloop and an old destroyer, four days out of Gibraltar, headed towards Liverpool. Knowing that *Hipper* was at sea and not far away, Vice-Admiral Karl Dönitz, commanding Germany's U-boats, had tried to arrange for a joint attack on the convoy, but was rebuffed: 'Group Command West was asked whether there was any question of Hipper operating (she was in

62. February 1941 proved to be a high-water mark in commerce raiding by German warships. *Hipper* set out from Brest and found convoy SLS.64, sinking seven ships out of the nineteen in the convoy, including this large, modern freighter afire from end to end. (Actually, this victim does not particularly resemble any of *Hipper*'s victims on this voyage, making this identification of time and place somewhat suspect, but, looking at this unfortunate merchantman, set against a 10.5cm secondary mount similar to that carried by *Hipper* is sufficient to illustrate the damage a heavily armed warship could inflict on an unescorted convoy. It is fortunate for the British that this proved to be a very rare event.) (*NARA*)

an adjacent sea area); the reply was no. If however, the boat manages to shadow until morning it may be possible for aircraft to operate.'[9]

What followed the next day, 9 February, was the first of the very rare examples of inter-service co-operation on the part of the Germans. After sinking two ships by torpedo, *U37* trailed the convoy and radioed a beacon used by five Fw200 Condors based at Bordeaux to find the convoy and sink four more ships and damage another (which subsequently sank in a gale six days later). On 10 February, Clausen sank one more ship from the convoy and reported his intent to continue trailing the convoy, leading to the following report for the next day: 'U 37 lost contact at midnight, but pressed on . . . Contrary to their original intentions, Group Command West decided to operate Hipper against the convoy after all. U 37 received orders to search again and when contact was made to make beacon-signals every 2 hours, . . .'[10]

And, finally, on 12 February: 'Towards midday Hipper encountered a convoy (presumably U 37's) in CF 80 and apparently annihilated it. Thus, for the first time in naval history, a combined operation between U-boats, aircraft and surface forces has reached a successful conclusion.'[11]

Dönitz was only partially correct. *Hipper* had indeed vectored in on Clausen's beacons, but these soon ceased, because *U37* was unable to re-establish contact with HG.53. Arriving at the last broadcast position at approximately midday on the 11th, *Hipper* crossed the wake of the convoy, but had not missed it entirely. She intercepted SS *Iceland*, an old steamer carrying 962t of oranges from Sevilla to Bristol, which had been part of HG.53, but had suffered a major engine casualty and was adrift when *Hipper* approached.

Having taken off *Iceland*'s crew and dispatching the abandoned steamer with gunfire and a single torpedo, *Hipper* turned northeast at economical speed, hoping to overtake HG.53, but also because she was already running low on fuel and that course took her towards Brest. Shortly after midnight, multiple radar contacts were reported dead ahead at a range of 16,000yd. Assuming this was indeed the remnants of HG.53, Meisel worked his way around the port side of the contact at maximum radar range. His plan was to break out a Royal Navy white ensign and approach from head-on at first light, hoping this would allow him to get close to the convoy before his true identity was detected. (This kind of *ruse de guerre*, of which flying a false flag is perhaps the most common example, is a time-honoured tradition of naval warfare dating back centuries, and was practised (and condemned) by all sides in the Second World War.)

Meisel's ploy worked, *Hipper* approaching within 3,000yd of the ship leading the convoy's port column before the alarm was raised and the signal to disperse given by the convoy's commodore. What followed was sheer slaughter. The convoy was in fact not HG.53, which still had two escorts, but was SLS.64, a slow convoy of nineteen merchantmen out of Freetown heading for Great Britain with no escort whatsoever. In the mêlée that ensued, *Hipper* steamed into the middle of the confused mass of targets, firing every gun she had. Three of the merchantmen are known to have fired back: one of them, the Norwegian freighter SS *Borgestad*, obtained a hit on *Hipper*'s tower mast before being smothered by gunfire. When the firing died down after a little over an hour, Meisel surveyed a scene of carnage, sinking and burning ships and scores of men in the water, many of them wounded, and he realised that, as much as he may have wanted to rescue survivors, his low fuel state and depleted magazines, and the certainty that British warships and aircraft were headed his way, left him no choice but to depart the scene and head for Brest. When he arrived there on the 15th, having taken an evasive course skirting the Spanish coast, he claimed to have sunk fourteen ships and damaged two more. The actual score was more modest, but still disastrous for the British: *Hipper* actually sank seven ships and damaged three more. In all, 110 men died in the sunken ships; 107 were rescued by two of the convoy's ships that courageously remained at the scene.

Hipper would never again raid in the Atlantic. Her limited endurance and fragile powerplant made her ill-suited for such duty. On 15 March, she left Brest, refuelled southwest of Cape Farewell, passed through the Denmark Strait on 24 March and arrived at Kiel four days later. A long-overdue and lengthy refit awaited her, which would last until November.

Scheer Slips Home

Scheer rounded the Cape of Good Hope on 2 February 1941 and, after failing to find any traffic south of Madagascar, headed for the northern entrance to the Mozambique Channel. There she captured a British tanker and sank a Greek freighter off Zanzibar on 20 February. Two more freighters followed the next two days, but these were able to make raider reports. Just four and a half hours after sinking SS *Rantau Pandjang* on the 22nd, *Scheer* was sighted by an aircraft launched from HMS *Glasgow* (21), which was 140nm to the northwest. All available Royal Navy ships were immediately ordered to concentrate on *Scheer's* position, including the old aircraft carrier *Hermes*, but Krancke headed east and then southeast before swinging south and was not sighted again. Now in serious need of docking, *Scheer* headed back into the Atlantic on 2 March, and spent three days in company with *Nordmark* and the newly arrived *Alsterufer*, replenishing, refuelling and tuning her engines for the long haul home. Taking advantage of the distraction caused by the two battlecruisers, she passed due north up the middle of the North Atlantic in the third week of March and transited the Denmark Strait in fog on the night of the 27th, reaching Kiel unmolested on 1 April. Her raid had lasted over five months and claimed sixteen merchant ships and one auxiliary cruiser sunk or captured. Like *Hipper*, her yard work would last until November and, also like *Hipper*, she would never again wander free in the Atlantic.

The High Point of German Commerce Raiding

In the middle of March 1941, the Royal Navy was indeed distracted by *Scharnhorst* and *Gneisenau*. Having been chased away from HX.106 by *Ramillies* on 8 February, the two battlecruisers rendezvoused with the oilers *Esso Hamburg* and *Schlettstadt*, and remained west of Cape Farewell until 17 February when they again moved south to sweep the Halifax convoy route. After several days of fruitless searching, Lütjens' luck changed mid-morning on 22 February, when he chanced upon part of the dispersed westbound convoy OB.285. (At this stage of the war, the Royal Navy did not have sufficient long-range escorts to escort convoys all the way across the North Atlantic. OB.285 was typical in that it comprised forty-four merchantmen and six escorts, which left Liverpool on 11 February and was dispersed in mid-ocean on the 17th. Dispersal did not mean the ships simply scattered: those heading to a common destination and capable of maintaining the same speed tended to stay together.) Starting at 1055 and not ending until just before midnight, the two battlecruisers combined to sink five ships, totalling more than 25,000GRT, and took 180 sailors captive.[12]

Aware that their position had been reported, Lütjens led his ships south into the Central Atlantic, where they again refuelled, and then east towards the Cape Verde Islands, where they hoped to feast on the Freetown traffic. On 7 March, they found a large southbound convoy, SL.67, escorted by the battleship *Malaya*. The battlecruisers were sighted by *Malaya*'s aircraft and by the battleship herself, but managed to shadow the convoy long enough to radio their position back to Germany, where it was passed along to Dönitz, who ordered three U-boats to converge and, if possible, eliminate *Malaya*, allowing Lütjens to attack.[13] The plan almost worked; *U124* (Lieutenant Commander G-W Schulz) and *U105* (Lieutenant Commander Georg Schewe) found the convoy that night and between them sank five ships, but not *Malaya*, and the next morning both the U-boats and Lütjens' battlecruisers broke off contact with the convoy. While en route to another mid-ocean refuelling, they found and sank a large Greek freighter. They then headed northwest back towards the North Atlantic convoy routes.

Here they again found rich hunting. As before, they came upon part of a dispersed westbound convoy of forty-two merchant ships, OB.294, on 15 March. They found a group of tankers in ballast heading for the Caribbean oil depots. *Gneisenau* singlehandedly captured three tankers and sank another, while *Scharnhorst* sank two more. Prize crews were put on board the captured ships and they were directed to make for Bordeaux.[14] Continuing on to the northwest, the two battlecruisers sighted ship silhouettes against the horizon and, at dawn on the next day, they found themselves in the midst of the remainder of the convoy. In almost leisurely fashion, they picked off targets one-by-one. Between 0428 and 1550, *Gneisenau* sank five ships and *Scharnhorst* four more.

As the sun was lowering in the west, a curious incident occurred. An independently sailing motorship, the Danish MV *Chilean Reefer*, a tiny (1,830GRT) food transport, appeared directly in the midst of the carnage. Sighting and being sighted by *Gneisenau* at 1710, she tried to escape, but was rapidly overtaken. *Gneisenau* opened fire, but the surprisingly nimble transport eluded the gunfire and began returning fire with her own 4in gun. Hit repeatedly, the transport's captain finally decided at 1730 to abandon ship. Apparently fearing she might be some kind of torpedo-armed decoy, Lütjens ordered that fire be continued, even as the transport's crew was taking to their boats. For a full ten minutes, *Gneisenau* sat stopped, continuing a methodical pounding of the tiny transport. Then, for no reason that was obvious to the transport's crew watching from the lifeboats, the battlecruiser ceased fire and headed off to the east into the gathering gloom at high speed. It was only after the transport's surviving crew was rescued by HMS *Rodney* that it became clear that, for the third time during this voyage, Lütjens' battlecruisers had departed in haste rather than face a British battleship. *Chilean Reefer*, last seen ablaze from end to end, sank during the night. It had taken *Gneisenau* seventy-three 28cm rounds to sink the tiny transport. Twelve men died due to an accident while launching one of the transport's two lifeboats.[15]

Now low on munitions, the two battlecruisers set course for Brest. The passage was eventful, as the Royal Navy was alert and eager to exact revenge for the devastation the battlecruisers had wrought. Spotted by a reconnaissance aircraft off *Ark Royal* late on 20 March, they altered course to the north, but resumed an easterly heading after dark. Royal Navy forces converged on the Bay of Biscay overnight and RAF Coastal Command picked up the search at dawn on the 21st, but bad weather and bad luck dogged the search and it was not until evening that the battlecruisers were sighted again, and by then they were under German air cover.

The completion of this cruise marked the high point of German surface-ship commerce raiding. Between the two battlecruisers, they had accounted for twenty-two merchant ships of over 113,000GRT. It certainly appeared that, with fast, elusive warships, supported by a network of supply ships throughout the Atlantic and an active fleet of auxiliary cruisers to distract the enemy, there was little to prevent the success from continuing. In May, however, just when it looked like the Kriegsmarine was about to play its masterstroke, the tide turned suddenly and decisively, though not without terrible cost to the Royal Navy.

63. Operation Berlin came to a successful conclusion when *Gneisenau* (seen here) and her sister *Scharnhorst* arrived at Brest on 22 March 1941. The joy on the faces of the officers greeting the raiders would not last, as the Kriegsmarine's fortunes in the Atlantic soon took a turn for the worse. (*NARA*)

Germany's Newest and Best Take the Stage

As successful as these raids had been, SKL was certain they were just a prelude to what would be accomplished by Germany's two newest, most powerful ships. While the Germans assumed attention had been riveted elsewhere, these ships had been completing their working up in the Baltic, preparatory to a planned breakout into the Atlantic, codenamed Rheinübung (Rhine Exercise). One was a near-sister of *Hipper*, named *Prinz Eugen*. She differed from *Hipper* in many details, being marginally larger in all dimensions, though her armament, armour and the basic design of her powerplant remained the same. The larger dimensions gave her 15 per cent greater range, but they shared the same set of issues concerning the reliability of their high-pressure steam turbine propulsion.[16] (Famously, *Prinz Eugen* broke down completely on her last voyage to Bikini Atoll in 1946 and had to be towed on the final legs of that voyage.) Nevertheless, she was a handsome and powerful ship, the cause of much concern to the British.

However, it was the second ship working up in the Baltic that winter that really worried the British Admiralty. She was the first new battleship built by Germany since the First World War. *Bismarck* was fast (30kt), heavily armoured and, in typical German fashion, extensively sub-divided internally. Yet, in many ways, she was anachronistic, her design simply an update to the last designs of the previous war. Most noticeably, like those designs, her main battery was eight 38cm guns arranged in four twin turrets, a very unusual and wasteful arrangement, especially when other major navies had adopted triple and even quadruple turrets for their main battery. Less noticeable, but ultimately more important, her armour scheme, which, while doing an adequate job of protecting the central 'citadel' between her forward and after main-battery barbettes, would provide little protection fore and aft of this. While in principle, this was not

64. One of the reasons hope was high in the Kriegsmarine was the entry into service of the massive ship seen here during her commissioning on 24 August 1940. *Bismarck* was large, fast, heavily armoured and well-armed, and looked the part. Yet, her design was in some ways anachronistic and she had unseen weaknesses that would be exposed when she first went into action. (*NARA*)

unusual among contemporary designs, it was taken to an extreme in *Bismarck*'s design and represented a weakness the British would be able to exploit.[17] More unusual was *Bismarck*'s very limited endurance, a weakness that would prove decisive during Rheinübung. Compared to contemporary American, though not British, battleship designs, *Bismarck* had a very limited radius of action.[18] Despite a displacement more than double that of *Prinz Eugen*, *Bismarck* had a cruising range barely 18 per cent greater.

The reader must understand that this analysis includes a great deal of hindsight. Facing the prospect of containing this powerful pair of warships loose in the open ocean in real time was frightening indeed. Having just withstood the depredations of *Scheer*, *Hipper* and the two battlecruisers in three independent cruises, which had seriously disrupted convoy schedules, the Royal Navy was terrified that their activities might be co-ordinated with the two new ships in such a way as to entirely stop that vital traffic. It is easy in retrospect to conclude that such concern was exaggerated, given what the British knew in the spring of 1941. Analysis of the activities of German raiders to date should have revealed that, while they had scored some spectacular successes, those successes were isolated instances that would be difficult to repeat. The British had reason to believe that *Scheer* and *Hipper* were both out-of-service for the foreseeable future and that *Scharnhorst* at Brest was likewise indisposed.[19] Of the four ships that had been raiding in the Atlantic, the only one seen actively exercising was *Gneisenau* and, on 6 April, she was torpedoed by an RAF Beaufort bomber and put out of action for almost a year.[20] The German plans to support Rheinübung, originally scheduled for the end of April, with a sortie by one or both battlecruisers from Brest, thus had to be scrapped. Even the reduced plan of just *Bismarck* and *Prinz Eugen* breaking out on their own had to be postponed when the cruiser ran onto a mine approaching Kiel on 23 April, requiring repairs lasting three weeks. There was discussion of perhaps waiting for *Scharnhorst* to be ready, which was expected to happen in mid-June, but Raeder and Lütjens, who was put in charge of Rheinübung with his flag on *Bismarck,* decided that to wait would allow the Royal Navy too much time to prepare. So, as soon as *Prinz Eugen* was once again ready, she sailed to Gotenhafen, where she replenished; departing on 18 May, she met *Bismarck* the next morning off Cape Arkona (Kap Arkona) and together they proceeded through the Belts and the Kattegat.

The British were well aware of these activities. While still unable to read German naval cyphers in anything resembling real time, they were able to tell from decrypts of Luftwaffe 'Red' network messages, which were being read concurrently, that additional ice reports for the waters between Greenland and Jan Mayen Island had been requested and a sharpened watch on Scapa Flow was being mounted.[21] They were also aware that Lütjens had boarded *Bismarck* in the second week of May, all of which pointed to an imminent operation. This was sufficient for Tovey to put the Home Fleet on alert and send HMS *Norfolk* (78), flagship of Rear-Admiral Frederic Wake-Walker, to relieve *Suffolk* (55), which was patrolling the northern entrance to the Denmark Strait, so the latter could refuel at Hvalfjordur and then quickly resume station. At 2058 on 20

May, the Admiralty received definite word of the passage of the German ships through the Kattegat from the British naval attaché at Stockholm. The Swedish cruiser *Gotland*, apparently on routine patrol off the naval base at Göteborg, sighted *Bismarck* at 1300 on 20 May and trailed her for about two hours. Lütjens assumed, quite correctly, that word of his passage would reach the British. For reasons that are not clear, he decided to change his original plan, which had been to proceed north up the Norwegian coast at high speed and refuel from a tanker waiting near Jan Mayen. Instead, he now decided to stop at Bergen, replenish there, and await the cover of bad weather before proceeding.

(The battle whose opening stages are being described – the Battle of the Denmark Strait – is one of the most studied and least understood battles in history. It involved only six ships, only four of them in the main action, yet important aspects of the battle are poorly understood, because, in a strange coincidence, neither commanding admiral survived to explain his actions, so many details of this engagement can only be surmised.)

On 21 May, Admiral Tovey received both the attaché's report and explicit confirmation of Lütjens' presence at Bergen, provided by photo reconnaissance aircraft. While the Germans' intentions were far from clear – in fact, their stop at Bergen muddied the picture – Tovey had to continue to assume that their plan was a breakout into the Atlantic.[22] Based on that assumption, he ordered, among other moves: *Suffolk* was to remain at Hvalfjordur until further notice to conserve fuel; the two light cruisers patrolling the Iceland–Faroes Gap were ordered into Kongshavn in the Faroes to replenish; and, most importantly, a detachment comprising the battlecruiser *Hood*, the brand-new battleship *Prince of Wales* (53) and six destroyers under Vice-Admiral Holland – last seen off Cape Teulada – was ordered to Hvalfjordur in order to be ready to support either group of cruisers.[23] Holland departed Scapa Flow just before midnight.

The weather Lütjens wanted to aid his breakout arrived earlier than he expected. Assured that he might benefit from several days of cloud cover if he acted quickly, *Bismarck* and *Prinz Eugen* departed Bergen at 1945 on 21 May, having spent less than nine hours there. During that brief stay, *Prinz Eugen* refuelled from a tanker, but *Bismarck* did not. There is much speculation as to why Lütjens chose not to refuel *Bismarck*; the explanation that makes the most sense is that there simply was not time to refuel both ships, as there was only one tanker available, and it was correct to top off the shorter-legged *Prinz Eugen* first. It is probable that Lütjens wanted to refuel *Bismarck* as well, but was persuaded to leave Bergen earlier than intended after being informed that the Arctic low front providing the providential cloud cover was narrow and fast moving and that he could not count on its protection if he delayed his departure even by a few hours. It is also likely, but impossible to prove, that he still hoped to meet the tanker waiting near Jan Mayen, but, again, was dissuaded from doing so by the necessity of keeping up with the weather front. In fact, the German squadron maintained an average of 24kt as it took a course that curved north and west around Iceland, a speed that was far from economical. Regardless of the reason, *Bismarck*'s failure to refuel at Bergen or later near Jan Mayen was to have far-reaching consequences.

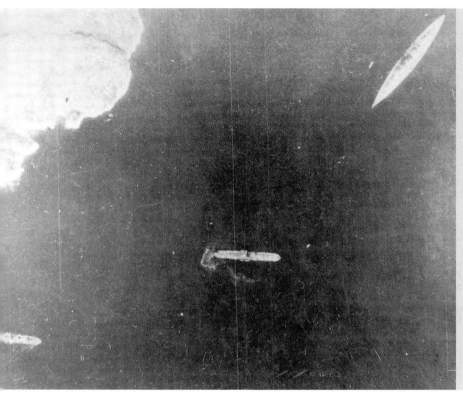

65. When the time came for *Bismarck* to break out into the Atlantic on her first commerce raid, she was accompanied by *Prinz Eugen*, a near-sister to *Hipper*, which shared many of that ship's shortcomings, including her inadequate range and unreliable powerplant. *Prinz Eugen*'s short legs caused Admiral Lütjens to interrupt his breakout from the Baltic long enough to stop in at Bergen, Norway in order to refuel his cruiser. Pressed by his meteorologist to leave immediately, he did not top up *Bismarck*, which was fortuitously caught here at Bergen by a photo reconnaissance flight on 21 May 1941.

A Cataclysmic Loss in the Denmark Strait

A single RAF reconnaissance aircraft managed to reach Bergen on 22 May and was able to establish that *Bismarck*, at least, had departed. With that knowledge, Tovey acted decisively. His flagship, *King George V*, along with the new aircraft carrier *Victorious* (38), plus four light cruisers and seven destroyers, were ordered to sea, leaving Scapa and heading west late in the day.[24] At the same time, Tovey released *Suffolk* to rejoin *Norfolk* in the Denmark Strait. This was critical because, while both cruisers were equipped with search radar, *Suffolk*'s brand-new Type 284 had an antenna mounted on her main-battery director, allowing nearly 360° coverage, while *Norfolk* was equipped with an older Type 286M with a fixed, forward-facing antenna. The two cruisers met late that afternoon off Hornstrandir, the northwesternmost part of Iceland. While the Denmark Strait is theoretically about 150nm wide at that point, shore-to-shore, a series of British minefields to the south and thick pack ice to the north limited the navigable width of the strait in places to less than 10nm. The weather was relatively calm for that latitude and the days already long – more than eighteen hours between sunrise and sunset, and even after the sun set it never got totally dark – but persistent fog off the pack ice and intermittent rain squalls often limited visibility to a few miles at most.

At 1922 on 23 May, the starboard after lookout on *Suffolk*, which was heading towards the southwest skirting the northern edge of the minefield, sighted two ships emerging from the fog to the north-northeast. *Suffolk* sent a sighting report, which was reported to Holland at 1939, and skillfully manoeuvred around behind and to the starboard side of the Germans, which turned a few degrees to port as they passed the last minefield and the ice-free passage widened. *Norfolk*, which had been patrolling a line further to the south, emerged from a fog bank at 2030, approximately 12,000yd off *Bismarck*'s port bow. She was brought under fire immediately by *Bismarck*, which got off five forward main-battery salvos before *Norfolk* wisely disappeared back into the fog, suffering only minor splinter damage. *Bismarck*, on the other hand, inflicted some more consequential damage to herself; the shock of firing her forward guns disabled the FuMO 23 sets mounted on her foremast and conning tower, leaving only a third, similar set mounted on her after fire control position in working order. In response, Lütjens ordered *Prinz Eugen*, with a functioning forward-facing radar, to take the lead.

The change in the German formation went unobserved by Wake-Walker's cruisers because of a snow squall that developed ahead of *Suffolk* at 2352. This caused sufficient interference with radar reception that all contact with the German ships was temporarily lost. At that same moment, a lookout on *Suffolk* reported a 'shadow' in the snowstorm ahead and, fearful that Lütjens might be taking advantage of the reduced visibility to double back and attack the trailing cruisers, *Suffolk* reversed course to the north. This would have been a sensible step for the Germans to take, as the cruisers represented a serious threat to their plans, but in fact Lütjens had continued steaming to the southwest. It only took a few minutes for the mistake to be discovered and for *Suffolk* to reverse course again, but, by then, the Germans were beyond the range of *Suffolk*'s radar.

(It is known that Lütjens was under the impression, due to faulty intelligence, that as of the previous afternoon the entire Home Fleet was at Scapa Flow, but even that cannot fully explain his lack of reaction to the trailing cruisers. After the one engagement at 2030, Lütjens made no further attempt to shake off the pursuit. This is particularly interesting, given that he had turned back in January when he encountered a cruiser during his last breakout attempt. It is possible to speculate that, because in this case the cruisers were across his route back to Norway and because any engagement with them, particularly at night, meant risking torpedo damage, he believed continuing to the south at high speed would give him a better chance to escape. Another possibility is that Lütjens had simply accepted that he would not be able to shake his pursuers, regardless of the manoeuvres he attempted. This was because he is known to have been deeply disturbed by the intercepted signals from *Suffolk*'s Type 284 radar which were much more powerful than any the Kriegsmarine had encountered to date.[25])

When *Suffolk* sighted the Germans at 1922, Holland's force was approximately 300nm due south, steaming just north of west on a course designed to bring it across the path of the Germans around 0200 the next morning. (His plan apparently was to engage Lütjens at that time, when he could bring all his guns to bear while the enemy approached head-on and while they were silhouetted against the pre-dawn gloom and his squadron would be hidden by the dark southern sky. It was a fine plan for a gaming table, but one that depended on precise timing and predictable behaviour by men and equipment,which rarely, if ever, occurs in real life.) As the squadron's speed gradually increased, the accompanying destroyers found themselves unable to keep up and they were instructed to follow as best they could. What can be divined of Holland's intentions at this point can be found in a message he sent to Captain John C Leach, commanding the *Prince of Wales*, at 0020, in which he stated that he wanted his two ships to engage *Bismarck* while Wake-Walker's cruisers took on *Prinz Eugen*. This was a workable plan, except that, because of Holland's insistence on radio silence, it was never communicated to Wake-Walker in *Norfolk*. When the battle was joined in the morning, the cruisers were unaware of the role they were expected to play, they were too far astern of the German ships to join in and, because they (and Holland) were unaware that *Prinz Eugen* was leading the German formation, they were closer to *Bismarck* than their intended target.

At 0008, a few minutes before he was informed of *Suffolk*'s loss of contact, Holland ordered a turn to 340°. It is most likely this was done to bring forward the time of the encounter.[26] But, after he found out about the loss of contact, he ordered a turn to due north at 0017 at 25kt, to be in position to intercept Lütjens should he bear away to the southeast.

In the event, Holland worried about overshooting the Germans in the dark, so, at 0203 he led around to 200°, putting him on a course that very nearly paralleled Lütjens'. Finally, at 0247, *Suffolk* regained radar contact with *Bismarck* and reported her course (220°) and speed (28kt) to Holland. Based on *Suffolk*'s reported position, this put the Germans 35nm to the northwest of Holland's position, moving slightly faster and diverging slowly from his course. Because the sun would not rise until a few minutes past 0400, Holland waited until 0340 before ordering a turn to 240°, which would narrow the gap, albeit slowly, and another thirteen minutes before increasing speed to match the Germans. (Having missed the opportunity to cross over to the westerly side of the German squadron, which would have given several advantages of visibility and wind in the early morning, Holland was now in no rush to begin the action as long as there was no risk of the enemy escaping.)

With the gap between the forces slowly dropping, Holland ordered action stations at 0510. Lütjens, informed about this at the same time that hydrophone operators on *Prinz Eugen* were picking up additional high-speed turbine sounds off to the southeast, turned to the south at 0521 and then back to 220° at 0532, his ships now making 27kt, with *Prinz Eugen* still leading by approximately 2,700yd.[27] Three minutes later, lookouts on *Prince of Wales* sighted smoke on the northeastern horizon and, in another two minutes, sent a sighting report to Tovey giving the range to the enemy as 17nm (approximately 35,000yd). At the same time, 0537, lookouts on *Prinz Eugen* got their first glimpse of the enemy. An intelligence officer, aboard *Prinz Eugen* specifically to identify enemy warships, declared the lead ship to be a light cruiser.

Each admiral faced a tactical problem. Lütjens' problem was simpler: he was now facing the very battle that his orders forbade him to fight and that he had very much hoped to avoid. Even if geography – specifically the proximity of the pack ice – did not prevent him from turning away from Holland, that course

66. One of the last clear images of HMS *Hood* (51), taken from the quarterdeck of HMS *Prince of Wales* (53) soon after dawn on 24 May 1941, the day of the Battle of the Denmark Strait. Holland's flagship is framed by three of the four barrels of *Prince of Wales*' quadruple 'Y' turret.

offered no benefit. He had no option but to fight and, with skill and luck, he might still win his way through.

Holland had many more choices available to him. He could have hung back at extreme visual range and, along with Wake-Walker's cruisers, shepherded the Germans to the south. While fuel consumption would limit how long this could be done, Holland knew that the Germans faced similar fuel issues and, while he had relief in the form of Tovey's squadron a day's sailing away and refuelling available at Iceland, Lütjens had no similar help. Alternatively, he could engage the Germans at extreme range, but this was the least attractive of his choices for three reasons. First, of the four main combatants, *Hood* had the shortest maximum main-battery range (29,850yd), so bringing his ships into gunnery range brought him well within the range of both of Lütjens' ships.[28] Second, he knew well that the Germans had gunnery optics, doctrine and training that gave them a decided advantage at long-range. This should have been at least partially offset by the fact that both of Holland's ships carried Type 284 fire control radar and that steering a course parallel to the enemy's would mitigate the great weakness of *Hood*'s antiquated MkV Dreyer Table, namely its inability to handle rapid changes in course. Finally, and undoubtedly foremost on Holland's mind, was the knowledge that *Hood*'s armour, particularly her deck armour, had not been strengthened in any of her refits, and she would be highly vulnerable to long-range plunging fire.[29] He no doubt also had firmly in mind the memory of the three Royal Navy battlecruisers destroyed by catastrophic explosions at Jutland, which seems to have persuaded him to adopt the third alternative, namely to steer a course that would rapidly reduce the range.[30] This seemed to offer several advantages besides the hoped-for result of moving his ships close enough to the enemy that their advantage in long-range gunnery and *Hood's* vulnerability to plunging fire would be neutralised – a key advantage being that by approaching at a relatively sharp angle, he presented a narrower target to the enemy.[31] Having decided on this course of action, Holland ordered a turn of 40° to starboard, to 280°, at 0537. (There can be little doubt that Holland was influenced in this decision by the official criticism he received after Cape Teulada for not handling his cruisers more aggressively.[32])

The distance between the two squadrons now dropped rapidly. To speed the process even more, at 0549, Holland ordered another 20° turn to starboard. This last turn caused the 'A' arcs of both his ships to 'close', meaning that their after turrets would no longer bear on the enemy until they turned back to port.[33] Two minutes before that, at 0547, Lütjens ordered the 'alarm' sounded on his ships, bringing them officially to battle readiness, although most men had long since found their way to their action stations. By 0550, the distance between the forces was 27,300yd and dropping steadily, now well within the extreme range of all four major combatants.[34] Still acting on the intention he had communicated to *Prince of Wales* over five hours earlier, Holland ordered fire from both of his ships to concentrate on the left-hand target, which was still believed to be *Bismarck*. (In defence of *Hood's* spotters, mistaking *Bismarck* and *Prinz Eugen* at extreme range and in hazy morning light was easy to do, as they had remarkably similar profiles.) In fact, the spotters in *Prince of Wales* recognised Holland's error and targeted the right-hand ship, *Bismarck*, from the beginning of the engagement. It would appear that, when fire was opened by *Hood* at 0552-1/2, her forward turrets loosed a two-gun half-salvo at *Prinz Eugen* at 25,000yd. The shells fell close to each other, close for range, but about 165yd ahead of the target. As per doctrine, *Prince of Wales* waited thirty seconds and then fired her first three-gun half-salvo at a range of 26,500yd.[35] These fell 1,500yd over and aft of *Bismarck*. (It is assumed that *Hood* used her Type 284 radar to help establish the range to *Prinz Eugen*; the similar set in *Prince of Wales* functioned only intermittently, and this was one of the periods when it was not working.) It was only when the large splashes of heavy-calibre shells erupted from the water around *Prinz Eugen* that the officers on that ship realised they were facing British capital ships.

Lütjens delayed returning fire, for reasons that are not entirely clear. In the meantime, each of the British ships fired a second half-salvo, which were closer, but still wide of the mark. At 0554, Holland ordered a 20° turn to port to reopen his 'A' arcs and to slow the rapid rate of closure which had brought the range down to approximately 23,000yd. Each of the British ships fired two more half-salvos before the turn was actually executed at 0555. *Hood's* fourth salvo was in line and over by only 150yd, sending shell splinters rattling against *Prinz Eugen's* starboard side. By *Prince of Wales'* fourth salvo, she had already lost the use of one gun in her forward quadruple turret.

It was only now, at 0555, that Lütjens gave permission to open fire on the British. Both German ships began firing alternating half-salvos, all four forward

67. Looking back from *Prinz Eugen* towards *Bismarck* as the latter opens fire on *Hood* at the Battle of the Denmark Strait, 24 May 1941. *Bismarck* was firing half-salvos, first her forward turrets, then her after turrets. (*NHHC*)

guns followed a few seconds later by all four after guns, all targeting *Hood*. They very quickly found the range. Remarkably, at 0556, a 20.3cm shell from *Prinz Eugen*'s fourth half-salvo (the second half of her second full salvo) hit *Hood* between her second funnel and mainmast and started a fierce fire that was seen to spread along her boat deck, apparently fed by ready-use rounds stored there.[36] While the fire burned brightly and created a thick plume of smoke, and exploding 4in shells and anti-aircraft rockets endangered nearby crewmen, it actually represented no great danger to the ship. The shells used for these first, ranging salvos were no doubt nose-fused HE shells and this one exploded on impact as designed, causing no damage to the interior of the ship.

68. Interested sailors on *Prinz Eugen* watch as shells from *Hood* fall just over. (*NARA*)

After the turn, the next several salvos from *Hood* were off target for deflection, no doubt due to the inability of her Dreyer Table to adjust rapidly to even minor changes in 'own ship' course. *Prince of Wales*, with her more modern AFCT, had no such trouble keeping her guns on target during the turn. One shell from her sixth salvo, fired at 21,150yd – just three shells because another two guns in her 'A' turret had malfunctioned – hit *Bismarck* well forward on her bow shell plating above the thin armoured deck extending forward from 'Anton' turret's barbette. The shell punched through this deck and out the starboard side without exploding, but it did significant damage along the way. The immediate effect was minimal: the holes on either side were within the bow wave when the ship was moving at high speed, causing the flooding of several forward compartments, including the forward fuel-distribution compartment, and the contamination of her forward fuel tanks with sea water. In the short-term, this had no effect on *Bismarck*'s fighting ability, but the loss of the use of 1,000t of fuel oil and the flooding forward would have important long-term implications.[37]

At 0557, *Hood* was hit twice more. One hit was by a 38cm shell from *Bismarck*'s third complete salvo, fired at 20,200yd, which passed through *Hood*'s fire control tower at her foretop. This shell did not explode and the hit went unnoticed in most of the ship, except at the bridge where it was noted that communication with the foretop was lost at that time. The effect on the fire control tower must have been devastating, despite the fact the shell failed to detonate. It is likely that most, if not all, of the occupants of the foretop were killed instantly; none survived the ensuing catastrophe. The second shell was from *Prinz Eugen*. It landed at the base of the starboard side of the forward superstructure, entering a compartment where perhaps two hundred men were assembled, awaiting assignment to damage-control parties. It is believed all were killed when the shell exploded and a localised fire added to the continuing munitions fire further aft on the boat deck.

The range had now decreased to approximately 18,600yd, and secondary batteries on *Bismarck* (three twin-15cm turrets on her port side) and *Prince of Wales* (four twin-5.25in turrets on her starboard side) were able to open fire. It is unlikely any achieved any hits. *Prince of Wales*, which from her ninth salvo fired, at 0557, was able to bring all three main-battery turrets to bear, only had the use of all four guns of 'Y' turret for two salvos before one of the four 14in guns failed. (After several more salvos, all four guns of 'Y' turret were out of action and *Prince of Wales* was reduced to firing three-gun salvos – one gun from 'A' turret and the two guns of 'B' turret – for much of the remainder of the engagement.) With her ninth salvo, *Prince of Wales* hit *Bismarck* again, this time under the waterline, below her main armour belt, in way of the transverse bulkhead separating her forward port turbo-generator room from her forward port boiler room.[38] This shell exploded outside the 45mm torpedo bulkhead that formed the outer, watertight shell of these compartments, perforating the bulkhead in places and fracturing welded seams that proved to be less strong than intended. The large turbo-generator room flooded immediately and the even larger boiler room began filling with water. While damage-control crews were able to prevent the complete flooding of that compartment, the two boilers had to be shut down and *Bismarck*'s maximum speed dropped to 28kt. Lütjens, realising that *Prince of Wales* was shooting so well in part because she was herself not under fire, ordered *Prinz Eugen* to switch target, which she did, starting with her seventh salvo.

At 0559, the range having come down to less than 17,000yd, Holland apparently decided that it was now dropping too fast and ordered another 20° turn to port. (This is a very curious decision, as so small a turn would only slow the closing rate by one-third. If he decided he was close enough to the Germans, a turn of 60° would have put him on a course parallel to theirs. It is very difficult to discern what advantage he thought he might gain from closing the enemy any further. Given the problems associated with his Dreyer Table, one big turn would certainly have been less disruptive to the accuracy of *Hood*'s gunfire than multiple smaller turns.) At the same time, *Prince of Wales* scored a third hit on *Bismarck*. One of the three shells from her thirteenth salvo, fired at approximately 16,500yd, struck *Bismarck* amidships between her funnel and mainmast, demolishing the bow of one of her cutters and then continuing over her starboard side without exploding. Debris from the damaged boat disabled her catapult, but did little other damage.

It appears *Hood* had just started executing the ordered turn, when, at 0600, one shell from the second half of *Bismarck*'s fifth salvo struck near the mainmast. The range was approximately 16,500yd.[39] It is possible, but not likely, that a second shell from that same salvo struck further aft, but, even if one did, it most likely had no effect on subsequent events. It is impossible to be certain whether the shell fell just short and pierced *Hood*'s side below her main armour belt or came in through one of her thinner upper-armour strakes (5in and 7in thickness). Either way it appears to have penetrated one of her 4in magazines just aft of the after engine room and ignited the propellant charges there. Capt Leach described what he saw and heard (or rather did not hear):

> I happened to be looking at 'Hood' at the moment when a salvo arrived and it appeared to be across the ship somewhere about the mainmast. In that salvo there were, I think, two shots short and one over, but it may have been the other way round. But I formed the impression at the time that something had arrived on board 'Hood' in a position just before the mainmast and slightly to starboard. It was not a very definite impression that I had, but it was sufficiently definite to make me look at 'Hood' for a further period. I in fact wondered what the result was going to be, and between one and two seconds after I formed that impression an explosion took place in the 'Hood' which appeared to me to come from very much the same position in the ship. There was a very fierce upward rush of flame the shape of a funnel, rather a thin funnel, and almost instantaneously the ship was enveloped in smoke from one end to the other . . .
>
> The explosion gave the impression of a vast blow lamp. I almost expected to hear the corresponding noise but I did not. I do not remember hearing any noise.[40]

Almost every witness agreed with Leach's description of the event being completely or almost completely silent, at least not loud enough to be heard over the 'normal' noise of battle, indicative of an extremely fast conflagration, but not the near-instantaneous combustion of an explosion. Apparently, the flames vented into the engine room and upwards through the vent system, accounting for the initial 'funnel' of flame seem by most witnesses, but it also spread aft into the 15in magazines for 'X' and 'Y' turrets, where approximately 94t of cordite propellant was stored, and the combustion of that material tore apart the aft end of *Hood*. Her forward part lurched to starboard and then back, as witnessed from his position on the compass platform by Ordinary Signalman Albert E Briggs:

> There was not a terrific explosion but the officer of the watch said to the Admiral that the Compass had gone and the Admiral said move over to the after control. During that she had listed 6–7° to starboard and shortly after what the Admiral said she listed right over to port. She had gone about 25° to port and the crew were trying to get away – by crew I mean people on the bridge, but the Admiral did not make any attempt to get away. I got out of the starboard door and there was the Navigator just in front of me and the S.G.O. just in front of him. I had just got out of the door and the water by that time had got level with the Compass Platform. I did not remember anything more then until I found myself on the surface. The bows of the HOOD were vertical with the water about 50 yards away.[41]

Hood's bow stood out of the water for, at most, two minutes, before slipping beneath the waves. She left behind several thick oil slicks, burning in places, and a thick cloud of smoke that was carried rapidly to the east by the wind. It is not known how many of her crew survived the cataclysm and rapid sinking to reach the water alive. *Prince of Wales*, which had also begun to turn, was forced to reverse the turn to avoid colliding with *Hood*'s bow. This brought her around the exposed, starboard side of the smoke cloud. Leach ordered her helm reversed again and she began a semi-circular turn to port around the wreath of smoke in which *Hood* was sinking.

The Germans were just as stunned. *Prinz Eugen* had switched to firing at *Prince of Wales* a minute earlier, but *Bismarck*, unable to respond fast enough, sent her sixth salvo at the now-sinking *Hood*, before resetting her sights on *Prince of Wales*. With remarkable speed, *Bismarck* found her new target. One 38cm shell from her eighth salvo, just her second aimed at *Prince of Wales*, hit the battleship's compass platform at 0602. By great good fortune, the shell did not explode, but very nearly every officer and man there was killed. Purely by chance, Leach was only stunned, although for about a minute the ship was not under command, continuing her counter-clockwise circle around *Hood*.

As bad as that was for *Prince of Wales*, worse was to follow. Other ships in other battles, some to be described later in this book, may have faced a fusillade of gunfire worse than she suffered in the next two minutes, but not at a range of greater than 15,000yd and at speeds of 27kt or better. In those two minutes, *Prince of Wales* was hit six additional times:

0603 Two shells from *Bismarck*'s ninth salvo hit. One struck below the waterline in way of her starboard diesel room. This failed to penetrate her inner torpedo bulkhead and did not explode. Had it detonated, the boiler room would have undoubtedly flooded and the effect on the subsequent course of the battle would have been serious. As it was, the hit was barely noticed at the time, given what else was going on, and, it was only when she was docked at Rosyth on 1 June that its potential seriousness was discovered. The second hit disabled her starboard high-angle (anti-aircraft) director well up on her forward superstructure.

0603 One shell from *Prinz Eugen*'s seventeenth salvo hit right aft below the waterline, above the rudder, causing little damage and minor flooding.

0604 One shell from *Bismarck*'s next salvo damaged *Prince of Wales*' starboard crane and detonated on striking the after side of her second funnel. There was considerable splinter damage to her boats and the surrounding area.

0604 *Prinz Eugen*'s eighteenth salvo yielded two more hits. One hit aft below the waterline, forward of the previous hit, also for minor damage. The second could have been very serious, hitting the handling room serving the two aft 5.25in twin-anti-aircraft mounts on the starboard side. Fortunately, for *Prince of Wales*, this one also failed to explode.

While this was going on, both sides were manoeuvring violently, though for completely different reasons. Sound operators in *Prinz Eugen* heard the high-speed screws of torpedoes at 0603 and two approaching tracks were seen by observers on her bridge, including her captain. Both German ships turned away briefly before returning to their original course of 220˚. There has been much

69. This photograph from *Prinz Eugen* shows *Prince of Wales* – the single trail of smoke to the left – probably at 0605, when the latter turned away making smoke. The smudge on the horizon to the right was all that remained of *Hood*. (*NHHC*)

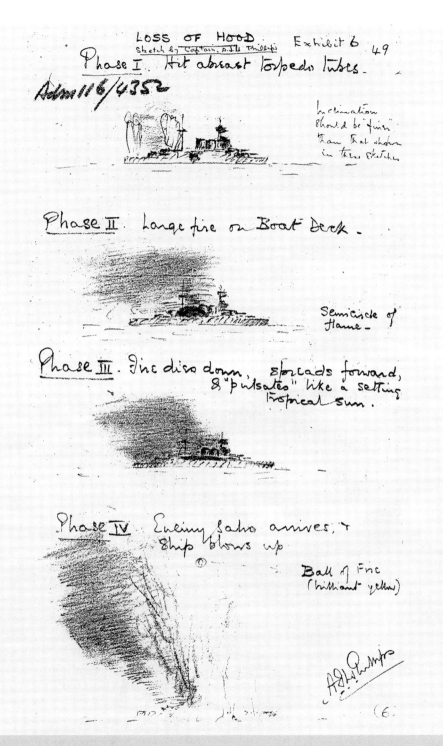

LOSS OF HOOD.   Exhibit 6 49
Sketch by Captain A.J.L. Phillips

Phase I. Hit abreast torpedo tubes.

Adm 116/4352

Inclination
should be finer
than that shown
in these sketches

Phase II. Large fire on Boat Deck.

Semicircle of
flame.

Phase III. Fire dies down, spreads forward,
& "pulsates" like a setting
tropical sun.

Phase IV. Enemy salvo arrives, &
Ship blows up

Ball of Fire
(brilliant yellow)

70. No photographs exist that show the loss of *Hood* in any detail, but the Admiralty asked several officer witnesses to sketch what they had seen and preserved them as exhibits in the several inquiries into the disaster. This set of four sketches by Captain A J L Phillips of HMS *Norfolk* (78), which was trailing *Hood* by approximately 10nm, show the initial hits by *Prinz Eugen*, the fire on her boat deck and, in 'Phase IV' the violent funnel of 'brilliant yellow' that accompanied her destruction.

71. Captain John C Leach of *Prince of Wales* had a much closer view of *Hood*'s demise, but created a very similar image, showing a spout or 'funnel' of flame shooting up from near the ship's mainmast, where an explosion of her after powder magazines, especially if it originated in the secondary battery magazine just aft of the engineering spaces, would have vented upward.

speculation as to the source of these torpedoes. Since there were no torpedo-carrying aircraft, destroyers or submarines in the vicinity, and the two trailing cruisers did not fire torpedoes during this engagement, the only possible source was the sinking *Hood*, which did have two fixed torpedo tubes on each broadside, which might have discharged accidentally as she was disintegrating. To say that this is unlikely is an understatement. It is most likely, in this author's opinion, that there were no torpedoes present. This is reinforced by the fact that torpedo sounds were heard, and the German ships turned away twice more – at 0607 and 0614 – which cannot in any way be attributed to *Hood*.

While the Germans were in the midst of their first torpedo-avoidance manoeuvre, Captain Leach was able to regain control of *Prince of Wales* and ordered a turn to starboard at 0604, which briefly brought her to a course paralleling the Germans' base course. This lasted only moments, as the German gunfire continued unabated despite their manoeuvres. Painfully aware that his ship was now badly outgunned, with little ability to strike back, and that his country would be poorly served by the loss of another ship and crew, he decided to make smoke and turn away to port.

This effectively brought the engagement to an end. *Prince of Wales* fired three more partial salvos from 'Y' turret, temporarily back in action, all of which fell short. The last was at 0605, after which she disappeared in her own smoke screen. *Norfolk* had joined in briefly at extreme range at 0602, firing three salvos which also fell well short. The Germans kept firing for four more minutes, before they too ceased fire. The engagement had lasted seventeen minutes. *Hood* had fired an estimated forty-four rounds and achieved no hits.

Prince of Wales actually fired fifty-five rounds and hit *Bismarck* three times for a hit rate of 5.5 per cent, quite respectable for a new ship with dodgy mechanical systems. (If all her guns had been working, she would have fired seventy-four rounds.) *Norfolk* shot, at most, twenty-four rounds, all of which missed. *Prinz Eugen* fired 157 main-battery rounds, of which five hit, for a hit rate of 3.2 per cent.[42] *Bismarck* fired ninety-three main-battery rounds, of which six hit, for a hit rate of 6.5 per cent. Considering that this was the first engagement for three of the four main combatants, the shooting was extraordinary, particularly by *Bismarck*.

The casualties this day, given *Hood*'s fate, were terrible. *Prinz Eugen* was not hit and suffered no damage or casualties. Despite being hit three times, *Bismarck* also suffered no casualties. *Prince of Wales* was less lucky: hit seven times, she suffered thirteen dead and nine wounded. *Hood*, because of her cataclysmic demise, suffered terrible losses. The best estimate is that she had 1,418 crew and flag staff aboard her when she sank; of that number, only three survived. It is not known how many men reached the freezing water alive. These three survived because they were able to find rafts and each other in the oil-covered water, and, even though they drifted apart as they fought hypothermia, they were found alive by HMS *Electra* (H27) a little more than two hours after *Hood* sank.

Another Anticlimactic Ending

Given the high drama of the engagement on the morning of 24 May, the story that enfolded from that point until the sinking of *Bismarck* three days later was remarkably anticlimactic, starting with Lütjens' refusal to pursue the wounded *Prince of Wales* as she turned away. *Bismarck*'s captain, Ernst Lindemann, pleaded with him, but Lütjens cited his orders, which forbade him engaging enemy capital ships, ignoring the fact that those orders had been invalidated by that morning's events. Instead, Lütjens continued to the south at the now-best speed of 28kt, with occasional changes in course and speed that he hoped might shake his pursuit. By 0801, he had made up his mind as to his next course of action, because, at that time, he signalled SKL his intention to head for France after detaching *Prinz Eugen* to operate independently in the Atlantic.

Prince of Wales was now officially part of that pursuit. At 0615, Wake-Walker, now senior officer on the scene, ordered her to fall in with his cruisers and the three ships together shepherded the Germans to the south. At 1600, while still some 400nm to the southeast, Tovey detached *Victorious* with a cruiser screen to make a high-speed run towards Wake-Walker, while he turned towards the southwest with *King George V* and *Repulse* with the idea of intercepting Lütjens sometime after dawn the next day.

Lütjens acted on his intention of detaching *Prinz Eugen* at 1614; when his ships were shrouded in a fog bank, *Bismarck* turned back on her pursuers while the heavy cruiser continued south at high speed. For the next forty-five minutes, the two sides exchanged sporadic long-range gunfire until, assured that *Prinz Eugen* was well clear, *Bismarck* turned south again at 1700. Nether side achieved any hits in these exchanges. By 2210, *Victorious* had drawn within 200nm, close enough that she was able to launch a strike of nine Swordfish torpedo-bombers.

72. Perhaps the last image to show *Bismarck* intact, this photograph was taken from *Prinz Eugen* as the two ships parted company in the afternoon of 24 May 1941. The battleship is well down by the head, the result of the hit by *Prince of Wales* that penetrated her weakly protected forepeak, flooding compartments in her bow and contaminating vital fuel tanks. (*NHHC*)

Flying through abysmal weather, they not only managed to find their target, but one of them put a torpedo into *Bismarck*'s starboard side. The torpedo ran rather shallow and detonated against her main armour belt in way of her forward starboard turbo-generator room, directly opposite where she had been hit earlier in the day. The damage on the starboard side was actually rather minor – one man was killed and six more injured – but the shock effect on the damage repairs on the port side was more serious, including the complete flooding of the forward boiler room on that side.

After midnight on 25 May, Wake-Walker's cruisers began zigzagging out of concern that they were being drawn into a U-boat 'trap'. At the southeastern end of each 'zig', *Suffolk* briefly lost *Bismarck* on her radar, re-acquiring her when she turned back. Taking advantage of this, at 0306, Lütjens ordered *Bismarck* into a wide loop back to the west and then around behind the pursuit, finally settling on a course 130°, heading for St-Nazaire. When Wake-Walker realised he had once again lost *Bismarck*, he ordered a sweep to the west and south, followed by *Victorious*, whose aircraft searched to the west and north. Tovey continued towards the southwest, passing approximately 100nm ahead of *Bismarck*.

Lütjens had managed to make a clean escape and might have been able to reach France undetected, had she been favoured by luck and overcast weather. Most Royal Navy searchers were looking in the wrong direction, but Force 'H', ordered up from Gibraltar to escort a southbound troop convoy, was redirected to sweep north across the Bay of Biscay after *Bismarck* was lost and might well have located her, even without Lütjens' help. In fact, *Bismarck* was 'lost' for only about four hours. Having successfully exploited the limitations of *Suffolk*'s radar in making his escape, Lütjens now blundered badly. Still able to detect the signal from *Suffolk*'s Type 284 radar, Lütjens assumed he was still being tracked, when, in fact, he was far beyond the range at which a useable return could be received by *Suffolk*.[43] At 0700 and again at 0852, he sent out radio messages, the second one over half an hour in length, which allowed British radio direction finders to pinpoint his location and confirm that he was heading towards France.

73. HMS *King George V* (41), class-leader and sister of *Prince of Wales*, was one of two battleships that took part in the battering of *Bismarck* on 27 May 1941. She is seen here much as she looked on that occasion. (*NARA*)

From that point on, *Bismarck's* fate was all but sealed – only the most absurd ill-luck or blundering would have allowed her to slip through the net that began to close around her. The British did make mistakes, including misplotting *Bismarck's* location in the flagship and attacking one of their own cruisers by mistake. *Bismarck* was not precisely located until 1030 the next morning, and she was not hobbled until a torpedo from a Swordfish off *Ark Royal* disabled her rudder at 2105 that night, but she really had little chance once her destination became clear. Sadly, her actual demise took the form of a battering by gunfire

74. The other major participant in the sinking of *Bismarck* was HMS *Rodney* (29), shown as she appeared in August 1940. *Rodney* was built between the wars to a striking design, with three triple main-battery turrets grouped forward to allow for a more compact (and robust) armoured citadel. She and her sister were well-armed, but sacrificed armour and speed to meet treaty tonnage limits. (*NARA*)

75. Operation Rheinübung ended with the arrival of *Prinz Eugen* at Brest on 1 June 1941. Any joy at her arrival was muted, not only by the loss of her partner *Bismarck*, but also by the repeated powerplant problems she suffered during her sortie, a problem shared by many German major warships. (*NHHC*)

76. *Prinz Eugen* would require immediate docking to repair her powerplant. She was covered by nets and any exposed surfaces elaborately camouflaged, but this did not prevent her presence being detected by the British and her becoming the target of bombing raids by the RAF. (*NHHC*)

and torpedoes that lasted almost two hours on the morning of 27 May, still more than 400nm west of the French coast. By the time she sank, the death toll had soared: out of an estimated complement of 2,249, only 116 were saved.

Opinions understandably differ regarding Lancelot Holland's tactical decisions at the Battle of the Denmark Strait, but he did leave behind one accomplishment that had a greater impact on German surface warfare in the Atlantic than any outcome at Denmark Strait would have achieved. Before raising his flag in *Hood* in May 1941, Holland was still in command of the 18th Cruiser Squadron, with the mission to capture the German weather boat *München*, a modified fishing trawler operating alone east of Iceland. The reason why three cruisers and four destroyers were detailed to intercept one converted fishing boat was because she used an Enigma machine to encrypt the regular weather reports she sent from her position equidistant from Iceland, Norway and the Faroes. This meant that she not only had the machine itself, but also the ancillary books of settings and code words for the months of May and June. The capture went as planned on 7 May. The German crew was able to dispose of the Enigma and many documents, but enough were captured to give GC&CS at Bletchley Park the cribs it needed to break into Kriegsmarine message traffic for most of the month of June. Between 3 June and 23 June, the Royal Navy caught and sank or captured six tankers and two supply ships in the German resupply network in the Atlantic. This, plus the dismay at the loss of *Bismarck*, caused all immediate plans for raiding by major surface naval units to be cancelled.

4 A CLEAN SWEEP
IMPERIAL JAPANESE NAVY VS ABDAFLOAT IN THE SOUTH SEAS, FEBRUARY–MARCH 1942

ON 6 DECEMBER 1941, THE US Navy was at war and had been for at least four months, even if many, perhaps most, Americans were unaware of it. That war was in the Atlantic against Hitler's U-boats. On 7 December 1941, that war was suddenly overshadowed by one that every American knew about, one in the Pacific against the Japanese, one for which America should have been better prepared.

In this the Americans were no different than the other navies on the receiving end of the Japanese onslaught at the end of 1941. Even the Royal Navy, with more than two years of hard fighting behind it, was unprepared for the speed and ferocity of the attack unleashed on South Asia. The British had seen the storm clouds building and had tried to gather forces in the Far East sufficient to defend India, Ceylon (Sri Lanka), Malaya and Singapore – if not to discourage the Japanese from making more aggressive moves against French and Dutch outposts in Indochina and the East Indies – but competing demands from other theatres and the need to replace damaged ships meant that few ships could actually be spared. The battlecruiser *Repulse* was sent to the Indian Ocean in October, where she joined the ancient aircraft carrier *Hermes* and an old light cruiser. As tensions in South Asia increased, additional forces were earmarked to join *Repulse*. The newly commissioned aircraft carrier HMS *Indomitable* (92) was supposed to go east, but she ran aground in November while working up in the Caribbean and her departure was delayed, which probably was fortuitous.[1] Less lucky was *Prince of Wales*. Having survived her brush with *Bismarck*, she served with the Home Fleet until tapped to join *Repulse* at Colombo, whence the ships departed on 29 November for Singapore, escorted by four destroyers, where they arrived on 2 December. This meager squadron was given the grandiose title Force 'Z' once it arrived at Singapore. The veteran heavy cruiser *Exeter*, met before at the River Plate, was detached from escort duty in the Indian Ocean and also ordered to join Force 'Z'.

The US Asiatic Fleet was small and scattered over a wide area of the Philippines and the northern East Indies. As war approached, the heavy cruiser USS *Houston* (CA30) was at Iloilo on the southern coast of Panay in the central Philippines, the modern light cruiser USS *Boise* (CL47) was not far away at Cebu and another light cruiser, the ancient USS *Marblehead* (CL12), was at Tarakan, Borneo, along with five old destroyers, with two more divisions, each comprising four more flush-deckers of First World War vintage, at Cavite (Manila) and Balikpapan, Borneo.[2] The destroyer division at Balikpapan was sent to Singapore on 6 December to bolster Force 'Z's escort.

The Dutch had a small surface force, comprising three light cruisers (Hr. Ms. *De Ruyter*, *Tromp* and *Java*) and seven destroyers, based at Tanjung Priok, Batavia (Jakarta) on the north coast of Java. The Australians also operated a small number of ships, cruisers and destroyers, mainly out of Fremantle and Darwin, supporting Royal Navy activities in the Indian Ocean.

Force 'Z' Overwhelmed

Besides the force of six fleet aircraft carriers and supporting ships that attacked Pearl Harbor on 7 December 1941, the Japanese had multiple task forces at sea carrying invasion forces towards Malaya, the Philippines and numerous islands in the Central and South Pacific.[3] While the movements of the Kido Butai, the main carrier strike force, remained opaque to Allied intelligence, the ability of the Allies to analyse Japanese message traffic allowed the Allies to follow the movement of army units, aircraft and ships southward along the coast of China and Vietnam. By 27 November, the intelligence was solid enough for a 'war warning' message to be sent by CNO Admiral Harold Stark to all relevant Pacific commands, including Admiral Thomas Hart, commanding the US Asiatic Fleet.[4] There was little Hart could do to prepare for war except recall most of the small patrol force deployed on the China coast.

Admiral Sir Tom Phillips, commanding Force 'Z' and recently arrived at Singapore, flew to Manila on 5 December to meet with Hart. The meeting resulted in an agreement to co-ordinate the activities of the British and American forces and, more specifically, to send aid in the form of the four American destroyers at Balikpapan to Singapore to bolster Force 'Z'. In the event, they were not to arrive in time. In co-ordination with the carrier air attack on Pearl Harbor, Japanese air

attacks were made on American bases on Luzon, Guam and Wake Islands, as well as British positions in Malaya and China. Landings began in southern Thailand and northern Malaya, to which Phillips responded by sortieing Force 'Z' from Singapore, despite knowing that he would have no air support at the time of his planned arrival off the landing beaches at dawn on the 10th.[5] After being sighted several times by Japanese aircraft on the 9th, Phillips turned south again. Receiving a false report of Japanese landings further south at Kuantan, he turned southwest, arriving off the coast soon after dawn on the 10th to find no enemy activity. That peaceful state would not last long: Japanese air attacks began soon after 1100 and continued in seven waves until after noon, by which time both capital ships had been mortally wounded; Phillips and *Prince of Wales'* Captain John Leach were not among the 2,081 rescued from the two ships that day.

With this attack and the devastating Pearl Harbor raid, it would seem that the dominance of air power over surface warships had been definitively established, and that the only chance for operating surface ships would be within range of friendly land airbases or accompanying aircraft carriers. Yet, it turned out that the Pacific theatre was vast, the number of aircraft carriers still quite small and the speed of advance of the initial Japanese moves so fast that the naval forces of Japan and of the Allies arrayed against them would in fact meet and fight most often without significant interference by aircraft.

A Small Measure of Revenge at Balikpapan

Even before the destruction of Force 'Z', Hart had made the decision to withdraw his meager naval forces to the south in an attempt to defend the Dutch East Indies. *Houston* arrived at Darwin, by way of Balikpapan and Surabaya, on 28 December. Political decisions made half a world away ordained that the surviving Allied forces would be brought together at Surabaya in a unified coalition command dubbed ABDACOM (American–British–Dutch–Australian Command) under British General Sir Archibald Wavell. The ABDACOM strategy was to defend Australia by holding the so-called 'Malay Barrier', an arc of islands running from Singapore in the west, through Java, Bali, Flores and Timor, as far east as New Guinea. The naval forces (ABDAFLOAT) were put under the command of Hart, but split into three areas of national interest. A British-led task group was based at Singapore with orders to resist Japanese moves south towards that island and Sumatra; a Dutch squadron at Surabaya covered the Java Sea approaches; and the American TF5 at Koepang (Kupang), Timor, comprised the remaining surface forces of the US Asiatic Fleet.

They did not have to go hunting for the Japanese: the momentum of the Japanese advances, marked by the capture of Davao on Mindanao (20 December 1941), Hong Kong (25 December 1941) and Manila (2 January 1942), continued south with landings on the British-controlled northwest coast of Borneo. Three oil towns on the coast of Sarawak and Brunei were occupied as early as 16 December. The main thrust into the Dutch East Indies, however, did not begin until early January. The first Dutch towns to fall were Tarakan on Borneo's northeast coast and Menado (Manado) near the northern tip of Celebes (Sulawesi).

It was from Koepang that TF5, under the command of Rear-Admiral William Glassford Jr, left on 21 January, in response to reports that a Japanese invasion convoy would be heading south from Tarakan into the Makassar Strait between Borneo and Celebes. Already in place were nine submarines – seven American and two Dutch – deployed to patrol the strait. The main Japanese force, which in fact departed Tarakan that same day, 21 January, was heading for Balikpapan,

79. Some US Navy ships spent long periods between the wars assigned to duty with the Asiatic Fleet, the only major fleet unit permanently stationed outside US continental waters. One of those ships was the flush-decker destroyer *Pope* (DD225), seen here at Tsingtao (Qingdao), China, probably in 1924. She would have looked little different, except for painting out her large white hull numbers, when she sailed from Manila to the Netherlands East Indies at the outbreak of war in December 1941. (*via navsource.com*)

most of the way down Borneo's east coast, a big step closer to Java and Australia beyond that. It was commanded by Rear-Admiral Nishimura Shoji.

Both the American and Japanese task forces would have their share of misadventures before they finally met. Glassford's force, led by *Boise* and *Marblehead* and escorted by six old destroyers, got no farther than Sape Strait between Flores and Sumbawa Islands before it quite literally ran into trouble. *Boise* came up on an uncharted rock and ripped out part of her bottom, requiring her to retire westward toward Tjilatjap (Cilacap) on the south coast of Java and eventually Mare Island Navy Yard via Colombo, Ceylon. Glassford transferred his flag to *Marblehead*, but she meanwhile had suffered an engineering casualty that limited her to a best speed of 15kt. One destroyer accompanied *Boise* westward and another escorted the hobbled *Marblehead*, which left the four destroyers of DesDiv59, under Commander Paul H Talbot to oppose Nishimura. Glassford ordered Talbot to proceed as far as the Postillion (Sabalana) Islands at the southern exit of the Makassar Strait to await further orders.

Nishimura's 1st Protection Fleet comprised one old light cruiser (*Naka*) and nine modern destroyers in support of the Imperial Army's Sakaguchi detachment carried in sixteen transports and cargo ships with a close escort of four minesweepers, three patrol boats (ex-destroyers converted to patrol boats and then re-converted to high-speed transports similar to to the US Navy's APDs) and three submarine chasers. Attacked by Allied aircraft and submarines, only fourteen transports actually anchored off Balikpapan after dark on 23 January, and one of those was on fire and would eventually be abandoned. Just before midnight, the Dutch submarine *KXVIII* fired a spread of torpedoes at *Naka*; they all missed, but one hit another of the transports, *Tsuruga Maru*, which settled stern-first in the mud, her bow remaining out of the water. This

80. The flagship of Rear-Admiral Nishimura's 1st Protection Fleet escorting invasion transports to Balikpapan, Borneo in January 1942 was the old light cruiser *Naka*, seen here before 1934 when an aircraft catapult was added aft. Nishimura had a rather undistinguished part to play in the Battle of Balikpapan on the night of 23–24 January. He will show up again playing a major role in the last chapter of this book. (*NHHC*)

was fortuitous for Talbot, as the submarine alarm drew *Naka* and the destroyers out towards deeper water and they played no part in the subsequent action.

Even before reaching his patrol position, Talbot was ordered to attack the Japanese landing force at Balikpapan, so DesDiv59 simply continued north, keeping to the eastern side of the strait, passing close off Cape Mandar after dark on the 23rd and then turning northwest to bring them off Balikpapan at approximately 0300. Talbot ordered a line-ahead formation, with the flagship, USS *John D. Ford* (DD228) leading *Pope* (DD225), *Parrott* (DD218) and *Paul Jones* (DD230) at 27kt, their maximum sustainable speed. None of these ships were equipped with radar, but all had TBS shortwave, short-range tactical radio, which allowed Talbot to pass an explicit battle plan to his captains as they headed towards the Japanese, the first American ships to enter a surface engagement with an enemy force since 1898.

Talbot did not want a gunfight with a force that he believed, correctly, to be far stronger than his four flush-deckers. His only advantage would be surprise and speed and he intended to take maximum advantage of both. His orders were to attack first with torpedoes, using guns only after all torpedoes were expended and only if the opportunity presented itself.[6] As such, this would seem to be simply the first of a succession of night torpedo fights in tropical waters that spanned the next several years, and, as such, it should fall outside the purview of this narrative, but, unlike many of those engagements, this one ended with a brief, but interesting, gunfight.

The beginning of the engagement went as well as Talbot could have hoped. The American line approached from the southeast. Two rows of Japanese transports were anchored parallel to the shore which ran roughly southwest to northeast. A Japanese attempt to capture the oil port intact earlier in the evening by *coup de main* had failed utterly and fires burned along the shore, which alternately silhouetted the transports or obscured them in thick black smoke. Talbot's line was first sighted at 0245 by minesweeper *W15*, which initially mistook *Ford* for *Naka*, because both had four funnels, but this was soon cleared up when three more four-funnelled shapes followed the first. (*Naka* was the only four-funnelled Japanese ship in the vicinity.) The minesweeper reported the presence of enemy warships in the anchorage by radio – a report that took twenty-five minutes to reach Nishimura – but otherwise did nothing to interfere with Talbot's destroyers.[7]

For the next hour, the line of American destroyers steamed at high speed around the Japanese anchorage, looping first around to the south, then east, then making another left-hand loop around to the north, all the while firing off torpedoes, thirty-nine in all, of which as many as ten hit a target. Three merchantmen were destroyed and one patrol boat damaged to the extent that she was written off as a 'constructive total loss'.[8] Then at 0339, while heading north for a third pass at the anchored transports, lookouts on *Ford* spotted a 'destroyer' 2,500yd off the port bow which was seen to fire torpedoes in *Ford*'s direction.[9] (It is impossible to determine what *Ford*'s lookouts saw, but it is certain that it was not a Japanese (or American) destroyer and that no torpedoes were fired at *Ford* at this or any other time during this engagement.[10]) Regardless,

Ford reacted as if to avoid torpedoes, with hard left rudder and backing her port engine full to swing the ship sharply to the left.

One result of this sudden manoeuvre, which dropped *Ford*'s speed to a crawl, was to throw the following line of destroyers into chaos. Each captain, coming up suddenly on the nearly stopped *Ford*, had to make a split-second decision to avoid a collision.

Pope turned even more sharply to the left, sweeping rapidly around *Ford*'s port side and then turned right, crossing ahead of the flagship. She sighted a destroyer on her port bow and briefly opened fire. She continued turning to starboard and soon joined up with *Parrott* and *Jones* heading south, away from Balikpapan.

Parrott and *Jones* turned sharply to the right to avoid *Ford*, coming under fire as they continued their turn. *Parrott*'s action report states that, at 0350, 'it was reported on PARROTT bridge that shells were falling astern and that one had just passed ahead.'[11] Any confusion as to the source of the gunfire was soon cleared up:

> From POPE 'Am firing to port at destroyer.'
> From PARROTT 'Believe you are firing at us; am clearing area, course
>   180°.'[12]

That left only *Ford* still engaged with the Japanese. After very nearly coming to a complete stop, she went ahead full on both engines and resumed her previous course of 320°, which very quickly brought her up to the inner line of anchored transports between the large transport *Asahi Maru* to starboard and *Tsuruga Maru*, which had already settled stern-first in the mud, to port. With two torpedoes remaining in *Ford*'s port tubes, Talbot was determined to take one last swing at the enemy before retiring.

The torpedoes were fired to port, one hitting the bow of *Tsuruga Maru*, causing another large explosion. Meanwhile, she opened fire with her four single-4in/50 mounts at three targets in succession. The first to be hit was *Tamagawa Maru*. This cargo ship had been near the northern end of the outer line when the first of the American torpedoes hit with a spectacular explosion. She got under way and steamed slowly south and west, down the inner line of transports, reaching a point just in-shore of *Tsuruga Maru* when *Ford* opened fire.[13] 'Nine hits were observed in the first target opening up a large hole in her quarter as if all shots hit in the same vicinity. When last observed it was settling rapidly by the stern and had at least a ten degree list to port.'[14]

The action progressed so rapidly, with *Ford* turning towards the right and her gunners switching to another, closer target to starboard after firing at *Tamagawa Maru* for no more than a minute, that they can be excused if they overestimated the effectiveness, if not the accuracy, of their gunfire.[15] Japanese records indicate that *Tamagawa Maru* was indeed hit approximately ten times, with six crewmen injured or dead, but she was not seriously damaged.[16]

Ford's second target was *Asahi Maru*, which was hit three times aft as the destroyer sped up her port side. Again, the damage was minor, but these hits landed among a concentration of troops preparing to debark, causing

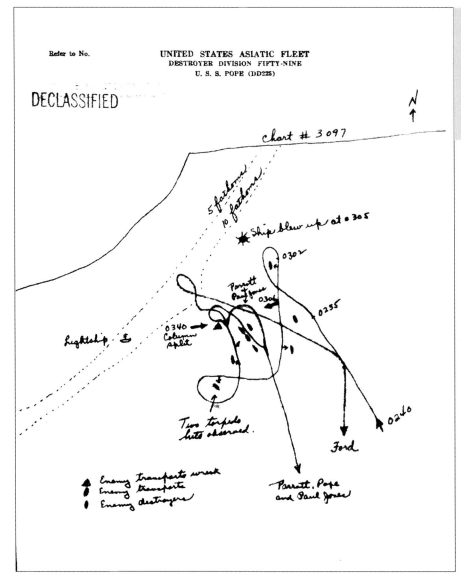

81. This chart of the Battle of Balikpapan, 23–24 January 1942, is reproduced from the action report of *Pope*. Nishimura's ships remained off the map to the east throughout the action. (*NARA*)

approximately fifty casualties. Four hits were claimed on an unidentified third target, firing over open sights at a range of approximately 200yd. Japanese records make no mention of a third ship being hit by gunfire at this time.[17]

It really was an unfair fight. In total, *Ford* fired twenty-five rounds of 4in common shells. To obtain sixteen or seventeen hits was extraordinary shooting, but she was firing at extremely close range at stationary targets. It was more remarkable that the Japanese managed to exact a small measure of revenge, *Tamagawa Maru* hitting *Ford* once with a shell, probably of 3in calibre.[18]

At 0347 a minor caliber shell struck the port side of the torpedo workshop about two feet above the deck and exploded wounding four men and doing considerable damage of a minor nature.[19] A fragment pierced the auxiliary radio gasoline tank, setting this gasoline free and starting a fire on the deck in that vicinity. Fragments punctured two drums of consol in the racks and consol was freed on deck but was not observed to burn. A drum with 30 gallons of gasoline, a drum with 2 gallons of kerosene, and 2 drums of consol were dumped over the side. The fire was brought under control in about 1½ minutes. The ship firing this shot was under fire from the FORD and hits obtained on her by the FORD apparently silenced her battery.[20]

Ford turned left around the burning *Tsuruga Maru* and now exited the scene at 0400, the last of the American destroyers to do so. It had been an hour and fifteen minutes since *Ford* was first sighted by *W15*.

Four wounded men, only one seriously enough to require hospitalisation, was a very small price to pay for over an hour marauding inside an enemy anchorage guarded by a force far superior to DesDiv59 in everything but initiative. It is difficult to comprehend why the Japanese failed to react with any force either while the Americans were attacking or to chase them after they withdrew. Nishimura and all nine destroyers, after being drawn out into the main strait by *KXVIII*'s attack hours earlier, were still milling around well off-shore when the Americans arrived. Even before he received *W15*'s sighting report at 0310, Nishimura had seen *Samanoura Maru* explode in a massive fireball, but he barely reacted, radioing at 0328 for all his ships to be 'Aggressively alert against enemy submarines and torpedo boat attacks'.[21] Despite this warning message, he did not order *Naka* or any of his destroyers into the anchorage. Incredibly, at 0350, while three of Talbot's destroyers were already departing to the south, he ordered one of his two destroyer squadrons to sweep north of the anchorage for possible enemy intruders. It was only with dawn, at which time Talbot's line had reformed and rejoined *Marblehead* near the southern exit from the Makassar Strait, that the magnitude of the defeat finally sank in. The Japanese lost four ships – five if you count *Tsuruga Maru* torpedoed by both *KXVIII* and *Ford* – and approximately two hundred men were killed or wounded.

Paul Talbot was in poor health and was hospitalised after reaching port; deservedly, he was awarded the Navy Cross for his leadership off Balikpapan. Nishimura, despite his lacklustre performance that night, retained his command. He will appear again in these pages.

Cruisers vs Bombers – An Unequal Contest

The Japanese setback at Balikpapan barely slowed their advance through the Dutch East Indies. Moving south from Menado, the Japanese occupied Kendari on the southeast coast of Celebes on 24 January. Under political pressure, Hart named Dutch Rear-Admiral Karel Doorman to command ABDAFLOAT's surface forces. While leading a force that included *Houston*, *Marblehead*, *De Ruyter* and *Tromp*, with four American and four Dutch destroyers, against a concentration of Japanese transports sighted south of Balikpapan on 4 February, Doorman had the misfortune to encounter a force of thirty-seven Japanese land-based naval bombers recently forward-based at Kendari. *Marblehead* was hit

82. The Royal Netherlands Navy produced several classes of scout cruisers intended for service in their remote colonies, particularly the Netherlands East Indies. Hr.Ms. *Java* was designed during the First World War, but not completed until the mid-1920s, after which she served in the Far East until war broke out in December 1941. (*Allan C. Green Collection – State Library of Victoria*)

83. Another First World War vintage scout cruiser caught in the Far East by the outbreak of war was the American light cruiser *Marblehead* (CL12). This image shows her during a visit to Australia with one of her sisters (in the distance to the right) sometime before 1932, when the lower aft 6in casemates were deleted. (*Allan C. Green Collection – State Library of Victoria*)

84. On 4 February 1942, while patrolling east of Surabaya, Java, an ABDAFLOAT squadron of four cruisers and seven destroyers was bombed by Japanese aircraft. The two American cruisers in the squadron, the heavy cruiser *Houston* (CA30) and *Marblehead*, were both hit and damaged, and were directed to head for Tjilatjap (Cilacap) on the south coast of Java. This photograph, taken from *Marblehead* two days later, shows *Houston* moored at Tjilatjap, her colours at half-mast while her burial party is ashore. *Houston* received a single bomb hit at the base of her after superstructure, causing the visible damage to her deck and disabling No. 3 turret, jamming it over to port. (*NARA*)

twice aft and near-missed for damage forward, leaving her on fire aft with her rudder jammed, steaming in circles. *Houston* took one hit that disabled her after main-battery turret. *Marblehead* suffered fifteen dead and eighty-four seriously injured. She limped into Tjilatjap, eventually reaching New York via Trincomalee and South Africa; she would be out of the war until October. *Houston* should have joined her, but remained part of the ADBA fleet; she suffered approximately fifty dead, including all but two of the crew of turret No. 3.

On the same day, the Asiatic Fleet was formally disbanded, its remaining units being assigned to Naval Forces, Southwest Pacific Area under the command of now-Vice-Admiral Glassford. Hart would be replaced as commander of ABDAFLOAT by Dutch Vice-Admiral Conrad Helfrich on 12 February. Hart was placed on the retired list upon his return to the US in March, although he served on the General Board of the Navy into 1944 and conducted the Hart Inquiry into the Pearl Harbor attack between February and April of that year.

Night Melée in Badung Strait – Part 1

The next major Japanese move was an attack on Palembang, Sumatra, in the middle of February, which was contested by Doorman with a force that included all three Dutch light cruisers, *Exeter* and the Australian light cruiser HMAS *Hobart* (D63) – near-sister to *Ajax* and *Achilles* – accompanied by ten destroyers (four Dutch and six American). This force sailed from Tanjung Priok on 13 February, losing one Dutch destroyer which ran aground that night east

85 & 86. *Marblehead* was raised in a floating dry dock at Tjilatjap to inspect her damage and effect what repairs could be made to her damaged steering. One bomb made the hole seen in her deck just aft of her after 6in turret; the explosion of that bomb buckled her quarterdeck and jammed her rudder. In the second image, the damage caused by a near-miss which caved in part of her shell plating forward is being assessed, but nothing could be done to repair it with the time and facilities available. (*NARA*)

87. While *Marblehead* was out of the battle, *Houston*'s damage was not sufficient to cause her to be ordered home. She is seen here at Darwin, Australia, mid-February 1942, before departing for Timor escorting reinforcements for the garrison there. (*NHHC*)

of Bangka Island. Air attacks the next day damaged two American destroyers and *Hobart* with multiple near-misses. Allied strength was being whittled down.

Thus it was that when word came of a Japanese invasion force approaching Bali, east of Java, from Makassar on 18 February, the ABDA reaction was small and poorly co-ordinated. The Japanese force, under the command of Rear-Admiral Kubo Kyuji in the light cruiser *Nagara*, comprised two transports and a squadron of eight destroyers. Expecting Allied intervention such as had occurred off Balikpapan, Kubo expedited the unloading of the transports in Sanur Roads, a shallow bay on the southeast coast of Bali, near the southern entrance to the Badung Strait, the western branch of the Lombok Strait that divides Bali from Lombok Island. As midnight approached on 19 February, one of the transports and all but two of the Japanese destroyers had already departed for Makassar.

The geographic dispersion of the ABDA forces would not, in Helfrich's opinion, allow those forces to be united for a single blow; instead his plan called for three separate waves of attacks against the landing forces.

> The general plan was to attack Japanese forces in Badoeng Strait in three waves. The first wave to start at about 2200, February 19, 1942 and consisted of de RUYTER, JAVA, two Dutch destroyers and U.S. Destroyers J.D. FORD and POPE.[22] The second wave consisting of TROMP, STEWART, PARROTT, J.D. EDWARDS and PILLSBURY, and to start from a point three miles south of Taefel Hoek at 0100, February 20, 1942.[23] The third wave consisted of a detachment of motor torpedo boats . . . to start attack at 0200, following the second wave.[24]

The ABDA forces continued to be dogged by bad luck. As the first wave – two Dutch light cruisers (*De Ruyter* and *Java*), two Dutch destroyers (Hr.Ms. *Piet*

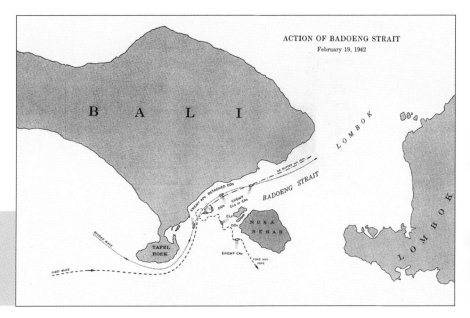

88. This chart gives an overview of the two waves of Allied ships that fought the Battle of Badung Strait, 19 February 1942.

Hein and *Kortenaer*) and two American destroyers (*Pope* and *John D. Ford*) – was departing Tjilatjap in the dark on 18 February, *Kortenaer* ran aground and had to be left behind. The remaining forces continued south of eastern Java and Bali during the afternoon and early evening on the 19th and assumed tactical formation as they turned north into Badung Strait, the two cruisers in line-ahead, led by Doorman's flagship *De Ruyter*, followed by *Java*, and then at 5,500yd, the limit of visibility, by *Piet Hein*, *Ford* and *Pope*. The Americans, from Glassford down to Lieutenant Commander E N Parker in *Ford*, commanding the two American destroyers, had serious reservations about this plan, which counted on the cruisers' gunfire to disable whatever ships might be found at Sanur, before the destroyers got their shot with torpedoes and guns.[25] Parker and his captains believed that reliance on gunfire at night was a mistake, as was the plan of leading with the heavier ships, which would, they feared, guarantee the destroyers would encounter an alert and prepared enemy, exactly the opposite of how they thought a night engagement should be fought. Destroyers, they felt strongly, would benefit far more than cruisers from the element of surprise that came with being first on the scene. They did not like, but understood, Doorman's plan for his cruisers to make a single, high-speed pass through the bay and then retire to the north.[26] After all, there was a second wave due three hours later and he worried about the danger of fratricidal interference. This was because the Dutch had no tactical radio equipment like the American TBS – even had there been a means of real-time communication during battle, the Dutch commanders and the American destroyermen did not speak each other's language. Doorman opted to keep his battle plan simple and clean.

When, at 2130, the Allied force rounded the south cape, turned north into Badung Strait and increased speed to 27kt, Doorman had no idea how many enemy ships lay ahead or where exactly they would be encountered, so he ordered *de Ruyter*, the lead ship, to turn all turrets to starboard and *Java*, the next in line, to

89. The least fortunate ship that night was Hr.Ms. *Piet Hein*, seen here just before the outbreak of the war in the Pacific. The only difference between this and her appearance on 19 February 1942 would have been the painting out of the prominent identification letters on the sides of her forecastle.

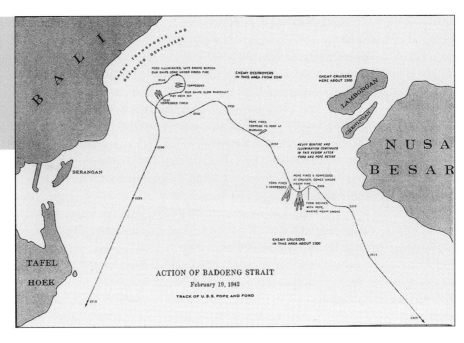

90. This second chart shows the tracks of *Pope* and *John D. Ford* (DD228), which, along with *Piet Hein* followed the two Dutch cruisers of the first wave at the Battle of Badung Strait, 19 February 1942.

aim most of her guns to port. In fact, as noted above, most of the Japanese landing force had already departed. Remaining in Sanur Roads were the transport *Sasago Maru*, anchored well offshore awaiting the return of her landing barges, and two modern destroyers under Captain Abe Toshio – *Asashio*, idling closer in towards shore southwest of the transport, and *Oshio*, making slow sweeps 3,000yd to the north. The Dutch cruisers were small by contemporary standards, but both were three times the size of the Japanese destroyers and carried more and larger guns (15cm/50 versus 12.7cm/50). If, however, the Japanese destroyers could survive the attack of the Dutch cruisers intact, they stood a better chance against the three ABDA destroyers, which were all older, smaller and more lightly armed.

Asashio and the Dutch cruisers sighted each other at just about the same time, just before 2225, at a range of 6,500yd. Both sides reacted slowly – *Asashio* because she was at a dead stop and, although she had steam raised, still took a few minutes to gain sufficient headway to manoeuvre; the Dutch because *de Ruyter*'s guns were pointing the wrong way and *Java*'s captain initially refused to open fire without orders from Doorman. Thus, approximately five minutes passed as the range rapidly dropped, the Dutch steaming northeast at high speed, *Asashio* paralleling their course but much more slowly, at least at first. Finally, at 2230 (or just before), still without orders from Doorman, *Java* opened fire with starshells followed by common rounds at a range of about 2,200yd. At the same time, *Asashio* switched on her searchlight, illuminating *Java*. In a brief exchange of gunfire, the two ships managed to do minor damage to each other. A Dutch shell, probably a 40mm round from her secondary battery, hit *Asashio*'s searchlight platform, destroying the light, killing four crewmen and wounding eleven. *Java* took a 12.7cm shell on her port side aft, causing minor damage and wounding two men. *Sasago Maru* may have been hit by one shell from *Java*. *De Ruyter* appears to have got off several salvos at *Oshio*, all of which missed, before the high speed at which the Dutch cruisers were travelling carried them beyond visual range, and their part in this multi-part engagement came rapidly to an end.[27] It had lasted all of two minutes.

Abe may have briefly considered chasing Doorman, but he soon had closer and more inviting targets to the south. Lieutenant Commander J M L I Chömpff, commanding *Piet Hein* and leading the three destroyers approaching from the south, watched the lightshow taking place to the north and, at 2230, having sighted shapes off to port, fired torpedoes and bore away in that direction, followed by the two Americans.[28] Then, as *Oshio* crossed her path from left to right, *Piet Hein* turned sharply to starboard, again followed by the Americans. The Dutch destroyer became obscured by smoke – her class was known to leave a dense trail of funnel smoke at high speed – which temporarily hid her from the Americans, but not the Japanese. During that brief period, at 2238, she was hit in her after boiler room by a 12.7cm shell from *Asashio*, which was trailing *Oshio* and was, at this point, much closer to the ABDA destroyers. That hit severed her main steam line and caused an immediate loss of power. Slowing rapidly, she was hit by several more salvos from *Asashio* and perhaps some from *Oshio* as well. The Americans emerged from the smoke, only to be greeted by *Piet Hein* dead in the water and afire straight ahead and *Asashio* close off their port beam.[29] *Ford* immediately slowed to avoid hitting *Piet Hein*, which, in turn, forced *Pope* to come to a full stop at 2239. A shell, probably from *Asashio*, cut the after falls of *Ford*'s whaleboat, leaving it dangling in the water, and leaving Lieutenant Commander Cooper in *Ford* no choice but to order it cut loose.

Now in control of his two ships and under fire from both sides, Parker ordered full speed, smoke and a hard left turn away from the enemy. *Ford* led *Pope* around a tight left-hand circle, coming around to a northeast heading to follow the cruisers up the strait. Finding their path again blocked by the Japanese destroyers, Parker bore away to starboard until settling on a course of 150°, which would take them south of the several islands that formed the eastern side of Bandung Strait and out into the more open Lombok Strait. All the while *Pope* was under fire from *Asashio* trailing on her port quarter.

At 2258, *Ford* was illuminated by a ship on her starboard bow that she identified as a large cruiser. Not expecting any ships from that direction and, concerned that it might be *Tromp* from the second wave arriving earlier than planned, she turned on identification lights, as did *Pope*. This was greeted by a barrage of gunfire that caused the Americans to launch torpedoes and turn away. This outburst lasted three minutes until the searchlight was switched off and the firing ship disappeared into the gloom. Still convinced they had engaged an enemy heavy cruiser, *Ford* and *Pope* resumed a southeasterly course and exited the area at high speed. Their departure was disturbed briefly at 2315 by the sight of searchlights and gunfire in the area they had just vacated.[30]

Several illuminated destroyers could be observed bows on and under heavy gunfire. Hits and fires on two were observed and one blew up.[31]

A third destroyer emitted a large burst of steam upon being hit.[32]

91. The last major Allied warship to enter Badung Strait that night was Hr.Ms. *Tromp*, which received numerous 12.7cm hits along her upperworks, sufficient to cause her to be withdrawn to Australia for repairs, ensuring she would survive the general disaster that overwhelmed most of the rest of ABDAFLOAT. *Tromp* was very modern-looking, even in this image taken in 1946; equipped with British and American radars and painted in a late-war Admiralty-standard camouflage scheme, she nevertheless looks not very different from how she would have appeared at Badung Strait. (*Allan C. Green Collection – State Library of Victoria*)

While observing this fierce gunfight, Parker assumed that he was seeing the American destroyers of the second wave fighting one or more Japanese ships, including the large cruiser he believed he had just escaped. At no point does it appear that he considered turning back to their assistance.

The reality of what had just happened was far simpler, and confused, than either side imagined at the time. The 'cruiser' encountered by *Ford* was *Oshio*, which had crossed in front of the American destroyers, and was now circling back west to the south of their path. As Parker turned away, making smoke, *Oshio*'s captain, Commander Kikkawa Kiyoshi, assumed she was sinking and, concerned about the safety of *Sasago Maru*, broke off the brief firefight and continued towards the roadstead. She circled to the north when she found another ship approaching on her starboard side. These two briefly exchanged fire before they realised it was *Asashio* also heading back towards the anchorage.

Except for the loss of *Piet Hein*, which cost the lives of sixty-four officers and men, all of the shooting of guns and torpedoes had caused remarkably little damage. *Sasago Maru* had been hit a few times by shells from *Piet Hein* and the Americans, but not seriously damaged. *Java* and *Asashio* had each been hit once, the Americans not at all, but the battle was not over.

Night Melée in Badung Strait – Part 2

As soon as Rear-Admiral Kubo learned of the battle taking place off Sanur Roads, he set out with *Nagara* and three destroyers from his covering position near Makassar, but there was no chance they would arrive before dawn. Of more practical use to Abe was Kubo's decision to release destroyers *Arashio* and *Michishio*, which were escorting a damaged merchant ship in the Bali Sea, with instruction to head for Sanur at best speed. *Asashio* and *Oshio* remained on patrol off Sanur Roads while *Sasago Maru* attempted to patch several holes in her hull near the waterline.

At the same time, the second wave of the ABDA attack was approaching from the south. Under the command of Captain J B DeMeester in *Tromp*, it included the four American destroyers of DesDiv58 under Commander Thomas H Binford in USS *Stewart* (DD224), followed by *Parrott*, *J.D.Edwards* (DD216) and *Pillsbury* (DD227). DeMeester, with a better understanding of the relative night-fighting capabilities of destroyers and cruisers, reversed the formation adopted by Doorman, leading with his four destroyers, with *Tromp* following by a full 5nm. Despite the fact that four Allied ships had been in these waters two hours earlier, it would appear no attempt was made to inform DeMeester or Binford what they might expect to find in Badung Strait. Binford saw the flash of gunfire and the glow of searchlights silhouetting Bali's mountains as DesDiv58 steamed east along that island's south coast, but all attempts to communicate with Parker failed and Binford had absolutely no idea what to expect to find as he turned northeastward at 0112 on the 20th.[33]

In fact, what awaited Binford was exactly the same set of three Japanese ships that met Doorman, although haze and smoke from the previous engagement clinging to the shore reduced visibility into the anchorage. The Japanese were in much the same formation as two hours earlier, with *Sasago Maru* anchored in towards shore and the two destroyers patrolling at slow speed somewhat further out in the strait. At 0132, having tracked several lights off her port bow, *Stewart* opened fire with torpedoes and gunfire at two silhouettes, followed immediately by *Parrott* and *Pillsbury*. The two silhouettes, identified as cruisers, were in fact *Asashio* and *Oshio* once again taking on superior numbers of enemy ships, as seen from *Parrott*.

> 10.   About 0138 STEWART reported a ship coming back along her port side. About a minute later STEWART turned on searchlight in an effort to reveal target on her port quarter. At practically simultaneous moments fire was opened by STEWART and enemy. A few seconds later, PARROTT joined the fire with her own gun battery. Enemy salvoes began straddling our formation immediately. Several straddles were seen to light near stern of STEWART. The enemy fire control was amazingly accurate.[34] The STEWART seemed suddenly to slow, and I believed that she had been seriously hit and was settling. Many salvoes continued to straddle the column just ahead of our bow. PARROTT sheered out to starboard. About a minute later fire was broken off by both sides. Two of our own destroyers were seen to port and PARROTT eased back into column, not knowing who she was following, or how many ships were now in the column.[35]

The following gives a good idea of American gunnery practice during these last 'pre-radar' days, as seen from *Parrott*.

> During first engagement, rangefinder range of enemy searchlight was 5800 yards. Fire was opened under director fire and initial spread of three salvoes, 6300 yards, 5800 yards, 5300 yards were fired. Down 500 was applied to second salvo, at same time rangefinder gave 5400 yards.

Enemy speed 15, target angle 130 were assumed giving a slowly opening range rate. Actual range apparently was opening faster and result was that our fire seemed to draw across target. Deflection setting remained almost constant at about 96 and was not corrected. About thirteen salvoes were fired. 200 yard rocking ladder was used on later salvoes.[36]

During this exchange of gunfire that lasted perhaps six minutes, the only damage was to *Stewart*. At approximately 0146, she was peppered amidships by shell splinters from a 'short' that caused no serious material damage, but killed one enlisted man and wounded two officers, including her XO. Moments later, *Stewart* received the only direct hit suffered by an American ship this night, the hit that caused her to slow and threw the line of destroyers into confusion. The damage was significant, but not as serious as it appeared from *Parrott*.

> . . . STEWART was engaged with the enemy and sustained a shell hit on the port side of the steering engine room. This shell exploded on contact and made a hole about three feet in diameter on the port side. Shell fragments entered the steering engine room, severed the wheel ropes to after steering station, punctured the exhaust steam line and three fragments passed through the starboard side making three holes five to eight inches in diameter. Steering control from the bridge was maintained until arrival Sourabaya.[37]

Stewart rapidly regained speed and continued her passage to the northeast. *Parrott* and *Pillsbury* both swerved to starboard, very nearly colliding; *Edwards* remained in column behind *Stewart* and was apparently the ship that *Parrott* then 'eased' behind. *Pillsbury* made her own way northeastward further to the east. The Japanese destroyers briefly crossed the wake of the abbreviated American column and then recrossed back in towards shore, also heading to the northeast, for the time being just shadowing the Americans.

This state of affairs could not last long, with *Tromp* approaching from the south and two more Japanese destroyers were speeding south at best speed. At 0205, *Tromp* switched on her fighting lights to inform Binford of her location, but this had the contrary effect of giving the Japanese a target to shoot at. *Asashio* rapidly hit *Tromp* at least ten times along her superstructure, starting fires and injuring crewmen, but none of the damage was serious; *Tromp*'s revenge was to put one shell into *Oshio*'s bridge structure, killing seven men in an anti-aircraft gun crew.

This action quickly died down, only to flare up again as *Arashio* and *Michishio* spotted, and were spotted by, *Stewart* at 0215. *Michisio* switched on a searchlight and was greeted by 4in rounds from the American column and also from *Pillsbury* steaming independently off to the east. *Pillsbury* struck first, disabling *Michishio*'s main-battery gun house No. 2. This was followed by a shell from *Edwards*, which hit her bridge and wounded her captain. *Tromp* arrived on the scene in time to put three rounds into *Michishio*'s engine room, bringing her to a halt and killing or wounding ninety-six of her crew. The scene was witnessed first-hand by Watanabe Daiji, a chief rangetaker posted in the gun director position above *Michishio*'s bridge.[38]

The runner shouted up to the bridge, 'Hit on No.2 Mount! All dead!' Many men died in the fire as a result of the explosion of powder charges and shells in the mount. At the same time, we received another hit on the bridge. This shell reached the bridge after passing under the Chief Searchlight Operator's post and penetrating the bulkhead of the forward radio room. Cdr Ogura Masami was wounded by this shell. The moans of the wounded could be heard from all parts of the ship.

Three shells hit the engine room at the same time. The explosions and escaping steam killed all the engineers and seamen in that compartment. Most of the crew sustained burns or other wounds; some of them died. The electrical system shut down; we could no longer use the automatic fire control system. We had to use manual control. Furthermore, we were unable to control the maneuvering of the ship because the rudder was damaged. After a while, however, the fighting ceased. We just now drifted on the very quite sea . . . Our ship was drifting, submerged to sea level at the middle to rear deck. The ship seemed to be ready to split into two pieces at the No.2 mount. We could not communicate between the forward and after parts of the ship. I couldn't see any ships. The sea was so calm and peaceful. I felt as if I had just had a bad dream.

The upper deck was crowded with the dead and wounded. There was no space to walk. There were over 50 casualties. But this deceptively peaceful time ended very quickly. As soon as night was over, enemy airplanes appeared and started attacking us mercilessly. We could not maneuver to avoid the attacks. We fired back at the attacking planes even though that added to the risk of the ship breaking in two. We shot down one light bomber. The pieces of the enemy airplane hit the surface of the sea and some ricocheted on to the ship . . . During this attack, three sailors were thrown into the sea, but we were too occupied defending ourselves to have any chance of rescuing them. The only thing we could do was to release a rescue boat with one pistol and one pack of biscuits to them while shouting, 'Stay alive, we will come to rescue you!'[39]

This brought the battle to an end, but not the night's excitement. While the ABDA force was steaming clear of the Japanese destroyers, before the gunfire had died down, *Parrott* found herself in mortal danger.

In the midst of it all, PARROTT's steering control jammed with the rudder left and the ship swinging left. As the helmsman made the announcement the searchlight on our column illuminated several large rocks immediately ahead of us and certainly not more than a thousand yards away. The ship was going ahead at about twenty-eight knots and we continued to be subjected to heavy gunfire while replying with our own. The ship seemed lost. I leaped to the engine order telegraph and rang up emergency full speed astern. The engines responded immediately. I heard someone say we were aground. However, in a moment I detected that we had gathered sternway and were getting clear of the shore.[40]

Using her engines, *Parrott* was able to resume heading northeastward into the broader Lombok Strait and away from the Japanese. All the Japanese destroyers (and *Sasago Maru*) made port, *Michishio* towed to Makassar by *Arashio*. All fought on in this and subsequent campaigns. All would be war losses before the end. Except for *Piet Hein*, all the ABDA participants survived, but their fates were more mixed. *Tromp* was damaged to the extent that she departed for repairs at Sydney three days later, avoiding the devastation that overtook the rest of the Dutch forces in the theatre. All six of the American destroyers which fought in Badung Strait would fight again in this or later campaigns, five of them under the American flag. *Stewart* suffered one of the most unusual fates of any warship in this war. Placed in a commercial floating dry dock upon arrival at Surabaya, the ship slipped off her blocks as the dock was raised, causing damage that could not be repaired in time to make her seaworthy before the port fell to the Japanese on 2 March. Once it was clear she could not be repaired, attempts were made to render her irreparable, but the Japanese did indeed repair *Stewart* and commissioned her into the IJN as *Patrol Boat No.102*, in which capacity she served in the East Indies and later in

92. Damaged at Badung Strait, *Stewart* (DD224) was raised in a commercial floating dry dock at Surabaya, but slipped off the blocks and was captured in this condition by the Japanese, who repaired her and put her to work as a local patrol craft. (*NHHC*)

home waters before being laid up in a bay near Kure, where she was taken over again by the US Navy and recommissioned on 29 October 1945.[41]

As in all naval battles, men were injured and killed on both sides in Badung Strait, but there were also instances of survival against long odds. A crewman off *Parrott*, Raymond Padgett, CWT, was part of a group passing ammunition to one of the midships 4in guns when he disappeared overboard, last seen at approximately 0220, about the time when *Parrott* suffered her steering casualty. By the time his absence was noticed, it was far too late to consider a rescue attempt. When *Parrott's* CO submitted his action report the next day, all he could do was note that Padgett was a good swimmer and was believed to be uninjured, so there was 'a strong possibility he may have reached shore'.[42] In fact, Padgett did swim to shore, where he found a party of Dutch soldiers and was evacuated with them to Java a few days later, where he rejoined *Parrott* at Surabaya before she sailed for Tjilatjap on 28 February.

Perhaps luckier still were a group of survivors from *Piet Hein*. At first light, a group of thirteen men floating together found themselves in the vicinity of *Ford's* cast-off whaleboat, intact and upright. Over the next few hours they found twenty more survivors, some clinging to a gasoline drum, and all thirty-three made their way to at least temporary safety at Surabaya.

Exeter at the Java Sea

The climactic battle of East Indies campaign was on 27–28 February in the Java Sea to the north of Surabaya, as the combined strength of ABDAFLOAT – two heavy cruisers, three light cruisers and nine destroyers – attempted to block the full-scale invasion of Java. The resulting Battle of the Java Sea lasted seven hours and shows neither side in a good light regarding either gunnery or firing torpedoes. (It is described well in many other sources, and will not be recounted in detail here.[43]) ABDA lost five of the fourteen warships to join the battle at 1525, only one of them, the destroyer *Electra*, by gunfire; the others were lost to torpedoes or mine. Two ships, the Japanese destroyer *Asagumo* and *Exeter*, suffered significant gunfire damage. Doorman lost his life along with some 2,300 other Allied sailors; Rear-Admiral A F E Palliser, RN, took over tactical command of Allied naval forces.

The damage to *Exeter* from a single 20cm AP Type 91 round from Japanese heavy cruiser *Haguro* was extraordinarily extensive.[44] This shell type weighed 277.4lb with a 6.9lb bursting charge, although the fact that it was found in relatively large pieces would indicate that the charge never exploded, all the damage being done by the kinetic energy of the projectile.

A few minutes later Exeter suffered her first hit. This was an 8in projectile, which entered the ship from a direction slightly abaft the starboard beam. It passed through the shield of the starboard after 4in. HA guns, killing four of the crew, thence through the forecastle deck and passed through the fore and aft bulkhead of ' B ' boiler room air intake immediately below the access door on the upper deck. Smashing the armoured grating, it went through the forward impeller and casing of the starboard inner fan. It then

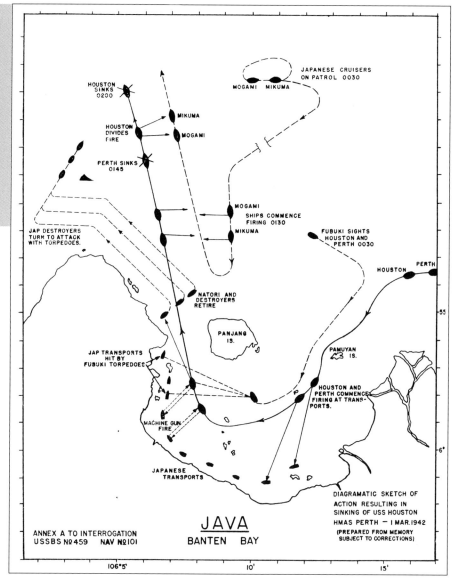

93. This very much simplified sketch of the Battle of Sunda Strait, 28 February–1 March 1942, is based on the postwar recollections of the captain of *Mogami*, Captain Shoji Akira. It leaves off many details, including the presence of Babi Island northeast of Panjang Island, around which *Fubuki* turned. (*USSBS Interrogation No. 495/101*)

pierced the uptake casings over 'B2' boiler and entered 'B' boiler room through the lower deck. At this point it struck the fore and aft 'I' beam on the centre line below the lower deck and removed a large part of it. It carried away two oil fuel pipes on the cold-oil fuel-discharge system to both 'B' port and starboard units, removing two pairs of flanges on these pipes completely. The main steam pipe leading from 'A' port unit was pierced almost exactly through its centre line. At this point the projectile appears to have broken up and, after hitting gratings, handrails, etc., and the pieces entered 'B1' boiler casing and smashed through generator and superheater tubes. Large pieces of the projectile and the complete base plate were found later on the furnace floor.[45]

Besides the four men killed at the anti-aircraft mount and ten men in 'B' boiler room, all but one of the men in the compartment at the time were killed.

Slaughter in the Sunda Strait

Soundly defeated and scattered to Surabaya and Tanjung Priok, the survivors of the Battle of the Java Sea were ordered to make their way to Tjilatjap as best they could. HMAS *Perth* (D29) and *Houston* arrived at Tanjung Priok at noon on the 28th, where they were ordered to take on what little fuel was available and leave while it still appeared possible to reach Tjilatjap safely. *Hobart*, which had missed the Java Sea battle, had entered the Sunda Strait at 0616 on 28 February, headed for Ceylon. She had found the strait clear and reported that information to Captain Hector Waller in *Perth*. (He was senior to Captain Albert H Rooks in *Houston* and therefore had command of the small squadron that comprised the two cruisers and the Dutch destroyer Hr.Ms. *Evertsen*.) *Houston*'s off-duty crew spent the afternoon manhandling 8in rounds from the after magazine under the disabled turret No. 3 to a common magazine space improvised between the two forward turrets. When the two cruisers were ready to depart at 1830, the promised harbour pilot did not appear, nor was *Evertsen* ready to leave. An hour later, neither circumstance had changed, and Waller, impatient, decided to head out through the swept passage without either. The two cruisers negotiated the exit safely and set course to the west at 20kt, a slow enough speed that *Evertsen* should have been able to catch up with them before they entered the strait.

Waller had been informed that 'an aerial reconnaissance had been made that afternoon and the Sunda Strait area had been found to be free from any enemy forces.'[46] The only known nearby enemy force was a small convoy sighted earlier in the day 70nm northeast of Batavia heading east, away from the Sunda Strait. Thus, the two cruisers had reason to hope for a safe passage to the south. Sadly, their hope was ill-founded.[47] Not only were there enemy forces in the area, Waller's force was steaming into a hornet's nest. The entrance to the Sunda Strait was swarming with a massive invasion fleet and its escort. The geography of this area plays a role in the story, so it is worth describing in some detail. The northwestern tip of Java, marking the entrance into the strait, was known as St Nicholas Point. It also formed the western shore of the deep semi-circular Banten Bay. Close to that western shore was a large, roughly circular island named Panjang, while north of the eastern edge of the bay was long, narrow Babi Island. The Japanese under tactical command of Rear-Admiral Hara Kenzaburo were arrayed to protect a fleet of more than fifty transports, most of which were anchored close to St Nicholas Point, behind Panjang Island. The destroyer *Fubuki* was patrolling west of Babi Island, watching the eastern approaches to the bay. Three old destroyers – *Harukaze*, *Hatakaze* and *Asakaze* – were, respectively, patrolling east, west and northwest of Panjang, controlling the direct approaches to the landing beaches. North of St Nicholas Point, blocking the entrance to the strait, were the old light cruiser *Natori* and destroyers *Hatsuyuki*, *Shirayuki*, *Shirakumo* and *Murakumo*. Finally, 20nm further to the north, the heavy cruisers *Mogami* and *Mikuma* and destroyer *Shikinami* provided backup.

Thus, it was *Fubuki* which first sighted *Perth* leading *Houston* south of Babi Island at 2239. The Japanese destroyer was not seen from either cruiser; *Fubuki* turned east and slipped behind Babi while the two cruisers continued west along the south side of the island. *Fubuki* emerged around the eastern end of the island and fell into a shadowing position behind *Houston*, still unobserved by either cruiser. It was not until 2306 that lookouts in *Perth* sighted a ship 10,000yd fine off her port bow. Waller hoped it might be a Dutch patrol boat and flashed a challenge, but it proved to be *Harukaze* in her patrol position east of Panjang, which replied by turning north and making smoke in an attempt to hide the landing operation taking place behind her. *Perth* turned to starboard and opened fire.

What followed was a mêlée in the truest sense of the word, a confused struggle in which the Japanese destroyer captains attempted to set up torpedo shots only to find their set-ups disturbed by other destroyers; the two ABDA cruisers looped first to starboard and then to port, firing at whatever targets were illuminated by searchlight, starshell or explosion.[48] Between 2306 and approximately 2350, the two cruisers stood off a concentrated attack by the light cruiser *Natori* and eight destroyers without suffering significant damage. *Perth* took a shell in her forward funnel at 2326, another on the flag deck at 2332 and a third near the waterline in way of her crew's mess at 2350. None of these seriously affected her fighting ability.

The Japanese attacked mainly with torpedoes – swarms of them. In that period of about forty-five minutes, the Japanese launched more than fifty torpedoes, not one of which hit its intended target. The Allied cruisers had better luck. At approximately 2340, *Harukaze* was hit right aft, damaging her rudder, probably by a 6in shell from *Perth*. In the next few minutes, as *Harukaze*, *Hatakaze*, *Hatsuyuki* and *Shirayuki* pressed home torpedo attacks, the first of those was hit twice more – once in the engine room and once in the bridge – resulting in three dead and more than fifteen wounded, and the last was hit once, in the bridge, killing one and wounding eleven.

Having expended their ready torpedoes, most of the Japanese destroyers and *Natori* withdrew to the north to regroup and reload.[49] This cleared the way for the two Japanese heavy cruisers, which had been racing down from the north. Finding the scene to the south obscured by smoke, *Mikuma* led *Mogami* and *Shikinami* around to the east at approximately 2345. The two ABDA cruisers were starting a sweeping starboard loop north of Panjang, so the two formations were on roughly parallel courses perhaps 12,200yd apart, the Japanese roughly northeast of the Allies. At 2349, seeing they were bearing down on Babi Island, Captain Sakiyama Shakao reversed course to port, both *Mikuma* and *Mogami* firing six torpedoes back at the Allies before they turned. Those twelve torpedoes, like all the others fired up to that point, seem to have harmlessly missed all targets, friend or foe.

Starting shortly after 2350, this exercise in relative futility began to get deadly serious. As Sakiyama's cruisers settled on a course roughly west-southwest, *Perth* was leading *Houston* around to the northwest just north of Panjang Island (meaning the range between the pairs of cruisers began dropping rapidly). At the same time, the Japanese destroyers were renewing their torpedo attacks.

94. The light cruiser HMAS *Perth* (D29) saw some action in the Mediterranean, but spent most of the early war, up until Pearl Harbor, operating in the Indian Ocean and Pacific. She fought at Sunda Strait with *Houston* and was overwhelmed there at the same time. This image shows her in the camouflage scheme she wore during her Mediterranean deployment in early 1941. At the time of her loss, her starboard side carried a different disruptive pattern, while the port side was painted in two almost identical shades of blue-grey very similar to US Navy Sea Blue (5-S). (*NHHC*)

Events began to occur so rapidly that it is perhaps best to simply list them in chronological order (with the understanding that all these times are best estimates by the participants and the actual sequence may have been somewhat different than that described here).[50]

2355   *Houston* made one (perhaps more) 8in hit on *Mikuma*, killing six, wounding eleven and temporarily knocking out electrical power, dousing her searchlights and silencing her main battery.

2357   *Mogami* launched six more torpedoes at the Allied cruisers. Unlike all previous salvos, these found targets.

2400   *Perth*'s Gunnery Officer, Lieutenant Commander P S F Hancox, reported to Waller that his ship was almost out of main-battery rounds. Waller resolved to set a course to round St Nicholas Point and enter the Sunda Strait. This meant remaining on a steady heading of north-northwest.

2400   *Mikuma* restored electrical power and resumed firing on *Houston* at a range of 9,800yd. *Houston* received a 20cm hit in her forecastle, which started a persistent fire.

2400   *Houston* observed three Japanese destroyers cutting her wake at 3,000yd, firing torpedoes. She was able to steer between the torpedoes passing to either side, one missing her port side by ten feet. (These were probably *Harukaze* and *Hatakaze*, perhaps joined by *Asakaze*, though this identification is speculative.)

0005   Torpedoes, almost certainly those fired by *Mogami* at 2357, hit four Japanese transports and one minesweeper, sinking all five ships (although two of the transports were later salvaged).

0005   *Perth* was hit by a torpedo on the starboard side in way of her forward engine room, immediately cutting her speed in half, killing all but one of the engine room crew. Given the timing and position of the hit, this is most likely one of the torpedoes fired at *Houston* at 2400.

0007   *Perth* was hit by another torpedo on the starboard side beneath her bridge. Captain Waller ordered the ship abandoned.

0010   *Houston* was hit by a torpedo on the port side in the after engine room. By this time, she had passed *Perth* and was continuing on to the north-northwest.[51] This were most likely from a salvo of eighteen torpedoes fired by *Shirakumo* and *Murakumo* at long range from north of St Nicholas Point at or just before 2400. Escaping steam from the engine room forced the abandonment of the midships secondary battery.

0012   *Perth* was hit in rapid succession by two torpedoes on her port side, one in way of 'X' turret and one under her bridge. These were almost certainly also from the salvo of torpedoes fired by *Shirakumo* and *Murakumo*. *Perth* very rapidly rolled on her port side and sank.

0020   *Houston* was hit by a 20cm round on the upper face of turret No. 2, which 'produced a large brief flare extending well above the bridge'. As fire spread into the handling rooms, it became necessary to flood the *ad hoc* magazine space used by both forward turrets, which meant that turret No. 1 was now limited to those rounds already in the hoists on their way to the turret.

0025   By this time, *Houston* had been hit by innumerable shells of 20cm and 12.7cm calibre and possibly by more torpedoes. With no effective means of continuing the fight, Captain Rooks ordered the ship abandoned. However, she still had 20kt of way on and the first attempts to launch boats and rafts were disastrous. At about this time the captain was killed by a shell hitting a 1.1in mount he was standing near, and, the XO, informed of this fact, rescinded the abandon ship order at 0029.

0033   The ship having slowed sufficiently, *Houston*'s XO again ordered the ship abandoned. She heeled over on her starboard side about 0045 and sank on an even keel.

There were reports of seamen being machine-gunned by circling destroyers as they prepared to leave their sinking ships and even in the water, but also reports of perfectly correct treatment of survivors by the Japanese. It is undeniable, moreover, that surviving the sinking of one's ship and rescue by Japanese seamen was hardly a guarantee of humane treatment on shore. Out of a complement of 680 men (plus six RAAF passengers), approximately 330 of *Perth*'s crew were captured by the Japanese and 215 survived the war.[52] Of *Houston*'s complement of over 1,000, only 368 were captured; 266 survived the war.[53]

Evertsen, which had left Tanjung Priok almost two hours after the two cruisers, saw the lightshow in Banten Bay and opted to swing north around the scene of *Perth*'s and *Houston*'s agony. Lieutenant Commander W M DeVries radioed Helfrich with news of the battle and received orders that any ship not engaged should help in any way possible, but by then the lights had died down

95. The Dutch destroyer Hr.Ms. *Evertsen* was supposed to accompany *Perth* and *Houston* on 28 February 1942, but was delayed leaving Tanjung Priok. She attempted to make her way separately through the strait, but was caught by a pair of Japanese destroyers and ended up aground at Sebuko Island.

and *Evertsen* was probing the entrance to the strait. Attempting to reach the far shore and then skirt the coast of Sumatra to the south, *Evertsen* was sighted by *Shirakumo* and *Murakumo*, and lost a very brief running gunfight. Six of the crew were killed in the engagement.

Escape through the Bali Strait

The four American destroyers of DesDiv58 that had fought at the Battle of the Java Sea – *Edwards*, *Alden* (DD211), *Ford* and *Jones* – separated from the rest of the ADBA force at about 2100 on the day of the battle with orders to make for Batavia, but Binford opted to head first for Surabaya as it was a closer and more reliable source of fuel and supplies. Once there, he found *Exeter* undergoing emergency repairs, preparatory to departure that evening for Ceylon via the Sunda Strait accompanied by HMS *Encounter* (H10) and *Pope*.

Out of torpedoes and low on ammunition, and with no reloads available north of Fremantle, Binford pressured Glassford to allow him to take his destroyers south as rapidly as possible.[54] The four destroyers departed Surabaya at 1700 on 28 February and proceeded at 22kt towards the Bali Strait to the east, hugging the Java shoreline. Four Japanese destroyers, all newer, bigger, better armed and faster than Binford's flush-deckers, were on patrol across the southern exit of the strait, although only three actually engaged the Americans. Binford had the advantage of surprise and better visibility; the Japanese were plainly visible in mid-channel while the American destroyers were harder to spot against the background of the dark coastline. It was only when the Americans were forced away from the coast by a reef off the eastern tip of Java that they became visible.[55] The following account is by the CO of *Alden*.

At 0230 we had to pull away from the coast in order to clear the coast reef on the eastern side of the Blambangan Peninsula. At 0231 gunfire was seen to port and a few seconds later splashes, apparently from five inch guns from size of splashes were seen about one thousand yards short.[56]

All ships opened fire with four inch guns at this time. A running gun fight of about five minutes duration ensued. This vessel fired a total of thirty-one rounds with two guns. The forward gun was not used due to the tightness of the navigation and the necessity for having good visibility on the bridge. No hits were observed and apparently we were shooting about 500 yards short. The target was crossed several times by firing spotting ladders.[57]

No hits or even near-misses were achieved by either side and no casualties suffered.

At 0245 came to course 210° true and cleared the area at maximum speed. No further ships were seen. At about 0250 gunfire was observed astern, and it was presumed enemy was attempting to draw our fire in order to locate our position. Fire was not returned. Rest of night was uneventful, and no further contacts were made.[58]

The four destroyers reached Fremantle safely on 4 March after a passage that was interrupted only by minor engineering casualties, only to be expected with ships so old and hard-driven.

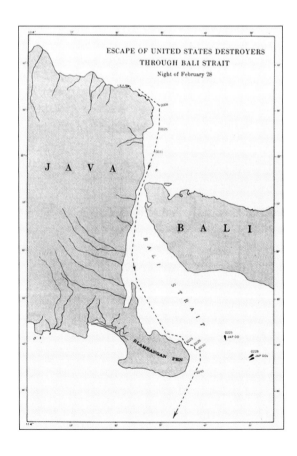

ESCAPE OF UNITED STATES DESTROYERS
THROUGH BALI STRAIT
Night of February 28

96. The same night that the Japanese were enjoying such success in Sunda Strait, four American destroyers managed to break south from Surabaya through the Bali Strait at the other end of Java by a combination of speed, stealth and luck.

No Escape from Surabaya

The only major warships left on the north side of the Malay Barrier were *Exeter*, *Encounter* and *Pope* at Surabaya. They left port at 1900 on 28 February, with orders to head west to Sunda Strait (the much closer Bali Strait was considered to be too shallow for *Exeter*) with the eventual goal of reaching Ceylon, where *Exeter* would receive more-permanent repairs. A Dutch destroyer, Hr.Ms. *Witte de With*, was supposed to accompany them, but was not ready to leave on time and, like *Evertsen*, was left behind.[59] Knowing that *Exeter* was slowed by damage to her after fire room – when she left Surabaya, she could initially only make 16kt, though this gradually improved to 24kt – her CO, Captain O L Gordon, hoped she could find a safe passage by heading north, away from the Java coast, not turning west until north of Bawean Island, about 80nm north of Surabaya. (*Pope* was also hobbled; she had missed the Java Sea battle because of a damaged condenser, only partially repaired before departing Surabaya, and she suffered the loss of one-quarter of her ability to generate steam early in this battle when a near-miss caused the collapse of No.3 boiler's firebrick .)

Gordon's plan did not work. The three ships passed 25nm east of Bawean at dawn, 1 March 1942, but continued to the north for another hour before turning west-by-north. At 0750, masts were spotted on the southern horizon. With no chance that the ships were friendly and no hope of greater speed, Gordon could do little but wait and prepare his crews as best he could as the masts resolved into the shapes of two Japanese heavy cruisers. They were *Nachi* and *Haguro*, the same two cruisers that had fought Doorman's ABDA force at the Battle of the Java Sea a day and a half earlier. Indeed, it had been *Haguro* whose 20cm shell had so badly damaged *Exeter*'s 'B' boiler room and knocked out six of her eight boilers.

97. *Exeter* is seen at Calcutta, probably in October 1941. She has the antennas for the Type 279 air-search radar at her two mastheads. If any ship deserved a quiet posting, it was *Exeter*, which had probably seen more enemy action that any in the Royal Navy, and that might have been why she was selected for transfer to the East Indies Squadron in May 1941. At the time, that was as quiet a posting as could be found, but it would not remain so for long.

Although the two cruisers, under Rear-Admiral Takagi Takeo, were more than enough to take on Gordon's force with good odds of success, he nevertheless held his fire until the other two cruisers of 5th Sentai (Cruiser Division), *Ashigara* and *Myoko*, commanded by Vice-Admiral Takahashi Ibo, approached from the northwest at 0935.[60] Turning away to the east only delayed the inevitable. *Encounter* and *Pope* skirmished inconclusively with Takahashi's escorting destroyers, *Akebono* and *Ikazuchi*. Finally, at 1020, with Takagi on her starboard beam and Takahashi on her port quarter, the Japanese opened fire at 25,000yd. The range rapidly dropped to 18,000yd. *Exeter's* escorts made smoke that effectively hid her from Takagi, but Takahashi kept up a deliberate and accurate fire that finally paid off around 1120 with a shell that burst in *Exeter's* 'A' boiler room and brought the cruiser to a stop. *Exeter's* end was now not long in coming. This gallant ship, which had fought *Graf Spee* and now the overwhelming superiority of the Japanese, succumbed to innumerable 20cm hits and a final torpedo from *Ikazuchi* at about 1150. Fifty-four of her crew were killed in this action, a surprisingly small number, and 651 went into captivity.

After his ship had been disabled, Gordon set the destroyers free to do their best to escape. *Encounter* did not last much longer than *Exeter*. At 1135, her powerplant was damaged by a shell splinter and, as she lost way, her captain ordered the ship scuttled and the crew overboard. She went down at 1155; 149 of her crew were rescued, of which 37 died in captivity.

Pope had better luck, at least initially. Against impossible odds, Lieutenant Commander W C Blinn and his crew kept fighting, even though they were now out of torpedoes and running low on 4in rounds. Sighting a fortuitous rain squall to the east, *Pope* was chased all the way by shell splashes, but managed to reach the concealment of the downpour at 1145 without suffering serious damage. Finding another squall on the other side of the first, hope briefly was raised that perhaps the old flush-decker could hop-scotch from squall to squall until dark, but, coming out of the second squall, the sky to the east was clear and a spotter aircraft were seen circling overhead. Forty-five minutes later, a flight of six 'Vals' were approaching from the west.[61] The light aircraft carrier *Ryujo* had accompanied the invasion force heading for Sunda Strait. Compared to the fleet aircraft carriers that had raided Pearl Harbor, *Ryujo* was small and cramped, carrying half the number of aircraft and handling those much more slowly. The six dive-bombers that attacked *Pope* represented nearly half her available strike group. None of the bombs hit her, but one near-miss in way of No.4 torpedo tube mount punched a hole in her side and bent her port propeller shaft, forcing the shutdown of that engine. A follow-on attack by six 'Kates' did no further damage, but none was necessary.[62] The ship was starting to settle from the earlier near-miss, to the point that Blinn ordered *Pope* abandoned at 1250. As the crew was pulling away, *Ashigara* and *Myoko* pulled within range and finished the destruction of the old destroyer with six salvos of their 20cm guns. *Pope* rapidly settled stern-first.

Only one man died in *Pope's* sinking; 151 officers and men survived to make it into one whaleboat and a string of rafts. Still defiant, some crewmen took a few potshots with Browning automatics at Japanese floatplanes sweeping low to investigate the scene, which led to several strafing passes. No-one was

98. The proximate cause of *Exeter*'s demise was a 20cm shell from *Ashigara*, seen here prewar, or her sister *Myoko*, fired as the Royal Navy cruiser, damaged at the Battle of the Java Sea, attempted to escape from Surabaya on 1 March 1942. Note the sinuous sheer line of her weather deck, characteristic of Japanese warships built after the First World War. (*NHHC*)

99. *Exeter* met her end after damage to her remaining boiler capacity brought her to a halt. After that, it was inevitable that she would succumb to an overwhelming barrage of gunfire and torpedoes. (*NHHC*)

100. *Pope* put up a gallant fight, but she too was overwhelmed on 1 March 1942, the day the Japanese cleaned out all remaining ABDA warships north of the Malay Barrier. She had stayed alive chasing rain squalls, but finally ran out of squalls and luck and succumbed to attacks from the air and from *Ashigara* and *Myoko*. (NHHC)

hit on either side in this exchange. They spent nearly three days adrift before being picked up by a Japanese destroyer and delivered intact to Makassar. Unfortunately, as with all of these accounts, a number of men, 27 in this case, failed to survive their incarceration on Java or the Celebes, succumbing to malnutrition or one of the diseases that often accompanies it.

A Clean Sweep

There now remained no Allied ships north of the Malay Barrier and only a few in the waters between the East Indies and the north coast of Australia, and those latter ships were not much safer than those to the north had been. Beyond the four destroyers of DesDiv58, very few of the major Allied warships caught in the Indian Ocean south of Java at the beginning of March 1942 survived the next few days. Besides the Japanese land-based air units moving rapidly to operate from bases captured in Java and Sumatra, four large aircraft carriers moved south through the Malay Barrier west of Timor on 26 February supported by two fast battleships and five heavy cruisers. The purpose was to raid Allied posts in Western Australia and southern Java, as far west as Christmas Island, and to clear these waters of any Allied ships.

There were not many ships to be 'cleared away'. USS *Langley* (AV3), carrying USAAF P-40 fighters to Java, had been sunk south of that island by Japanese aircraft on 27 February. The destroyers USS *Edsall* (DD219) and *Whipple* (DD217) picked up the survivors and headed west to transfer them to the oiler *Pecos* (AO6) near Christmas Island. However, Glassford ordered *Edsall* to keep thirty-two pilots and mechanics aboard and make a high-speed run to Tjilatjap. When *Edsall* parted from *Pecos* and *Whipple* on the morning of 1 March, as far as the Allies were concerned she might as well have disappeared off the face of the earth. No word reached America regarding her fate, or that of any of her crew, until after the war; indeed, it was not until 1952 that definitive proof of her fate came to light.

Edsall had the singular misfortune of stumbling across the wake of the Japanese main carrier task force (Kido Butai) as it steamed southwest of Tjilatjap. Spotted by a CAP fighter from *Akagi*, *Edsall* was initially misidentified as a '*Marblehead*-type' light cruiser, an understandable mistake given that both the flush-deckers and *Marblehead* were narrow-hulled ships with four funnels. At 1552, Admiral Nagumo Chuichi ordered Vice-Admiral Mikawa Gunichi to investigate with battleships *Hiei* and *Kirishima*, accompanied by heavy cruisers *Chikuma* and *Tone*. It took only ten minutes to sight *Edsall* and another minute for *Chikuma* to open fire at extreme range. The ensuing engagement is one of the least skillful examples of naval gunnery ever recorded. *Edsall*, incapable of maximum speed due to a collision suffered early in the Java Sea campaign, was manoeuvred skillfully by her captain, Lieutenant Commander Joshua Nix, laying down a dense smoke screen from which she emerged occasionally to fire off 4in rounds at her pursuers, making use as well of a fortuitous rain squall. All four of the Japanese pursuers fired at *Edsall* more or less continuously for almost an hour before *Hiei* managed to obtain a hit at 1654. Even this did not slow down the destroyer; it took the efforts of twenty-six Vals launched from the aircraft carriers to slow *Edsall*. They managed to hit her with several bombs, damaging her powerplant and starting fires that could not be controlled. The destroyer finally was overwhelmed by her pursuers, capsizing at 1731, almost an hour and a half after *Chikuma* began the engagement. The Japanese battleships had fired 297 36cm/45 rounds (210 by *Hiei* and 87 by *Kirishima*), obtaining the one hit recorded at 1654, and 132 15cm/50 rounds (70 by *Hiei* and 62 by *Kirishima*) with no recorded hits. If anything, the heavy cruisers shot far worse; they fired off 844 20cm/50 rounds for one recorded hit, by *Tone* at 1705. The destroyer was finished off by the secondary battery of *Chikuma* with sixty-two 12.7cm/40 rounds fired at point-blank range; presumably most of them hit.

It is known that five survivors of *Edsall* reached Kendari on 11 March; on that date or shortly thereafter, they were executed by beheading.

Pecos was sunk by Japanese carrier aircraft also on 1 March. *Whipple* turned back to rescue survivors, eventually rescuing 231 men who were safely landed in Australia. A British destroyer, HMS *Stronghold* (H50), was caught on 2 March by a force comprising the heavy cruiser *Maya* and two destroyers 300nm south of Bali and dispatched in yet another sloppy gunfight.[63] Approximately fifty survivors were picked up by a Dutch merchantman and later transferred to *Maya*, where, reportedly, they were well treated. Later on 2 March, *Pillsbury* was intercepted by a force of two Japanese heavy cruisers, *Atago* and *Takao*, and sunk with relative efficiency, requiring only 166 20cm rounds. *Pillsbury* sank very rapidly at 2232; there were no survivors. The final victim in this surgical sweep of the seas south of Java was USS *Asheville* (PG21), a gunboat that had served long and well along the Chinese coast. She cleared Tjilatjap on 1 March, but two days later was caught 300nm to the south by destroyers *Arashi* and *Nowaki*, which made short work of the venerable patrol boat. Sadly, her sole survivor perished in a Japanese POW camp in 1945.

AN OLD-FASHIONED GUNFIGHT

IMPERIAL JAPANESE NAVY VS US NAVY IN THE NORTH PACIFIC, MARCH 1943

WHEN THE JAPANESE WENT TO WAR with the Allies, they had a plan to win the war, just not a very good one. For the most part, they had no illusions regarding their ability to defeat America in a long war.[1] It was simply that their planning assumed that a series of rapid, spectacular victories would convince the Americans to accept a compromise peace that left Japan in control of most of the territory it had gained in the first months of the war. When it became obvious that the Americans had no interest in a negotiated peace, the Japanese had to decide how to consolidate the gains they had made, particularly in South Asia.

The Naval General Staff wanted to continue pushing south, completing the conquest of New Guinea and establishing a strong enough presence in the Solomon Islands to threaten the American hold on Espiritu Santo (Vanuatu) and New Caledonia and the sea lane between New Zealand and Australia. The leadership of the Combined Fleet, in particular Admiral Yamamoto Isoroku, felt strongly that the initial Pearl Harbor attack had failed in its primary aim of hobbling US naval strength because none of America's aircraft carriers had been damaged or sunk in the attack.[2] Yamamoto wanted to lure the American carriers into battle with the concentrated might of the Kido Butai. His plan to bring this about was to strike at a target which the Americans would not expect to be attacked, but could not refuse to defend, where they would have to rush into battle at a time and place of his choosing. His chosen target was Midway Island.

Timed to coincide with Yamamoto's move against Midway, the Japanese also planned the occupation of three islands towards the western end of the Aleutian Island chain. The reason for this was their concern that the Americans might be planning to move strategic bombers, and possibly even large military units, to those islands, where they could attack Japanese positions in the Kuriles or even Hokkaido.[3]

On 7 June 1942, Japanese troops were put ashore on the islands of Attu and Kiska.[4] The plan, what there was of one, was that these men would construct airbases from which aircraft could keep an eye on the American base at Dutch Harbor and defend against air or naval raids. This failed to take into account the nature of the landscape in the western Aleutians, where there are few natural sites for airstrips and no readily available materials from which they could be constructed, where the ground is either frozen solid or a muddy quagmire, where all supplies had to be brought in across 650nm of open water from Kataoka Bay, Paramushiro and where some of the worst weather in the world made such transport a challenge without even taking enemy activity into account.[5]

Between the landings in June 1942 and March of the following year, the Japanese found just how hard it would be to maintain even small garrisons in the Aleutians. Three valuable loads carried on three even more valuable transports were lost between November and January to attacks by American aircraft and nearly every other ship sent to Attu or Kiska was attacked. More critically, the fast transport *Akagane Maru* was intercepted on her way to Attu on 18 February 1943 by USS *Indianapolis* (CA35) and two destroyers, which had earlier in the day bombarded that island. This smacked of a naval blockade which the Japanese found more threatening than sporadic air attacks.

It was therefore decided that, from then on, all transports to the Aleutians would be formed into convoys, rather than sailing independently, and that Vice-Admiral Hosogaya Boshiro's 5th Fleet would provide the necessary escort. This worked well in early March; Hosogaya successfully delivered a convoy to Attu on 9 March and shepherded the empties back to Paramushiro. When word of this reached the Americans, they were equally determined that it would not be allowed to happen again. Thus, when radio intercepts indicated another convoy movement in the second half of the month, the admiral commanding US forces in the North Pacific, Rear-Admiral Thomas C Kinkaid, ordered his task force commander, Rear-Admiral Charles 'Soc' McMorris, to take his force of one old light cruiser – USS *Richmond* (CL9), sister to *Marblehead* previously encountered in the East Indies – and two new destroyers – USS *Bailey* (DD492) and *Coghlan* (DD606) – out from their forward base at Adak on 17 March.[6] They were joined on the 22nd by the recently repaired and refitted USS *Salt Lake City* (CA25), nicknamed 'Swayback Maru' because her extreme sheer line did make her appear to sag in the middle, and two more destroyers , the much older *Dale* (DD353) and *Monaghan* (DD354). This composite force, variously known as TG16.6 or Task Group Mikc, now set out to patrol a line west of Attu.

Japanese Convoy No.21-RO from Kataoka Bay to Attu was divided into two parts.[7] The first part departed on 22 March and comprised the destroyer *Usugumo* and the cargo ship *Sanko Maru* (5,491GRT). This part left first because *Sanko Maru* was the slowest of the cargo ships. The second part, comprising two faster transports, *Asaka Maru* (7,399GRT) and *Sakito Maru* (7,158GRT), departed the next day. The former had been built as a reefer which had been converted into an AMC and, as a result, could carry only a small amount of cargo; the latter was an IJA transport fully loaded with three hundred troops, munitions and foodstuffs. Both were capable of maintaining 15kt. They were escorted by Destroyer Squadron 1, commanded by Rear-Admiral Mori Tomokazu in the old light cruiser *Abukuma*, leading destroyers *Ikazuchi*, *Inazuma*, *Hatsushimo* and *Wakaba*. Finally, the day after, Hosogaya set out with his main force – his flagship, heavy cruiser *Nachi* – last seen off Borneo engaged with *Exeter* – her near-sister *Maya* and the old light cruiser *Tama*. Hosogaya's plan was for both parts of the convoy and his cruiser force to rendezvous the next day, 25 March, 60nm south of the Komandorski Islands and 200nm west of Attu. (More importantly, this was 600nm west of Adak, and believed to be beyond the range of American air search.[8]) From this point, he intended to fight the convoy through whatever opposition the Americans might mount. He certainly could have no doubt there would be opposition. As early as 21 March, a Japanese reconnaissance aircraft had overflown, and drawn fire from, McMorris' squadron.

The plans of both sides were disrupted by the one constant in these waters – bad weather. A violent storm on 23 and 24 March delayed both parts of the convoy, the slow section more than the two faster transports. The fast section of the convoy met Hosogaya around noon on 25 March, but when the sun set that evening, *Sanko Maru* and her escort were nowhere to be seen. Hosogaya led his ships, now four cruisers, four destroyers and two transports arrayed in line-ahead, on a roughly north–south loop course south of the Komandorskis to wait out the night, assuming he would sight the missing merchantman and her escort at first light on the 26th. He then planned to make his run-in to Attu a day behind schedule. As the southeastern sky began to lighten before dawn, the Japanese were executing a starboard turn in order – *Nachi, Maya, Tama, Wakaba, Hatsushimo, Abukuma, Ikazuchi, Asaka Maru, Sakito Maru* and *Inazuma* – through 180° from south to north, to head back to the planned rendezvous.

McMorris, in the meanwhile, had his own concerns. Half of his ships having been on patrol since the 17th, he was concerned about fuel and, with this in mind, he planned on having *Salt Lake City* refuel *Bailey* and *Coghlan* on the 23rd. The two days of bad weather that delayed the Japanese convoy played similar havoc with McMorris' plans. It was not until the morning of 25 March that the refuelling operation could commence. Soon after the

101. The Japanese light cruiser *Tama* is seen in original condition in 1925. She did not look much different when she fought at the Battle of the Komandorski Islands on 27 March 1943. The main difference would have been the addition of an aircraft catapult before her mainmast. She would have been wearing a grey-and-white deceptive camouflage, one of the few Japanese ships to carry such a scheme. (*NARA*)

start of that operation, a message was received from Kinkaid ordering Task Group Mike back to port. McMorris acknowledged receipt and told Kinkaid he would comply when the refuelling was complete.[9] This delay proved fortuitous, as the order was presently countermanded; that same morning, Kinkaid received further confirmation from Pearl Harbor that a Japanese convoy was approaching, and he gave McMorris authority to continue his patrol at his discretion. A quick calculation showed that *Monaghan* and *Dale* had sufficient fuel to go three more days before they would need refuelling and *Richmond* could last until the 29th before having to head for Adak. He informed Kinkaid of his decision to continue the patrol and as the day drew to a close, put his ships in a standard scouting formation, six miles between ships, on a roughly north-northwest–south-southeast axis heading just east of north at 15kt, *Coghlan* at the northern end of the line. His position was due south of Hosogaya's and, until the Japanese began their turn to the north, steadily closing.

Contact in Half-Light

At 0730, an hour before sunrise, *Coghlan* made radar contact with two ships just east of north at a range of 14,500yd. Moments later, *Richmond*, next south in the scouting line, picked up three contacts at 24,000yd, almost exactly due north.[10] As the contacts could only be the enemy, McMorris immediately ordered all ships to concentrate on *Richmond*, a prearranged manoeuvre that would bring them from the extended scouting line into a battle formation with the two cruisers in line-ahead, with a pair of destroyers ahead and another pair astern. The manoeuvre may have been prearranged, but it still was one that would take time to complete, because of the distances involved: *Monaghan*, the last ship in the scouting line, was 24nm south of *Richmond*.

McMorris had no time to spare. Every one of the six American ships involved in this battle carried at least three radar sets serving both search and fire control functions, while none of the Japanese ships had yet been radar-equipped. Despite this advantage, the Americans had been spotted by the Japanese a full half-hour before *Coghlan* and *Richmond* made contact.[11] At 0700, lookouts on *Asaka Maru*, which was in the process of turning to the north, and *Inazuma*, which had not yet turned, sighted masts on the southern horizon at a range of 27,300yd.[12] At first these were taken to be the expected merchantman and destroyer, but when a third and fourth set of masts were detected, Hosogaya ordered a turn to the southeast. The passing of this order by flag and lamp was a bit ragged in the pre-dawn half-light, with the result that *Nachi* came about smartly, but the rest of the line, minus the two merchantmen which were ordered to head away on a reciprocal course, became confused, taking almost as much time to reform a line of battle as did the Americans.[13]

With the battle lines forming, the Japanese steaming southeast, led by *Nachi*, the Americans just slightly west of north in three columns – *Richmond* leading *Salt Lake City* in the centre column, *Bailey* and *Coghlan* off *Richmond*'s port bow and *Dale* and *Monaghan* off *Salt Lake City*'s starboard quarter – the engagement was about to begin. Within minutes of the first sighting, the Japanese knew they were up against an enemy cruiser force, one over which they had an advantage in firepower and speed, and Hosogaya was eager to get the battle started. It took the Americans much longer to appreciate the danger they were facing. The first visual sighting of the Japanese was not made until 0811, and, as late as 0830, the captain of *Salt Lake City*, Captain Bertram J Rodgers, still had a completely erroneous tactical picture.

> At about 0830 when still several thousand yards from the flagship, Spot I sighted smoke on the horizon at 345° (T). Then the tops of three destroyers, a possible merchantman and a tall mast came into view. To the left appeared the tops of four more ships. There were now in sight two merchantmen, two light cruisers and about five destroyers. The destroyers were apparently in a sound screen covering the after sector. Good clear visibility and gentle swells made this look like an easy day's pickings.[14]

It was about this time that the full Japanese force came into focus from the American line and any illusion that this was a weak enemy force that might be quick overwhelmed finally dispelled. McMorris wrote: 'The situation had now clarified . . . but it had also radically and unpleasantly changed.'[15] As if to put an exclamation point on that assessment, *Nachi* opened fire with her forward two turrets at 0840 at a range of 20,000yd, followed seconds later by *Maya*. The battle that ensued is known to the Americans as the Battle of the Komandorski Islands and to the Japanese as the Sea Battle off Attu Island.

(These Japanese heavy cruisers carried a main battery of ten 20cm/50 guns in five twin turrets. This led to an awkward arrangement of three turrets forward, the second one superfiring over Nos. 1 and 3, which were sited on the main deck. This meant that a full ten-gun salvo could be fired only if the target was bearing more than approximately 30° off the bow or stern of the ship. At less than this angle, only four guns could bear forward or astern. *Salt Lake City* was also armed with ten 8in/55 guns, but in only four turrets, two forward and two aft. Both superfiring turrets were triples, while the main deck mounts were twins. The awkward arrangement of turrets on the Japanese cruisers led Hosogaya to steer a weaving course that allowed him to alternate between paralleling the American course and turning away sufficiently to permit a full broadside to be fired. This contributed significantly to his inability to take advantage of his superior speed and gain a more advantageous tactical position.)

Richmond, still leading *Salt Lake City* by over 1,000yd, opened fire at 19,700yd at 0841. This was extreme range for her 6in/53 main battery. *Salt Lake City* followed a minute later. The shooting on both sides appeared to be spectacularly accurate from the initial salvos. *Richmond* was straddled on *Maya*'s second salvo at 0845, shaking the ship so violently that many aboard believed she had been hit: 'Enemy salvo straddled. Estimated we were hit in the bow and amidships. Ordered Central Station to inspect for damage.[16] Commenced zigzagging to throw off enemy fire. Central reported no hits and no damage.'[17]

Moments later, the Americans witnessed what they thought was a spectacular success from their first salvos, which proved just as illusory. Starting at 0844, *Salt Lake City* believed she scored one or more hits on the leading enemy ship, *Nachi*, confirmed at 0849 by heavy black smoke rising from that ship's midsection.[18] This observation was correct, but was not caused by American gunfire. The smoke was due to the aircraft on *Nachi*'s starboard catapult, a Mitsubishi F1M Type 00 'Pete', catching fire, caused by the muzzle blast from the cruiser's No. 4 turret firing at *Richmond* at full forward bearing.[19] This was a common enough occurrence in naval battles at the time, and the problem was solved by simply launching the burning aircraft overboard. While this commotion was going on, *Nachi*'s starboard torpedo crew, a deck below, fired eight torpedoes at 0843. These would be the first of forty-eight torpedoes fired this day (forty-three known to have been fired by the Japanese and five by the Americans), not one of which found a target. The American commanders went the entire day blithely unaware the Japanese had fired so many torpedoes at them; though torpedoes from this first salvo were sighted off *Bailey*'s starboard quarter and crossing ahead of *Richmond* at 0856, they were dismissed, as in this from *Richmond*'s CO, Captain T M Waldschmidt:

> The usual reports of periscopes and torpedo wakes were reported but it was not believed that any torpedoes were fired at this force at any time. The supposed torpedo wake ahead of the RICHMOND was observed by the commanding officer and consisted of the splash of a school of small fish in a comparatively straight and narrow path.[20]

Now fully aware of the danger facing him with a superior force crossing to his starboard bow, moving to cut him off from his base to the east, and the range down to under 18,000yd and dropping fast, McMorris made the only move he could, ordering a turn to the left, to 250° at 0848 and to 220° at 0850. By now both Japanese heavy cruisers had clearly identified the enemies they were facing and *Maya* switched targets, so that both were now firing at *Salt Lake City*. Nevertheless, the first hit of the battle was scored by the Americans. At approximately 0850, a shell struck the after end of *Nachi*'s flag bridge, killing eleven and wounding twenty-one, though sparing Hosogaya and his staff.[21] This shell also ruptured the communication leads from the forward main-battery fire control director, seriously impacting the accuracy of her gunfire for some time. A small fire resulted from this hit, but it was rapidly extinguished. Two minutes later, *Nachi* was hit again, this time on her aircraft deck aft. The shell penetrated this deck and exploded in the torpedo-handling space immediately below, killing two and wounding five. Another hit, possibly from the same salvo, severed the starboard after leg of *Nachi*'s tripod mainmast. This hit severed the leads from the ship's main antenna and the after radio room, temporarily silencing seven different pieces of radio equipment, but rapid work by damage control crews maintained uninterrupted radio communications between the flagship and all other Japanese ships.[22]

Both American cruisers claimed these hits.[23] The case for *Richmond* is based mainly on the enemy having left her to enjoy some undisturbed target practice, albeit at extreme range. Also, one of the two Japanese eyewitnesses, Commander Miura Kintaro, states emphatically that all the hits on *Nachi* at this stage of the battle were by 6in shells. Almost all the remaining arguments point towards *Salt Lake City*. These included her firing a larger shell at less than maximum range, which would have tended to increase accuracy. Having more modern fire control radar and a rudimentary Combat Information Center (CIC) might have helped, but perhaps the most persuasive evidence is from the second Japanese eyewitness, Commander Hashimoto Shigefuso, who stated that the hit was by a 'blue dye loaded shell'.[24] *Salt Lake City* was firing blue-dyed AP shells that day; *Richmond*'s AP shells carried orange dye.

A Curious Loss of Power

At about this time there occurred (or perhaps did not) an event of some significance affecting *Nachi*'s ability to fire her main battery. According to Commander Miura (and echoed by many other accounts of the battle), after one or two salvos, *Nachi*'s engineers switched her electrical generators to a cold boiler, which cut electrical power to her turrets, and which took approximately half an hour to restore.[25] In fact, this could not have happened, as none of *Nachi*'s five generators were steam-powered.[26] This does not, however, mean that there was not an interruption of power to her turrets. The hit that cut the electrical connection from her foremast main-battery director could only be repaired by temporarily shutting down the power in those cables, and it is possible that that might have required the temporary cutting of power to the hydraulic motors that elevated and trained her guns. (Although *Nachi* had a second, identical main-battery director on her after superstructure abaft her second funnel, it was poorly placed to direct her gunfire in what quickly became a stern chase. The guns also could have been fired under local control, but in the poor visibility caused by smoke, haze and low overcast, that would have seriously degraded accuracy. There was good reason for *Nachi*'s damage control crews to attempt to repair the electrical connection to her foremast director, even if that meant the temporary interruption of main-battery gunfire.)

The two Japanese sources that give a timeline for *Nachi*'s gunfire tell very different stories.[27] One shows *Nachi* opening fire only at 0930, and then only for three minutes, before falling silent for another nineteen minutes; the other shows *Nachi* opening fire at 0842, stopping for four minutes between 0852 and 0856 (which would coincide with the hit on her bridge), then resuming until 0943, when fire ceased for fourteen minutes. It should be noted that, according to both charts, *Maya* ceased fire for an even longer period (twenty-seven minutes) at this time. It is most likely that this slackening of Japanese gunfire, as noted below, was entirely unrelated to *Nachi*'s electrical problems.

It is this author's opinion that it is simply not possible to be certain, but it is likely that for some period (or periods) between 0852 and approximately 0925, when, according to Lorelli, repairs on *Nachi*'s foremast electrical circuits were completed, she did indeed cut power to her main-battery turrets, but that this was intermittent rather than being one continuous outage.[28] Over the course of the entire engagement, *Nachi* fired 197 fewer main-battery rounds than *Maya*. The Japanese were manoeuvring so that they were generally firing full ten-round broadsides, so that *Nachi* fired approximately twenty fewer salvos than *Maya*. These ships were capable of firing between two and three salvos per minute, so if they were firing as rapidly as possible, which they were doing for much of the initial phase of this battle, that meant that *Nachi*'s guns were silent for a total of between seven and ten minutes during this period, which would be consistent with a process during which power was intermittently shut down to her main-battery turrets.

Salt Lake City in Trouble

These problems did not prevent *Nachi* from launching the aircraft on her port catapult, a 'Jake' three-seat floatplane, at 0856. This aircraft attempted to spot fall of shot for the Japanese, but did a poor job of it, coming under anti-aircraft fire from the Americans on a number of occasions. Hosogaya reacted to the American turn to the southwest by detaching *Abukuma* and the four destroyers, which he ordered to shape a similar course to the southwest, staying on the Americans starboard quarter and remaining in a position to block any move McMorris might make to double back towards the east. For the moment he kept his heavy cruisers heading south-southwest so that they could continue to hurl broadsides at *Salt Lake City*, even though this allowed the range to steadily increase and would inevitably put him in a trailing position when he finally turned to follow McMorris. This increase in range did help the Japanese in that it put them beyond the reach of *Richmond*'s 6in guns, which would be silent from 0903 until 1044.

At 0910, *Maya* hit *Salt Lake City* with what initially felt like solid blows forward and amidships.

> Several shocks were felt forward to starboard. Immediately thereafter several shocks were felt aft to starboard. Repair parties were despatched immediately to investigate in forecastle and midships. The after engine room reported fire and a few moments later belayed the word. The after engine room was taking water through the after bulkhead.[29]
>
> The hit aft at 0910 proved to be a hit on the port side at frame 102. The shell penetrated below the water line just below the third deck (first platform), penetrating inward and exploding. Shaft alleys 3 and 4 were flooded. The pipe lines leading from the after bulkhead of the after engine room port side in the hold carried away causing the after engine room to take water.[30]

Shell fragments from this hit punctured fuel tanks in way of the after engine room, causing oil to leak into that compartment and sea water to enter the bunkers.

Having opened a considerable lead on the enemy heavy cruisers, McMorris began a sweeping right-hand turn at 0930 that gradually led his line towards the north. Depending on how Hosogaya reacted to this turn, McMorris might have several options, including chasing the transports last seen fleeing to the northwest or turning east towards Adak. For the next twenty minutes, the fire from the Japanese heavy cruisers slackened considerably, as they had fallen well behind the Americans and they could only fire broadsides by turning to one side or the other, which meant falling further behind. At about 0950, Hosogaya brought *Nachi* and *Maya* around to the north-northwest and resumed a rapid and effective bombardment of *Salt Lake City*. The Americans did not respond because, at the same time, McMorris noticed that *Abukuma* and her destroyers were approaching on a course that would bring them into position for a torpedo attack from the starboard quarter. At approximately 1000, *Salt Lake City* opened fire on the light cruiser, causing her to loop away, ending that threat for the moment.

The American cruiser was allowed no chance to admire her success. At 1002, as the cumulative result of the 0910 hit aft, repeated near-misses and the pounding caused by the firing of her own aft guns, *Salt Lake City* lost her primary rudder control. Fortunately, she was able to make a relatively orderly shift of rudder control to the emergency steering system over the next twenty minutes. While this was happening, she was hit again, fortunately well forward so it did not aggravate her steering problems, hitting her main deck at frame 7 at 1010.

> This hit penetrated the starboard side of the center line main deck at a high-angle impact, striking the starboard anchor windlass, deflecting forward and downward and sheering the chain pipe, deflecting more forward and downward to the overhead of the chain locker, A-301-E, two or three feet below the water line. There were two shrapnel holes besides the shell hole in the second deck, one hole in the hull to starboard in A-302-A, a shell hole in the deck at frame 5, A-400 the starprojectile leaving the ship's hull at frame 4, at the juncture of the overhead chain locker to bulkhead of A-1-W forward peak tank and hull plating. No fire resulted.[31]

Four forward compartments were flooded; the bulkhead at frame 10 was immediately shored to prevent the flooding spreading aft.

Increasingly concerned about the condition of *Salt Lake City* and finally acknowledging that there was no chance of either catching the transports or immediately turning east, McMorris began a series of small turns to the west and, at 1013, ordered *Bailey* to begin making smoke to cover the cruisers. Fortunately, the cold air and relatively windless conditions made the smoke screen by *Bailey* and other American ships surprisingly effective, and, once again, the fire from the Japanese slackened.[32] Lacking radar, the Japanese had to wait for a break in the smoke screen before they could take a shot at the Americans. The Japanese light cruisers, particularly *Tama*, manoeuvred actively, searching for the breaks in the smoke, and were successful to the extent that many Americans believed the Japanese were using fire control radar.[33]

The engagement now settled into a stern chase to the west-northwest, periodically punctuated by gunfire from the Japanese heavy cruisers, who trailed the Americans by slightly more than 20,000yd. At approximately 1040, *Tama*, which was at this point well ahead of the heavy cruisers, turned the northern edge of the smoke screen and got a clear view of *Bailey* just south of west at 14,000yd. A brief firefight ensued as *Tama* took on *Bailey*, which was soon joined by *Coghlan* and *Richmond*, at relatively close range. This exchange of gunfire continued until 1100. *Bailey* was straddled by a salvo of 14cm/50 rounds from *Tama* at 1046. This was enough to disable her gyros, but did not prevent her zigzagging successfully back into the smoke without further damage. It was probably during this exchange that *Tama* sustained the two 5in hits in her superstructure she received during the battle, probably fired by *Bailey*.

At approximately 1050, McMorris, well aware that every passing minute was taking him further from his own base and air support – and closer to the enemy's – decided that the time had come to attempt to extricate his squadron from this engagement.[34] He ordered a 90° turn to the left, to a course of 240° at 1053, followed by successive smaller changes that had them heading 160° by 1107. It is possible Hosogaya did not see this course change; it is more likely he saw it but misunderstood its significance, thinking it yet another minor perturbation in the generally west-northwest course the two forces had been holding for the past forty-five minutes. Perhaps he hoped that continuing to the west after the Americans turned south would allow him to get clear of the smoke. For whatever reason, he continued on his previous course for more than fifteen more minutes before he began a very gradual turn to the south. However, before the American turn had succeeded in putting much additional distance between the two forces, the Japanese scored two more hits on *Salt Lake City*.

At 1059, she was hit on her starboard catapult. The shell, most likely a 20cm round, detonated on impact, causing mostly superficial damage.

> A hit was received at frame 67-68 setting the plane on the starboard catapult on fire. This shell exploded on impact on the starboard catapult. Fragments penetrated the well deck (center line), and forward stack and superstructure. Fire party was dispatched immediately and the fire was put out. The plane was jettisoned after having been badly shattered. It is believed it was at this time that the First Lieutenant was killed by a flying fragment on the port quarterdeck.[35]

Besides the first lieutenant, one other officer and one seaman were killed and four more were injured.

Six minutes later, at 1105, *Salt Lake City* was hit a glancing blow on the port side by a 14cm shell fired by *Abukuma*. This shell did not penetrate the hull, rather it ricocheted back into the water and exploded there, driving in the shell plating at frame 98 to a depth of nine inches, and fragments punched numerous new holes in the hull above and below the waterline. This compounded the damage caused by the earlier hit at frame 102 at 0910; the cumulative damage was becoming serious.

The A.A. Switchboard (After Gyro Room) began taking oil through fragment holes. This was apparently caused by the hit on the port side at frame 102. Oil and water were flooding at a moderate rate. No fires. Electrical circuits to A.A. Switchboard and gyro killed. Flooding proceeded to completely fill the A.A. Switchboard room, after 5-inch handling room, after 5-inch ammunition stowage and shaft alleys 3 and 4. The ship began to take a four or five degree list to port. Shoring of after bulkhead of after engine room was immediately undertaken but due to the many pipe lines and manifolds, shoring was not very successful in stopping flooding. The engine room was not able to control the flooding by her pumps. A submersible pump was dispatched immediately from repair station.[36]

Between 1105 and 1115, the Japanese fired sixteen more torpedoes at McMorris, all of which passed aft of the American line. Finally, at 1115, Hosogaya began a slow, sweeping turn to the south-southeast, crossing the wake of the American squadron at 1123. At that point, he trailed *Salt Lake City* by 22,000yd. All of his forces now were well to the north of McMorris, who could turn east at any point with no interference from the Japanese. Neither side could know that the 'crisis' of the battle was about to occur.

The progressive flooding in *Salt Lake City*'s after engine room had reached the point where it was necessary to temporarily shut down those engines and take steps to correct the ship's list. As the engineering crews worked feverishly to transfer fuel oil from port to starboard tanks and to pump the cold, slimy oil–water mix from the compartment, by 1125 the ship's speed had dropped to 20kt. It took McMorris a few minutes to react to *Salt Lake City* slowing, by which time *Richmond* was 6,000yd in the lead. At 1129, he ordered three of Riggs' destroyers to cover the heavy cruiser with a torpedo attack, the fourth remaining behind to continue making smoke. Due to confusion between *Dale* and *Monaghan* as to which was to remain behind, the attack was mounted by only *Bailey* and *Coghlan*, which immediately attracted every Japanese gunner. They were soon charging through a seeming forest of shell splashes. Fortunately, their exposure to this danger did not last long. By 1132, Rodgers' engineers had managed to bring one of the two after engine room turbines back on line and *Salt Lake City*'s speed had increased to 26kt; at 1135, the torpedo attack was called off and the destroyers ordered to resume screening the heavy cruiser. Despite never reaching attack position and launching no torpedoes, the charge of DesRon14 caused Hosogaya to turn away to the west-southwest, which gave *Salt Lake City* a chance to again increase her distance from the Japanese. Incredibly, *Bailey* and *Coghlan* resumed their post on *Salt Lake City*'s starboard quarter without suffering so much as a scratch.

No sooner had this crisis been resolved than another clamoured for attention. At approximately 1140, Rodgers was informed that his after turrets, which had been doing the vast majority of the American shooting, were running low on AP rounds. Although it went against all safety doctrine, Rodgers ordered the transfer of shells and powder charges from the forward

102. This photograph shows *Salt Lake City* (CA25) at about 1150 on 27 March 1943, as she was losing way due to salt-water contamination of her fuel oil. (*NARA*)

magazines aft, which meant the opening of closed watertight doors and the movement of explosives through unarmoured passageways. Before the first of these transferred shells could reach the after turrets, turret No. 3 ran out of AP shells and started firing HC, which had almost six times the bursting charge. These exploded spectacularly on contact with the water as they landed near the Japanese cruisers and they exploded without the blue dye that marked the heavy cruiser's AP shells, which must have led them to believe they were under air attack, because observers on *Salt Lake City* saw a barrage of anti-aircraft fire blossom over the enemy heavy cruisers.[37]

Aircraft were indeed on Hosogaya's mind at this time. At 1145, he received word from Tokyo that 'several score' American aircraft were on their way to attack him.[38] This was not unexpected, as American land-based bombers had become increasingly active west of Attu over the preceding months. What Tokyo had heard was the radioed orders to Adak and Amchitka to send three small groups of USAAF B-25 Mitchells against Hosogaya, but these flights were slow to get off the ground and all of them turned back long before reaching the Japanese. Nevertheless, the belief that they were on their way would soon have decisive influence on Hosogaya's decision making.

This would not occur, however, before Hosogaya would have within his grasp the chance for the victory that so far had eluded him. Starting at approximately 1150, sea water contamination in the oil tank fuelling the boilers in *Salt Lake City* began to douse the fires one by one. By 1153, her speed had dropped to 8kt, and by 1155, she was dead in the water, all boilers out.[39] As she was losing way,

Rodgers turned *Salt Lake City* to the right so her starboard broadside would face the expected Japanese attack.

All hands knew the ship's peril when it was compelled to hoist, 'MIKE SPEED ZERO', with the enemy heavy cruisers about 19,000 yards on the port quarter and the light cruiser about the same on our starboard quarter. The enemy heavies continued to fire at every opportunity, and only Divine Providence enabled this ship to avoid severe damage . . . The Commanding Officer ordered fire checked to conserve ammunition for a final attack on the closing Japanese forces.[40]

Whether or not supernatural aid saved *Salt Lake City*, in what appeared to be the most dire of straits, she was not hit during these critical minutes or indeed during the rest of the engagement – the proximate cause of her salvation was the failure of *Nachi*'s spotter aircraft to report *Salt Lake City*'s distress in a timely manner. She was aided too by McMorris, who ordered another torpedo attack by DesRon14 at 1154.[41] This attack was much better organised than the first and developed rapidly. *Monaghan*, which was on *Salt Lake City*'s port quarter along with *Dale*, looped quickly across the cruiser's bow and fell in behind *Bailey* and *Coghlan* as they headed west-northwest towards the Japanese. (*Dale* was again designated to remain behind and continue making smoke across the cruiser's starboard side.) What none of the Americans could have known was that, two minutes before *Salt Lake City* drifted to a stop, at approximately 1153, Hosogaya ordered a turn away to the southwest. He had decided to disengage and retire towards Paramushiro. (The reasons for Hosogaya's decision included not only his belief that an air attack was imminent, but also several other factors, including the depletion of stocks of ammunition, particularly his heavy cruisers', and the fuel state of his ships, particularly his older destroyers, *Inazuma* and *Ikazuchi*.)

Regardless of that decision, the Japanese had to react to the charge of DesRon14, and they did so with every gun that could bear. The American destroyers, particularly *Bailey* leading the line, were again smothered in shell splashes. Amazingly, it was *Bailey* who scored first. Just before 1200, she put a 5in round on the front face of *Nachi*'s turret No. 1 after glancing off one of the gun barrels. The shell did not explode, but the impact disabled the turret, killing one man and wounding another.

The Japanese quickly evened the score, and then some. A 20cm shell hit *Bailey*'s midships superstructure, carrying away her starboard galley door, exploding in the passageway, destroying the ship's main pantry, killing four instantly and wounding four more seriously and three less so. One of the seriously wounded died later. The men were all members of repair parties waiting outside the galley to carry sandwiches to the gun crews.[42] A large fragment from a 20cm shell that fell just short entered her hull in way of her forward fire room; the 3in-by-6in hole in her hull was patched with a mattress and any flooding controlled by her bilge pumps. At about the same time, another fragment from a 20cm shell pierced the hull somewhat further aft,

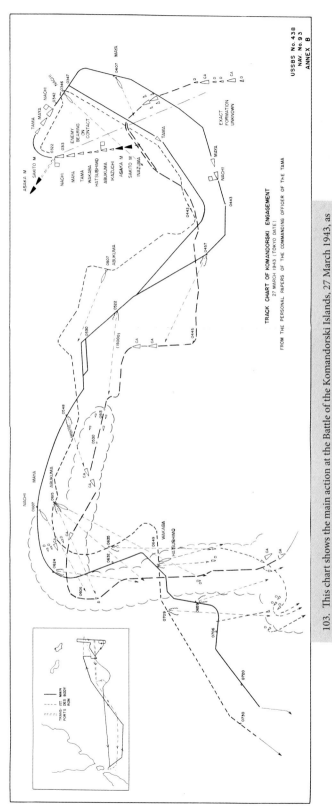

TRACK CHART OF KOMANDORSKI ENGAGEMENT

27 MARCH 1943 (TOKYO DATE)

FROM THE PERSONAL PAPERS OF THE COMMANDING OFFICER OF THE TAMA

USSBS No. 438
NAV. No. 9 3
ANNEX B

103. This chart shows the main action at the Battle of the Komandorski Islands, 27 March 1943, as recorded by the CO of *Tama*. (*USSBS Interrogation No. 438/93*)

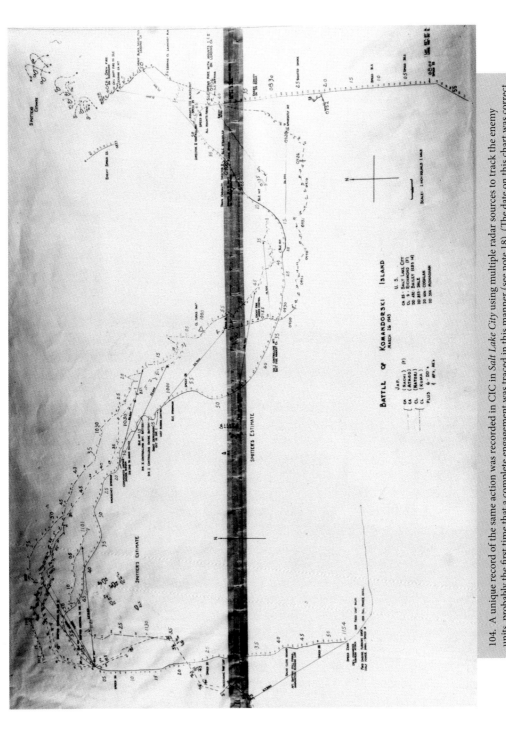

104. A unique record of the same action was recorded in CIC in *Salt Lake City* using multiple radar sources to track the enemy units, probably the first time that a complete engagement was traced in this manner (see note 18). (The date on this chart was correct for the Aleutians, where *Salt Lake City* was based, but the local date of the engagement, which took place west of the International Date Line, was a day later.) (NARA)

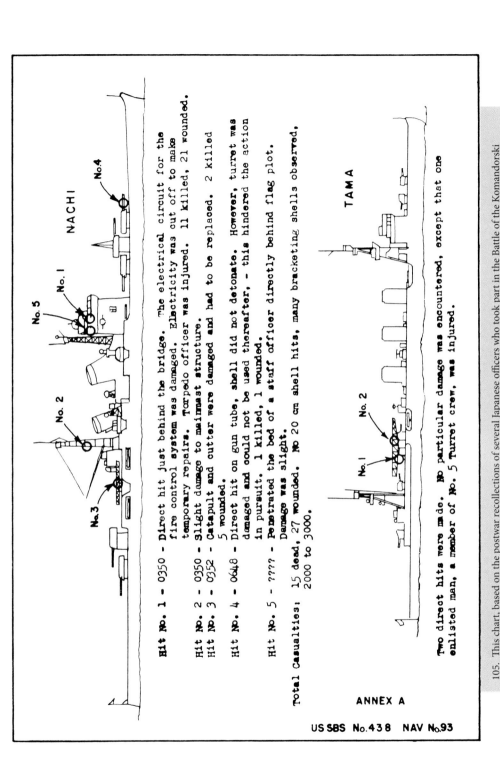

105. This chart, based on the postwar recollections of several Japanese officers who took part in the Battle of the Komandorski Islands, including the CO of *Tama*, represents a relatively accurate record of the damage done to the Japanese participants in the engagement. The comment that there were no 20cm (8in) shell hits is almost certainly incorrect. (*USSBS Interrogation No. 438/93*)

in way of the forward engine room; it may have even been part of the same shell that damaged the fire room. This 6in-by-20in hole proved difficult to reach, being behind the oil purifier pump. Another 20cm shell hit her after deck a glancing blow, dug a furrow in the deck plating, caromed off mount 54 and continued over the port side without exploding.[43] Despite taking this continual pounding, *Bailey* managed to obtain another hit on *Nachi*, this one on her signal platform.

At 1203, having reached 9,500yd from the Japanese line, *Bailey* turned to port and launched five torpedoes at *Maya*. Like every other torpedo fired that day, they missed. As *Bailey* turned away, still surrounded by shell splashes, *Coghlan* and *Monaghan* also turned; their captains judged the distance too great to fire torpedoes. *Coghlan* was near-missed by a 20cm shell; fragments left her XO unconscious and bleeding from a deep cut over his left eye and wounded two other men less seriously. They also knocked out her air search and fire control radars. Another near-miss destroyed *Bailey*'s motor whaleboat and carried away the after davit on her starboard side. The three destroyers now ducked into the safety of their own smoke screen and set a course to rejoin *Dale* and *Salt Lake City*. At 1204, the Japanese ceased fire. They maintained their previous course, to the southwest, away from the Americans.

Salt Lake City's engineers had been working frantically to find an uncontaminated fuel bunker and to flush the sea water from the pipes feeding the fire rooms. By 1200, just five minutes after drifting to a stop, she had way on again and in another seven minutes, all boilers had been relit and she was making 17kt. At 1202, seeing that the Japanese showed no interest in closing his hobbled ship, Rodgers allowed his after turrets to open fire on the retreating enemy. Two minutes later, she ceased fire again, as the range had become too great. *Dale* fired off the last shots of the battle at 1205. *Richmond*, which had again pulled some distance ahead of the rest of Task Group Mike, now doubled back and began making smoke to cover *Salt Lake City* at 1207. At 1210, McMorris ordered a course of 060°, almost the reciprocal of Hosogaya's. Realising that the battle was indeed finally over, McMorris ordered *Richmond* to stop making smoke at 1211.

Little to Feel Good About

All that was now necessary was the return to port and the sorting out of what had, and perhaps more importantly, what had not happened south of the Komandorski Islands. For the Japanese, there was little to feel good about. The attempt to reinforce Attu had failed, though at least no ships had been lost. But a significantly weaker American force had been encountered in a battle free from interference by aircraft or submarines and had been allowed to escape intact. Hosogaya, rightly or not, was held to have been insufficiently aggressive and was retired from active service. None of the Japanese ships had been seriously damaged, but *Nachi*, as the most damaged, was taken in hand at Yokosuka Navy Yard from 3 April to 11 May for damage repair and a general refit which included strengthening her AA battery and adding a No. 21 air search radar to her foremast.

The Japanese fired a prodigious amount of ammunition at the Americans for very little result. *Maya* fired 904 main-battery rounds; *Nachi* fired 707; *Tama* fired 136 and *Abukuma* 95. (*Maya* had a maximum magazine capacity of 1,260 rounds and a normal load-out of 1,200 rounds.) Out of this total of 1,842 main-battery rounds, six actual hits – four on *Salt Lake City* and two on *Bailey* – occurred, along with two or three near-misses close enough to cause damage to *Bailey* and *Coghlan*. Even counting those near-misses, that is a hit percentage of 0.5 per cent. To understand this poor shooting, it must be remembered that, despite the relatively clear and clement weather for the latitude and time of year, between the smoke of battle and the smoke screens generated by the Americans, the Japanese often had poor visibility of their targets. Also, unlike the Americans, they only had visual rangefinding to guide their gunnery.

Additionally, the Japanese heavy cruisers had a known issue with excessive dispersion of salvo fire.[44] This was found to be caused by interference between the shells fired simultaneously from a single turret, and, counter-intuitively, by too much time elapsing between the firing of individual turrets. (Exercises

106 and 107. This pair of images show *Salt Lake City* at Dutch Harbor two days after the Battle of the Komandorski Islands. The white patches on her hull, particularly on the starboard side, are rime ice. These clearly show the multiple radar systems carried even by an older US warship in a lesser theatre. *Salt Lake City* has two FC main-battery fire control radars (on her foretop and on the aft end of her stub mainmast), two FD secondary-battery fire control radars (on her two Mk19 AA directors) and an SC-2 air-search and SG surface-search antenna atop her foremast. (*NARA*)

showed that the older Japanese three-turret heavy cruisers of the *Furutaka*- and *Aoba*-classes fired tighter salvos with a significantly higher hit probability than the newer five-turret cruisers.) As a result of this problem, these cruisers, which had a theoretical maximum range of 31,700yd and a practical maximum of 21,900yd, were in practice limited to 16,800yd. In 1939 a system was installed that attempted to resolve both issues by introducing a maximum salvo spread of 0.2sec, while at the same time separating the firing of the two barrels of each turret by 0.03sec. This was found to improve accuracy to the extent that a hit rate of 6 per cent was anticipated, although, in practice this rate was never achieved and, on this occasion, never even approached. Rodgers, in *Salt Lake City*, noted that there was a noticeable difference between the accuracy of the two Japanese heavy cruisers. One, using a 'bilious green dye', was consistently off-target.[45] 'One of the enemy, firing blue-dye projectiles was very effective, and it was estimated after the battle that 200 of her shells fell within 50 yards of this ship. Her pattern was approximately 200 yards in range and 30 yards in deflection.'[46]

109. *Salt Lake City* fired so many 8in rounds from her main-battery turrets during the Battle of the Komandorski Islands that the paint on the barrels peeled away and the burning powder left a distinctive scorch pattern at the guns' muzzles. (*NARA*)

110. A normal part of post-battle routine since guns became the main armament of warships was swabbing out the barrels of the guns to remove powder residue from the bore. A pair of gunner's mates on *Salt Lake City* perform this arduous task after the Battle of the Komandorski Islands at Dutch Harbor. (*NARA*)

111. A sadder post-battle duty was the burial of the dead. Here, two of *Salt Lake City*'s dead are carried ashore for interment at Dutch Harbor across the bleak, snow-covered terrain of the Aleutians after the Battle of the Komandorski Islands. (*NARA*)

'Getting the Hell out of Here'

The retirement of Task Group Mike towards Adak should have been uneventful, but it was not. The trouble began immediately for *Bailey* as she attempted to make speed back towards the rest of the squadron. Despite the best efforts of her engineers and damage control parties, it proved impossible to stanch the inflow of water into her forward engine room. The decision was made to evacuate that compartment and secure the boilers in the forward fire room. This was completed by 1207. Although now steaming on two boilers and one engine, *Bailey* was still capable of making 25kt.

Salt Lake City's speed was gradually increasing, reaching 24kt at 1212, but her list was also increasing, reaching 9°. When the pumps in her after engine room failed at 1215, she was forced to reduce speed again, informing McMorris at 1224 that she believed she could maintain 20kt. *Monaghan* had her own engineering problems, with grating noises coming from her starboard reduction gearing and the steam lines to her fuel pumps failing, which combined to reduce her speed temporarily to 24kt. Nor were *Bailey*'s problems resolved. A problem with the main feed-water line to her after fire room forced her after engines to be shut down for four minutes, but a switch over to an emergency line brought the after engine back on line; her best speed after this was 15kt. The attitude of all participants was best summed up in the entry for 1226 in *Salt Lake City*'s log: 'Changed course to 090° (T) and are getting the hell out of here.'[47]

A Lot of Shooting; Not Much Hitting

The Americans fired a total of 3,465 rounds of ammunition of all calibres that day, which included 483 rounds of 5in, 3in and 40mm AA fired at the Japanese spotting plane. All of those rounds missed, although they were effective in reducing the spotter's effectiveness. Of the remaining rounds expended, 832 were fired by *Salt Lake City*, 271 by *Richmond*, 482 by *Bailey*, 750 by *Coghlan*, 203 by *Monaghan* and 444 by *Dale*. If Miura's first-hand testimony is to be believed, all of the hits achieved that day were by *Richmond* or the destroyers. In his opinion, all *Salt Lake City* contributed was some irritation of the eyes.

> These heavy shells made many close misses. But the vast majority landed just forward of the ship's bow, drenching the bridge with water. He complained of smarting eyes, which he attributed to the dye in these shell splashes. He was eloquent on the subject of the American destroyers' gunnery, saying their 13cm (5 inch) shells landed aboard like rain.[48]

> On closer examination, it now appears likely that the three hits obtained early in the engagement were all fired by *Salt Lake City*, and that the four known 5in hits (two on *Tama* and two on *Nachi*) were most likely all fired by *Bailey*. If this assessment is correct, then *Salt Lake City* shot slightly better than 0.36 per cent and *Bailey* about 0.8 per cent, which, even accounting for battle conditions, was unexceptional, especially given the presence of fire control radar on every American participant.[49] The presence in *Salt Lake City* of an early example of a CIC seems to have had little, if any, impact on the engagement. This may have helped Rodgers while he was chasing salvos, but likely had no effect on the accuracy of her gunfire; the CIC and *Salt Lake City*'s Ford Range-keeper, which actually generated fire control solutions, were not directly interconnected.

Unlike Hosogaya, McMorris was acclaimed upon his return from this battle. 'Soc' McMorris was rewarded by being appointed Chief of Staff to Admiral Nimitz, a post he held for the rest of the war.

6

AN UNFAIR FIGHT I
ROYAL NAVY VS KRIEGSMARINE IN THE FAR NORTH
MARCH 1942–DECEMBER 1943

THE SINKING OF *BISMARCK* IN MAY 1941 actually did little to allay British fears for the safety of their Atlantic convoys and the newly assumed responsibility to run supplies to their 'strange bedfellow', Soviet Russia. Following the time-honoured logic that 'the enemy of my enemy is my friend', the Soviets suddenly became an ally of the British on 22 June 1941 when Hitler invaded Russia. Not only an ally, but an ally in desperate need of aid of all kinds lest they collapse and free Hitler to turn his undivided attention on the British Isles. Ignoring the building crisis in the Atlantic, where beleaguered Royal Navy escort groups, with a small, but increasing, amount of aid from the US Navy, were trying to hold off Dönitz' wolfpacks, this chapter looks at the threat to the movement of vital supplies to Russia by sea around Norway's North Cape (Nordkapp) represented by those German surface forces that remained after *Bismarck*'s demise.

The remaining German major surface units were, for various reasons, largely inactive for the rest of 1941. As of the beginning of March 1942, *Tirpitz*, sister-ship to *Bismarck*, and *Scheer* were at Trondheim, where *Hipper* would join them later in the month. *Lützow*, *Prinz Eugen* and *Scharnhorst* were all in various stages of working up in the Baltic and would head for Norway later in the year. Of the major German naval units, only *Gneisenau* was missing from the list. Badly damaged during an RAF raid on Kiel on 26 February 1942, her forecastle was gutted by fire. She was never again operational.

SKL had learned the hard way that the French Atlantic ports, such as Brest and La Pallice, were not practical bases for their capital ships, being within easy reach of RAF bombers based in Britain. In fact, the same was true for the main north Germany ports such as Wilhelmshaven, Bremen or Kiel. To be safe from threat from the air, they had to be moved east to Baltic ports such as Gotenhafen, or north to Norwegian ports such as Trondheim, or even better to Narvik or Alta. There they were, for the moment, beyond the range of RAF bombers, and they were well positioned to threaten the new Russian convoys.

The Dispersal of the Royal Navy

The positioning of even a few capital ships in the far north of Norway was a serious threat to the ability of the Royal Navy to protect the convoys to and from Murmansk. The British fleet was not much bigger or stronger than it had been a year before, and now there was a new enemy in the Japanese. The third of the new *King George V*-class battleships, HMS *Duke of York* (17) had joined the fleet, but *Prince of Wales* had been needlessly lost off Malaya along with *Repulse*, so there were still only two modern battleships with the armour, speed and armament capable of standing up to *Tirpitz*. Besides *King George V* and *Duke of York*, the main units of the Home Fleet, which had responsibility for the containment of any Kriegsmarine units on the Norwegian coast, were, at the beginning of March 1942, the battlecruiser *Renown* and the aircraft carrier *Victorious*. There was a squadron of three heavy cruisers and two squadrons totalling seven light cruisers.[1] Most of the Royal Navy's aircraft carriers were in the Indian Ocean watching the Japanese sweep into the East Indies and South Asia, while the bulk of the cruiser force and the remaining old battleships were in the Mediterranean, trying to keep Malta alive and Rommel out of Egypt.

A Desperate Shot at *Tirpitz*

The first eleven convoys between Iceland and Russia, labeled with the prefix 'PQ', (and the first seven QP convoys returning empty) had been relatively unmolested by the Germans for a variety of reasons, including the long darkness of Arctic winter nights, but with the concentration of German warships at Trondheim, it became obvious to Admiral Tovey that PQ.12/QP.8, which left Reykjavik and the Kola Inlet respectively on 1 March, would not likely be so lucky. Not only would the longer March days make them easier to locate, but the still-extensive pack ice would force them to pass through the relatively narrow waters (215nm wide) between Bear Island (Bjørnøya) and North Cape, which would further limit their ability to avoid detection or interception. Tovey decided, despite the fact that air reconnaissance showed *Tirpitz* and *Scheer* still in port, to support these convoys with a large part of the strength of the Home Fleet. The 2nd Battle Squadron, comprising *Duke of York*, *Renown*, *Kenya* and four destroyers, under the command of Vice-Admiral A T B Curteis, was sent to provide distant cover for the convoys, arriving at Hvalfjordur the afternoon of the 2nd and departing again early the next morning.

Tovey's plan was for the remaining strength of the Home Fleet to stay at Scapa Flow until the Germans actually started moving. The advantage of this plan was that Tovey would be ideally placed to react to any move in strength against the convoys, while also guarding against a possible breakout into the Atlantic. The greatest advantage of remaining in port as long as possible was that, at Scapa, Tovey was connected to GC&CS by telephone, and thus could be apprised instantly of the latest ULTRA decrypts. Once he left port, the stringent rules restricting how and to whom ULTRA-derived information could be disseminated by radio came into play. However, for neither the first nor the last time, First Sea Lord Admiral Sir Dudley Pound intervened.[2]

At 0136 on 3 March, Pound ordered Tovey to join Curteis. *King George V*, along with *Victorious*, *Berwick* and six destroyers, sailed from Scapa Flow at 0730 on 4 March, although *Berwick* and one destroyer were soon detached due to engine trouble. The two halves of the Home Fleet met at 1030 on 6 March, at which time they were less than 100nm south-southeast of the outbound convoy. At almost exactly the same time, *Tirpitz*, flying the flag of Vice-Admiral Otto Ciliax, weighed anchor and started her slow passage from Fættenfjord to the

Norwegian Sea. Four hours later, now accompanied by four destroyers and two torpedo boats, *Tirpitz* turned north-northeast into open water and increased speed. This operation was given the grandiose name Sportpalast (Sports Arena).

Neither admiral had a totally clear tactical picture. A German reconnaissance aircraft had spotted PQ.12 at 1300 the day before, giving Ciliax a reasonably good idea where the convoy would be about midday the next day, when he could expect to reach the latitude of North Cape. He had no idea, however, that the Home Fleet was out in force.[3] Tovey was somewhat better served by his information sources. At 1801, HMSub *Seawolf* (N47) sighted *Tirpitz* soon after she emerged from Frohavet Channel, the outer approach to Trondheim, but was forced to dive and could not report the contact for several hours. Tovey did not receive the news until after midnight, at 0010 on 7 March.

The two convoys and the two squadrons converged throughout the night. At dawn, Tovey had hoped to fly off a search to the east and southeast that would have likely found Ciliax, but heavy icing made *Victorious'* flight deck unusable. *Tirpitz* was unable to launch her reconnaissance aircraft for the same reason. Shortly after 0900, Ciliax detached the three destroyers that remained with *Tirpitz* with orders to sweep to the north-northwest, while he turned more to the northwest. At one point at noon on the 7th, the two convoys and the two squadrons were within 90nm of each other.[4] Ciliax crossed south to north just a few miles behind PQ.12 and ahead of QP.8, but in the prevailing haze was utterly unaware of that fact. His destroyers, making slower progress approximately 30nm to the east, cut the wake of the two convoys after they had passed each other. At 1630, *Hermann Schoemann* (Z7) stumbled upon a straggler from QP.8, the Russian MV *Ijora*, and attempted to sink her with a torpedo.[5] When this failed, *Schoemann* started shelling the small motorship, soon joined by *Friedrich Ihn* (Z14). *Ijora's* distress signal was picked up by Tovey, who had spent the day loitering to the southwest, but contained no decypherable location information. At 1830, the three destroyers rejoined *Tirpitz*, which was 150nm northeast of the Home Fleet and about midway between the two convoys which were steering away to the northeast and west-southwest.

As the day lengthened on 7 March, the destroyers on both sides began running low on fuel, which affected the actions of both admirals. At 1750, Tovey released two destroyers to head for Iceland, leaving him with seven. At 2000, with six more approaching the point when they would have to follow, he decided to send them on a run to the southeast towards the Lofoten Islands, with orders to sweep to the north starting at 0400 the next morning, after which, if they found nothing, they too would head for Iceland. This left his main force, now comprising two battleships, one battlecruiser and one aircraft carrier, covered by one remaining destroyer (HMS *Lookout* (G32)). At 2113 on the 7th, Ciliax sent *Friedrich Ihn* to Harstad, and at 0740 the next morning, after spending the night steaming east at about 72°N, a latitude just north of that of North Cape, released his other two destroyers to head for Tromsø, leaving *Tirpitz* to continue alone.

Tovey steamed south after midnight 7–8 March. Ciliax continued east, turning north at 0700, thus the distance between the forces grew, as both stumbled about, ignorant of each other's location. QP.8 was well to the west by this point and out of danger from *Tirpitz*; PQ.12 was north-northwest of Ciliax and steering north, but turned to the southeast at noon to clear Bear Island, and, encountering pack ice, turned more to the south at 1700. Ciliax turned west-southwest at 1045, which brought him across the convoy's path at around noon, around 80nm to the south. That was as close as *Tirpitz* got to PQ.12; she continued to the west-southwest and the convoy bore away to the southeast, so the distance between them grew from noon onward.

By 0400 on 8 March, Tovey, convinced that Ciliax had abandoned the chase, turned to the southwest, hoping to shorten the distance to Iceland and his refuelled destroyers and, at the same time, remove his ships from waters known to contain U-boats. For much of the day, the two squadrons steamed parallel courses, the British approximately 400nm southwest of the Germans. This continued until 1800, when Tovey received a signal from the Admiralty containing ULTRA intelligence gleaned from a message sent from SKL to Ciliax instructing him to break off his search south of Bear Island and return to Trondheim if the convoy was not sighted before nightfall the next day.[6] With this knowledge in hand, Tovey turned northeast twenty minutes later.

The Germans vacillated, fearing for *Tirpitz*' safety so far from help of any kind. Ciliax turned southeast at 1800 and then at 2130 due south, signalling at 2352 that he was aborting the mission and heading for Trondheim. Again, GC&CS decyphered this message in a timely fashion, and, at 0240 on 9 March, Tovey was informed of *Tirpitz*' new course and destination. Three minutes later he turned to the southeast and increased speed to 26kt with every expectation of being in position to launch an airstrike on the German battleship at dawn.

At 0640, *Victorious* flew off six reconnaissance aircraft with instructions to search out to 150nm, and, without waiting for contact to be made, twelve torpedo-carrying Albacores were launched, starting at 0730.[7] *Tirpitz* was sighted at 0802 and the report received by the strike force, which made contact at 0842. By this time, *Tirpitz* had turned east towards Vestfjord and Narvik, and had increased speed to 29kt. The Albacores, which were now approaching from astern and flying into the wind, had a maximum loaded speed of approximately 135kt; it took them over half an hour after sighting *Tirpitz* to reach an attack position. The attack was from astern and the torpedoes were dropped at too great a distance from their target. Although carried through bravely, it was ultimately futile, as none of the torpedoes hit and two of the attackers were shot down.

This brought to an unsatisfactory end the best chance the Royal Navy ever had of catching *Tirpitz* at sea. In reality, though, it was not all that great an opportunity. Even had one or more torpedoes hit, *Tirpitz* was well inside the protective 'umbrella' of Luftwaffe air control. *Victorious* simply did not carry a sufficient number of sufficiently capable aircraft to protect herself or the remainder of the Home Fleet had they attempted to approach a hobbled *Tirpitz* in Vestfjord. It would, in all likelihood, have not been a repeat of the sinking of *Bismarck*; it is more likely to have resembled the sinking of *Prince of Wales*. In the event, Tovey was spared the difficult decision whether to pursue a damaged *Tirpitz* into coastal waters. At 0940, the Home Fleet turned to the west. At 1545, as if to emphasise the point, three Ju88s bombers attacked the squadron. One put a bomb close astern of *Victorious*.

Nervous Watching

The story of a pair of Arctic convoys and of two fleets stumbling about in poor visibility, as exemplified by PQ.12/QP.8, would become a model for a number of later engagements, almost all of which ended as disappointingly. The story of PQ.12/QP.8 also marked the beginning of a concern over *Tirpitz* on the part of the British which can rightly be described as obsessive. Certainly, the German battleship was individually superior to any single unit the British could put against her, but the Home Fleet always had the advantage of superior numbers to offset the individual quality of German units such as *Tirpitz*, *Scharnhorst* (after March 1943), *Hipper* and the pocket battleships. The Germans had the advantage of 'inner lines' and the strategy of a 'fleet in being', meaning simply that the threat they represented was constant, and the choice of when to act on that threat was entirely theirs. This advantage, however, was significantly offset by British codebreaking and aerial reconnaissance, which often gave the Admiralty significant warning of German movements.

The next attempt by the Germans to use their heavy units to interfere with an Arctic convoy came at the beginning of July, when the biggest of the convoys to date, PQ.17/QP.13, set out from Iceland and Russia, covered by close and distant cover forces including an American battleship – *Washington* (BB56) – and two American heavy cruisers – *Wichita* (CA45) and *Tuscaloosa* (CA37). The Germans took the bait with Operation Rösselsprung (Horse Jump), massing all available forces. *Tirpitz*, *Scheer*, *Hipper*, seven destroyers and two torpedo boats deployed through Altenfjord.[8] They were to have been joined by *Lützow* and three more destroyers, but those ran aground while staging through Narvik. The threat of this force was enough to cause Admiral Pound to order the convoy dispersed – with disastrous results. The German squadron sailed from Altenfjord just before noon on 6 July, but was ordered to break off the operation only a few hours later, before they encountered any Allied surface ships. (The decision to terminate the operation was influenced by the sighting of an RAF Catalina not long after they reached open water.) All the German ships were back at Kaafjord the next morning. In the event, the action of German surface ships proved unnecessary. U-boats and Luftwaffe aircraft had their way with the scattered merchantmen.

Arctic Convoys Resumed

So complete was the destruction of the dispersed PQ.17, that the decision was made to halt the Arctic convoys, at least until the end of summer brought longer nights. In the meanwhile, the British continued their efforts to hobble the German heavy units in Norwegian waters, particularly *Tirpitz*. Launching periodic air raids on the anchorages in southern Norway, particularly Trondheim, had the effect of forcing the Germans to move their base of operations further north, to Narvik, Tromsø and Altenfjord.

When the British next tried moving a pair of Arctic convoys, PQ.18/QP.14, in mid-September, the nights were longer, but apparently still not long enough. The Home Fleet provided its usual three-layer protection – close escort by numerous corvettes, minesweepers, trawlers, a light cruiser, sixteen destroyers and, for the first time, an escort aircraft carrier; middle cover was provided by three heavy cruisers and distant cover by two battleships (*Duke of York* and the newly commissioned HMS *Anson* (79)), the new light cruiser HMS *Jamaica* (44) and four destroyers. The Germans responded by moving *Scheer*, *Hipper*, the light cruiser *Köln* (only recently moved forward to Norway) and two destroyers from Narvik to Altenfjord, but, interestingly, not *Tirpitz*, which remained behind at Narvik. Nothing came of this massing of large ships. Thirteen merchantmen were lost out of PQ.18 and four merchantmen and one destroyer from QP.14; all were lost to aircraft and U-boat attacks.

Bloody Bumbling in the Barents Sea

Except for one home-bound convoy run in late November, there would be no more Arctic convoys again until mid-December, with the running of JW.51A and B from Loch Ewe, Scotland, and RA.51, which left the Kola Inlet on 30 December. Besides having a new numbering sequence with new letter designators, these convoys had several advantages not shared by the last PQ/QP convoys. The onset of winter brought long Arctic nights; just as importantly, the Allied invasion of western North Africa siphoned away most of the Luftwaffe units previously based in northern Norway. Additionally, the accelerated programmes of escort production in both the US and Great Britain were starting to bear fruit, with each of these convoys having more escorts than cargo ships. Despite all this and the presence of the usual Home Fleet middle and distant cover forces, the Germans rose to the challenge.

The Germans had been moving ships around in the last months of 1942. *Scheer* returned to Germany for a refit; she would not return to Norwegian waters. *Tirpitz* was moved to Trondheim for an extended refit. The light cruiser *Nürnberg* and *Lützow* moved to northern Norway, joining *Hipper* and *Köln*, to compensate for the loss of those two major units. The Royal Navy was concerned that *Lützow* might make a break for the open ocean where, because of her power and endurance, she might do great harm (although that would be much more difficult without the network of supply ships that had supported *Scheer's* long raid over a year earlier). To protect against this eventuality, the Home Fleet re-instituted cruiser patrols in the Denmark Strait and moved *Anson* to Hvalfjordur, where she might better cover the passages out of the Norwegian Sea. In fact, the Germans were seriously considering such a move for *Lützow*, but only after she took care of other business.[9]

JW.51A left Loch Ewe on 15 December with fifteen merchantmen, a fleet oiler and a massive close escort (seven destroyers and five other escorts). Two light cruisers and two destroyers under Rear-Admiral Robert L Burnett provided more distant cover, following the convoy all the way through to Murmansk. Between the length of the winter nights and the reduced German aerial reconnaissance, this convoy slipped through unmolested. The second half of the convoy left Scotland a week later and had a harder time.

JW.51B comprised fourteen ships, with a close escort of three *Hunt*-class escort destroyers and six smaller escorts. The *Hunts* were replaced in the close escort on Christmas Day by six destroyers of Captain R St V Sherbrooke's

17th Destroyer Flotilla. Burnett (Force 'R') sailed from the Kola Inlet on 27 December, with *Jamaica*, *Sheffield* and two destroyers, intending to steam west past North Cape, and past the convoy, to a point roughly northwest of Tromsø on the morning of the 29th. Fuel considerations would require his destroyers to be detached at that time; the two light cruisers would then turn back to the east and sweep along the southern flank of the convoy until late on the 30th, at which point Burnett would turn again, this time to the northwest and cross the wake of the convoy, before turning yet again and trailing it into Murmansk. Distant cover was provided by Admiral Sir Bruce Fraser, second-in-command to Tovey, coming out from Iceland in *Anson*, along with *Cumberland* and five destroyers.

As is almost always the case with complex naval operations that depend on forces from widely separated starting points, co-ordinating movements with little or no inter-communication, especially in the Arctic in winter, meant that the timing of the various forces soon became confused. The convoy ran into a severe gale seven days out from Scotland that slowed its progress and caused two escorts and five merchantmen to become detached. The minesweeper HMS *Bramble* (M11) was dispatched to round up the stragglers. When Force 'R' arrived at its first turning point on 29 December, it was much closer to the convoy than planned. It was barely 30nm away, but the prevailing poor visibility prevented contact from being made, and Burnett rapidly pulled ahead of JW.51B, to the extent that by noon the next day, Force 'R' led the convoy by almost 150nm. Fraser and the distant cover force had turned back the day before and played no part in subsequent events.

This situation was about to go from confusing to dangerous very quickly. The British knew that *Lützow* and *Hipper* had moved forward from Narvik to Altenfjord on 19 December and that, as of 0045 on 30 December, they were still at anchor.[10] Burnett also knew that the Germans were aware that he was at sea, but not of his exact position. However, in one of the sadder coincidences of the war, the next day, 31 December 1942, proved to be one of those rare days at the end of 1942 when no ULTRA decrypts were obtained.[11] Thus, Burnett was not informed that *U354* (Herbschleb) had sighted the convoy south of Bear Island around noon on 30 December, nor was he told that *Hipper*, flying the flag of Vice-Admiral Oskar Kummetz, *Lützow* and six destroyers had debouched from Altenfjord at 2145 that day and swung around to the northeast. (This operation, as seemingly were all German movements aimed at the enemy, was given a grandiose title – Operation Regenbogen (Rainbow).) Kummetz, as usual, was strictly limited in how and when he could attack the convoy. He was prohibited from attacking at night and from engaging any force of equal or superior strength. The importance of emerging from the convoy battle unscathed was stressed all the more because *Lützow* was supposed to follow the convoy attack by an immediate raid into the Arctic Ocean.[12]

To further confuse the picture, Kummetz devised a complex scheme of his own. Fearing the convoy might be scattered over a large area and hoping to better his chances of finding targets, at 0240 on 31 December, he split his force. *Lützow* continued to the northeast with three destroyers while he took a more northerly course with the other three destroyers. Then, when they reached the expected latitude of the convoy, *Lützow* would turn north and *Hipper* east, and the two German forces would, if all went as hoped, trap the convoy between them.

The Germans, it turned out, because of *U354*'s sighting, had a far better idea of the convoy's position than did Burnett. Believing he was just south of the convoy, Force 'R' turned to the northwest at 1800 on 30 December with the intent of cutting the convoy's wake. On the assumption that, if a German force was chasing JW.51B, it would be approaching from astern, this move would put Burnett between the enemy and the convoy at first light the next morning, the time he deemed it most likely they would attack. Burnett's assumptions were uncannily correct, given that he had no direct knowledge if or when Kummetz had sailed. What he did not know was that his estimation of the convoy's position was off by more than 150nm, so that, in the dark soon after midnight, he crossed well ahead of the convoy, rather than behind it, and, at 0830 on 31 December, he was approximately 30nm due north of JW.51B.

The situation at that hour could hardly have been more confusing, with no group knowing exactly the position of any of the others. The largest group was the convoy itself, now comprising twelve merchantmen and eight escorts, heading east approximately 130nm north-northeast of North Cape. The smaller escorts were close in to the convoy, while Sherbrooke's destroyers, now five in number, ranged around more loosely.[13] The trawler *Vizalma* (FY296) with one straggler was 45nm to the north. The minesweeper *Bramble*, still looking for additional stragglers, was on her own 15nm northeast of the convoy. Finally, Burnett's cruisers, unaware

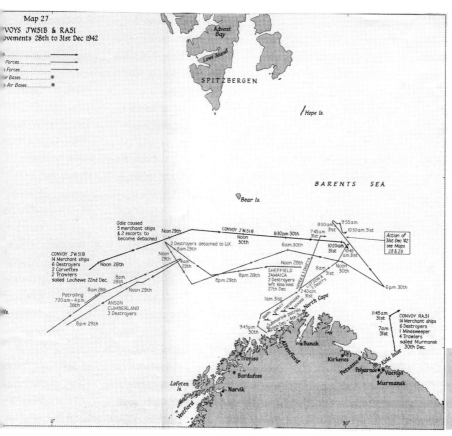

112. This chart shows the tracks of the forces that converged on convoy JW.51B on the last day of 1942.

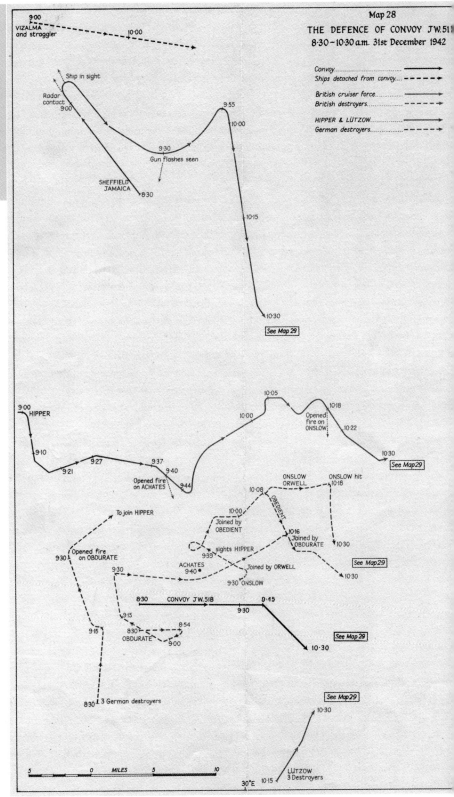

113 and 114. This pair of detailed charts shows the various forces as they chased each other around in the haze of the brief Arctic day in the Barents Sea on 31 December 1942. Each time cruisers of one side or the other stumbled upon smaller ships of the other side, the smaller ships invariably paid dearly.

Map 28
THE DEFENCE OF CONVOY JW.51
8·30 – 10·30 a.m. 31st December 1942

Convoy ....
Ships detached from convoy ....
British cruiser force ....
British destroyers ....
HIPPER & LÜTZOW ....
German destroyers ....

9·00
VIZALMA
and straggler
10·00

Ship in sight

Radar contact
9·00

9·55
10·00

9·30
Gun flashes seen

SHEFFIELD
JAMAICA
8·30

10·15

10·30
See Map 29

9·00 HIPPER
10·05
10·00
10·18
Opened fire on ONSLOW
10·22
10·30
See Map29

9·10
9·27
9·37
9·40
9·21
9·44
Opened fire on ACHATES

ONSLOW
ORWELL
ONSLOW hit
10·18

To join HIPPER
10·08
OBEDIENT
10·00
Joined by
OBEDIENT
10·16
Joined by
OBEDURATE
10·30

9·30 Opened fire on OBDURATE
9·30
sights HIPPER
9·39
ACHATES
9·40
Joined by ORWELL
9·30 ONSLOW
10·30
See Map 29

8·30
CONVOY JW.51B
9·15
9·30
10·30
See Map 29

9·15
9·15
8·30
OBDURATE
8·54
9·00

8·30 3 German destroyers

See Map29
10·30

5   0   MILES   5   10

30°E   10·15
LÜTZOW
3 Destroyers

BIG GUN BATTLES

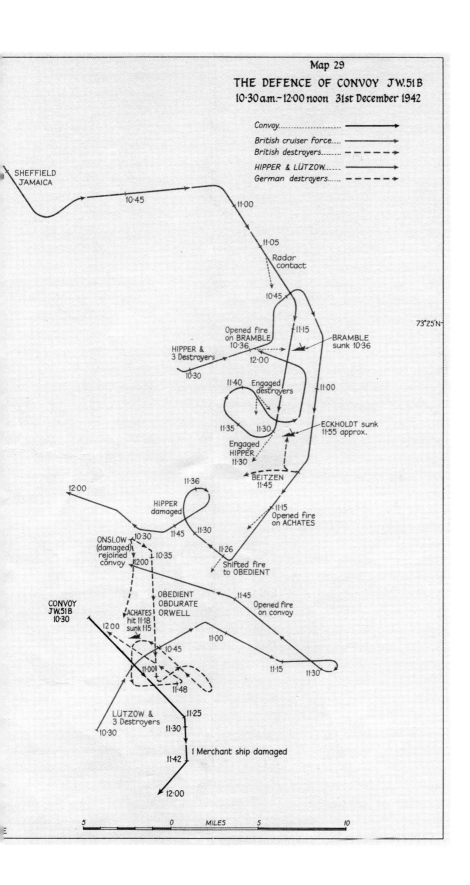

Map 29

THE DEFENCE OF CONVOY JW.51B
10·30 a.m.–12·00 noon 31st December 1942

Convoy ....
British cruiser force ......
British destroyers ....
HIPPER & LÜTZOW ......
German destroyers ......

SHEFFIELD
JAMAICA

10·45

11·00

11·05

Radar
contact

10·45

11·15

73°25′N

Opened fire
on BRAMBLE
10·36

BRAMBLE
sunk 10·36

HIPPER &
3 Destroyers

12·00

10·30

11·40 Engaged
destroyers

11·00

11·35   11·30

ECKHOLDT sunk
11·55 approx.

Engaged
HIPPER
11·30

BEITZEN
11·45

11·36

HIPPER
damaged

11·45   11·30

11·15
Opened fire
on ACHATES

12·00

ONSLOW
(damaged)
rejoined
convoy

10·30

10·35

11·26

12·00

Shifted fire
to OBEDIENT

OBEDIENT
OBDURATE
ORWELL

11·45
Opened fire
on convoy

CONVOY
JW.51B
10·30

ACHATES
hit 11·18
sunk 1·15

12·00

11·00

10·45

11·00

11·48

11·15   11·30

LÜTZOW &
3 Destroyers

10·30

11·25

11·30

1 Merchant ship damaged

11·42

12·00

5   0   MILES   5   10

of the presence of any of these ships around them, were steaming northwest approximately 30nm north of the convoy and 15nm southeast of *Vizalma*.

At 0718, a lookout in *Hipper* spotted shadows on the northern horizon and, while the heavy cruiser hung back, Kummetz sent his three destroyers on a loop to the east and then north to investigate the contact. He was in no rush at this point; dawn, what there was of it, was still an hour off. So it was that *Friedrich Eckoldt*, leading *Richard Beitzen* and *Z29*, came up upon the southern inner screen of the convoy just before 0820 and were sighted by the corvette *Hyderabad* (K212). This ship, expecting the arrival of Soviet reinforcements, failed to report the contact. It was only when one of Sherbrooke's destroyers, *Obdurate* (G39), sighted the German destroyers crossing the convoy's wake ten minutes later, that the alarm was raised.

Sherbrooke, to his credit, never hesitated. He ordered *Obdurate* to investigate and 'sent his own ship's company to breakfast and ordered them to change into clean underclothing'.[14] That bizarre order was a hangover from earlier days of the Royal Navy, when crew sanitation was marginal, and it was considered beneficial to order the crew into clean undergarments before battle. As Roskill so elegantly put it: 'It must have been one of the few occasions when that traditional order before battle was actually given during the last war.'

The visibility that day was so bad that, although *Obdurate* made best speed in pursuit of the unidentified intruders and cut corners as she too crossed the wake of the convoy heading north, it was not until 0930, when she was within 4nm of the German destroyers, that she was able to make a positive identification, and that only because they opened fire. Sherbrooke in *Onslow* (G17) immediately turned to support and ordered *Obdurate*, *Orwell* (G98) and *Obedient* (G25), the last two from ahead of the convoy, to join him on the northern flank of the convoy. Lieutenant Commander C E L Sclater, in command of *Obdurate*, up against three enemy destroyers, needed no persuading. He turned back east towards Sherbrooke and the convoy; the German destroyers did not follow him. This left only the destroyer *Achates* (H12) and three smaller ships to provide close escort for the convoy.

At 0939, *Onslow*, joined by *Orwell*, was heading northwest when *Hipper* emerged from the mist barely 14,000yd dead ahead and opened fire. Her target was not Sherbrooke's ships; Kummetz had his sights on *Achates*, which was making smoke on the convoy's port quarter, perhaps 4,000yd southwest of *Onslow*. *Hipper* snapped off several salvos, achieving several near-misses for damage that started some hull plates and reduced her speed, before *Achates* was able to turn back into her own smoke screen. To take the pressure off *Achates*, Sherbrooke led *Orwell* towards *Hipper*, feinting a torpedo attack. Kummetz reacted as expected, turning away to the northeast and changing target to *Onslow* and *Orwell*, soon joined by *Obedient*. Afraid that the German destroyers might be working around behind him, Sherbrooke detached *Obedient* at approximately 1000 to join *Obdurate* to the southeast, to provide closer cover for the convoy, which had turned to the southeast at 0945.

Sherbrooke broadcast a general alarm at 0941 announcing *Hipper*'s presence, which was picked up by *Sheffield*. Burnett, stubbornly clinging to the belief that he was south of the convoy, despite having seen gunfire further south at 0930, continued searching to the northeast for another fourteen minutes before finally accepting that the only ships north of him were *Vizalma* and her straggler and he turned south-southeast at 0955.

After trading inaccurate salvos in the diminishing visibility, Kummetz and Sherbrooke, steaming parallel courses towards the northeast and then, after approximately 1005, towards the east, both ceased fire for nearly fifteen minutes until, at 1016, the mist parted and *Hipper* was able to obtain a clear fix on *Onslow*. Opening fire, she rapidly straddled the destroyer, seriously wounding and temporarily blinding Sherbrooke with a shell splinter. The next few salvos registered hits that toppled *Onslow*'s funnel and started fires in the handling room under 'B' turret and further forward. She rapidly turned away; covered by smoke from these fires and a smokescreen from *Orwell*, *Onslow* retired towards the convoy. Sherbrooke ordered Lieutenant Commander D C Kinloch in *Obedient* to take command of the flotilla.

The situation at 1030 looked favourable for the Germans. Kummetz had damaged two of Sherbrooke's destroyers and knew that the convoy was to his south whence *Lützow* was approaching. In fact, at 1030, *Lützow*, commanded by Captain Rudolf Stange, was just five miles due south of the convoy and headed on a course to intercept in just a few minutes, but in the prevailing poor visibility, neither had yet seen the other. Burnett was heading southeast and was, at 1030, approximately 15nm northwest of *Hipper*, but he was so uncertain of the situation he was facing that a few minutes later he turned east, in the apparent hope that delaying his approach would bring the clarity he lacked. Even when gunfire erupted again on his starboard bow, he did not turn to investigate.

The gunfire was occasioned by the sudden appearance out of the haze of the minesweeper *Bramble* just after 1030, barely 5,000yd dead ahead of *Hipper*. The cruiser's overwhelming gunfire rapidly reduced *Bramble* to a wreck, but the minesweeper stubbornly refused to sink and inadvertently played a crucial role in protecting the convoy. Rather than just leave *Bramble* to expire on her own, *Hipper* slowed and circled north around the wreck, continuing to pump 20.3cm and 10.5cm rounds into the burning hulk for nearly half an hour, before Kummetz finally decided that he had wasted too much time and ordnance on this small target. At 1106 he ordered full speed and a course of south-southwest, hoping to find the convoy.[15] Even then, he could not leave *Bramble* well enough alone. He ordered two of his destroyers, *Beitzen* and *Eckoldt*, to remain behind and finish her off.

In the meanwhile, *Lützow* finally, belatedly, made her presence known. Coming up from the south at a time when all eyes and almost every gun were pointing north, she should have been able to wreak havoc on an essentially defenceless convoy. Once again the corvette *Hyderabad* was the first to sight the enemy and once again she failed to make a report, allowing *Lützow* to approach within 6,000yd before she was spotted and reported by the corvette *Rhododendron* (K78) at 1045. But, instead of bearing in, Stange turned to the northeast and passed ahead of the convoy, blaming an intervening snow squall which reduced his

115. One of those ships that paid a heavy price was HMS *Bramble* (M11), a minesweeper detached from the escort of JW.51B to round up stragglers. She had the misfortune to stumble on *Hipper* in the haze and was rapidly reduced to a burning wreck, but she refused to sink quickly and led indirectly to the sinking of a German destroyer by HMS *Sheffield* (24). (*via David Doyle*)

visibility and confused his radar picture. Even though he was plainly visible for several minutes from the injured *Onslow*, Stange did not open fire.

Lützow reappeared on the other side of the snow squall soon after 1100 steaming southeast, roughly paralleling the convoy about 14,000yd to the northwest, with Kinloch's line of three destroyers in between. Inexplicably, Stange still did not fire and, at 1130, reversed course to the northwest. Meanwhile, at 1115, *Hipper*, bearing down from the northeast, caught sight of *Achates* just clearing her own smoke screen on the convoy's port quarter, and, unlike her companion, did not hesitate. Her first salvo hit the destroyer's bridge, killing her captain and destroying her boiler room and forecastle. On fire and losing way, *Achates* dropped behind, wreathed in smoke. *Hipper* immediately switched target to *Obedient*; several salvos straddled the destroyer, knocking out her radios, forcing Kinloch to pass command of the flotilla to *Obdurate* and Lieutenant Commander Sclater. It was only yet another feigned torpedo attack by *Obdurate* leading *Orwell* and *Obedient* that forced *Hipper* to loop away at approximately 1130 and brought this burst of accurate gunfire to a close.

Now, finally, as *Hipper* was swinging to the northeast, Burnett's cruisers arrived on the scene. At a range of approximately 14,000yd, the British cruisers sighted *Hipper*, turned to parallel her course and opened fire. With far more sophisticated fire control radar, specifically the Type 284 sets carried by both cruisers, and with a total broadside of twenty-four 6in/50 main-battery guns, they very rapidly made their presence known to the German. *Hipper* was turning to starboard at high speed when she was hit in way of her No.3 boiler room. (The shell hit her hull below the waterline because she was heeled over due to her high-speed turn.) The damage from the shell exploding and the subsequent flooding when she settled on a northwesterly course briefly reduced her speed to 15kt. She was hit twice more in rapid succession, once by a shell that passed through her hull amidships without exploding and again by a shell that started a fire in her aircraft hangar. At exactly this moment, Kummetz received a message from his coastal commander reminding him to avoid unnecessary risks, but he certainly needed no persuading to duck into a fortuitous snow squall and attempt an escape.

At almost this same moment, at 1138, Stange, in *Lützow*, was granted so clear a view of the convoy that even he could not pass it up. Opening fire at 16,000yd to the southwest, he was able to damage the steamer *Calobre*, but do little other damage before Sclater intervened with his three destroyers. At approximately 1200, *Lützow* loosed a few salvos in the direction of *Obdurate* and managed to inflict significant splinter damage. At 1203, Stange received Kummetz' order to withdraw to the west; that brought Stange's participation in this engagement to an end, an action he clearly had little heart for from the beginning.

One more bloody encounter remained before this long and confused Battle of the Barents Sea would come to an end. Even as Burnett's cruisers lost sight of *Hipper*, at approximately 1143, the destroyers *Beitzen* and *Eckoldt*, having finished off *Bramble*, emerged from the mist 4,000yd to the south. *Sheffield* hit *Eckoldt* with her first salvo and disabled her with her third. After her sixteenth, it was obvious the destroyer was sinking and *Sheffield* ceased firing her main battery, though the wreck was raked with secondary battery and anti-aircraft gun fire as the cruiser passed the now-drifting hulk. *Beitzen* reacted quickly and turned away to the west, undamaged, disappearing again into the mist. *Jamaica* fired a few rounds at the fleeing destroyer, but obtained no hits. By the time Burnett's cruisers looped left and returned to the pursuit of *Hipper*, the latter was 27,000yd to the southwest and had regained most of her speed.

Briefly, at 1230, Burnett's cruisers caught sight of *Lützow* and the three ships exchanged reasonably accurate fire that achieved several straddles, but the light was rapidly fading and neither side had the desire for night engagement in Arctic waters, so the two sides separated by mutual consent around 1400. The last fight of the day was lost as, at 1315, *Achates*, which had seemed to be in stable condition, capsized and sank with little warning. Of the three ships lost this day, she was the only one with survivors. Eighty-one of her ship's company of 194 were rescued, although one additional man died later. *Bramble* sank with her entire complement of 121 men, as did *Eckoldt* with her entire crew of 340. Seventeen men were killed in *Onslow*.

The shooting this day was often very good, with short ranges and radar assistance to gunnery, particularly on the British side. Typical of German shooting, always good when their excellent optics and mechanical controls could be brought to bear, was *Hipper*'s engagement with *Onslow*, in which she expended forty-eight 20.3cm and 72 10.5cm rounds to obtain three hits, for a hit percentage of 2.5 per cent.

Hipper had sustained sufficient damage that she could not be repaired in Norway. She was patched up at Alta, but then transferred by stages to Wilhelmshaven, where she was docked in February. This was not safe from RAF raids and, as soon as possible, she was towed to Pillau (Baltiysk, Russia) where repairs were to be completed. She would never again be fully operational. *Lützow* remained in northern Norway until September when she too transferred to the Baltic.

The Battle of the Barents Sea was disastrous from the point of view of the German surface fleet. Hitler was furious at the lost opportunity — he had been

116. Heavily damaged at the Battle of the Barents Sea, 31 December 1942, HMS *Onslow* (G17) is seen here in the foreground with a larger *Tribal*-class destroyer in the background. Royal Navy destroyers were often smaller, less well-armed and shorter-legged than their contemporaries in other navies, but their ability to handle the rough seas common in northern waters was without equal. (*NHHC*)

promised a great victory — and, in one of his classic rages, he sacked Raeder, replacing him with his U-boat commander Admiral Karl Dönitz, whom he assumed would be more compliant. Hitler ordered that all warships larger than destroyers were to be scrapped. Curiously, neither Kummetz or Stange was penalised for their behaviour that day; both received promotions and responsible commands right up to the end of the war.

Another part of the reason for Hitler's rage was that the British press, with the full support of the Admiralty, portrayed the battle as a great victory for the Royal Navy. Sherbrooke received the Victoria Cross and Burnett, despite behaviour that can be most charitably described as extremely cautious, was awarded the DSO, as were the captains of the participating cruisers and destroyers.[16]

The Royal Navy's Continuing Obsession with *Tirpitz*

Admiral Dönitz quite unexpectedly proved to be a persuasive defender of the Kriegsmarine's surface fleet and not only convinced Hitler to rescind his scrapping order, but managed to convince him to allow *Scharnhorst* to be moved to northern Norway in March 1943 to join *Tirpitz*. Together at Altenfjord, the two remaining German capital ships proved to be a great distraction for the Admiralty, but, in fact, they were almost entirely inactive for almost all of 1943. The only time the two sortied together was Operation Sizilien (Sicily) in September 1943.[17] In fact, the entire Arctic theatre had been relatively quiet since March, when the regular running of convoys to north Russia was halted due to the almost perpetual daylight along the route and the desperate need for all available escorts in the North Atlantic as the 'crisis' in the U-boat campaign escalated.

With no convoys to contest, attention in the far north turned to the Svalbard Archipelago and, in particular, to the island of Spitsbergen. It was nominally German territory since Germany had conquered Norway, which held legal sovereignty of the islands. With the German invasion of Russia in June 1941 and the planned running of regular supply convoys through the Barents Sea, the Admiralty became concerned that the Germans might have garrisoned Spitsbergen in some force and might have been using it, at a minimum, as a weather station. A Royal Navy squadron reconnoitred the islands in July 1941 and found some Russian coal miners, a few Norwegian fishermen and no Germans at all. These were evacuated in August and, at the same time, demolitions rendered the settlements and mines unusable to the Germans without considerable effort. The Germans finally got around to establishing a small weather station of their own well up the western coast of Spitsbergen in late 1941, a considerable distance from the Isfjorden where mines and fishing villages were located. A small squadron of Norwegian soldiers arrived in the spring of 1942 at Isfjorden, apparently unaware of the German weather station further north, and was periodically resupplied by Royal Navy missions, all called some variant of Operation Gearbox. The German weather station was evacuated in August 1942 for reasons unrelated to establishment of the Norwegian garrison a few months earlier. That is how the matter rested until September 1943.

For reasons that, as much as anything, reflected Dönitz' need to demonstrate his warships' ability to do something useful, *Tirpitz*, *Scharnhorst* and nine destroyers departed Altenfjord late on 6 September, the most powerful German squadron to put to sea in at least a year and a half. The destroyers were carrying a battalion of grenadiers, strong enough to easily overwhelm the tiny Norwegian garrison at Barentsburg, but the aim never was to re-establish a permanent German presence on Spitsbergen.[18] The squadron arrived on 8 September, landed their troops, causing most of the Norwegian garrison to surrender (although some did escape into the surrounding wilderness), destroyed all the garrison's facilities and equipment, and then withdrew. The squadron arrived back at Alta the next evening. It would be the only occasion on which *Tirpitz* fired her guns in anger.

The Royal Navy, in its obsession with *Tirpitz*, had been planning a truly daring (which can be read as 'dangerous' or perhaps 'desperate') attempt to disable the battleship. The plan, called Operation Source, called for the use of 'X'-craft, four-man midget submarines, to penetrate Altenfjord and plant large mines under *Tirpitz*.[19] Set to begin any time after 6 September, a photo reconnaissance flight over Alta the next day revealed the absence of the German squadron and gave the British their first inkling that Sizilien was underway. The submarine HMSub *Tantalus* (P98) was dispatched to check into Isfjorden late on the 8th, arriving after the German squadron had already departed, but able to pass the first word to the Admiralty of the destruction of Barentsburg. When the next reconnaissance on 10 September showed the German ships back at Altenfjord, Source was initiated. Six 'X'-craft departed Loch Cairnbawn on 11 September; only two reached a position where they were able to place charges near *Tirpitz* on 22 September. The damage done by the mines was sufficient to put the battleship out of action for six months. The operation cost the Royal Navy nine men dead and six more captured. A small Allied squadron with the heavy cruiser *Tuscaloosa* and one American and three British destroyers arrived at Barentsburg on 19 October with fresh Norwegian troops and construction materials to re-establish the garrison there. This is believed to be the farthest north any major American warship ventured during the war.

A Final Tragedy off North Cape

There was to be one final operation in the north by a German capital ship, which would give the heavy units of the Royal Navy one final chance to prove their worth against their intended foe. By the end of the year, the only remaining major operational unit of the Kriegsmarine outside the Baltic was *Scharnhorst*. The Arctic convoys were restarted at the beginning of November, and Admiral Fraser, who took over the Home Fleet in May, fully expected fierce German opposition, including the commitment of *Scharnhorst*. After the first convoys of the new series slipped through undetected in foggy weather, the next eastbound convoy, JW.55A, was detected by Luftwaffe aircraft and Fraser ordered full support, in the form of *Duke of York*, *Jamaica* and four destroyers to follow the convoy all the way through to the Kola Inlet, where they arrived on 16 December. This was actually six days ahead of the convoy; because *Scharnhorst* had not risen to this bait, Fraser wanted to return to Iceland as rapidly as possible to refuel and be ready to support the second half of the convoy, which was due to depart Loch Ewe on 20 December.

Even for Dönitz, much more in Hitler's favour than Raeder had ever been, obtaining permission for *Scharnhorst* to move against a convoy was a struggle. At a conference held on 19–20 December, it was agreed 'that the *Scharnhorst* and destroyers of the task force will attack the next Allied convoy headed from England for Russia via the northern route, if a successful operation can be assured.'[20] No doubt Dönitz gave Hitler all the necessary assurances.

The pace of events noticeably quickened the next day. JW.55B had sailed on schedule, with nineteen merchantmen and a close escort of ten destroyers and at least three smaller escorts, and was sighted by a Luftwaffe weather flight the next day.[21] Fraser was informed of this sighting soon after midnight on 23 December and he met with the captains of his squadron, now called Force '2', on his flagship at 1800. The instructions he gave them anticipated a night surface action against *Scharnhorst*. He explained that he wanted his destroyers – HMS *Savage* (G20), *Saumarez* (G12), *Scorpion* (G64) and HNoMS *Stord* (G26) – to form into two-ship sub-divisions and to find attack positions relative to *Scharnhorst*, but to refrain from attacking until *Duke of York* and *Jamaica* had reduced the enemy's firepower. At 2300, *Duke of York* led Force '2' out of Akureyri on the north coast of Iceland.

As the shortness of the days at this latitude and time of year made the odds of encountering *Scharnhorst* in darkness very great, Fraser decided to practise his battle tactics as Force '2' made its way to the northeast at 15kt. *Jamaica* was detached with two destroyers and instructions to swing ahead and approach the battleship from various angles. *Duke of York*'s Type 273Q surface search radar was able to detect the cruiser easily at well beyond visual range and her Type 284M gunnery radar had no trouble distinguishing *Jamaica* from her accompanying destroyers.[22] Meanwhile, other forces had been moving towards a meeting off North Cape, after which the coming engagement would be named. On 22 December, Force '1', comprising HMS *Belfast* (35), *Norfolk* and *Sheffield*,

under Vice-Admiral Burnett, departed Kola Inlet as part of the distant cover for westbound convoy RA.55A.

Although there was no sign of *Scharnhorst* moving on the 23rd, Fraser was concerned about his late start from Iceland and the shrinking distance between JW.55B and Altenfjord. Therefore, at 1400, Fraser took a step his predecessor had always resisted, often to the detriment of British fortunes: he broke radio silence with a request that JW.55B reverse course to the west for three hours. He also took the equally daring step of increasing Force '2's speed to 19kt. The original, slower speed had been maintained in order to allow his short-legged destroyers maximum endurance at the anticipated interception point south of Bear Island. Increasing speed meant his big ships would be nearer the convoy sooner, but at a heavy cost in terms of the reduced time his destroyers could remain 'on station'.

As expected, the Germans intercepted and fixed the origin of Fraser's transmissions. The local area commander, Rear-Admiral Otto Klüber, correctly deduced that the transmission had come from a major force supporting the convoy and signalled to Captain Erich Bey his assessment that the necessary preconditions for a successful interception of the convoy were not present. SKL, however, reached an entirely different conclusion, declaring that the message had come from a straggler from the convoy and that it represented no threat to the planned sortie, now dubbed Operation Ostfront (Eastern Front). (Bey, who would be promoted to rear-admiral the next day, should not have been the man commanding Ostfront. He was the commander of destroyers for the Kriegsmarine and was at Alta in command of the five destroyers of the 4.Zerstörerflottille – Z29, Z30, Z33, Z34 and Z38. As the next most senior officer present, he was acting as the temporary replacement for the regular squadron commander, Admiral Kummetz, who was on leave. Bey and his staff had accommodations in *Tirpitz*.)

Shortly after midnight on Christmas Day, still concerned about the exposure of JW.55B, Fraser again broke radio silence and requested that RA.55A, which had not been sighted by the Germans, divert to the north after clearing Bear Island, which would happen that morning, and, in the meanwhile, detach four destroyers to supplement eastbound convoy's escort.[23] The four destroyers of the 36th Division – HMS *Musketeer* (G86), *Matchless* (G52), *Opportune* (G80) and *Virago* (R75) – reached JW.55B shortly after noon that day in what had now grown into a Force 8 gale out of the southwest.[24] The storm was sufficient to affect Force '2's progress that day and the following night:

> 5. During the night of 25/26th December, the Battlefleet steamed eastward at 17 knots. There was an unpleasant sea and conditions on DUKE OF YORK were most uncomfortable, few people obtaining any sleep.
>
> . . .
>
> 21. On the course and speed of Force 2 and in the following sea my destroyers had much difficulty in avoiding broaching to and the DUKE OF YORK'S bows were constantly under water.[25]

Finally, at 1427 on 25 December, Bey received the order to initiate Ostfront at 1600. As this required him to move himself and his staff over from *Tirpitz*, Bey was not underway in *Scharnhorst* until 1855. As he moved up the winding passage from Langfjord through Altenfjord and Sørøysund into the Norwegian Sea, he collected the five destroyers of the 4th Flotilla. On reaching open water, he set a course of due north at 25kt, a speed the destroyers could maintain only with the greatest difficulty. In the midst of all this, at 2025 he received the following message from Dönitz, intended to be broadcast to his crews:

> 1. Enemy attempting to frustrate the heroic struggle of our Eastern Armies by sending valuable convoy of supplies to the Russians.
>
> 2. SCHARNHORST and destroyers will attack convoy.
>
> 3. Tactical situation must be used skilfully and boldly. Engagement not to be broken off with only partial success achieved. Every advantage must be exploited. Best chance lies in SCHARNHORST's superior fire-power. Therefore endeavor to deploy her. Destroyers to operate as seems suitable.
>
> 4. Disengage at your discretion but without question if heavy forces encountered.
>
> 5. Inform crew accordingly. I rely on your offensive spirit.[26]

It would be difficult to imagine a less rousing, more confusing message to send to men about to fight for their lives in some of the worst weather on the face of the earth. Dönitz seems mainly concerned with covering himself in case the operation went sour, which, given recent history, was a very real possibility.

This message failed to address Bey's most immediate concern, which was the weather, and at 2116 he signalled Klüber his worry that in the present conditions the destroyers would unable to manoeuvre, much less fight. Already overruled by Berlin, Klüber immediately pushed the decision 'upstairs' to Dönitz, who replied immediately that Bey was to continue with the operation, but, at his discretion, he could order the destroyers back to base and continue with *Scharnhorst* alone.[27]

It would have required a stronger man than Bey to act decisively under these circumstances. He knew the convoy's approximate position and knew he was on course to intercept it just before the onset of the weak Arctic daylight, which would begin at approximately 0830 and last until about 1520. The various reports he had been receiving from the aircraft and U-boats shadowing the convoy led him to believe that it was escorted by three cruisers, five destroyers and four smaller escorts.[28] In fact this overstated the escort close to the convoy; at 0400, JW.55B's immediate escort was fourteen destroyers and three smaller craft. Force '1' with three cruisers was about 160nm east of the convoy and closing at 18kt; Force '2' was 230nm to the southwest and had just increased speed to 24kt.

Thus, despite Fraser's best efforts, his heavy squadron was out of position to intervene in the expected interception of the convoy by *Scharnhorst*. It would be late afternoon at the earliest before *Duke of York* could reach the convoy, which was making an effective 6kt into the weather, steering 070°. At 0401, he again broke radio silence to order the convoy to turn to the north and for Burnett and Captain J A McCoy in *Onslow* to radio their positions, courses and speeds. It took over two hours for Force '1' and the convoy to receive and comply with this request and for the responses to be plotted in the flagship, but once Fraser had a complete picture of the disposition of his own forces, he broke silence a third time to send out updated orders at 0628. The convoy was ordered back onto a northeasterly course to bring it closer to Force '1' and Burnett was ordered to make for the convoy at best speed.[29]

At 0730, having reached almost 74°N, north of the expected latitude of the convoy, Bey turned his force to the southwest, ordering his destroyers to form a sweep in line abreast ten miles ahead of *Scharnhorst*. This put him on a reciprocal course northeast of the convoy by approximately 50nm and slowly closing. If nothing disturbed the movements of either the convoy or Bey's force, they would pass each other, the closest approach being at approximately 0900, when the westernmost of the German destroyers would be about 15nm east of the convoy, well beyond visual range. *Scharnhorst* had a recently upgraded FuMO 26 radar mounted on her foremast which could have easily detected the convoy at that range, but it was standard German practice to turn on radars only when a target was known to be within range, and Bey was one to follow standard procedures. *Scharnhorst* did have radar detectors, particularly her FuMB 7 Naxos, and, at approximately 0800, this gave Bey his first definite warning of the approach of Force '1'.[30] (It is unlikely that *Scharnhorst*'s radar detector gave Bey any useful indication of Force '1's direction or proximity. His actions over the next few hours were certainly those of a man unsure of his enemies' location.)

Bey turned *Scharnhorst* to the northeast at 0820 upon hearing word of a contact by *U716* (Dunkelberg); Captain Rolf Johannesson, commanding the

German destroyers, failed to notice the turn and 4th Flotilla steamed away to the southwest, playing no further role in the ensuing engagement. About ten minutes later, *Scharnhorst* reversed course to the south-southwest. At 0840, at a range of 35,000yd, *Belfast*'s radar registered a large echo at a bearing of 295°, which was correctly identified as being the enemy battlecruiser, but nothing in *Scharnhorst*'s sensors would have informed Bey of this fact. Without enough information to act on, Bey moved seemingly without purpose, continuing to the south-southwest at 18kt until just after 0900 and then again turning northeast. Meanwhile, Burnett led his three cruisers towards the northwest with the intent of putting his ships between the enemy and the convoy. As Bey remained unaware of Burnett's location, he let the range drop until 0921, when, 13,000yd to the south, *Sheffield*, the middle ship in a line of bearing 160° to port of the flagship, reported sighting *Scharnhorst* through the gloom. Three minutes later, *Belfast* fired starshells to illuminate the battlecruiser, taking Bey completely by surprise, and at 0930, *Norfolk*, the southernmost of the cruisers, opened fire at 9,800yd. Because *Scharnhorst* was on an opposite heading and turned away to the south-southeast as soon as she came under fire, Burnett's choice of a port line of bearing proved unfortunate: *Norfolk* masked the guns of the other two cruisers throughout this initial phase of the engagement.

Force '1' turned due west while *Scharnhorst* increased speed and turned away more sharply to the southeast. This had the effect of rapidly increasing the range to the point that at 0940, ten minutes after opening fire, *Norfolk* ceased shooting and Force '1' did a quick 180° turn to an easterly heading. A few minutes later, *Belfast* led around to the southeast and Force '1' increased speed to 24kt, the maximum speed it could maintain in the prevailing conditions. *Scharnhorst*, bigger and faster, rapidly worked up to 28kt. Bey turned left to the northeast at about 0950 and then left again to just short of due north at 1000. Burnett, realising he had no chance of catching *Scharnhorst* in a stern chase, turned back to the northwest at 1000, intending to stay between the German and the convoy. Radar contact was lost at 1020, ending the initial phase of the engagement.[31]

Norfolk was the only British ship to fire in this phase. She obtained at least one and possibly two hits. The one definite hit was high on *Scharnhorst*'s tower foremast and it disabled her forward radar, causing several casualties. This proved to be a serious loss. *Scharnhorst* still had a second radar, a FuMO 27, mounted aft, but it was sited poorly and could not detect a target more than 30° forward of amidships. The second hit, believed to have been in the forecastle, was not substantiated by survivors. If it hit, it failed to explode and caused no discernible damage. After recovering from her surprise, *Scharnhorst* fired several salvos at the cruisers from her after 'Cäsar' turret, achieving no hits. Johannesson saw the gunfire, but made no attempt to intervene, continuing to the southwest until 1027.[32]

At 0951, in response to a request for escort from Burnett, the 36th Division, recently borrowed from RA.55A, was ordered to join up with Force '1', which they reached at 1024. At 1030, when it was clear to Fraser that Burnett had lost touch with *Scharnhorst*, but that he had succeeded in gaining a blocking position east of the convoy, he ordered the convoy to turn northeast again.

It is necessary to ask at this point why Bey did not take advantage of his situation, having lost contact with Burnett's cruisers, to simply turn south and head for Alta. He must have understood that, even without knowledge of the approaching Force '2', he was in much the same situation *Graf Spee* had been in more than three years earlier, a single powerful ship facing a number of enemy cruisers with smaller, but much more numerous guns. (It is believed that, at this point, Bey was still not certain whether he was facing two or three enemy cruisers.[33]) He did have one advantage Langsdorff had not had: *Scharnhorst* was faster than any of his main adversaries. But he also must have known that it does not take much damage to nullify a speed advantage. While it will never be possible to know his reasons with certainty, it is possible to speculate that two factors may have led him to continue attempting to reach the convoy. One, of course, was Dönitz' exhortation to attack unless 'heavy forces' were encountered, and certainly two or three cruisers could hardly be described as such. Probably just as important is the very real possibility that Bey was unaware that Burnett had lost contact. The great disadvantage of reliance on radar detectors as sensors is that, while they can tell you when there is a radar in the vicinity, they cannot tell you whether that radar is tracking you. It is highly likely that, as *Scharnhorst* steamed north for the next hour and forty-minutes, her Naxos registered Burnett's radars continually. Finally, at noon, aware that he must make a move against the convoy soon or lose any chance of acting in the pale Arctic daylight, Bey turned to the northwest and a few minutes later to the southwest. (In fact, his run to the north had in no way decreased the distance to the convoy. When he turned at noon, the convoy was 30nm to the west-southwest; it had been 5nm closer at 0930.)

At 1050, Force '1' made contact with the convoy and took a position 10nm ahead of it, with the four destroyers of the 36th Division 2nm further ahead. Fraser's concern that *Scharnhorst* might escape into the Atlantic led him to order Force '2' to reverse course to the west at 1150, a manoeuvre that was very difficult for his destroyers to execute in the southwesterly gale; it was a full fifteen minutes before Force '2' settled on 260° at 18kt.

Even as that manoeuvre was completing, Fraser received the news he most desired. At 1205, *Belfast* established radar contact to the east-northeast at 30,500yd, exactly where Burnett expected *Scharnhorst* to be found. Her course was determined to be 240° and speed approximately 20kt. At 1219, Burnett led his squadron around to east-by-south in line abreast with *Belfast* at the northern end and *Norfolk* at the southern; the destroyers of 36th Division were in line-ahead off *Belfast*'s port bow. A minute later, *Scharnhorst* altered to a course of due east. It is not known whether *Scharnhorst*'s one remaining radar was active; given that the forces had been approaching on almost reciprocal courses, Force '1' would have been in that radar's blind spot. Thus, once again, Bey was surprised when, at 1221, *Scharnhorst* was sighted from *Sheffield* at 11,000yd and Burnett ordered his cruisers to open fire and destroyers to attack with torpedoes.

Scharnhorst immediately reversed course to port and put on speed, soon reaching 28kt. The two leading destroyers, *Musketeer* and *Virago*, opened fire with their 4.7in guns at a range of 7,000yd, which quickly dropped to 4,100yd, but never reached a position from which they could fire torpedoes at the rapidly retreating battlecruiser. All three cruisers fired at *Scharnhorst*, at ranges that fell to 9,100yd as she was turning and then opened up to over 16,000yd when firing ceased after twenty minutes. Spotters on Burnett's cruisers claimed at least six hits, plus a number of 4.7in hits by the destroyers. Survivors uniformly reported only one hit, port side aft, which failed to explode, though they also 'agreed that the cruisers' fire was unpleasantly accurate and filled the air with fragments'.[34]

On this occasion, *Scharnhorst*'s return fire was equally 'unpleasant'. Straddles were obtained on *Virago* and *Sheffield*, but it was *Norfolk*, which had the misfortune of being loaded out with smokeless powder, that attracted the most attention. The bright flashes of her gunfire stood out vividly in the half-light of the Arctic winter day. She was hit twice by 28cm rounds. One passed through her 'X' turret barbette and roller path and out the other side without exploding. Nevertheless, the damage was extensive, disabling the turret, starting a fire in the ammunition path from the magazine that caused a vivid plume of flame above the turret and necessitated flooding the magazine. This put 'Y' turret out of action as well. The second hit was amidships, passing most of the way across the ship before exploding near the shell plating on the far side of the ship. This hit killed seven men. Neither hit slowed *Norfolk*, however, and she was able to remain with *Belfast* as Burnett followed *Scharnhorst* around to the south.

Bey had finally decided that he had done his best to reach the convoy and now he decided to head for home. By 1300, he was heading southeast at 28kt and over the next three hours gradually wore around to south-southeast, but he was not able to shake Burnett's pursuit. All three of the British cruisers were able to keep up the same speed as *Scharnhorst*, trailing her by just over 15,000yd off her port quarter, until 1603, when a smoldering fire in a wing compartment in *Norfolk* threatened to spread out of control, forcing the cruiser to slow while fire crews contained the flames. This was done efficiently and she was able to rejoin

118. Burnett's flagship was *Sheffield*, seen in close escort of a convoy sometime in 1943 in typical northern weather, hazy with choppy seas. She carries a typical Royal Navy mid-war radar fit: besides a Type 284 mounted on her main-battery fire control director, she has Type 281 air-search antennas at her mastheads, a Type 273M surface-search antenna in its perspex lantern atop the radar office just in front of the foremast and a Type 285 secondary-battery fire control radar antenna on her HA director aft of the mainmast. (*NHHC*)

Belfast at 1700. More serious was a failure in the bearings of *Sheffield*'s port inner shaft, which caused her speed to drop to 10kt for half an hour. After that she was gradually able to build her speed back up to 23kt, but she trailed the action for the rest of the day.

Now reduced to *Belfast* and the destroyers of the 36th Division, Force '1' continued to shadow *Scharnhorst* until 1617, when *Duke of York*, coming up from the west, made radar contact with the battlecruiser at 46,000yd, bearing just east of north. Forces that had been spread over vast distances had now converged. Multiple story lines now resolved themselves into a single thread, and the pace of events accelerated. For the sake of clarity, the remaining events in this phase of the engagement are listed below in chronological order.

1632   *Scharnhorst* was detected on *Duke of York*'s Type 284 fire control radar at 29,700yd.

1637   Force '2's destroyers, which were formed up in sub-divisions of two each on either bow of the flagship, 'were ordered to take up the most advantageous position for torpedo attack, but not to attack till ordered to do so'.[35]

1640   *Belfast* detected *Duke of York* at 40,000yd, bearing 176°. Range from *Belfast* to *Scharnhorst* was then 19,300yd. Fraser ordered Burnett to illuminate the enemy.

1642   *Scharnhorst* altered course to southeast. There is no indication Bey was aware of Force '2's presence off his starboard bow, which would have been in *Scharnhorst*'s radar 'blind spot'. This was almost certainly simply another of the periodic minor course changes done in an attempt to complicate Burnett's pursuit.

1644   Force '2' tuned to 080° to open *Duke of York*'s 'A' arcs.

1647   *Belfast* opened fire on *Scharnhorst* with starshells. *Duke of York* did likewise a minute later.

1650   *Scharnhorst* was illuminated from two sides. From *Duke of York*, she appeared 'of enormous length and silver grey in colour'.[36] *Duke of York* and *Jamaica* opened fire at 12,000yd. *Scharnhorst* gave every indication of being caught by surprise once again; her main-battery turrets were still trained fore-and-aft and her initial return fire was slow and erratic.

Scharnhorst immediately turned away to the north, followed by Force '2'. She almost immediately encountered Force '1'. *Belfast* and *Norfolk* opened fire and reversed course to the north-northwest; *Scharnhorst* returned fire and turned away to the east. Force '2' followed suit and fell into a stern chase, with destroyers attempting to overtake *Scharnhorst*, a pair on each quarter. Force '1' remained to the northwest until 1727 before turning southeast, concerned lest the German attempt to break back to the west.

Duke of York shot very well at this stage of the engagement, obtaining hits on her first and third salvos. The initial hit was in the forecastle near 'Anton' turret, jamming that turret. Turret 'Bruno' was temporarily disabled as well. The second detonated in her hangar space, killing a large number of anti-aircraft gunners. *Jamaica* also claimed a hit during this period, though the specifics are not known; she continued to fire sporadically until 1742, but rarely had a good view of the enemy, always being on one quarter or the other of the flagship.

Scharnhorst's return fire was generally accurate, frequently obtaining straddles on *Duke of York*, but no direct hits on her hull. The battlecruiser steered a zigzag path, turning sharply, generally to starboard, to fire off a broadside, and then resuming her easterly course. The 28cm shells passed through both of *Duke of York*'s masts but failed to explode. The one that passed through her mainmast disabled her radar jamming set; *Scharnhorst*'s gunnery was seen to improve after this hit.[37]

At 1713, Fraser ordered his destroyers to attack.[38] They chased Bey, gaining very little, for over an hour. At 1820, the two Force '2' destroyer sub-divisions were still 12,000yd from their quarry and the 36th Division was even farther away to the north. Throughout this period of just over an hour, *Duke of York* continued a steady fire at *Scharnhorst* and scored at least two more telling hits: one at 1815 which damaged 'Bruno' turret's ventilation system and forced that turret to be temporarily abandoned, and one from that salvo or the next which passed through her starboard forward 15cm secondary battery turret and exploded near her waterline, blowing a large hole in her shell plating.[39]

Neither of those hits decreased *Scharnhorst*'s speed of 26kt, and, despite the zigzag course she was steaming, she was gradually pulling away from her pursuers. At 1800, Fraser turned south-southeast and, at 1820, southeast, hoping

120. A rarely seen image of HMS *Duke of York* (17) taken at Scapa Flow on 4 July 1943. In celebration of the day, she flies an American flag at her masthead. Her radar suite is very similar to that seen on *Sheffield*. Note the lack of radar on her after main-battery director and the fitting of a Type 285 on each of her four HA directors, three of which are visible. (*NARA*)

against hope he might lure Bey into following him. At 1820, *Scharnhorst* ceased firing, the range to *Duke of York* having reached 20,000yd. Fraser's flagship kept firing for four more minutes before she checked fire too, but, unbeknownst to Fraser at the time, one shell from one of her final salvos had decided the battle.[40] This 14in/45 APC round penetrated *Scharnhorst*'s upper side armour (3cm of Wh (Wotan hart) homogeneous armour steel) and her armoured deck (15cm of the same material) and exploded in her forward fire room, damaging the boilers there and, more seriously, blowing out high-pressure steam lines, causing her speed to rapidly drop to 10kt. *Scharnhorst*'s engineers reacted quickly and, within minutes, steam lines were re-routed and her speed was back up to 22kt. So fast were the repairs accomplished that her reduction in speed was not immediately apparent to Fraser. To Bey, *Scharnhorst*'s situation was absolutely obvious, her fate now unavoidable. At 1825, he signalled SKL: 'To the Führer, we shall fight to the last shell.' To Fraser, the situation appeared equally obvious. He composed a message that was radioed to Burnett at 1840: 'I see little hope of catching *Scharnhorst* and am proceeding to support convoy.'

But before he could order that turn, he was informed by his plotting room that *Scharnhorst* had slowed and that the destroyers were finally gaining on her. Instead of turning back towards the convoy, Fraser ordered a turn to the northeast, directly at the enemy, and closed in while Force '2's destroyers attacked. *Scharnhorst* opened fire on two of the destroyers while the other two approached unobserved. *Scorpion* and *Stord* fired sixteen torpedoes at 1849–1850 and turned away to the northeast firing their 4.7in guns as they retired.

Savage and *Saumarez* lined up to the west. Both destroyers were targeted by the battlecruiser's main and secondary batteries, *Saumarez* received most of the attention and almost all of the damage. *Savage* took no direct hits and suffered no casualties. *Saumarez* was hit at least twice by 28cm rounds; one passed through her director and another just below her rangefinder. Neither exploded. Splinter damage from multiple near-misses was far more devastating. The crew of one of her banks of torpedo tubes was incapacitated and damage to her engineering spaces reduced her speed to 10kt. In total, eleven of her crew were killed and a like number wounded. *Savage* got off eight torpedoes at 1855; *Saumarez* managed to fire only four. Both also exited to the northeast.

It is estimated that *Scharnhorst* was hit by four of the twenty-eight torpedoes fired by the four destroyers, one from the first sub-division and three from the second. Her speed again dropped and was again restored, but the torpedo damage was causing serious flooding, particularly aft. Completing a turn to the south at 1901 to parallel *Scharnhorst* at a range of 10,400yd, *Duke of York* and *Jamaica* opened fire again, immediately obtaining hits on her superstructure and hull. They re-engaged at this time because the Force '2' destroyers had now cleared the immediate vicinity of the target.[41] The trajectory of *Duke of York*'s 14in/45 APC rounds, fully capable at that range of penetrating *Scharnhorst*'s 35cm of KC n/A (Krupp cemented new type) main belt armour, was so flat (approximately 7°) that a shell striking the side above the waterline would not damage the ship's vitals, and shells hitting the water short would ricochet rather than plunging into the water and striking the ship's side underwater.[42]

121. This photograph is somewhat blurred, understandably so since it was taken by a photo-reconnaissance aircraft making a high-speed, low-altitude pass over the anchorage at Langfjord near Alta, Norway, late 1943. It is nonetheless a valuable image in that it shows *Scharnhorst* in her final appearance, with light-grey fore and aft and dark-grey amidships, the way she looked when she sailed north against convoy JW.55B at the end of the year. (*NHHC*)

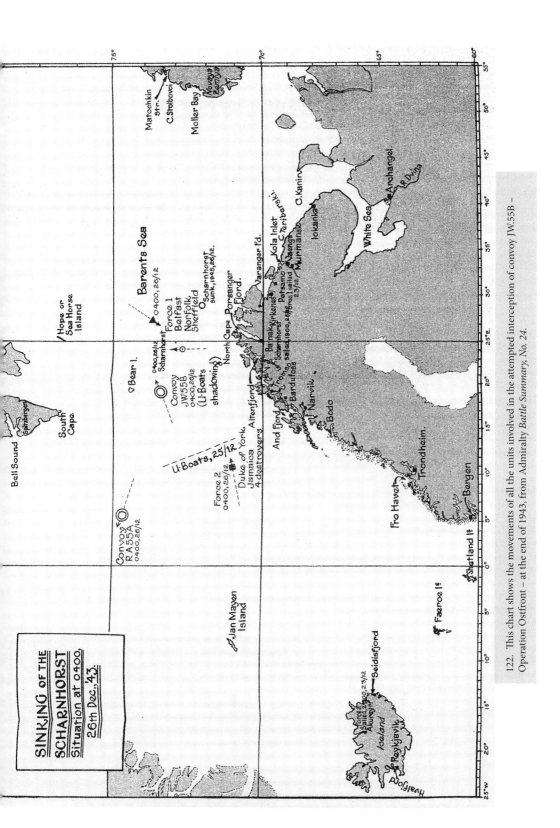

122. This chart shows the movements of all the units involved in the attempted interception of convoy JW.55B – Operation Ostfront – at the end of 1943, from Admiralty *Battle Summary, No. 24*.

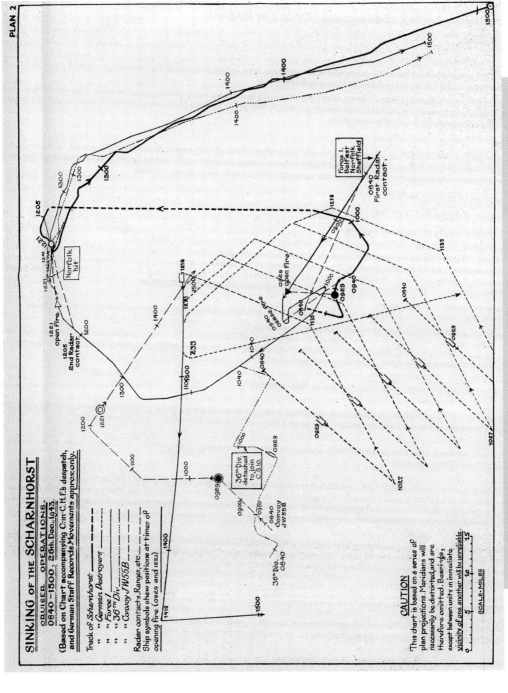

PLAN 2

SINKING OF THE SCHARNHORST

CRUISER OPERATIONS.
0840–1500, 26th Dec. 1943.

(Based on Chart accompanying C-in-C H.F.'s despatch,
and German Staff Records. Movements approx. only.)

Track of *Scharnhorst* ──────
" " German Destroyers ──────
" " *Force I* ──────
" " *36TH Div.* ⋯⋯⋯⋯
" " Convoy JW55B ─·─·─·─

Radar contacts, Ranges, etc.
Ship symbols show positions at times of
opening fire (0929 and 1221)

CAUTION
This chart is based on a series of
plan projections. Meridians will
necessarily be distorted, and are
therefore omitted. Bearings,
except between units in immediate
vicinity of one another will be unreliable.

SCALE: MILES
0   5   10   15

Force I.
Belfast
Norfolk
Sheffield

0840
First Radar
contact.

Norfolk
hit

1205
2nd Radar
contact

1221
open fire

36th Div. detached
to join C.S.10.

Convoy
JW55B

36th Div.
0840

123 and 124, (these pages) and 125 (overleaf). This is a series of three charts, also from Admiralty *Battle Summary*,

SINKING of the SCHARNHORST

Cruiser Shadowing and Battleship Action.
1500 - 1900, 26th Dec., 1943.

Based on Chart accompanying C-in-C.H.F.'s despatch.

ALL TIMES ARE ZONE -1

KEY

Track of Scharnhorst ....
,,   ,, Duke of York ....
,,   ,, Belfast and Norfolk ....
,,   ,, Sheffield when not in company ....
,,   ,, 36th Division ....
,,   ,, Savage, Saumarez ....
,,   ,, Scorpion, Stord ....
Radar contacts, Ranges, etc. ....
Ship symbols show positions at times of Duke
of York opening and checking fire (1860 & 1824)...

CAUTION

This chart is based on a series of plan projections.
Meridians will necessarily be distorted and are
therefore omitted. Bearings, except between units
in immediate vicinity of one another, will be unreliable.

Scale - Miles

0   5   10   15   20   25   30

1500 Force 1

1500, Scharnhorst

1500 36" Divn.

1600

1600

1600 Sheffield

Norfolk } reduce speed.
Sheffield }

1650 Sheffield

1700

1650

Belfast check fire

Belfast open fire

Norfolk open fire

D of Y open fire

Duke of York - 1st Radar contact

Destroyers ordered to take up most
advantageous position for firing torpedoes,
but not to attack.

Destroyers ordered to attack with
torpedoes as soon as possible. (1713)

1617

1600 Force 2

1800

1800

1800

1900

Sheffield

1800

1824

1800

1900

1900

See Plan 4

1900

1900

1824

1824

1800

1824

1862 A

1900

D of Y open fire 1900

1824

125. This is the third in a series of three charts, also from Admiralty *Battle Summary, No. 24*, which show successive stages of the confusing action of the Battle of the North Cape, 26 December 1943. (The first two charts are on the previous pages.)

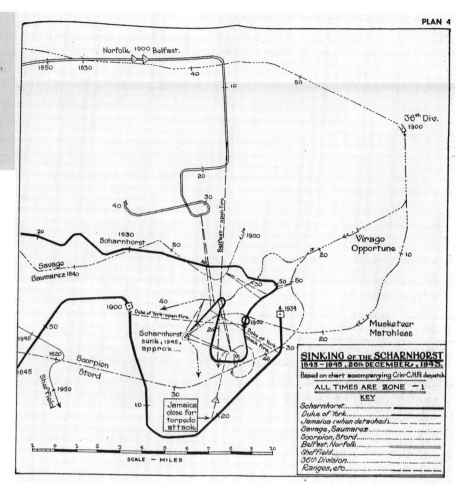

It very quickly became obvious to Fraser that, while he would be able to do great damage to *Scharnhorst*'s upperworks, he would not be able to sink her by short-range gunfire alone. *Norfolk* fired two salvos from 23,000yd to the north, but checked fire again because her gunners could not be sure whether they were firing at *Scharnhorst* or Force '2'.

At 1908, *Scharnhorst,* her speed starting to drop again, turned to the west. She steadied on this course only for five or six minutes before turning north. It is not clear whether these turns were intentional or due to a loss in control of her steering. By this point, *Scharnhorst*'s gunfire had become ragged and inaccurate. Only 'Cäsar' turret was firing regularly. 'Bruno' continued to fire periodically, still plagued by ventilation problems. Most of her secondary battery had been silenced.

Belfast opened fire at 17,000yd at 1915. When it was observed that *Scharnhorst* had turned to the north, *Belfast* led *Norfolk* around to the west. At 1919, Fraser ordered *Jamaica* to approach *Scharnhorst* and attack with torpedoes. A minute later the same order was sent to *Belfast*. *Jamaica* turned to the north-northeast, while *Duke of York* continued to the northeast. *Belfast* led around to the south and then the east to set up her torpedo attack. At 1928, *Duke of York* checked fire in order to avoid firing at the cruisers. She then turned to the north and played no further part in the engagement. It is estimated she scored at least ten main-battery hits for having fired twenty-five full salvos.[43]

The two light cruisers fired five torpedoes between them, all of which missed. At 1931, the destroyers of the 36th Division began to attack and a second pass by *Jamaica*, starting at the same time, finally overwhelmed *Scharnhorst*. At 1935, she fired her last shots, to no effect. At 1948, *Belfast* came around again to attempt to fire her remaining torpedoes. She fired starshells to illuminate the target but *Scharnhorst* was nowhere to be seen. Apparently *Scharnhorst* sank, unobserved by any other ship, at about 1945. It was likely that she had been hit by seven more torpedoes in the final ten minutes of her life.[44] *Scorpion* picked up thirty survivors and *Matchless* six more, all that lived out of a complement of 1,968.

The conditions in which this battle was fought were appalling, testing men and ships, making this a very difficult engagement. On top of that, the British faced an obstinate foe in *Scharnhorst*, which, like *Bismarck* before her, proved very hard to sink. This was the last time a Royal Navy battleship would perform its intended duty, fighting an enemy capital ship. The battle concluded with the interesting and, to many long-serving naval officers, disturbing lesson that the naval long rifle simply was not the best weapon with which to sink a well-designed and well-built enemy vessel of large size – at least not from close range. Not even with all the advantages that fire control radar gave the shooter. At long range, plunging fire could still be decisive, but the odds of achieving a hit remained very low even with electronic assistance.[45] It proved fortunate for Fraser that he had torpedo-bearing destroyers and cruisers along with *Duke of York* (and that *Scharnhorst* did not).

An Unfair Fight II
Imperial Japanese Navy vs US Navy in the Philippines, October 1944

To witness the final large-scale naval gunfire engagement of the Second World War, it is necessary to fast forward ten months and travel halfway around the world. The Allies, mostly Americans, faced a failing and desperate Japanese fleet, now stripped of the naval air power that had helped make it so potent three years earlier. The Imperial Japanese Navy was reduced to conventional pre-aviation assets – battleships, cruisers and destroyers – with which to react to the invasion of the Philippines. Not only were the forces that converged on Leyte Gulf from the south at the end of October 1944 utterly conventional, but they were relatively few in number and almost all of them dated to before Japan's entry into the war. Most of the Allied ships that faced them were brand new, launched since the attack on Pearl Harbor, the products of the prodigious industrial capacity of the United States. Ironically, however, five of the six American battleships that waited at the northern end of Surigao Strait on the night of 25 October had been at Pearl Harbor when the Japanese attacked almost three years earlier and two of those five had been left resting in the mud at the bottom of the harbour by Nagumo's airmen.

A Losing Proposition

The path that brought the Japanese to this pass was marked by mistakes of strategy, tactics and intelligence, highlighted by great failures, such as Midway and the Philippine Sea, but even more so by battles in which they had given as good as they got, most notably the protracted Solomons Campaign from late 1942 through to the end of 1943. Ultimately, the Japanese had neither the resources nor the population to trade punches with the United States. The US Navy could replace each lost ship and crew with ten new ones; the Japanese could not even replace their losses one for one.

After losing the Solomons, Gilberts and Marshalls, the Japanese proclaimed the Marianas as a defensive line that must be held, but Guam, Saipan and Tinian all fell in mid-1944 and the decisive naval battle in the Philippine Sea that was intended to blunt Admiral Chester Nimitz' Central Pacific advance turned into the 'Great Marianas Turkey Shoot', so-named because so many Japanese naval pilots fell so easily to their better-trained and better-mounted American counterparts.

It was obvious to the Japanese where the Allies should strike next. The two lines of advance – one up the Solomons chain and along the north coast of New

Guinea, led by General Douglas MacArthur, and the other across the Central Pacific – would most logically meet at the Philippines. By capturing those islands, the Americans would hold the eastern flank of the vital Japanese sea lane to the East Indies. From there they could strike west to Hainan or mainland China, south to the Indies or north to Formosa and the Home Islands. While the Japanese made plans in case the Americans bypassed the Philippines, they considered this unlikely, especially given MacArthur's very public promise to return when he had been forced out in March 1942.

Even if they guessed right in assuming that the Philippines would be next, there still were many possible points at which the Americans could land. The archipelago comprises over seven thousand islands stretching approximately 1,000mi north to south. Given the Allied bases to the southeast at Manus and to the east at Majuro and Eniwetok (Enewetak), they could land anywhere along that length, although in practical terms the choices were Luzon in the north, where the capital Manila and most of the usable airbases (as well as the bulk of Japanese defenders) were located, Leyte in the centre or Mindanao in the south.

MacArthur, not surprisingly, wanted to hit Mindanao first, in October 1944, then Leyte in November, followed by a series of small landings by his and Nimitz' forces, culminating in the invasion of Luzon at Lingayen Gulf in April 1945.[1] American CNO Admiral Ernest King and Nimitz objected, saying this would take too long and tie up fleet assets needlessly, proposing instead to bypass the Philippines and move directly to Formosa and then mainland China. It took a grand conference moderated by FDR in Hawaii at the end of July to hammer out a compromise, which was essentially MacArthur's plan minus the landings on Mindanao and involving none of Nimitz' amphibious assets.

Characteristic Complexity

The losses in aircraft and aircraft carriers at the Battle of the Philippine Sea were devastating to the Japanese, but possibly even more damaging to the Imperial Japanese Navy was the steady attrition of merchant shipping caused by Allied submarines. By the autumn of 1944, there simply was not enough tanker capacity to move the oil needed between the wells and refineries in the East Indies and the IJN's bases in the Home Islands. Increasingly, the Japanese were forced to base their remaining warships closer to the oil, at places like Lingga Roads, south of Singapore.[2] Thus, when the Japanese drew up their plans for their response to the next Allied move, it was with only remnants of the once-proud carrier fleet still based in the Inland Sea. The bulk of the Japanese fleet was under Vice-Admiral Kurita Takeo based at Lingga.

The Japanese plans were numbered 'Sho-1' through 'Sho-4', with Sho-1, the plan for repelling an invasion of the Philippines, being considered the most likely.[3] When activated, the plan called for the so-called Main Body, the carrier force, to sortie from the Inland Sea and 'drag its cape' ostentatiously northeast of Luzon to draw the American carriers away from Kurita's 1st Striking Force.[4] This force was to leave Lingga, stop at Brunei long enough to refuel and then proceed northeast along the west coast of Palawan Island, turn southeast into the Mindoro Strait, weave its way east through the island-strewn Sibuyan Sea and out into the Philippine Sea through the San Bernardino Strait. If Kurita got his force that far more or less intact, he would turn south along the coast of Samar and then west into Leyte Gulf to fall upon the landing fleet trapped inside. It was a relatively simple plan that, if the Japanese were very lucky and the Americans very lax, had a chance of working. As was often the case, though, the Japanese could not resist the temptation to make this simple plan much more complex. The added complexity, in this case, may have actually helped the Japanese, as it caused the Americans to divide their forces in a manner that left them vulnerable to Kurita's attack. At the same time, it set the stage for the engagement described in this chapter.

MacArthur's Navy

The mass of warships and transports that departed Seeadler Harbor, Manus, on 12 October 1944 for Leyte Gulf were all part of now-Vice-Admiral Kinkaid's Seventh Fleet, otherwise known as 'MacArthur's Navy'. Kinkaid received this unenviable assignment because he had success commanding US Navy forces in the Aleutians, a posting requiring extraordinary patience and diplomacy in dealing with his US Army counterparts. Unlike Nimitz' Central Pacific Force, designated the Third Fleet when commanded by Admiral William F Halsey (as it was in the autumn of 1944), which included the Pacific Fleet's fast carrier units (TF38) and all of the US Navy's new battleships, the Seventh Fleet was a far less glamorous contingent.[5] Seventh Fleet had aircraft carriers, but they were not the fleet carriers and light carriers of TF38: they were the eighteen escort carriers of Rear-Admiral Thomas L Sprague's TG77.4, which

126. Two of the American battleships which fought at the Battle of Surigao Strait on 25 October 1944 are seen in this image on 8 December 1941. *West Virginia* (BB48) in the foreground rests in the mud of 'Battleship Row' at Pearl Harbor, having been hit by seven torpedoes in her port side and two bomb hits. Only superb damage control allowed her to settle on the bottom in an upright position. In an equally remarkable achievement, she would be refloated in only five months, but it would be two more years before her repair and reconstruction was completed. *Tennessee* (BB43), in the background, was protected from torpedoes by *West Virginia*, and did not sink, but she nevertheless received two bomb hits and suffered hull damage from burning oil leaking from other battleships. Surrounded by damaged ships, *Tennessee* was not able to move for nine days. She left for Puget Sound and permanent repairs on 20 December. (*NARA*)

BK

SG

FH

FD

SC

FH

BL-2

FD

FD

127. Having spent most of 1942 protecting the US West Coast from Japanese attack, *Tennessee* returned to Puget Sound for a major reconstruction that lasted eight months. In this dockyard photograph, taken 1 May 1943, just days before she rejoined the fleet, the radars on her completely rebuilt superstructure are called out. The antennas not seen earlier are the two FH (Mk8) microwave main-battery fire control radars on Mk34 directors and the BL-2 and BK ESM antennas. (NARA)

between them brought over five hundred aircraft for support of the landings and defence of the fleet. In the place of the six new battleships in Vice-Admiral Willis A Lee's TF34, Kinkaid had six old battleships in Rear-Admiral Jesse B Oldendorf's TG77.2. To give an idea of the relative age of the battleships comprising TF34 and TG77.2, the oldest of Lee's battleships was *Washington*, in commission barely three years; the youngest of Oldendorf's 'battlewagons' was *West Virginia* (BB48), completed in December 1923.

The official title of TG77.2 was 'Central Philippine Attack Force Bombardment and Fire Support Group'. Besides the six battleships, it comprised three heavy cruisers, three light cruisers and fifteen destroyers.[6] They took up station at the entrance to Leyte Gulf on 17 October, supporting the landings on Suluan and Dinagat islands and Homonhon the next morning, clearing the approaches to the main landing beaches inside the gulf. The 19th was spent bombarding the Leyte beaches while minesweepers cleared paths through the gulf and 'frogmen' worked on clearing beach obstacles. The main landings on Leyte, including MacArthur's several staged walks through the surf to announce his return to the Philippines, took placc on 20 October.

128. *West Virginia* came out of her reconstruction looking similar to *Tennessee*. The idea behind the compact superstructure was to open clear arcs for her anti-aircraft battery. This photograph, taken 20 October 1943, shows 'Wee Vee' providing fire support from San Pedro Bay for the northern landing beaches on Leyte Island. She is wearing Ms32/7D camouflage, one of a series of disruptive schemes developed mid-war to make visual tracking by submarines and surface ships more difficult. Here it is badly faded and corroded, losing much of its effectiveness. (*NARA*)

Assigned to protect Sprague's carriers, but available to support the landings, was Rear-Admiral Russell S Berkey's TG77.3 – two heavy cruisers, two light cruisers and a squadron of destroyers.

Shima's Meanderings

The addition of new complications to the basic Sho-1 plan started well before Oldendorf's battlewagons showed up off Suluan. On 10 October, Halsey's TF38 began a series of raids on Japan's inner defences – called the 'connecting zone' by the Japanese – starting with Okinawa.[7] These were followed over the next several days with attacks on northern Luzon and Formosa. The Japanese reacted by committing all available land-based aircraft and even threw in the partially trained air groups off their four remaining aircraft carriers. The result was, if possible, even more disastrous than the Philippine Sea battle in June, leading to the loss of over five hundred aircraft, including nearly all the carrier aircraft, at the cost to the Americans of less than a hundred aircraft and damage to a pair of cruisers.[8]

The surviving Japanese fliers reported the Philippine Sea strewn with damaged and sinking American carriers, and, incredibly, they were believed to the extent that a squadron of cruisers and destroyers was ordered to sortie from the Inland Sea to rescue surviving aircrew and finish off disabled enemy ships. The unit selected for this duty was the former 5th Fleet, the same force until recently responsible for the defence of Japan's northern frontier, which, under Vice-Admiral Hosogaya, had fought at the Komandorski Islands battle. Now commanded by Vice-Admiral Shima Kiyohide, 5th Fleet had, at the end of July, been transferred to the Inland Sea for refit and training, with the intent of being incorporated into the Main Body carriers' screen for the Sho operation.

129. Two-thirds of Rear-Admiral Jesse B Oldendorf's CruDiv4, part of the Fire Support Unit South, itself part of TF79, the Southern Attack Force carrying out the landings at Dulag on Leyte Gulf, is seen in this image taken on 19 October 1944. In the foreground is *Minneapolis* (CA36) and in the left background is *Louisville* (CA28), Oldendorf's flagship. The most noticeable difference is that *Louisville* is still painted in a Ms32/6d disruptive camouflage. With the re-emergence of aircraft as the primary threat to surface ships, the US Navy was reverting to painting its warships in Ms21, an overall Navy Blue (5-N) scheme that was deemed more effective against observation from the air. (*NARA*)

Departing Kure just before midnight on 14 October, Shima took his flagship *Nachi*, sistership *Ashigara* and the *Abukuma*, leading seven destroyers of the 1st Destroyer Squadron.[9] When attacked by aircraft the next day from the still-intact TF38, Shima realised how exposed he was and turned west towards Amami-O-Shima, a large island group midway between Kyushu and Okinawa, entering Satsukawa Bay at 1630 on 17 October, his escape helped by bad weather.

Before leaving Amami-O-Shima, Shima was given new orders. Alarmed by the previous day's attack on the islands at the entrance of Leyte Gulf and under pressure from their IJA counterparts to provide transport for the immediate reinforcement of Japanese forces on Leyte, orders were sent out by Combined Fleet Chief of Staff Vice-Admiral Kusaka Ryunosuke, acting in the absence of CinC Admiral Toyoda Soemu who was on an inspection tour of the Philippines and Formosa, assigning Shima's 5th Fleet to the Southwest Area Fleet of Vice-Admiral Mikawa based at Manila. (Mikawa was last seen in these pages leading the force that sank *Edsall* on 1 March 1942. He is best known for leading the Japanese force that won a spectacular, but incomplete, victory at the Battle of Savo Island, 8–9 August 1942.) Shima's cruisers and destroyers were to be put at the disposal of the Southern Area Army to carry troops from Luzon to Leyte.[10] Because the army did not yet have a definite schedule for moving troops, Shima was instructed to head to Mako (Makung/Magong) in the Pescadores Islands off the west coast of Formosa, where he would find fuel and, it was hoped, clarification of his orders.

At the same time, the 16th Sentai, comprising heavy cruiser *Aoba*, light cruiser *Kinu* and one destroyer, was detached from Kurita's 1st Striking Force and also assigned to Mikawa for transport duty. They were instructed to head immediately to Manila.[11]

130. The other heavy cruiser in Oldendorf's Left Flank Force at the Battle of Surigao Strait was *Portland* (CA33), seen here completing a dockyard availability at Mare Island on 16 July 1944. She had an SK air-search and an SG surface-search antenna on her foremast and another SG on her main mast. Such duplication of radar sets was frequently made necessary by interference resulting from the proliferation of radars aloft. She had FH sets on her main-battery directors and lightweight Mk28 dishes on her old Mk33 secondary-battery directors. (*NARA*)

131. *Portland* is seen again a few weeks later making her way westward across the Pacific towards the Philippines. She has been freshly painted up in an Ms32/7d disruptive camouflage scheme. The Ms32 series of schemes were considered the most effective against surface observation in clear, sunny weather. (*West Virginia*'s camouflage, seen earlier, would have had similar contrast when new. The purple-blue pigments used by the US Navy to tint the white base paint were expected to last only a few months of exposure to sun and salt air before losing all of their bluish cast and fading to various shades of grey.) (*NARA*)

BIG GUN BATTLES

Kusaka's Interference

The order alerting Kurita to expect the activation of Sho-1 went out early on 17 October, and the actual activation order followed later the same day. The 1st Striking Force began to manoeuvre the swept channel leading east out of Lingga at 0100 the next morning. His force was sighted by an American search plane as it began dispersing to several separate anchorages in Brunei Bay early on 20 October, but the report never was passed on to Kinkaid or Halsey. Nevertheless, Allied radio interception and decryption of Japanese fleet transmissions was sufficiently timely by this stage of the war that the American commanders had a good idea that Kurita was on the move with most of the Japanese fleet and that the Main Body was preparing to exit the Inland Sea.[12]

The day of 20 October proved to be critical in setting the stage for the action in the Surigao Strait six days later. About midday, Kurita received a message from Kusaka, in which the latter 'suggested' he split off part of his force to make a separate simultaneous penetration of Leyte Gulf from the south, through Surigao Strait. This was met with displeasure and resignation by Kurita, who had already complained to no avail about the loss of the 16th Sentai. Although he had no choice but to go along with this 'suggestion', the decision as to which ships to assign this task was left to him.

That same day, Shima arrived at Mako early in the morning and began refuelling again, but the only orders waiting there were the unwelcome detachment of three of his destroyers – Destroyer Division 21, comprising *Wakaba*, *Hatsushimo* and *Hatsuharu* – which were sent to Takao (Kaohsiung), Formosa to pick up the ground elements of the 2nd Air Fleet, whose aircraft had flown ahead to Luzon. This left Shima with just four destroyers – *Akebono* and *Ushio* of Destroyer Division 7 and *Kasumi* and *Shiranuhi* of Destroyer Division 18.

Still lacking firm tasking from the army, both Shima and Mikawa had radioed Combined Fleet multiple times over the previous twenty-four hours, proposing that what remained of 5th Fleet be assigned to Kurita, but no reply was forthcoming. Nevertheless, his refuelling complete by mid-afternoon, Shima was so confident that his request would be approved that he held a command conference for his officers on *Nachi*, giving sailing orders for the morning and drinking the traditional pre-battle toasts with Imperial sake. It was only after the conference broke up and the officers returned to their ships that the long-overdue response arrived from Combined Fleet simply repeating the previous order that Shima remain attached to the Southwest Area Fleet and wait at Mako for further orders.[13]

Kurita's Easy Choice

While Shima spent the morning of 21 October fuming at Mako, events proceeded at Brunei Bay. Kurita apparently had little difficulty selecting which ships to designate to satisfy Kusaka's suggestion. When he convened a conference of all his commanding officers at 1600 on 21 October, he indicated that he had chosen Battleship Division 2, comprising *Fuso* and *Yamashiro*, commanded by now-Vice-Admiral Nishimura Shoji, – last seen milling around aimlessly off Balikpapan. This was an easy choice because this was the division of battleships most recently added to his force, which therefore had had the least opportunity to integrate with the rest of his force and, no doubt, also because they were the oldest and slowest battleships in the fleet.[14] These battleships were so old and slow – they could theoretically steam at a maximum of 24kt, but had not seen that speed in many years – that Kurita was probably just as glad to send them off on their own.[15] For this mission, Nishimura's squadron was designated 'C' Force or 3rd Section, indicating it was still technically part of Kurita's 1st Striking Force.

Along with the two old battleships, 3rd Section comprised the seaplane cruiser *Mogami* and four destroyers: *Michishio, Asagumo, Yamagumo* and *Shigure*. *Mogami*, last seen at Sunda Strait, had been seriously damaged aft at the Battle of Midway, and, rather than repairing her demolished after turrets, the Japanese decided to rebuild her stern as a space for storing and launching as many as eleven reconnaissance seaplanes. It was in this form that she was recommissioned on 30 April 1943 and she sailed with the six other ships of 3rd Section from Brunei shortly after 1500 on 22 October. Their mission was to penetrate Surigao Strait in co-ordination with Kurita's approach from the north.

Shima's Plans

Shima remained idle until 1600 on 21 October, when the 5th Fleet departed Mako and headed south towards the Philippines. The record is not entirely clear whether at that time he believed he was heading towards Manila, still under orders to transport troops to Leyte, or was heading for Coron Bay in the Calamian Group southwest of Mindoro to refuel before following Nishimura into Surigao Strait. His course leaving Mako would have been the same for either destination. That afternoon, Combined Fleet finally responded to the various entreaties from Shima and Mikawa, most recently a message from Mikawa's Chief-of-Staff explicitly expressing the strong suggestion that 5th Fleet be subordinated to Kurita's 1st Striking Force and ordered to Leyte Gulf via Surigao Strait.[16] This finally garnered a response from Combined Fleet headquarters. Mikawa was informed simply that Combined Fleet concurred with his suggestion. The message said nothing about transferring Shima from Mikawa's control. Shima was not an addressee, nor were any instructions included for him other than to co-ordinate his actions with Kurita's. It is not clear whether Mikawa had been able to pass this information to Shima before he left Mako. One of the few survivors in a position to know, Commander Mori Kokichi, who was torpedo officer on Shima's staff, stated after the war that Shima was aware of his new assignment before sailing.[17] This tends to be supported by his use of the Mako radio station to attempt to communicate with Kurita regarding the latter's intentions for the 5th Fleet.[18] (It is about this time that Shima's squadron took on the additional designation 2nd Striking Force.)

On his way south towards the Philippines, Shima attempted to decide how best to carry out his new assignment. Other than informing Shima of his own plans and timetable, Kurita gave him no orders or even suggestions. Shima became aware of Nishimura's assignment sometime during the 22nd while steaming south. '. . . NISHIMURA's movement became known after we left . . . We expected to make [the] approach alone until we learned of NISHIMURA's movement.'[19]

Because he understood that his slender force of seven ships was insufficient to force Surigao Strait against the expected opposition – the Japanese had a fairly accurate idea of Kinkaid's strength – Shima counted on being able to reunite with the three destroyers carrying support troops to Manila. Even after learning of Nishimura's assignment, he still lacked any details of the 3rd Section's plans or schedule. Hoping to resolve both problems, he dispatched two floatplanes to Manila with a message for Captain Ishii Hisashi, the officer commanding the detached destroyers, ordering him to proceed to Coron Bay as soon as he had deposited his passengers, and with a request for additional information to be radioed to Nishimura. He also hoped to confirm that oilers would be waiting for him at Coron Bay. In the event, his messages never got through. Rough water in Manila Bay caused one of the floatplanes to overturn and sink on attempting to touch down; the other turned back.

132. As long as ships have had metal bottoms, sailors have had to chip away at old paint and marine growth and apply fresh paint to control corrosion and keep a ship steaming well. Here sailors off *Phoenix* (CL46) perform this unpleasant, but necessary, task in a floating dry dock at Espiritu Santo on 10 August 1944. *Phoenix* was one of the light cruisers in Rear-Admiral Russell S Berkey's Right Flank Force at the Battle of Surigao Strait. US Navy warships had a black stripe of boot-topping, below which red antifouling paint covered the bottom. (*NARA*)

Despite this, Shima learned the basics of Nishimura's plans in a radio message sent before noon, which was received by *Nachi* only at 1930.[20] In this message, Nishimura stated that the 3rd Section would turn through the Balabac Strait between Borneo and Palawan at approximately 1000 on the 23rd, cross the Sulu Sea by a deceptive course that started by following Palawan's east coast to the northeast until nearing Panay, after which they would turn southeast and, skirting Panay and Negros, reach the southern entrance of the Surigao Strait at 0100 on 25 October.[21] The reason for this major diversion to the north, rather than simply steaming east across the Sulu Sea, was two-fold. Nishimura feared that American submarines were waiting east of the Balabac Strait. Additionally, the northern swing would increase the distance from the known Allied reconnaissance airbase on Morotai Island, northeast of Halmahera, approximately 600nm southeast of the centre of the Sulu Sea.

With this information, Shima could make his own plans. He would reach Coron Bay that evening. There he would refuel and gather the detached Destroyer Division 21, leaving again before dawn to begin his own transit of the Sulu Sea, passing south of Negros and into the Bohol Sea (also called the Mindanao Sea) and reach the southern entrance of Surigao Strait at 0600 on 25 October, five hours behind Nishimura. Shima sent only a single message to Nishimura, among other addressees, at 2000, giving the bare outline of his plans. None of the recipients, which included Combined Fleet, Kurita and Mikawa, as well as Nishimura, saw any reason to respond.

A Lack of Initiative

Much effort has been spent trying to understand why Nishimura and Shima apparently failed to co-ordinate their movements. The simplest course of action would have been for the two forces to merge and act as a unified command. There is no evidence that either commander suggested this or wanted it to happen. It may have been nothing more than a desire on the part of both admirals to avoid the many radio messages back and forth that would have been necessary to accomplish such a junction. It has also been suggested that there would have been some friction deciding who would lead such a combined force.[22] Nishimura and Shima knew each other, having been classmates at Etajima, the Japanese naval academy. There is no indication that they had much interaction in the years since graduation, Nishimura having spent almost all his time at sea, while Shima had mostly shore postings. Nevertheless, Shima had sixth months longer in grade, which is the normal method of determining who would command a joint squadron.[23] Also, Shima was in command of a fleet, while Nishimura commanded a section, which would have also given Shima precedence, despite the fact that Nishimura had significantly greater experience in combat leadership. It is likely that it came down to concern on Shima's part about potential crowding in Surigao Strait and Leyte Gulf, where Nishimura and Kurita were scheduled to arrive within an hour or so of each other.[24] (When Kurita doubled back in the Sibuyan Sea due to American air attacks on 24 October, thus delaying his scheduled arrival in Leyte Gulf, Shima increased speed to reduce the gap between his force and Nishimura's.) However, it is most likely that the ultimate reason why neither Shima

nor Nishimura attempted to unite their forces is because neither was ordered to do so by their respective superiors – Mikawa or Kurita – and to have done so on their own initiative probably never entered either man's mind.

No Oiler at Coron Bay

Shima's 2nd Striking Force arrived at Coron Bay just before dusk on 23 October.[25] Neither the tankers nor the destroyers he was hoping would be waiting were there. In fact, Ishii's destroyers had completed their transport run to Manila that day and had departed to rejoin Shima, but, not having received his orders, they headed south, skirting Mindoro, and planned to intercept the 2nd Striking Force off Negros. The absence of the oilers left Shima with no choice but to refuel his destroyers and *Abukuma* from the two heavy cruisers. While this left *Nachi* and *Ashigara* with more than adequate fuel to reach Leyte Gulf and return if they maintained economical cruising speed, this would not necessarily be true at higher speed, a fact that entered into Shima's calculations the next day. Refuelling complete, 2nd Striking Force departed Coron Bay heading generally south at 0200 on 24 October.

Approaching from the South

As the sun rose on 24 October, both 3rd Section and 2nd Striking Force were crossing the Sulu Sea. Nishimura was approximately 120nm west of the southern tip of Negros Island and the entrance into the Bohol Sea; Shima was just exiting the Cuyo West Passage between Dalanganem Islands and the Cuyo Islands, one of the northern entrances into the Sulu Sea, putting him about 120nm north-northeast of Nishimura. The distance between them would close during the morning because Shima was steaming south-southeast at 18kt, while Nishimura was making about 16kt heading northeast. Ishii's three destroyers were trailing Shima off Mindoro, heading for the Cuyo East Passage.

The Americans were well aware, in general terms, of the Japanese movements of the previous few days, but the pinpointing of the exact locations of the various groups approaching from the west came about in piecemeal fashion. Kurita's 1st Striking Force was found by, and attacked by, American submarines early on 23 October in the Palawan Passage. Shima had been sighted by submarines a day earlier in the Luzon Strait, but lost again. Neither his force nor Nishimura's would be sighted by the Americans on the 23rd, but they were found early on the 24th.

Of Halsey's three available carrier groups on 24 October, the southernmost was Rear-Admiral Ralph E Davison's TG38.4, comprising fleet carriers *Franklin* (CV13), *Enterprise* (CV6) and two light carriers. The other two groups spent the day attacking Kurita in the Sibuyan Sea; Davison's group was initially given responsibility for everything further south, including the Sulu Sea. Knowing there were enemy ships to be found, a major search sweep was launched from his position 60nm east of Samar at 0600; aircraft off *Franklin* headed for the west coast of Panay, while a strike force off *Enterprise* was directed further south towards Negros. *Franklin*'s aircraft drew first blood, catching Ishii's destroyers off Panay, sinking *Wakaba* at 0805 and convincing the other two to turn back towards Manila.[26] The rendezvous with Shima would never occur.

Exactly an hour later, *Enterprise*'s aircraft found Nishimura. They achieved a near-miss off *Yamashiro*'s fantail that caused some flooding, several hits on *Fuso* of considerably greater severity, strafing damage to *Mogami* that started a gasoline fire and a hit on *Shigure*. *Fuso*'s hits were one bomb forward abreast No. 2 main-battery turret that detonated deep inside the ship near her shell plating, starting leaks that were never fully controlled, and a second bomb right aft which demolished her wardroom and set off a depth charge that blew a hole in her side, as well as igniting an avgas fire on her fantail. When *Enterprise*'s aircraft departed, they thought they had done considerable damage to the 3rd Section,

134. A generation newer than *Phoenix* or *Boise*, the light cruiser *Columbia* (CL56) mounted one fewer main-battery turret, but had a much heavier 5in secondary battery, making them far better anti-aircraft platforms. *Columbia* is seen her from *Pennsylvania* (BB38) in Leyte Gulf, 19 October 1944, painted in Ms33/1d, the lighter disruptive scheme. Along with *Denver* (CL58), *Columbia* was part of Oldendorf's Left Flank Force. (*NARA*)

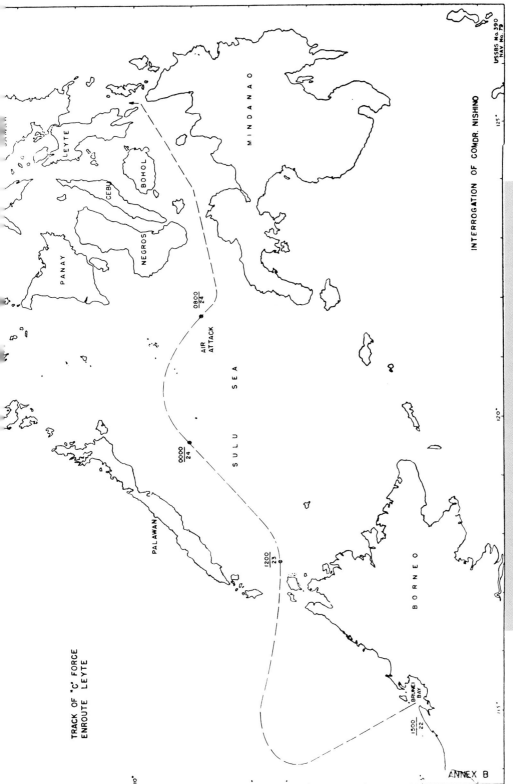

TRACK OF "C" FORCE
ENROUTE LEYTE

LEYTE

BOHOL

CEBU

PANAY

NEGROS

MINDANAO

PALAWAN

S U L U   S E A

AIR
ATTACK

0800
24

0000
24

1200
23

BORNEO

BRUNEI
BAY

1500
22

ANNEX B

INTERROGATION OF COMDR. NISHINO

USSBS No.390
NAV No.79

135. This chart shows the approach route taken by Vice-Admiral Nishimura Shoji's 3rd Section from Brunei Bay to the southern entrance to Surigao Strait. (*USSBS Interrogation No. 390/79*)

as smoke and flames were streaming from *Fuso*, *Mogami* and *Shigure*. In fact, the damage was relatively minor; fires were extinguished and, except for the case of *Fuso*, any flooding stanched. All three ships were able to continue eastward towards Surigao Strait.

In the case of *Shigure*, there is some confusion about how serious her damage was. This is caused by the changing testimony of her captain, Commander Nishino Shigeru. At the time and immediately after the war, he was quite certain about the damage received by his ship:

> The SHIGURE received a direct hit on No. 1 turret, an armor piercing bomb which exploded in the turret and killed five and wounded about six. This bomb hit on SHIGURE had no effect on speed or navigability, but forced them to borrow personnel to man the gun, and the gun was inefficient; it was not put out of action but we had to borrow radar personnel to man the gun.[27]

Apparently, he recanted this story in 1980, thirty-five years later, claiming that the bomb only glanced off the turret and exploded away from the ship.[28] Regardless, *Shigure* maintained her place in Nishimura's formation, which was spotted again that morning by a Navy PB4Y 'Liberator' flying from Morotai, but not attacked again that day. Shima's force was also sighted by a reconnaissance aircraft from Morotai, but was not attacked on the 24th. Davison's carriers were called to the north to join the attack on Kurita and paid no further attention to the forces approaching Surigao Strait. The attacks on Kurita in the Sibuyan Sea were of sufficient persistence and ferocity as to force him to temporarily turn back to the west. After just over two hours, he turned back eastward again at 1714, but now was well behind schedule. Nishimura continued eastward at his squadron's cruising speed, 16kt.

As Nishimura entered the Bohol Sea at approximately 1600 on 24 October, he had a reasonably good idea of the forces awaiting the Japanese in Leyte Gulf. A reconnaissance floatplane had been launched from *Mogami* before dawn and reconnoitred the gulf soon after 0600, returning to the 3rd Section soon after the American attack departed. The report it gave was generally accurate, if a bit on the low side. It reported that there were four battleships, two cruisers, four destroyers, fifteen aircraft carriers, fourteen PT boats and eighty transports in or near the gulf.[29] There also were reports of additional enemy patrol boats off the west coast of Panaon Island near the entrance to the strait that had Nishimura concerned. Equally concerned that he might not be able to clear the strait before dawn, given that the air attacks earlier in the day had slowed 3rd Section's progress, he ordered speed increased to 18kt during the afternoon. For reasons that are not clear, Shima also decided mid-afternoon to increase speed, narrowing the gap between his force and the 3rd Section. At 1352 he increased speed to 20kt, which would have him entering Surigao Strait an hour earlier, at 0500.[30] Then at 1645, he increased speed again to 22kt, the fastest speed he could maintain given the now-reduced fuel state of his cruisers; this now put his projected arrival time at the entrance to Surigao Strait at 0300, just two hours behind Nishimura.[31]

136. 3rd Section was attacked by aircraft off the most battle-tested US aircraft carrier in the Pacific – *Enterprise* (CV6) – early in the morning of 24 October 1944 in the Sulu Sea. Here bomb splashes bracket *Yamashiro*, whose main battery is raised to full elevation and rotated all the way to starboard to fire Common Type 3 IS (*sankaidan*) shells. These were anti-aircraft rounds intended to be fired from the 36cm main battery of Japanese battleships in a desperate attempt to fend off the swarms of American carrier aircraft they found themselves facing. *Yamashiro* was lucky and suffered only near-misses on this occasion. (*NARA*)

137. A more distant view shows *Yamashiro* and *Mogami* manoeuvring under attack from aircraft of *Enterprise*'s CVG-2, Sulu Sea, 24 October 1944. The large puff of smoke over *Yamashiro* indicates she has just fired at least a partial salvo of main-battery Type 3 IS shells. The smoke pouring from *Mogami* was caused by the avgas fire aft started by strafing fighters. (*NARA*)

Shima and Nishimura probably received word of Kurita's delay in the Sibuyan Sea only at around 1730 or 1800. It is not certain if either ever knew the details of Kurita's manoeuvres.[32] What is certain is that neither changed course or plan based on this information. Had either been considering altering their plan by, perhaps, also delaying their approach to Leyte Gulf or arranging to merge their forces, this would have been put aside by the message from Combined Fleet they intercepted at approximately 1900, admonishing Kurita in very uncharacteristically harsh terms to continue the advance to Leyte Gulf with all possible speed.

At approximately 1830, *Mogami* and three destroyers were detached by Nishimura and sent ahead to check out the reported enemy patrol boats near Panaon Island.[33] These ships quickly accelerated to 26kt and passed between the first two groups of PT boats waiting between Bohol and Camaguin Islands without being spotted. The remaining three ships of Nishimura's force – the two battleships and *Shigure* – edged closer to Bohol Island to the north, concerned that the central channel approaching the southern entrance to Surigao Strait might be patrolled by submarines. (It was not.)

Plugging the Northern Exit

Kinkaid was dealing with his own problems caused by incomplete information, particularly regarding the intentions of other American formations. Well informed of the approaching Japanese forces, he knew that it would be his responsibility to block Surigao Strait, but he assumed, as did Nimitz back at Pearl Harbor, that Halsey's Third Fleet, and particularly Lee's TF34, were taking care of blocking Kurita's possible exit through the San Bernardino Strait.[34] That this was not the case, and that Kurita actually was able to approach the escort carrier groups operating off the coast of Samar the next morning without further interference from any Allied force, bears only peripherally on the story being told here. What is important was that Kinkaid felt free to concentrate on the defence of Surigao Strait without worrying about the eastern entrance into Leyte Gulf and, based on that presumption, at 1443 on 24 October, he ordered Oldendorf, in his role as CTG77.2, to prepare to meet a night attack at the northern exit from Surigao Strait.

This order was hardly unexpected, and Oldendorf had a plan in place. It aimed at nothing less than the annihilation of any enemy forces attempting to force their way through Surigao Strait. That enemy would have to run a gauntlet of successive attackers of greater and greater strength until they were met at the northern end of the strait by his battleships. First to greet the enemy would be thirty-nine PT boats, split into thirteen three-boat sections. Nishimura's information was correct that some of these lurked off the west coast of Panaon Island. Indeed, the westernmost sections were six boats waiting between the eastern tip of Bohol and Camaguin Island some 40nm west of the entrance to the strait. Another group waited off Limasawa Island 10nm west of Panaon, while no fewer than five groups lined the narrows at the entrance to the strait. The remaining five groups were deployed along both sides of the southern reaches of the strait. One squadron of destroyers, the five-strong picket group, Captain Jesse G Coward's DesRon54, was arrayed on either side of the strait, two on the western side and three on the eastern, near the northernmost PT boat groups, in line with Amagusan Point on the Leyte coast.

Oldendorf arrayed his remaining ships at the northern end of the strait, where it widened and split into two, divided by Hibuson Island. The eastern channel is narrow and relatively shallow and rarely used; Oldendorf posted a single destroyer to patrol there, placing the bulk of his forces to block the main, western channel. The western part of this channel, near the Leyte shore, was the responsibility of TG77.3 under Admiral Berkey, who commanded one heavy cruiser (HMAS *Shropshire* (C73)), two light cruisers (*Phoenix* (CL46) and *Boise*) and the six destroyers of DesRon24. The destroyers patrolled a north–south line anchored at the southern end at Bugho Point, Leyte. Berkey's cruisers comprised the Right Flank Force covering the western end of the battle line's patrol line approximately 2.5nm south of the battleships. Oldendorf himself directly commanded the Left Flank Force, comprising three heavy cruisers (*Louisville* (CA28), *Portland* (CA33) and *Minneapolis* (CA36)), two light cruisers (*Denver* (CL58) and *Columbia* (CL56)) and the nine destroyers of DesRon56. His cruisers extended Berkey's patrol line to the north of Hibuson Island. The destroyers were arrayed in three groups of three, north of Oldendorf's cruisers. Behind the two flank cruiser forces and DesRon56 was the battle line commanded by Rear-Admiral G L Weyler, six battleships in the following order: *West Virginia*, *Maryland* (BB46), *Mississippi* (BB41), *Tennessee* (BB43), *California* (BB44) and *Pennsylvania* (BB38). Also near the battleships were the six destroyers of DesDiv 'X-ray' assigned directly to protect the battle line. They were split into two groups of three, covering the eastern and western ends of the battle line's back-and-forth patrol line.

Every one of the American battleships, with the sole exception of *Mississippi*, had been at Pearl Harbor when the Japanese attacked. The first two in line were armed with eight 16in/45 guns, the rest with twelve 14in of varying calibres. Against this formidable broadside of sixteen 16in and forty-eight 14in guns, the two Japanese battleships carried twenty-four 36cm/45 guns in twelve twin-turrets. *Mogami*, since the removal of her two after turrets, carried six 20cm/50 guns; against this, the eight Allied cruisers mounted thirty-five 8in and fifty-four 6in main-battery guns. The disproportion of destroyer weapons, battleship and cruiser secondary armament and torpedoes was similar. Adding Shima's three cruisers and four destroyers would have done little to redress this imbalance.

An obvious question is why did Oldendorf jam so many of his ships into so small an area at the northern exit from the strait. In a 'box' no more than 15nm wide and 5nm deep, he positioned six battleships, four heavy cruisers, four light cruisers and thirteen destroyers, with another twelve destroyers not far to the south. Within this confined space, they were supposed to manoeuvre back and forth and, when the time came, fire towards the south, the battleships firing over the destroyers and cruisers arrayed between them and the enemy and in the direction of the other destroyers further south. All this was to take place in the middle of a tropical night, generally clear with scattered rain showers and a quarter moon setting just after midnight. By this point in the war the American ships all had multiple radars and enough experience using them that the night did not feel as dark as it might have to sailors only a year or two earlier, but, as the night unfolded, the wisdom of Oldendorf's crowded formation and reliance on radar would be called into question.

The Last Gunfight

The Battle of Surigao Strait about to be described was the last time that battleships of enemy nations lined up against each other. Indeed, it was quite likely the last major gun battle in naval history. But, it was also a battle largely decided by weapons other than naval long rifles. In keeping with the other accounts related in this book, the following description will cover only briefly the torpedo attacks that caused most of the damage in this battle, in order to concentrate on those few minutes when the action was between ships firing steel projectiles at each other with the still imperfect assistance of new-fangled electronics. It was a scene of thunder and lightning alternating with pitch-black conditions, in which ships were hit or missed more by luck than intent and sometimes the ship that was hit was not the intended target.

First Contact

At 2236 on 24 October, Section 1 of TG70.1, the PT boat squadrons attached to Seventh Fleet, made radar contact with a force of ships to its northwest, closer in towards the shore of Bohol Island. Lookouts on *Shigure* sighted the three PT boats fourteen minutes later and warned Nishimura who ordered a simultaneous turn to the southeast in order to present smaller targets for the PT boats' torpedoes. At the same time, *Shigure* fired starshells that illuminated what appeared to be four torpedo boats, and two minutes later the destroyer and *Yamashiro* opened an effective fire with their 12.7cm and 15cm batteries, effective enough to damage two of the three PT boats and cause all three to turn away without firing their torpedoes.[35] (These was the calibres of *Shigure*'s main battery and *Yamashiro*'s secondary battery.) *PT152* was hit by a round from *Shigure* that carried away her forward 37mm/56 gun and killed the gunner, wounding three others in the gun crew. A fire briefly flared up on *PT152*, which led Nishino to believe the boat might have been more seriously damaged, maybe even sunk.[36] *PT130* attempted to intervene, making smoke, and was rewarded with a 12.7cm round from *Shigure* that passed through her hull without exploding, knocking out her radios. It turned out that none of Section 1's radios was operable, so *PT130* was sent across the channel to the southern side where she found Section 2 and had them send a contact report, indicating two enemy battleships and three destroyers had passed their position heading east. Radio reception was such that this report was not received by the flagship *Louisville* until 0016.[37] This, however, gave Oldendorf more than adequate warning of what was coming.

Nishimura ordered Nishino in *Shigure* not to pursue the fleeing torpedo boats and the Japanese resumed their eastward movement. At midnight, Nishimura ordered speed increased to 20kt, very close to the best speed his old battleships could sustain. *Mogami* and her accompanying destroyers rejoined at 0040. At 0130, 3rd Section reached the southern entrance to Surigao Strait and turned north, and at the same time came under renewed PT boat attack. PT boats from Sections 6, 8 and 9 attacked in rapid succession, firing at least sixteen torpedoes, all of which missed their targets. The return fire from 3rd Section was mainly intended to interrupt the torpedo attacks, as the PT boats were far too fast and

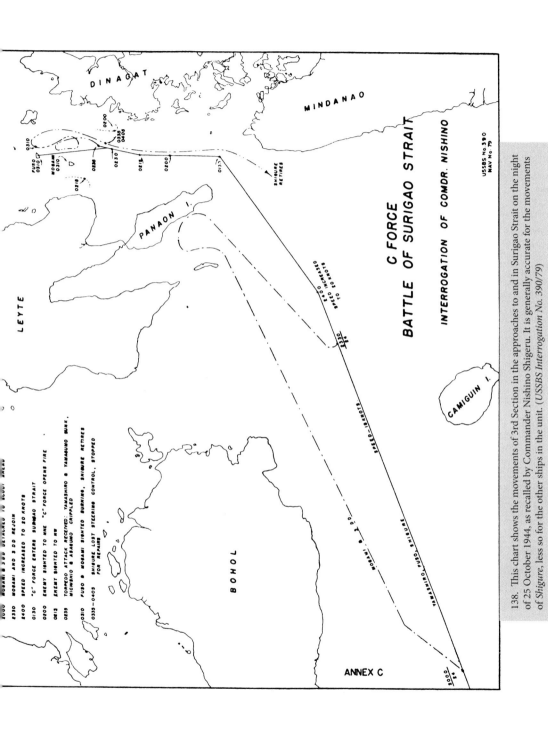

138. This chart shows the movements of 3rd Section in the approaches to and in Surigao Strait on the night of 25 October 1944, as recalled by Commander Nishino Shigeru. It is generally accurate for the movements of *Shigure*, less so for the other ships in the unit. (*USSBS Interrogation No. 390/79*)

elusive to make good targets, especially at night. Nevertheless, *PT490* of Section 9 was hit once, possibly twice, probably by *Michishio*. Badly damaged, though fortunately all the damage was above the waterline, she staggered away, aided by section-mate *PT493*. This boat put herself between *Michishio* and her target, making smoke, and paid a heavy price for her gallantry. Hit three times, she lost her charthouse and sustained a hit below the waterline that damaged the main engine and threatened to flood the boat; two men were killed outright and five more wounded.[38] Fighting flooding and a balky engine, *PT493* managed to crawl her way to the shore of Panaon Island, where she was grounded on a rocky outcrop. *PT491* stood off-shore and lent what aid she could, taking off the wounded and lending spare crewmen to help patch *PT493*'s hull as the tide rose. Soon after dawn, however, the battle was lost and, as the last crewmen swam to safety, *PT493* drifted away from shore and sank stern-first at 0743. She would be the only Allied vessel sunk in the Battle of Surigao Strait.

Fuso Out; DesDiv4 Devastated

One further trio of PT boats was approaching from the north, Section 11, but they were warned off by Captain Coward in *Remey* (DD688), commanding DesRon54. The picket squadron of destroyers deployed at the narrowest part of the strait was preparing its own torpedo attack. Arrayed three destroyers on the eastern side of the channel and two on the west, they established radar contact at 0240 and within five minutes had well-resolved targets showing on their SG surface-search radar scopes due south at 15nm. Coward, in personal command of the eastern group, had a slight lead over the western pair. They were perhaps 15,000yd north-northeast of 3rd Section when they were spotted by lookouts in *Shigure*, just ahead of *Yamashiro* in the Japanese formation. (There is some disagreement as to the exact formation of 3rd Section at this time. Nishimura wanted them to be in a single column, led by the four destroyers in the order *Michishio*, *Asagumo*, *Yamagumo* and *Shigure*, followed by *Yamashiro*, *Fuso* and *Mogami*. The single column would simplify identification of friend from foe. In reality, it appears that the Japanese had not yet achieved this formation and that the destroyers were well to the starboard of the battleships and *Mogami* somewhat to port.[39])

    Remey, leading *McGowan* (DD678) and *Melvin* (DD680), reached firing position at 0300 and began launching torpedoes immediately. Due to misfirings, only twenty-seven of thirty were launched and all but one (or possibly two) missed aft of *Yamashiro*. One torpedo, fired by *Melvin*, hit *Fuso* at approximately 0309 in way of her boiler room, causing her to lose power and speed. This started flooding that caused a starboard list and forced her out of line to starboard. It is possible she was hit by a second torpedo forward near her forward turret. The explosion of the torpedo(es) was quite visible to some, such as observers on *Mogami*, but was not seen from *Yamashiro* or *Shigure*. *Fuso* apparently lost all communications, because she did not report her damage to Nishimura, and *Mogami*, assuming the explosion must have been seen from the flagship, thought it unnecessary to report. The three American destroyers, under heavy fire from *Yamashiro* and at least two Japanese destroyers, escaped unharmed into the smoke screen they had laid on their way south with just this eventuality in mind.

139. No photograph of a night battle can hope to show the confusion caused by the crashing noise and flashing light of gunfire interrupting an otherwise pitch-dark night, 25 October 1944. This shot from *Pennsylvania* looks south over Oldendorf's Left Flank Force cruisers as they fire further south towards Nishimura. The low clouds are lit up by the gunfire, as is the lingering smoke from the gunfire, which was not much dispersed by the light northeasterly breeze. *Pennsylvania* was the one American battleship that did not fire in this battle. (*NARA*)

While not entirely brought to a stop, *Fuso* was reduced to limping along at about 10kt. For a while she continued to the north, but when the extent of her damage was understood, she turned first west and then south.

The two destroyers in the western group, *McDermut* (DD677) and *Monssen* (DD798), fired their twenty torpedoes, starting at 0309. This was seen clearly by the Japanese and Nishimura ordered a simultaneous 90° turn away to starboard, the correct move in such a situation. However, for reasons that will forever remain unknown, he ordered 3rd Section to turn back to the north after only ninety seconds, not nearly enough time for the torpedoes to have cleared his formation. All he achieved by this manoeuvre was to put his van destroyers in harm's way. At least four, possibly as many as six, of *McDermut*'s ten torpedoes found targets. At approximately 0320, *Yamagumo* was hit by two or three torpedoes, setting off a sympathetic explosion of her own torpedoes. She virtually disintegrated, sinking in less than two minutes; there were only two survivors. One torpedo hit *Michishio* in way of her port engine room, leading to the flooding of her engineering spaces and the loss of all power. (*Michishio* may have been hit by a second torpedo forward that carried away her bow.[40]) *Asagumo* was also hit by a torpedo from *McDermut*, which collapsed her forecastle under her No.1 main-battery mount. She could continue to make way, but only at a much reduced speed. After assessing the damage, her captain ordered her to continue to the north where, he hoped, her torpedoes and remaining guns could be of use.

One of *Monssen*'s torpedoes also found a target; *Yamashiro* was hit aft, starting a fire on her quarterdeck, but not affecting her speed or stability. Though not causing major damage, this hit did cause some serious confusion. Lookouts in *Shigure*, who had not seen *Fuso* hit, saw this detonation clearly, and reported serious damage to one of the battleships to Nishino. He then heard a voice radio message from Nishimura: 'We have received a torpedo attack. You are to proceed and attack all ships.'[41] Adding the tone of this message to observations reported by his lookouts, he concluded that *Yamashiro* had been disabled and that Nishimura was releasing the remnants of 3rd Section to continue the attack individually.

Confusion in 3rd Section

Even while the last of DesRon54's torpedoes were hitting, DesRon24's six destroyers began their attack. Coming south from Bugho Point, they split into two divisions of three, one led by squadron commander Captain Kenmore M McManes in *Hutchins* (DD476), the other by Commander A E Buchanan, RAN, in HMAS *Arunta* (D5). McManes wanted Buchanan to lead his three destroyers across the Japanese bow and attack from their starboard side while he swung inshore, hoping to remain undetected, pass the enemy formation and turn north again, delivering his attack from the port quarter. Buchanan had no enthusiasm for the risky manoeuvre assigned to his division, and opted for a direct attack from Nishimura's port bow, which commenced at 0323. *Arunta* and *Beale* (DD471) sent nine torpedoes towards *Shigure*, which was leading the shrunken Japanese formation. Nishino saw the attack forming, and, at 0324, he reversed course to the south and increased speed to 26kt, causing all torpedoes to miss. *Killen* (DD593) launched five torpedoes at *Yamashiro*; one of these hit, staggering the old battleship and temporarily reducing her speed to 5kt.

McManes' group started launching torpedoes at 0329; all fifteen of their initial salvo missed their targets.

Shigure continued south, passing *Yamashiro* and *Mogami*, mistaking the former for *Fuso*. His hope was:

> finding out what happened to the flagship and also the possibility of changing the flag to my ship. At 0255 I determined there was no more use looking for the YAMASHIRO and decided I must go to the van of the force.[42] We were unable to make telephone communication with YAMASHIRO. While searching for YAMASHIRO, the lookout informed me he had sighted what he thought was YAMASHIRO sinking. I did not attempt to pick up survivors, but shortly after this information proceeded to continue the battle. I was able to maintain communication with the FUSO.[43]

In the course of his communication with *Yamashiro* during his run to the south, he reported seeing *Fuso* (which was actually *Yamashiro*) gaining speed and heading north. When Nishimura received this news, he was elated, as it reinforced his mistaken belief that *Fuso* was still right behind him in line.

Shima Turns North

Shima's force, which by this time was trailing 3rd Section by only about forty minutes, had just turned north into the strait when it came under torpedo boat attack. At 0325, *PT137* of Section 6 put a single torpedo into *Abukuma*'s port side just below her bridge, causing serious flooding and reducing her to a crawl. In all, thirty of the thirty-nine PT boats present had attempted attacks on the Japanese forces, launching thirty-four torpedoes. This was the only one that hit. Shima opted to leave *Abukuma* behind and proceed up Surigao Strait towards the sound and sight of battle, increasing speed to 28kt.

Fuso and *Michishio* Sink Unseen

To wrap up this part of the action, before getting to the main gunfire action, it is necessary to look at the fate of two Japanese ships. *Fuso*, which had been taking water forward, apparently foundered just before 0340, sinking bow first. Her stern remained above water for some period of time. Oil leaking from ruptured bunkers ignited as she was sinking and burned fiercely on the surface around the upraised stern and perhaps in another separate patch nearby. These fires continued for several hours.[44] Only ten crewmen survived her sinking.

Some sources describe a large explosion accompanying *Fuso*'s demise. One of these was McManes in *Hutchins*. He had led his division south after the first attack at 0329. At 0338, his sound operator heard loud underwater detonations, which he took to be his torpedoes hitting, but were more likely the sound of bulkheads collapsing as *Fuso* sank. As McManes moved further south, he encountered two more targets – *Mogami*, which continued to trail *Yamashiro* by several thousand yards, and *Asagumo*, still struggling towards the north. (*Michishio*, which in some accounts is listed as one of McManes' division's targets, had most likely succumbed to her damage, sinking unseen at about 0335.[45]) McManes' destroyers kept up a steady fusillade of gunfire at *Mogami* and *Asagumo* for three minutes, between 0341 and 0343, scoring well on both targets. Before turning away, *Hutchins* fired five torpedoes at *Asagumo*. They appear to have all missed.

DesRon56 In; The Battle Line Prepares to Open Fire

Just as McManes was launching his first half-salvo of torpedoes, he sent a message to his immediate superior officer, Adm Berkey, who passed it on to Oldendorf: 'ComTaskGroup 77.3 reported that the western group had just fired and that the Destroyer Leader believed that the enemy was retiring.'[46]

McManes' belief was apparently due to seeing *Shigure* heading south. Oldendorf's reaction to this news was to have serious consequences. Fearful lest Nishimura escape to the south past destroyers and PT boats now out of torpedoes – or even worse, that he might join up with Shima for a more powerful lunge at the northern exit from the strait, he decided to send in the nine destroyers of Captain Roland N Smoot's DesRon56, which were still located between the battle line and the two cruiser lines further south. His orders, issued at approximately 0335, were simple; Smoot amplified the orders for the two sections he would not be personally leading: 'Launch attack at big boys. Section three (3) attack 270–315, section two (2) 090–045, medium speed setting for fish; fire half salvos.'[47] Smoot's intent was for his destroyers to accelerate past either end of Oldendorf's Left Flank cruisers and launch three simultaneous attacks, his group slightly off

Nishimura's starboard bow and the other two further out towards the sides as indicated in his message.

That was all well and good, but a second story line was being written even while Smoot's destroyers were heading south to attack. At almost exactly the same time Oldendorf was sending in DesRon56, Admiral Weyler ordered his battleships to prepare to open fire at 26,000yd.[48] (At this time, *Yamashiro* was approximately 32,000yd south of the battle line.) As early as 0336, McManes sent a message correcting his mistake, reporting that Nishimura was still heading north, yet there is no indication that Oldendorf made any attempt to cancel the orders to Smoot's destroyers.[49]

Men waiting in the battle line felt a strange combination of nervousness and confidence. Earlier in the morning, *West Virginia*'s log noted: 'Saw three starshells to NW of us, perhaps over land and fired in connection with troops operation. Wished they would stop as light might silhouette us.'[50]

Some of the Americans knew just what an advantage they had as they waited for Nishimura to come to them:

> There could be no doubt now. We were in the ideal position, a position dreamed of, studied and plotted in War College maneuvers and never hoped to be obtained. An enemy within medium gun range, on a comparatively steady course, in a column formation, steaming into a 'capped T' trap! Guns were on target, and voices and fingers were anxious to unload them.[51]

But, as the range shrank, there was also nervousness about the destroyers, both Smoot's and McManes', present in the target zone. Again, as seen from *West Virginia*, leading the battle line, the apprehension is a discernible subtext:

0333	4,000 yards to go. Gunnery officer reports range 30,000 and has solution on a large target.
0345	Saw explosion in target area. Talked with gunnery officer to be sure our target was not among our own DD's. Fire control stated he had been on target for some time. CIC stated our DD's were clear.
0349	Starshells in target area. Can't tell if our DD or enemy is firing them. Our range 24,000. Am hesitating to fire until certain target is enemy. ComBatDiv 4 directed open fire.
0351	Our cruisers on our right flank opened fire. Our gunnery officer says he has had same big target for a long time and it is enemy. Commanding Officer ordered commence firing.
0352-10	First salvo 8 guns range 2,800 yards AP projectiles.
0353	Could hear gunnery officer chuckle and announce hit first salvo. Watched the second salvo through glasses and saw explosions when it landed.[52]

Several points are worth noting about this account. One was Captain Herbert V Wiley's lingering concern about the presence of American destroyers in the target zone. (On this score, he actually had no reason to be concerned at 0345 or even 0353. McManes' squadron was clearing the immediate vicinity of 3rd Section and Smoot's destroyers were just working their way around the cruiser line during that period.) The second was the relief felt when the battle line, and the cruisers as well, actually got their chance to open fire.

Nishimura Overwhelmed

Having worked back up to 12kt after absorbing her second torpedo, *Yamashiro* headed north directly into the trap laid for her. *Shigure* was overtaking, but was well to the east of the flagship. *Mogami* trailed *Yamashiro* by at least 1,000yd. Shima was 10nm behind and closing the gap at 28kt.

Having reached this point, and apparently unaware that significant enemy forces blocked his immediate path forward, it is not surprising that Nishimura had no plan for how to respond when, at 0351, Oldendorf's cruisers opened fire, followed a minute later by the battle line and Berkey's cruisers. The effect must have been stunning (in the original meaning of that word). An eyewitness in *Bennion* (DD662), one of Smoot's destroyers racing south, saw much the same scene as Nishimura would have:

> All along the northern horizon, enormous billows of flame from . . . 16- and 14-inch main-battery guns lit up the battle line. Directly over our heads stretched a procession of tracers as the battleships' shells converged on the Japanese column. The apparent slowness of the projectiles was surprising. Taking 15 to 20 seconds in their trajectory before reaching the target, they seemed to hang in the sky. Through the director optics, I could clearly see the explosions of the shells bursting on the Japanese ships, sending up cascades of flame as they ripped away topside gun mounts and erupted in fiery sheets of molten steel tearing into the heavy armor plate.[53]

At first, it appears that every Allied ship that was firing had chosen *Yamashiro* to target, and she was literally smothered with a heavy and accurate fusillade as she bore around to port to open her amidships turrets. (The magazines supplying her two after turrets had been flooded after the second torpedo hit, so they were unable to fire.) Every one of the Allied cruisers participated in this slaughter, though *Shropshire* did not open fire for five minutes because her Type 284 radar was unable to obtain a usable firing solution until the range had dropped to 15,500yd. Three of the American battleships did almost all the firing for the battle line – *West Virginia*, *California* and *Tennessee*. This was in part due to the fact that these three had been fitted with the latest Mk8 (also known as FH) 10cm-band fire control radar. Of the other three American battleships, only *Maryland* contributed any significant amount of gunfire, six salvos, while *Mississippi* fired one salvo and *Pennsylvania* none at all. These three were all equipped with the older FC 40cm fire control radar, which proved to be poor at distinguishing ship targets from land returns and discriminating shell splashes from ships. An equally important factor was the movement of Oldendorf's cruisers in front of the battle line, which tended to block the radars of the ships further back in Weyler's line.[54]

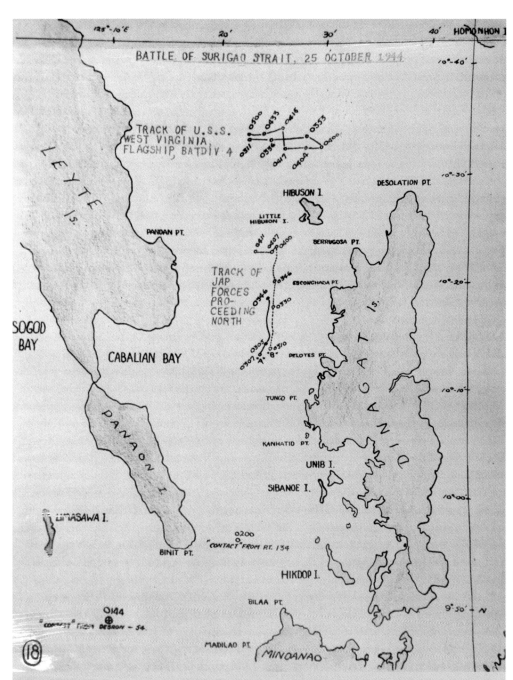

140. This chart shows the Battle of Surigao Strait as seen from *West Virginia*. The 'A' track appears to be that of *Mogami*; the 'B' track that of *Yamashiro*, through her approach and turn to parallel the Battle Line and up through the point she turned south, apparently being lost by *West Virginia*'s radar at that time. (*NARA*)

Mogami trailed *Yamashiro* by enough distance that she was ignored by all the major Allied units for the first seven minutes of the gun battle. Only McManes' destroyers continued to engage the cruiser as they moved north along the Leyte shore. Finally, one of the cruisers, *Portland*, noticed *Mogami* turning away and correctly deduced that she was preparing to fire torpedoes.

0356   Checked fire to shift targets as present target is under fire from many ships and burning brightly.

0358   Resumed fire at second ship in column which appeared to be retiring to south at high speed. Opening range 19,300, bearing 194° True.

0402   Check fire to shift targets. Target out of effective range.[55]

Mogami had indeed turned to fire torpedoes to the north; she was unable to pinpoint an exact target, so she put four Type 93 torpedoes in the water at 0401 aimed at the gun flashes to the north and continued her turn until she was heading south at her best speed. Before *Portland* ceased firing at *Mogami*, she hit her hard at 0402. Two hits in the bridge area killed her captain and other hits in her engineering spaces left her on fire and losing way.

Unlike most of the torpedoes fired this night, one of *Mogami*'s can actually be accounted for: its wake was spotted from one of Smoot's destroyers, *Albert W. Grant* (DD649).

0402-1/2 Enemy torpedo reported as missing astern by approximately 20 feet. This was a torpedo wake; hence torpedo should have been a hit. Miss probably due to deep submergence of torpedo.[56]

As would be the case with other Japanese attempts to strike back at the overwhelming force they were facing, with different luck, they might have had more success. In this case, a torpedo set to run deep for maximum effect on a cruiser or battleship ran harmlessly under a destroyer.

Shigure, which had taken a course about 1,000yd to the east of *Yamashiro*, also came under heavy gunfire, but had better luck than *Mogami*. Unable to find any targets with her radar and blocked by smoke from visual contact with the Allied squadron, Nishino gradually bore away to the east and then south starting at 0356, chased by shell splashes:

I was receiving a terrific bombardment. There were so many near misses that the gyro compass was out. The ship was constantly trembling from force of near misses, and the wireless was out . . .

At about 0315 SHIGURE received a 23cm hit on deck aft which penetrated to an oil storage tank but which did not explode.[57]

The 8in shell struck the hull aft, passing out the port shell plating underwater without exploding, but perforated several oil tanks and damaged her steering mechanism; it killed two men and wounded several more.

Grant Caught in the Middle; Yamashiro Brought to a Stop

Surprised and very quickly subjected to an overwhelming barrage of steel, the Japanese nevertheless responded with everything they had. *Yamashiro* turned sharply to port and opened fire with her 36cm main battery and 15cm casemates. As with *Shigure*, her radar proved to be of no assistance; she targeted enemy warships in both cruiser groups with her main battery when they became visible for one reason or another. As seen from *Boise* in Berkey's Right Flank Group: 'At about 0401, shell splashes were observed near HMAS SHROPSHIRE. The splashes were all short initially, then all overs. A few moments later, several salvos were heard passing directly over BOISE.'[58]

Shropshire was singled out by *Yamashiro*'s gunners for a reason: '. . . the U.S. Ships were all using flashless propellant, and when our first 8-inch broadside fired the flash was terrific. I consider that the Japanese ships fired several salvos in our direction, at our flash, mistaking us for a capital ship.'[59]

Columbia was targeted for a different reason:

0359   . . . Observed large-calibre shells falling close toward the stern of the ship.

0400   . . . Observed additional near misses and straddles aft.

0401   Additional straddles and near misses of a large calibre gun were observed aft. (This ship was plainly silhouetted to enemy by main-battery flashes of our BB's as our station was about abeam of 3rd BB in column.[)][60]

But, for all this shooting of her main battery, not one of *Yamashiro*'s 36cm shells found a target. She had much better shooting with her secondary battery. Their target was Section 1 of DesRon56.

Smoot's destroyers, once clear of the cruiser line, accelerated to flank speed, well aware they were entering dangerous waters where getting in and out fast might mean survival. Section 2, coming down the eastern side, fired fifteen torpedoes from relatively long range between 0354 and 0359, then retired towards Hibuson Island.[61] All of those torpedoes missed. Section 3, assigned the western approach, came within 6000yd of a target and fired their torpedoes.[62] Given what happened next, it's not possible to identify this target with any certainty. It may have been *Shigure*. It was more likely a false echo caused by shell splashes, a phenomenon to which the destroyers' Mk4 (FD) was susceptible.[63] As *Bennion* was turning away to starboard after launching her first half-salvo of five torpedoes, her gunnery officer, LT(jg) James L. Holloway III, was surprised by what he saw:

Suddenly, a large warship loomed on our port bow. Using the slewing sight, I swung the director to point directly at this new target, instructing the rangefinder operator to track and identify this contact. If hostile, the fire-control radar would be locked on and the plotting-room computer would then generate a target course and speed . . . It was at this juncture that the unidentified warship commenced firing what appeared to be its secondary battery. From the clearly visible tracers, I could see that the rounds were being directed at the USS *Albert W. Grant* (DD-649), a destroyer in our squadron . . .

When the unidentified large ship opened fire she had immediately established her identity as enemy, because her salvos were ripple fire. That was characteristic of Japanese naval gunfire, in contrast to the simultaneous salvos of U.S. Warships.[64]

Holloway's observations were correct. As Section 1, the middle of Smoot's three groups of destroyers, turned west at 0358, they became an excellent target for *Yamashiro*'s starboard secondary battery of seven 15cm guns. Indeed, Smoot's decision to turn parallel to the enemy's course must be seriously questioned. There is no doubt it made sense as far as delivering a torpedo attack was concerned. It put his three ships in an ideal position to launch a half-salvo of torpedoes at *Yamashiro*'s broad starboard beam from a range of less than 7,000yd at 0404. But that manoeuvre also put the three destroyers between *Yamashiro* and the Allied big guns, which meant that every salvo silhouetted them, making them the easiest target for the Japanese gunners. As Holloway noted, *Yamashiro*'s secondary battery was targeting Smoot's line soon after they turned, and shortly after 0404, *Grant* was being straddled by shell splashes.[65]

All three destroyers held a steady course to the west for three more minutes as they lined up their second half-salvo of torpedoes, making smoke all the while. Then, satisfied that the set-up was as good as it would get, Smoot ordered the remaining torpedoes fired and an immediate turn away to the north.

0407   Remaining five torpedoes ordered fired
0407   First hit aft landed among empty powder cases stacked across fantail. 5"/38 gun #5 out of commission from shrapnel. No fire started.[66]

The shell was fired by *Yamashiro*. Had she been the only ship firing at *Grant*, that would have been bad enough. Over the next several minutes, she was hit two more times by 15cm shells from *Yamashiro* and twice more by smaller-calibre Japanese shells. Three more Japanese shells exploded short but caused some degree of splinter damage.[67] The cumulative damage of all of these shots was serious, though in no way threatening to the survival of the ship: all the damage was above the waterline. Probably the worst hit was one which demolished the port-side whaleboat. Had *Yamashiro* been the only ship firing at *Grant*, she would have retired with the rest of her section in good order. The casualties due to this gunfire were relatively small.[68]

Unfortunately, the eyes of *Yamashiro*'s gunners were not the only ones tracking Smoot's destroyers. Some of those eyes were on Oldendorf's flagship:

8. The 5" battery had been coached to a single target approaching the formation at high speed at 14,000 yards on a course of about 330° T. Fire was opened at 0404 on bearing 183° T. range 7,000 yards. The enemy ship was observed to turn away to a southwesterly course and firing continued, with hits being made, until the target at 0409 bore about 200° T. . .[69]

It is very possible that *Louisville* experienced the same phenomenon as occurred to *Denver*, when a radar contact the gunnery officer had been following disappeared from their screens, only to reappear moments later on almost the same bearing, but much closer.[70] Shell splashes were erupting around *Denver* and *Columbia*, and *Denver* opened up on the closest target first with her secondary battery and then, at 0404, with her main battery, at what she believed was *Shigure* making a torpedo run. But it could not have been *Shigure*, which, by that time, had been heading south at high speed for more than five minutes well to the east of this scuffle. The ship that was the target of this gunfire recorded its effect.

0407-1/2 Commenced turn to 000°T. Still following in column. Several bad shell hits amidships. Steam began pouring out of #1 stack. Forward fireroom and forward engineroom out of commission. After fireroom abandoned due to excessive temperatures caused by rapidly escaping steam through two shell holes from forward engine room.

0408-1/2 Additional shell hits began to riddle ship. Hit forward at waterline flooded forward storeroom, frame 15, and forward crews berthing compartment. Hit in 40MM gun #1 exploded 40MM ammunition and started fire. Hit through starboard boat davit exploded killing Medical Officer, 5 radiomen, and almost entire amidships repair party. Other hits in forward stack, one hit in port motor whale boat, one hit and low order explosion in galley. One hit in scullery room, one hit in after crews berthing compartment, and one additional in forward engine room. All lights, telephone communications, radars, and radios out of commission. Steering control shifted aft.[71]

At 0408, Oldendorf received a message from Smoot reading: 'You are firing on ComDesRon56. We are in the middle of the channel.' Moments later, this was followed by another, more desperate: 'You are firing at us.' Oldendorf acted immediately, ordering all ships to cease fire at 0409.[72] But, in *Grant*, the damage had already been done. In a space of less than two minutes, she had been hit by ten American 6in AP shells, most likely all fired by *Denver*. That so much damage could be caused by one ship in so short a span of time was a testament to the speed and efficiency that gun crews guided by radar fire control had achieved by this point in the war. What would follow was a testament to the courage and determination of *Grant*'s crew as they fought to save their ship.

0411 Steadied on course 000°T. Still steering aft. Fire on 40 MM gun #1 extinguished. No light or power forward. Generator aft continued in operation by holding down trip until steam pressure dropped to 200 lbs. Investigation started to discover extent of damage. Ship began to lose speed.

0414 After fireroom entered and boilers # 3 and # 4 secured. Boilers had been steaming untended for about five minutes but high water was only trouble noted.

0420	Ship dead in water. No power or lighting to guns. All 5" battery except gun #5, all 40 MM except #4 and entire 20MM in commission and operating in manual. Enemy ships at estimated range of 7,000 yards sighted almost due south through occasional [sic] fires and explosions. Steps being taken to care for wounded, repair damage, and check flooding.
0421	Generator in after engineroom cut out due to loss of steam pressure. Diesel generator forward started in immediate operation furnishing emergency lighting to after part of ship and power to I.C. Room and after steering.
0440	Using blinker gun, following message sent to friendly cruiser to northward: ' From DD649 WE ARE DEAD IN WATER X TOW NEEDED.' Message was repeated several times as no acknowledgement was expected, this vessel being directly between the two battle lines.
. . .	
0455	Diesel generator cut out due to contamination of diesel oil with salt water through a split tank. No lights or power on the ship.[73]

Incredibly, *Grant* survived this ordeal, despite her forward engineering spaces being completely flooded and partial flooding in her after fire room, crew's mess and several compartments forward, leaving her down at the bow by more than 4ft and with a 9° port list. She was saved in part by her relatively light construction, and only three of the shells that hit her actually exploded. Nevertheless, her survival looked far from assured when Smoot's flagship *Newcomb* (DD586) came alongside at 0500 to send over her medical officer and two corpsmen. Fortunately, she had no major holes in her shell plating and, gradually, the flooding was brought under control. At 0505, boiler No.4 was relit, though it would be seventy minutes before it had enough steam pressure to cut in her generators. At 0543, *Newcomb* came alongside again and the transfer of *Grant*'s wounded began. *Newcomb* sent over power lines, submersible pumps and gasoline-powered handy-billies, all of which helped combat the flooding. After *Grant*'s generators were cut in at 0615, *Newcomb* cast off and began to tow *Grant* north at 0640. Still, it was not until 1245 that she was declared out of immediate danger of sinking.[74] When the casualties were counted, it turned out that 34 had died and an additional 104 had been wounded. Given the near-automatic excellence of American shooting and the unfortunate position Section 1 of DesRon56 found itself in, the question is not why was *Grant* hit by 'friendly fire', but rather why was *Grant* the only ship so hit?

Yamashiro had faced long odds when she came within range of Oldendorf's guns and it can be no surprise that, despite bravely fighting the ship, her crew was unable to keep her afloat for long under the pounding she was receiving. The volume of fire was so intense that it is difficult to identify the times that significant events occurred, but it appears likely that at about 0404, her No.3 turret exploded, set off by battleship gunfire penetrating the gun house. When the Allied lines ceased firing on Oldendorf's order at 0409, *Yamashiro* was ablaze all along her upperworks, but she was still under control, as she was seen to turn south. At about 0405 or shortly thereafter, she was hit by a torpedo, fired either

141. This chart shows the course of *Albert W. Grant* (DD649) as she wove her way between the battle line, the Left Flank Force and the enemy (*Yamashiro*), firing off two salvos of torpedoes, while coming under enemy and 'friendly' fire. It is very likely one of the torpedoes from the first salvo, marked on the chart with an asterisk ('*'), that hit *Yamashiro* and helped seal her fate. (*NARA*)

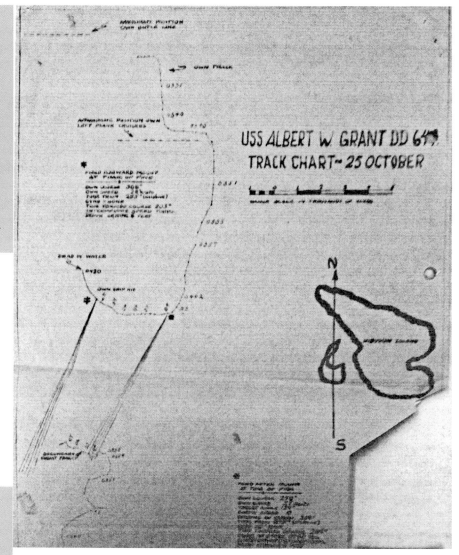

142. Four men of *Grant*'s Mk37 fire control director crew relax on top of the director under the FD radar antenna, 21 August 1944. The apparatus sticking up to the right is the slewing sight, used by the director control officer to quickly bring the director on to a target, after which the rangefinder and the three sighting scopes on the front face of the director used by the trainer, pointer and control officer (left to right) would be used to obtain a firing solution. (*NARA*)

by *Grant* or *Bennion*, which temporarily staggered the old battleship, but she was seen to increase speed again as she turned away.[75] *Yamashiro* was probably hit again by another torpedo as she was turning. This last hit appears to have left her without power and doomed her. As she drifted to a stop, she slowly rolled over to port and slid under at 0419. The best estimate of her losses is that 1,636 officers and men, including Nishimura, went down with the ship.

The question must be raised in this case, as in the case of *Bismarck* and *Scharnhorst*, whether *Yamashiro* could have been sunk by gunfire alone. While there are many similarities to the cases of those other two sinkings, there also are some striking differences. *Yamashiro* was a full generation older than the German ships, with all that implied in terms of less-adequate underwater protection and less complete internal subdivision. Also, *Yamashiro* faced six enemy battleships and eight cruisers, while the Germans faced much smaller Royal Navy forces. Still, it is hard to imagine how much pounding with short-range fire would have been required to disable *Yamashiro*, much less sink her. There is no question that the four or more torpedoes she absorbed were at least as important as all the gunfire aimed at her in accounting for her sinking.

The Remnants of 3rd Section Collide with Shima

That left *Mogami* and *Shigure*, both limping south – the former due to powerplant damage, the latter due to steering problems – as Shima was making his best speed north, his two cruisers leading the four destroyers. There is no question that Shima was alarmed by the wall of gunfire he saw in front of him starting at 0351, but he kept coming, hoping to somehow assist Nishimura before it was too late. The accounts of how and when *Shigure* encountered Shima's approaching squadron differ markedly. In some accounts, *Shigure* was still making 30kt and barely missed colliding with *Shiranuhi*, the lead destroyer of Shima's force. According to this version, *Shigure* kept going without communicating with *Shiranuhi* or any other of Shima's ships, only slowing due to rudder problems when well south of this point.[76] According to Nishino's testimony immediately after the war,

> About 0350, I sighted Admiral SHIMA's force advancing northward, while we were repairing the rudder.[77]
>
> . . .
>
> I signalled to Admiral SHIMA by blinker because the telephone was broken.
>
> . . .
>
> I signalled to the approaching force requesting them to identify themselves, as I was not sure but that they might be American surface units. The answer received was 'I am the NACHI'. I answered 'I am the SHIGURE, I have rudder difficulties.' There was no communication after this message.[78]

The interrogator at the time and many since have wondered that Nishino made no attempt to warn Shima about the maelstrom awaiting him to the north. He shrugged it off as not being his responsibility, since he was not under Shima's command.

143. This chart from a postwar damage report diagrams the damage done to *Grant* at the Battle of Surigao Strait, 25 October 1944. The top profile drawing shows all fifteen hits she sustained, five from *Yamashiro* and ten from *Denver*. The plan drawing at the bottom shows the flooded compartments. (USN)

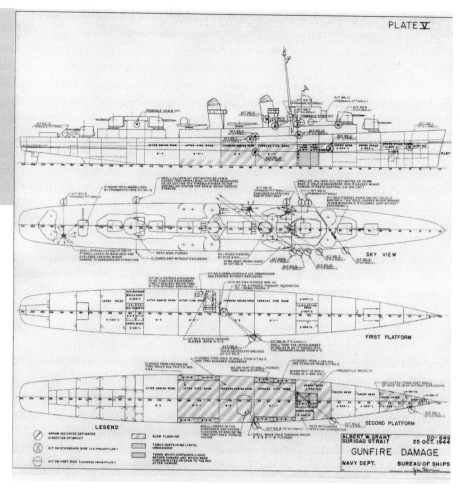

The further north Shima progressed, the more cautious he became about plunging ahead into the thick bank of smoke covering the entire width of the strait to his north, constantly lit by the flash of gunfire and flicker of burning ships. At 0330, he passed two fires about 22,000yd to the east.

Although we knew they were Japanese vessels on fire we did not bother with them, just progressed.[79] When we came to that place the smoke screen was very dense . . . and the Japanese radar on our ships were not working very effectively for search; we could detect no American ships on the radar. We knew however American forces were there because of the smoke screen and I judged from the situation that the American force was behind the smoke attacking NISHIMURA's force . . .
We knew that the other part of the NISHIMURA's fleet was there behind the smoke; there were flashes from gunfire and we saw the trail of the shells, but we could not see the body of the vessels.[80]

Shortly after passing *Shigure*, *Nachi*'s radar finally picked up the American cruiser line at 13,000yd and Shima put his plan into operation. 'We ordered the destroyers to conduct attack, the cruisers turned and delivered their torpedo attack and then ordered the destroyers to make their attack.'[81] Shima ordered the two cruisers to turn right and, at 0427, they launched a full salvo of torpedoes at the American line (regardless of any Japanese ships that might be hidden in the smoke). They were then to continue the turn, looping around and falling in behind the four destroyers which were to head north until they reached a point from which they too could launch torpedoes at the Americans.

At that moment, a burning apparition appeared out of the smoke on *Nachi*'s port bow. It was *Mogami*, afire and barely under control. With her captain dead, she was weaving such an uncertain course that observers in *Nachi* seriously misjudged her speed.

> . . . we thought at first that MOGAMI which was burning was stopped, but evidently it was not stopped but on a southward course; and after delivering the torpedo attack, NACHI, which was turning away, collided with MOGAMI on converging course about 10 degrees. We were all concentrating on the attack, so did not know the course of the MOGAMI until they collided. Although, we thought she was dead in the water, she was moving slightly and we simply over-estimated our own speed, and the MOGAMI was moving faster than we thought perhaps about eight knots, and in spite of hard rudder we collided . . .
>
> NACHI's speed was reduced to 18 knots as a result of the collision. ASHIGARA turned safely outside MOGAMI and fell in astern. The original intention was that NACHI would fall in astern of the destroyers but it was necessary to investigate damage, so we took southward course for about 10 minutes. We went south and then turned north again. The destroyers went to full speed of about 30 knots and closed further. At this time NACHI could not make any more than 20 knots which was insufficient to make the attack, and also by the smoke screen we could not guess exact position of your force, so Admiral SHIMA ordered to stop further attack of these cruisers at this time, called back destroyers, discontinuing attack.[82]

Nothing could have been further removed in spirit from Nishimura's dogged determination to break through to Leyte Gulf or die trying.

Mopping Up the Cripples

All that remained now was the retreat of the Japanese, the dispatching of the crippled ships by Allied forces, the praise for the victors, some deserved and some not, and the recriminations for the near-disaster off Samar. All the surviving Japanese ships were moving south towards the southern exit from Surigao Strait by at least 0435, with the exception of *Asagumo* and *Abukuma*. The former had got her flooding forward under control and turned north in pursuit of Shima's squadron at 0445.[83] This northward movement did not last long, as she soon encountered Shima heading south and came about to follow as best she could. *Abukuma* had repaired her damaged powerplant to the extent that she could make 20kt and she too had started making her way north.

As the dawn began colouring the eastern sky just before 0500, Shima's two heavy cruisers were heading south at 18kt, escorted by his four destroyers, still well within Surigao Strait. Remembering the PT boat attack that had damaged *Abukuma* near the southern tip of Panaon Island, Shima headed for the opposite side of the strait, closer to Mindanao. *Shigure* was ahead of Shima's force, moving slowly, still working on her balky steering. *Mogami* could make no more than 15kt and was trailing Shima by 3,000yd. *Asagumo* trailed even further behind. *Abukuma* had managed to build up to 20kt and was still coming north somewhat to the east of Shima on a converging course.

That was the situation when, at approximately 0455, *Shigure's* lookouts spotted torpedo boats 5,400yd to the west. These were the three boats of Section 11 that had been warned off by Coward more than two hours earlier. They had *Shigure* on their radars and made a slow, stealthy approach until she opened fire and increased speed, at which point they too increased speed and attempted to launch torpedoes.[84] Shima saw the gunfire to his immediate south and turned back to the north, followed by *Mogami*. *Asagumo* either missed or ignored the turn and continued to the south and soon joined *Shigure* in firing at the PT boats. One of the PT boats, *PT321*, suffered a 'hot-run' when attempting to fire a torpedo at 0459, and the resulting fire, fortunately of short duration, attracted the attention of the Japanese gunners. One man on *PT321* was wounded by shrapnel. Shima and *Mogami* turn south again at 0506. *Shigure* headed south at high speed, slowing again when this proved dangerous due to her on-going steering problems. *Asagumo* limped south behind Nishino, but, for the moment, ahead of Shima. *Abukuma* was sighted by Shima at 0515 and came about to the south at 0535; Shima assigned one of his destroyers, *Ushio*, to accompany her.

Oldendorf, in his capacity as commander of the Left Flank cruisers, gathered his ships and began a slow sweep to the south starting at 0450. He set his squadron's speed to 15kt, which unwittingly matched Shima's. His presumption was that the remaining PT boats and air strikes in the morning would catch any undamaged enemy ships; his task was to polish off any crippled ships he might come across. *Louisville* had continual radar bearings on multiple enemy targets to the south. At 0520, Oldendorf brought his cruisers right to 250° so they could fire broadsides at the various targets being tracked. He held off opening fire until he could be more sure of his targets. A message from Section 11's commander at 0525, reading: 'Three pips abeam Panaon Island. One burning brightly. Three large targets, 2 headed north, 1 south', seemed to satisfy him and he ordered fire resumed at 0530.[85] *Louisville* fired two full salvos at a target that proved to be illusory.

> At about 0530 the main battery fired 18 rounds on a huge flame that looked large enough to be coming from a large vessel broadside to the line of fire and burning from stem to stern. This was a burning ship of cruiser of [sic] larger dimension that evidently sank without further progress or was merely a pool of burning oil.[86]

That latter option was the only possible explanation as no ship was sunk in that area at that time, and there was at least one large persistent oil fire, often associated with the site where *Fuso* sank, repeatedly sighted during that night and morning, in the general vicinity of *Louisville's* phantom target. *Portland*, *Denver* and *Columbia* had found another target somewhat further south and *Louisville* switched to that target as well.

Occasionally the flame from this fire disclosed a destroyer stopped and apparently standing by. Shortly after we shifted . . . the fire of some other ship, it is believed the PORTLAND, apparently exploded this destroyer. When seen in the glow of firelight it had an intact bow . . .[87]

The ship targeted by the three American cruisers was not a destroyer and was not stopped; it was *Mogami*, now lagging some 2,600yd behind *Ashigara*. She had been hit multiple times and the fires in her amidships and after superstructure, which had been largely contained, once again flared out of control.

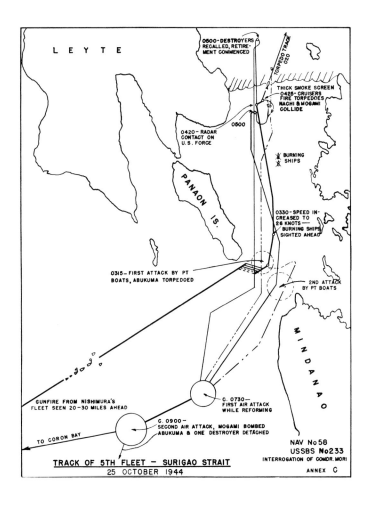

144. This chart, based on the postwar interrogation of Commander Mori Kokichi, shows the track of Vice-Admiral Shima Kiyohide's 5th Fleet during its approach to and penetration of Surigao Strait, 25 October 1944. (*USSBS Interrogation No. 233/58*)

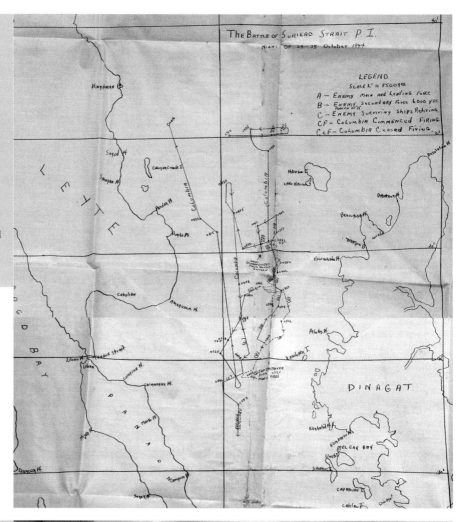

145. This chart shows the track of *Columbia*, one of the cruisers sent south to chase the retiring Japanese forces after the action died down at the north end of Surigao Strait, 25 October 1944. It shows the turn to the west at about 0530 and then to the north at 0550 when it was believed *Mogami* was making a torpedo attack. This was followed by a turn to the south at 0620 and the renewed chase after the retiring Japanese. (*NARA*)

146. *Denver* leads *Columbia* around to starboard as both fire their secondary battery at a target just barely visible at the left edge of this image. (Note the closely spaced puffs of smoke rising ahead of *Denver*.) The rising sun revealed several distinct smoke plumes on the southern horizon. The one on the left was probably from *Mogami*; the two larger on the right were likely the large oil fires burning over the site where *Fuso* sank. (*NARA*)

0530　Main battery commenced firing on target 'C', bearing 191°T range
　　　21,200, course 218°T, speed 16 knots. Visual observations disclosed
　　　Columbia's salvos to be striking large burning vessel believed to be BB.
　　　This ship was completely ablaze and burning worse than the Arizona
　　　burned at Pearl Harbor.[88]

Columbia's estimate of Mogami's size proved as faulty as Louisville's, but the
description of the damage being inflicted was probably only slightly exaggerated.
She was hit by between ten and twenty 6in and 8in rounds in a span of
approximately ten minutes. Nevertheless, Mogami showed no sign of giving up
the fight. Conned by junior officers, she wobbled south and then, apparently in
a desperate attempt to escape the punishment, turned west to 200° at 0535. This
manoeuvre was misinterpreted by Oldendorf as a torpedo attack and he ordered
his force to turn away, to the north, at 0540. At the same time, he ordered his
ships to cease firing. This proved fortuitous for Mogami, which probably could
not have stood up to much more of the pounding she had been receiving. She
turned to the south and, temporarily got lost in the pre-dawn gloom.
　　　Another Japanese ship was even closer to Oldendorf's cruisers: Asagumo was
3,000yd north of Mogami when gunfire started up, but being a smaller target, she
was ignored by all but one of the American cruisers. Minneapolis singled out the
destroyer for just a few rounds before also switching target to the larger Mogami,
but in those few rounds she hit Asagumo hard. Only one 8in round hit Asagumo,
right aft, but it started a fire and ruptured oil tanks, which proved to be a deadly
combination. She continued limping to the south at 7kt, but all efforts to contain
the spread of the fire proved futile and, at 0600, with dawn approaching, her
captain ordered her engines stopped and her crew to prepare to abandon ship.
　　　Over the next hour, this work progressed slowly, with the few undamaged
whaleboats slowly relaying crewmen to shore. This was interrupted half an hour
after dawn, when PT323, part of Section 13, the northernmost of the patrol boat
groups, attacked from the west, putting a single torpedo in Asagumo's starboard
quarter at 0700.[89] Enough crewmen remained onboard to man one gun in
the destroyer's No. 3 main-battery turret, and that defensive fire attracted the
attention of American destroyers further north screening Oldendorf's cruisers.
The following was reported by Sigourney (DD643):

0645　Number of smoke columns from enemy ships decreased to four (4) and
　　　were apparently drawing away. Sighted one enemy destroyer, believed
　　　to be SHIGURE class, with bow missing forward of forward gun mount
　　　and on fire aft, lying dead in water west of Tungo Point.[90]
. . .
0700　CONY, in Station #2, reported enemy destroyer (see 0645 entry) had
　　　opened fire and requested permission to return fire. Observed gun
　　　flashes from after gun mount of enemy destroyer; saw no shell splashes
　　　in vicinity of our formation.[91]
0706　CONY ordered to return fire. Several ships in the van commenced
　　　firing. Formation turned to course 210°T to unmask battery.

0708	Commenced firing on enemy destroyer.
0712	Ceased firing, having expended 5 rounds 5"/38 cal. AA Common and 20 rounds 5"/38 Common ammunition. Several definite hits observed at gun ranges from 12,000 to 7,000 yards.
0715	. . . Enemy destroyer observed to sink.[92]

In the end, there may have been as many as nine destroyers and two light cruisers firing at *Asagumo*, which returned fire from her after main-battery mount to the end. One hundred and ninety-one of her crew were lost; thirty-nine survived.

This ended the battle proper. By 0730, Oldendorf had received word of the action off Samar and all the Allied forces in Surigao Strait headed back to Leyte Gulf, with the exception of the PT boats still patrolling the southern reaches and two destroyers left to guard the northern exit. The remaining Japanese ships still had obstacles to overcome before they could find even temporary safety. They passed through the remaining PT boats without suffering further damage, but got caught several times by Allied aircraft as they tried to cross the Sulu Sea.

Mogami, by now lagging far behind, seemed especially vulnerable, and Shima detached the destroyer *Akebono* to escort her to Coron Bay. At 0830, her remaining engine broke down and she drifted to a stop approximately 25nm west of the Mindanao coast and about 30nm southeast of Panaon Island. At that point her fate was sealed. At 0902, she was hit by two bombs from attacking Avengers from TU77.4.1. She was ordered abandoned an hour and a half later and was finally scuttled by *Akebono*, taking 192 of her complement with her. *Shigure*, which arrived at Brunei on 27 October, was thus the only ship of the 3rd Section to survive the battle.

Art Become Science

It is worth a few lengthy excerpts from action reports to demonstrate how far naval gunfire had progressed from art to science. Typical of the American experience was *Phoenix*:

> At 0352, having received orders to commence fire when battleships opened . . . fire was opened with the main battery, to starboard . . . Full radar control, employing Mark VIII, was used.[93] Four spotting salvos, alternating forward and after 6" groups, using High Capacity shells, with steel nose plugs, were fired.[94] With hits observed on the fourth salvo, full fifteen gun salvos at fifteen second intervals were then initiated . . .
>
> The main-battery spotter reported at this time that the mean point of impact of all salvos was on target or slightly over, and good illumination was momentarily obtained by the explosion of the High Capacity shells on hitting the target. Tenth and subsequent salvos were fired using Armor Piercing shells. Flashless powder was used throughout the action. Force and direction of wind was such as to clear smoke between salvos and render optical spotting and observation possible.[95]

Columbia's report described the process somewhat differently:

> Mark 8 radar range and bearing using Mark 8 computer in normal fashion.[96] A smooth solution was obtained before opening fire. Fire was opened with an opening ladder, rapid salvoes. Radar spots were used and shift made to rapid continuous fire. When fires started in the target afforded an illuminated point of aim, radar bearing was checked optically and found to agree.
>
> After six minutes of continuous fire, shift was made to rapid salvoes and firing was continued in this manner until cease fire. Rocking ladder was used after opening ladder in accordance with doctrine.[97]

Both of these cruisers, and most of the American battleships at Surigao Strait, had Mk34 main-battery fire control directors. While not as sophisticated as the Mk38 GFCS installed in the post-treaty battleships, the Mk34 allowed some degree of 'closed-loop' operation with the Ford Range-keeper, so that when optical range-taking was possible, it would be fed into the Range-keeper as correction (if necessary) to the range supplied by the radar.[98]

Yamashiro had an equivalent fire control set up, but it was not nearly as centralised or automated as the American system. The work done by the Ford Range-keeper and its associated director was done in *Yamashiro* by three separate devices: Type 94 Hoiban director, which served a similar range and bearing data-gathering function as the Mk34; Type 92 Sokutekiban, linked to the director, calculated target course and speed; and Type 92 Shagekiban, which took inputs from the Hoiban and Sokutekiban, and calculated the gun set-up necessary to hit the target's predicted future position. Not only was this a more complex and slower arrangement, but it involved much more human interaction, with all the opportunity that brought for human error. The Hosen Shiki Sochi (low-angle fire control system) required eight men at the Sokutekiban and seven at the Shagekiban. The Ford Mk8 required a single operator.[99]

Despite this complexity, the Japanese system could perform well and had done so on other occasions, but it had its problems this night in *Yamashiro*, no doubt because the Hoiban and Sokutekiban, both located high up in her tall 'pagoda' foremast, were likely damaged or destroyed early in the gunfire phase of the engagement. The following comments are from *Columbia*'s action report:

> The enemy used both starshell and searchlight illumination . . . Just prior to the time this ship opened fire on target ABLE, several starshells were fired in the general direction of the formation in which this ship was steaming.[100] One of these starshells was about 2000 to 3000 yards short of this ship (but on in deflection). Since the starshells were between this ship and the enemy, they may have hindered rather than helped his control personnel . . . This ship was silhouetted by flashes of own battleship's gunfire. It is believed that this, plus own formation's flashes were responsible for the enemy fire experienced.
>
> The enemy's illumination was poor and his fire apparently confused. It is probable that his primary control stations had been hit. However, this did not prevent his placing shells uncomfortably close to this ship. A few minutes after our heavy ships opened fire, enemy major-caliber splashes were observed near this ship. Observers on this ship did not have good illumination (it being furnished mostly by gun-fire flashes) and it is considered that there were other splashes, (notably overs) which were not seen from this ship . . . Some observers stated they saw green dye, but its use cannot be confirmed. All splashes could not be clearly seen but enough were clearly seen to show that they were caused by heavy projectiles larger than 8". It is believed they were 14" splashes (At the time of observation they appeared even larger than 14"). Detonations were felt below decks.
>
> . . .
>
> The enemy appeared to be walking his salvos over and on, but not short.[101]

That account was followed by a chart listing fourteen salvos of near-misses from *Yamashiro*, five of which were straddles. It is testament to the quality of *Yamashiro*'s gunners that, amidst a rain of steel from at least half a dozen battleships and cruisers, they maintained a disciplined exercise of gunnery for as long as their guns would bear. *Columbia* was fortunate to have avoided damage or casualties.

Fates, Deserved or Otherwise

The fates of the major players in this sad drama need mention. Oldendorf, of course, received praise for his handling of the Allied forces inside Surigao Straits, but with the preponderance of forces he had, he could hardly have failed. He was awarded the Navy Cross and promoted to the rank of vice-admiral for his

148. Having appeared in these pages perhaps as many times as any ship, it is fitting that the heavy cruiser *Nachi* brings the story to a close. She reached as far as Manila Bay before the long arm of American naval airpower caught up with her on 5 November 1944. Manoeuvring frantically near Corregidor, she was hit by multiple bombs and torpedoes, breaking her in three pieces. Shima was ashore at Cavite and could only watch his flagship's demise. (*NARA*)

part in the action. He was never held responsible for his failure to recall Smoot's destroyers before opening fire on Nishimura. Nor was Smoot held responsible for his questionable decision to turn his section of destroyers into the potential line of fire between his own battle line and the enemy. In fact, Smoot was also awarded the Navy Cross for his actions in Surigao Strait and was promoted to rear-admiral soon thereafter.

The only Americans in any way questioned about their actions in the Battle of Leyte Gulf were Kinkaid and Halsey, both of whom were criticised by King for their joint failure to prevent Kurita exiting unopposed from San Bernardino Strait and attacking Sprague's carriers.[102] While this criticism may have stung, it prevented neither, especially Halsey, from having a full and successful naval career and considerable popular esteem.

Admiral Nishimura did not survive the battle. He was a respected combat leader, despite his less than stellar introduction in these pages, but had suffered grave personal loss, losing both his wife and only son during the war, and there is reason to believe he may have been seeking death in battle as he approached Surigao Strait.[103] If so, he found what he sought. Nevertheless, he was not universally admired: 'He was an old destroyer man . . . it was said of him he was clever and a capable Navy man. I will say this much, though, that there are some people who think NISHIMURA was very fortunate not to have returned from this battle.'[104]

Shima did return from Surigao Strait and survived the war. His conduct during this battle is the most open to question, as he made decisions that seem at odds with the Japanese spirit of strict adherence to orders and the active pursuit of death in battle. While his decision to retire from the battle after *Nachi*'s collision with *Mogami*, and to order his entire fleet to follow suit, stands in stark contrast to Nishimura's, it was by all lights a reasonable one. Shima lived for many years after the war and consistently defended his decision – at one point in 1958, responding to a letter from an American schoolboy, he stated: 'It was quite clear that we should only fall into a ready trap. I considered all such things – events, circumstances, possibilities. Then I came to my decision that it would be better to retreat from the strait and wait a chance to know how everything went.'[105]

Shima's actions at 0530, or lack of action, when he could have turned back to aid *Mogami* and *Asagumo*, is less understandable. Nevertheless, he, too, served out the war with distinction and lived the longest of any of the major players in this drama, dying at the age of eighty-three in 1973.

AFTERWORD

THE SECOND WORLD WAR WITNESSED MORE progress in the art of naval gunnery than had occurred in all the years since the Italians and English first mounted crude cannons on warships in the fifteenth century. Radars and optical rangefinders providing enemy range and azimuth; gyrocompasses, stable elements and pitometer logs providing own ship data; barometers and anemometers providing environmental data, all fed automatically into increasingly sophisticated analogue fire control computers such as the Ford Range-keeper, which integrated this data into enemy and own ship course and speed, and provided gun orders that could, if set to automatic, fire a salvo when the guns were all loaded. By 1944, this made it possible, at night, at ranges in excess of 20,000yd, to achieve hits with the first salvo, an achievement unthinkable even a few years earlier.

This success was the pinnacle of gunnery excellence and, at the same time, the harbinger of the end of naval gunnery as a major factor in warfare. With naval gunnery this effective, there was little point in battles between ships that could be assured of pounding each other to pieces regardless of sun, wind or weather. Add to this the increasing effectiveness of aircraft, submarines and small craft carrying torpedoes, and it is no wonder that within a few decades of the end of this war, the battleships and cruisers whose engagements are described in these pages had all but disappeared from the world's navies, never to reappear.

Notes

INTRODUCTION

1 Stern, *Destroyer Battles*, pp. 93–119; Stern, *The US Navy and the War in Europe*, pp. 118–39.
2 CSS *Virginia*'s iron casemate was built on the hull of the former USS *Merrimack*, which had burned to the waterline when union forces abandoned the Norfolk Navy Yard, and she is often referenced by her former name.
3 The information in this section is drawn primarily from Brooks, *Dreadnought Gunnery*, pp. 61–4 and 234–49, and Friedman, *Naval Firepower*, pp. 41–53, 68–81 and 85–99.
4 The Dumaresq was a mechanical instrument that, when pointed at the target and adjusted for own ship's and enemy's course, speed and range, produced the rate of change in range and bearing; the Vickers Clock, given the rates calculated by the Dumaresq, displayed the range to which guns should be set to allow for the time since the last setting of the Dumaresq; the plotting papers showed the range and bearing reported by each of the ship's rangefinders and allowed an operator to discard outliers and visually average the remaining readings, which could then be fed back to the Dumaresq, a process known as 'crosscutting'. Later versions of the Dreyer Table, such as some of those used at Jutland, adjusted also for wind, current and the time of flight of shells to the target.
5 For a given gun firing a shell of known weight and charge, the muzzle velocity and consequently the range of a shell would decrease by a known amount each time the gun was fired due to barrel wear.
6 Brooks, *Dreadnought Gunnery*, p. 243. During the 'run to the south', Hipper's battlecruisers hit the British ships at least twenty-two times, sinking two of Beatty's six battlecruisers, while being hit only six times.
7 Breyer, *Battleships*, p. 68, quoting from the gunnery officer of SMS *Lützow*. This officer commented that the lack of a fire-control director and plotting table was a serious detriment to German shooting later in the day when the visibility favoured the British.
8 The Argo Clock was not adopted by the Royal Navy, despite the fact that many considered it superior to the Dreyer Table, because it was significantly more expensive and more prone to breakdowns (and because Dreyer had better political connections). Pollen claimed that Ford had stolen his ideas, but was never able to prove his claim to the satisfaction of a court of law.
9 Friedman, *Naval Firepower*, p. 108.

10 Brown, *Technical and Military Imperatives*, pp. 42–3. The first recorded observation of this phenomenon in the US occurred in September 1922, when two engineers at a predecessor organisation to the US Naval Research Laboratory noted interference in radio signals across the Potomac River when the wooden steamer *Dorchester* passed between a transmitter and receiver.

11 Howeth, *History*, pp. 443–69.

12 Brown, *Technical and Military Imperatives*, p. 76. In general, there is an inverse relationship between wavelength and signal power in a given radar circuit.

13 Ibid, pp. 83–91.

CHAPTER ONE

1 Without counting any Allied contribution, the Grand Fleet in November 1918 comprised over forty battleships and battlecruisers, scores of cruisers and destroyers and even the world's first aircraft carriers.

2 As an example of the time that passed between commissioning and actual combat-readiness, HMS *King George V* (41) was commissioned for initial trials on 1 October 1940, she officially joined the fleet on 11 December 1940 and sailed on her first operational mission on 15 January 1941.

3 As was common practice among the major naval powers, the Germans 'cheated' when it came to displacement limits; the *Panzerschiffe* had an actual standard displacement of approximately 11,700t. Great Britain was probably the most strict about keeping within agreed treaty limits, but even they missed in some cases because displacement estimation during the design process is far from an exact science. The Japanese were the most notorious for understating displacements.

The designation '28cm/54' describes a naval gun that has a bore diameter of 28cm and a barrel length 54 times that diameter or, in this case, 15.12m (49.6ft) long.

4 Breyer, *Battleships*, p289. In fact, all three *Deutschland*s reached 28kt on trials.

5 Admiral of the Fleet the Right Honourable Lord John Arbuthnot Fisher of Kilverstone was First Sea Lord of the Admiralty between 1904 and1910 and again between 1914 and 1915, during which time he oversaw the development of Dreadnought battleships and battlecruisers, the latter being his favoured project.

6 There is no agreement among historians whether the *Dunkerque*-class or the *Scharnhorst*-class should be classified as battleships or battlecruisers. I have chosen to call them battlecruisers because they did not combine the large-calibre main battery and thick main armour belt characteristic of a battleship.

7 The theory behind a 'fleet in being' is that a small fleet, if kept ready for sea at all times, can force an opposing navy to tie down much larger forces to monitor and be ready to react to its moves.

8 Having given her formal name, this ship will henceforth be referred to by her more common name *Graf Spee*. In similar fashion, after being formally introduced, the second of the *Panzerschiffe*, *Admiral Scheer*, will be referred to in this text simply as *Scheer* and the heavy cruiser, *Admiral Hipper*, as *Hipper*.

9 Part of a class of five, *Altmark* was classed as a *Troßschiff*, literally a 'baggage train ship'. She was not officially commissioned into the Kriegsmarine, but

was in 'government service'; her crew comprised men retired from or on leave from the Kriegsmarine.

10 To put this speed in context, a merchantman was considered fast by the Allies if it could maintain 9kt, and, except for passenger liners, it was a rare merchant ship that had a maximum speed greater than 12kt.

11 Jones, *Under Three Flags*, pp. 44–6.

12 After completing this mission in mid-November, *Westerwald* was renamed *Nordmark*. A month later, *Deutschland* was renamed *Lützow*.

13 *Fuehrer Conferences*, p. 40: 'The *Fuehrer* . . . makes the following decisions . . . *(c)* The Graf Spee and the Deutschland are to hold back and withdraw for the present.'

14 Ibid, p43.

15 Roskill, *War at Sea, Vol. 1*, p. 43.

16 The rules regarding belligerent warships visiting neutral ports were well understood and scrupulously followed by Harwood, who maintained good relations with port officials all along the South American coast. His familiarity with these rules would soon become important.

17 Jones, *Under Three Flags*, pp. 29–37.

18 Captain Kennedy was the father of well-known Scottish journalist and author Ludovic Kennedy. The enemy warship was indeed initially identified as a battlecruiser, but this was changed in *Rawalpindi*'s later reports to *Deutschland*.

19 Admiral Charles M Forbes was CO of the Royal Navy's Home Fleet from April 1938 until December 1940.

20 Much of the description of this incident comes from Asmussen, http://www. scharnhorst-class.dk/scharnhorst/history/scharnnorthernpatrolattack.html.

21 Pope, *River Plate*, p. 67.

22 Ibid, pp. 91–5.

23 Because Port Stanley lacked even basic shipyard facilities, all maintenance was by own ship's crew using such parts as were carried or could be manufactured aboard.

24 Ibid., p. 98. These are parts of two separate signals sent to the three captains on 12 December. 'First Division' comprised the two light cruisers.

25 Ibid., p. 91.

26 O'Hara, *German Fleet at War*, p. 9.

27 Quoted in Waters, *Achilles at the River Plate*, p. 8.

28 No two sources seem to agree on exactly what time the sighting occurred. Roskill, *The War at Sea, Vol. 1*, p.118 says 0608, as does O'Hara, *German Fleet at War*, p. 9; Pope, *River Plate*, p. 107 says 0610; Waters, *Achilles at the River Plate*, p. 8 says 0614. Where there are disagreements between sources, I have tended to follow Waters, but not in this case.

29 Concentration firing simplified fire correction, since all shell splashes resulted from the same basic data and correcting for any splash corrected for all.

30 Royal Navy practice was to designate main battery turrets with letters, starting with 'A' for the turret closest to the bow and 'X' for those aft, but this system was very loosely applied. The Kriegsmarine designated turrets alphabetically as well, but used a continuous sequence and phonetic labels. Thus, *Graf Spee*'s two main battery turrets – one forward and one aft – were designated 'Anton' and 'Bruno'.

31 There is no agreement between sources as to how many times *Graf Spee* was hit, by what size shells or even what damage was done. This author has tried

to create a narrative that builds on points of agreement and make sense where sources disagree.

32 Waters, *Achilles at the River Plate*, p. 25. 'A.B.' is the Royal Navy abbreviation for able seaman.

33 Ibid., p. 26. O'Hara, *German Fleet at War*, pp. 11–12 says the duration of this problem was thirty minutes. Roskill, *War at Sea, Vol. 1*, p. 119 says the problem lasted from 0640 to 0708.

34 Millington-Drake, *Drama of Graf Spee*, pp182-3.

35 Howse, *Radar at Sea*, p45. *Graf Spee*'s radar, FuMG 38G, operated at 60cm with a nominal effective limit of 16,000yd. For most of this engagement, the range was at or beyond this limit.

36 Ibid., p. 457.

37 All of the gunnery analysis figures are from ibid., pp. 455–8.

38 www.naval-history.net/xDKCas1939-12DEC.htm.

39 Roskill, *War at Sea, Vol. 1*, p. 157.

40 The Germans suffered from continual problems with the high-pressure steam turbine propulsions systems used in their most modern cruisers, battlecruisers and battleships. They proved extremely unreliable even with regular maintenance, a condition only made worse as the Germans relied increasingly on 'conscripted' labour in their shipyards.

41 O'Hara, *German Fleet at War*, p. 26

42 For more details of these battles, see Stern, *Destroyer Battles*, pp. 93–119.

43 Most of the information in this section comes from www.fleetairmarchive. net/ships/glorious.html and from Howland, *The Loss of HMS Glorious*. Other sources include Roskill, *War at Sea, Vol. 1*, pp. 194–6 and O'Hara, *German Fleet at War*, pp. 54–9.

44 According to Howland, *The Loss of HMS Glorious*, at this time *Glorious* had twenty RAF aircraft aboard (ten Hurricanes of No. 46 Sqdn and ten Gladiators of No. 263 Sqdn), as well as sixteen aircraft of her own air group (ten Sea Gladiators of No. 802 Sqdn and six Swordfish of No. 823 Sqdn, one of which was unavailable).

45 'Action Stations' is the Royal Navy equivalent to the US Navy's 'General Quarters', a state where all hands are at their combat stations and the ship is made watertight preparatory to combat.

46 DiGiulian, *Longest Gunfire Hit*.

47 *Gneisenau* and *Lützow* were both added to the disabled list when they were torpedoed while returning to Germany.

48 Besides *Glorious*, the Royal Navy had lost HMS *Courageous* (50) to U-boat torpedoes, leaving only two full-sized aircraft carriers.

CHAPTER TWO

1 On 10 June 1940, President Roosevelt gave a commencement address at the University of Virginia that included the following comment: 'On this day . . . the hand that held the dagger has struck it in the back of its neighbor.'

2 Greene and Massignani, *Naval War in the Mediterranean*, p. 278, points out that while the eighteen 54t PT boats that comprised the first USN unit based in the Mediterranean (in January 1943) were each radar-equipped, the entire Italian fleet at the time had less than two dozen radar sets.

3 To a lesser extent, the Royal Navy suffered from the same problem. All British land-based aircraft, including aircraft used for maritime patrol, were part of the RAF; only those aircraft actually operated off ships were in the Fleet Air Arm, which, while technically still part of the RAF, took orders from the Admiralty. While the Royal Navy had few of the problems with air co-operation experienced by the Germans or Italians, it would be fair to say that relations with the RAF over control of the activities of RAF Coastal Command were not always smooth.

4 'Chasing shell splashes' was a tactic available to fast, relatively nimble ships (such as destroyers) fighting larger, slower-firing opponents (such as cruisers). On the assumption that the cruiser's fire control would attempt to correct for 'shorts' or 'overs', the target ship turned toward the most recent shell splashes in the hope that the enemy would 'correct' in the other direction.

5 *Diario Storico*, Vol. 1, p. 140.

6 Punta Stilo is a bulge in the Ionian coast of the 'toe' of the Italian 'boot'.

7 www.navweaps.com/Weapons/WNBR_15-42_mk1.htm and www.navweaps.com/Weapons/WNIT_126-44_m1934.htm. The Italian 320mm (12.6in) gun fired a 1,157lb AP shell, compared to *Warspite*'s 6crh shell, which weighed 1,938lbs. Also, the Italian 320mm guns could not be loaded at maximum elevation: they had to be lowered, loaded and re-raised to fire at long range.

8 Premature detonation of AP shells had plagued RN gunnery in the First World War, and was supposed to have been rectified by the redesigned APC shells in use in the Second World War.

9 Greene and Massignani, *Naval War in the Mediterranean*, p. 82.

10 *Battle Summaries, No. 2*, p. 32.

11 *The Second World War – A Day by Day Account*, 19 July 1940.

12 The times throughout this account are those kept by the Italians. British accounts give times an hour later. There is disagreement among sources about how to spell Commander Nicolson's name. Although *Battle Summaries, No. 2*, an official source, spells it 'Nicholson', most leave off the 'h' and I have as well.

13 This information came from Enrico Cernuschi, to whom I am extremely grateful.

14 Other factors contributing to this angular dispersion were the relatively light construction of the gun mounts within the turrets and the unusually close spacing of the two barrels, which may have caused some interference between shells despite a *c*.100ms delay introduced in salvo fire. Another factor was the ranging salvo doctrine of the Italians which included an azimuth spread as well as a range 'ladder'. This will be explained in greater detail later in this chapter.

15 *Battle Summaries, No. 2*, p. 34. The non-use of dye markers by the Italians was confirmed by Cernuschi, 29 Jan 2013. The apparent colours may have been a prismatic effect of sunlight on water droplets.

16 Casardi quoted in Gill, *Australia*, p. 188.

17 *Battle Summaries, No. 2*, p. 36.

18 According to emails from Enrico Cernuschi dated January 2013, referencing a report filed by *Colleoni*'s XO, Commander Eugenio Martini, now at the Archivio dell'Ufficio Storico della Marina Militare, Rome, in the *Fondo Scontri Navali e Operazioni di Guerra*, the ship was hit by only three 6in shells as described in this paragraph.

19 *Battle Summaries, No. 2*, p. 38.

20 Ibid., p. 38.

21 Commander Martini states that this torpedo was probably fired by *Havock*; this is possible, as *Havock* had joined the other destroyers at 0811.

22 RM practice was to designate main battery turrets fore-to-aft sequentially with roman numerals.

23 British sources report that *Colleoni* was hit by multiple 4.7in rounds from destroyers during this period, but Commander Martini's report makes no mention of these.

24 *Battle Summaries, No. 2*, p. 38.

25 Ibid., Appendix A, p. 43.

26 HMS *Ajax* carried a Type 279 radar, a first-generation air search radar with minimal surface search capability. See O'Hara, *Night Action*.

27 The destroyer was HMS *Hotspur* (H01), already a seasoned veteran, having fought at the First Battle of Narvik, where she was badly damaged. Repaired at Chatham, she was then assigned to the North Atlantic Command, but was most often employed on operations in the Mediterranean. It was on one such operation that she rammed and sank Italian submarine *Lafolé* on 18 October 1940. She was patched up at Gibraltar and was part of Force 'F' en route to Malta, where the repairs were to be completed.

28 Greene and Massignani, *Naval War in the Mediterranean*, p. 115; O'Hara, *Struggle*, p. 65.

29 *Battle Summaries, No. 9*, p. 4.

30 O'Hara, *Struggle*, pp. 66–7.

31 *Battle Summaries, No. 9*, p.5.

32 *Battle Summaries, No. 9*, p. 7.

33 Ibid., p. 8, n. 1.

34 Ibid., p. 8, n. 2.

35 Ibid., p. 6, nn. 1 and 2.

36 Ibid., p. 2.

37 Ibid., p. 9.

38 After *Renown* had initially opened fire on the cruiser leading Sansonetti's 'Western Group', which, having become disordered due to an earlier signal mix-up, was probably *Trento*, she next sighted two cruisers of Matteucci's division, mistakenly identified at first as battleships.

39 *Battle Summaries, No. 9*, p. 7.

40 Bragadin, *Sotto il segno di Barbara*, p. 41.

41 Woodward, *Context*, n. 70.

CHAPTER THREE

1 Winton, *ULTRA at Sea*, p. 6; Roskill, *The War at Sea, Vol. 1*, p. 287.

2 Jones, *Under Three Flags*, pp. 99–101.

3 Friedman, *Naval Radar*, pp. 205–6. FuMO 27 was one of several similar German surface search radars in the FuMO 22 series co-mounted with an optical rangefinder – in this case, the 7m Zeiss stereoscopic rangefinder at the top of *Hipper*'s forward tower mast.

4 O'Hara, *German Fleet at War*, pp. 70–2; www.naval-history.net/xAH-WSConvoys03-1940.htm. This was one of the longest nights of the year, being fully dark for fourteen hours at this latitude, with only nine hours of daylight.

5 Edwards, *Beware Raiders!*, pp.100–5.

6 HMS *Bonaventure* was, like the USN's *Atlanta*-class, intended as a large, fast, anti-aircraft platform. The British 5.25in/50 was not as successful as the American 5in/38, in part because it fired a heavier round (80lb versus 55lb) which made it more difficult to manhandle in the cramped, original-style gunhouse and because the gun itself was longer, heavier and therefore slower to train.

7 Jones, *Under Three Flags*, pp. 127–8.

8 Roskill, *War at Sea, Vol. 1*, p. 373.

9 *B.d.U. Op's WAR LOG*, PG/30282, p. 11. This is from the entry for 8 February 1941.

10 Ibid., p. 12. This is from the entry for 11 February 1941.

11 Ibid., p. 14. This is from the entry for 12 February 1941. 'CF 80' was a coded map co-ordinate designating an area west and slightly north of Gibraltar.

12 According to www.scharnhorst-class.dk/scharnhorst/history/scharnberlin. html, only eleven merchant sailors were killed in these attacks.

13 *B.d.U. Op's WAR LOG*, PG/30284, pp. 30–1. This is from the entries for 7–8 March 1941.

14 Two of the three tankers taken as prizes never reached Bordeaux, being stopped by HMS *Renown*, and were scuttled by their prize crews.

15 Much of this account was taken from the post-action report of the master of MV *Chilean Reefer* found at www.merchantnavyofficers.com/BFW.html.

16 Koop and Schmolke, *Admiral Hipper Class*, p. 28. *Hipper*'s range at 19kt was calculated to be 6,800nm; *Prinz Eugen*'s range at the same speed is given as 7,850nm.

17 Garzke, *Bismarck's Final Battle*, pp. 160–1: 'Unfortunately, the ship was extremely vulnerable to long range plunging shellfire, and major positions beyond the citadel were not as well protected as comparable positions on most foreign contemporary battleships.'

18 It seems like every source gives a different cruising radius for *Bismarck*, but the one closest to a median figure is 9,280nm at 16kt. Compare that to *North Carolina* (BB55), which had a cruising range of 17,450nm at 15kt. Compared to this, the contemporary HMS *King George V* (41) had a radius of 6,000nm at 14kt.

19 After examination at Brest, it was found that *Scharnhorst*'s boiler superheaters required repairs that would take a minimum of ten weeks.

20 *Gneisenau* was docked at Brest after being torpedoed and was then hit by four bombs four days later.

21 Winton, *ULTRA at Sea*, p. 24.

22 Ibid., pp. 25–6. Late in the day on 21 May, Tovey received word of an ULTRA decrypt of a month-old message reporting that *Bismarck* was to take aboard five prize crews with charts for the Atlantic ports, which provided solid confirmation of the Atlantic breakout hypothesis.

23 HMS *Prince of Wales* was so new that, despite having been in commission since January, she sailed this day with approximately 100 dockyard workers aboard to work on her two quadruple-14in main-battery turrets, which had proven far from reliable.

24 HMS *Victorious* was, if anything, even newer than *Prince of Wales*, and her aircrew, in particular, was inadequately trained, but there was no other aircraft carrier available for Tovey.

25 Brown, *Imperatives*, p. 126.

26 Woodward, *Context*.

27 Koop and Schmolke, *Admiral Hipper Class*, pp. 25–6. *Prinz Eugen* was equipped with an effective passive sonar array – *Gruppenhorchgerät* – which was able to detect Holland's force at a distance of 25nm.

28 Incredibly, *Prinz Eugen*'s 20.3cm/60 (8in) main battery outranged *Hood*'s 15in/42 guns by 3,000yd.

29 *ADM 239/268*, Table 5. This table, published internally by the Admiralty in 1939, shows that *Hood* had no immune zone against *Bismarck*'s 38cm (15in) main battery.

30 He could only have been encouraged in this choice by the standing 'Admiralty Fighting Instructions', which start by urging a 'strong offensive spirit'.

31 Garzke and Dulin, *Bismarck's Final Battle*, p. 185. Garzke and Dulin, further, on p. 166 state: 'In that era, long-range accuracy in deflection was much more readily obtained than accuracy in range.' This argues in favour of heading almost directly towards the enemy, as this would reduce the span of time during which range would be changing rapidly.

32 Woodward, *Context*, quotes the official Board of Enquiry after that battle (ADM 116/4351) as stating: 'The Board of Enquiry suggests . . . that the time chosen to give up the chase was slightly early . . . The Board of the Admiralty cannot emphasise enough that in all cases especially when dealing with an enemy who is reluctant to engage in close action, no opportunity must be allowed to pass of attaining, what is in fact, the ultimate objective of the Royal Navy – the destruction of main enemy naval forces when and whenever they are encountered. Only thus can control of the sea communications be properly secured.'

33 Jurens, *The Loss of H.M.S. Hood*, p. 9. Jurens make the point convincingly that a somewhat shallower approach would have exposed the British to little additional danger while allowing them use of their full main battery.

34 Bonomi, *Denmark Strait*, Pt 1.

35 The thirty-second delay was to allow for a time interval between the fall of shot of the two ships, aiding fire control. At 25,000yd, *Hood*'s shells would take approximately forty-nine seconds to reach their target. With a significantly higher muzzle velocity, but a somewhat longer distance to cover, *Prince of Wales*' shells would be in the air a few seconds less.

36 *Hood*'s boat deck (or shelter deck) was a partial deck one deck higher than her extended forecastle deck, extending aft from her forward superstructure, where many of her anti-aircraft guns and rocket launchers were sited.

37 Garzke and Dulin, *Bismarck's Final Battle*, p. 167.

38 Ibid.

39 Mention must be made of the almost total disagreement between sources as to the range at which this shot was fired. I have taken my range estimates mostly from Bonomi, *Denmark Strait*. O'Hara, *German Fleet at War*, p. 82, gives 17,000yd; Allen, *Pursuit*, gives 14,500yd; Jurens, *The Loss of H.M.S. Hood*, p. 143, gives 19,800yd. To this author, this may be the least interesting unanswered question relating to this engagement.

40 *ADM 116/4351*, questions 4 and 18.

41 Ibid, question 96. 'S.G.O.' refers to the Squadron Gunnery Officer.

42 Bonomi, *Denmark Strait*, Pt 2. Other sources put *Prinz Eugen*'s 20.3cm ammunition consumption as high as 183 rounds.

43 For a radar to detect a target, the radio pulse sent from the antenna must be reflected back by the target in sufficient strength to be distinguishable from background noise. Given that the reflected signal strength is reduced by many factors, such as target size, shape, speed and composition, as well as weather conditions, the effective range of a radar is far less than half the distance at which its signal can be detected.

CHAPTER FOUR

1 Speculative 'what-if' history is always a dubious exercise, but in this author's opinion, it is extremely doubtful that *Indomitable*'s fighter squadrons (nominally nine Sea Hurricanes and twelve Fulmars) would have been adequate to protect herself plus *Prince of Wales* and *Repulse* from the repeated waves of Japanese level and torpedo-bombers that attacked Force 'Z' off Malaya on 10 December, especially given the relative inexperience of her aircrews. The most likely outcome would have been the loss of *Indomitable* along with the other large ships.

2 *Boise* was not officially part of the Asiatic Fleet. She had escorted a convoy to Manila, which arrived on 4 December; once there, Hart contrived to keep her in Philippine waters for a few extra days and the arrival of war superseded any prior organisational arrangements.

3 A note on dates is appropriate at this point. The International Date Line falls between Hawaii and the scene of the action described in this chapter. The attack on Pearl Harbor famously occurred on 7 December 1941, but when war arrived later that same day in the Philippines and Singapore, it was 8 December on local calendars.

4 The full text of the message is as follows: 'This dispatch is to be considered a war warning x negotiations with Japan looking toward stabilization of conditions in the Pacific have ceased and an aggressive move by Japan is expected within the next few days x The number and equipment of Japanese troops and the organization of naval task forces indicate an amphibious expedition against either the Philippines [printed in ink, 'Thai')] or Kra Peninsula or possibly Borneo x Execute an appropriate defensive deployment preparatory to carrying out the tasks assigned in WPL 46 x Inform district and Army authorities x A similar warning is being sent by War Department x Spenavo inform British x Continental districts Guam Samoa directed take appropriate measures against sabotage.'

5 *Loss of Prince of Wales*, p1238. Adm Pound strongly urged Phillips on 1 December to move Force 'Z' away from Singapore, but in an uncharacteristic display of restraint, he left the final decision to the force commander on the scene.

6 Winslow, *Fleet Gods Forgot*, pp. 152–3.

7 *Senshi Sosho*, Vol. 26, p. 199. The Japanese reaction to the presence of enemy warships inside their anchorage was slow and unco-ordinated. This can be explained in the first few minutes by a concern that the ships they were seeing were friendly and also by the poor visibility, but once Japanese transports started exploding, no explanation seems to suffice.

8 These were *Samanoura Maru, Tatsugami Maru, Kuretake Maru* and *PC37* (ex-*Hishi*). The term 'constructive total loss' describes a ship that is afloat or aground, but so badly damaged that repair is considered uneconomical.

9 *DD228*, p. 2 of the attached XO's report.

10 Curiously, perhaps because *Ford*'s captain, Lieutenant Commander J E Cooper, realised that the torpedo sighting was improbable, he reported to the other ships in the division over TBS that *Ford*'s sudden manoeuvre was due to a suspected minefield. See *DD228*, p. 3. Equally curiously, this 'minefield' did not prevent *Ford* from immediately resuming her previous course and speed.

11 *DD218-1*, Enc. A, p. 8.

12 Ibid.

13 *Senshi Sosho*, Vol. 26, p. 199.

14 *DD228*, p. 3.

15 Ibid. 'All hits were observed to explode inside the ship's bulging the side and deck plating outward and upward.'

16 *Senshi Sosho*, Vol. 26, p. 201.

17 Ibid.

18 Ibid, p. 199. Most guns carried on Japanese merchantmen, especially early in the war, were 3in(8cm)/40 mounts that had been produced in large numbers during and immediately after the First World War.

19 The torpedo workshop was in the aft superstructure at the main deck level.

20 *DD228*, p. 2. Consol was described as 'Rust Preventive Compound – Grade A'; it was applied, usually by spraying, to unpainted metal surfaces exposed to seawater.

21 *Senshi Sosho*, Vol. 26, p. 200.

22 All these ships were together at Tjilatjap.

23 *Tromp* was coming from Surabaya; the four American destroyers were refuelling at Ratai Bay, Sumatra, and had to steam most of the length of the north coast of Java to meet *Tromp* before passing southward through the Bali Strait. Taefel Hoek was the Dutch name for a small cape on the coast of Bali approximately 8nm south of Sanur, at which point it is safe to turn north into Badung Strait.

24 *CDD58-1*, p. 1.

25 Roscoe, *Destroyer Operations*, p. 97; Morison, *Naval Operations, Vol. III*, p. 322.

26 *DD225-2*, Enc (B)(2).

27 Some accounts state that *De Ruyter* fired no shots.

28 Ibid, Enc (A)(1), p. 2. This enclosure was the XO's report of the action.

29 Some accounts, such as O'Hara, *U.S. Navy*, p. 29, say that *Piet Hein*, which sank at 2246, was finished off by a torpedo from *Asashio*, and this may indeed have been the case, but when she was last seen by the Americans, a few minutes before, there was no evidence of a torpedo hit. Note this from *Java Sea Campaign*, p. 41: 'Whether she had been hit by large-calibre gunfire or by a torpedo is not known, but *Ford* noted that she did not settle as if holed below the water line.

30 *DD225-2*, p. 3.

31 Ibid., Enc (A)(3).

32 Ibid.

33 *CDD58-1*, pp. 1–2. TBS was a 'line-of-sight' radio, and the intervening land mass prevented Binford receiving Parker's signals.

34 In *DD218-2*, Enc 'C', p. 2, *Parrott*'s XO states that *Stewart* was hit on the third Japanese salvo.

35 *DD218-2*, pp. 3–4.

36 Ibid, Enc 'C', p4. 'Rocking Ladder' is defined on www.navweaps.com/Weapons/Gun_Data_p3.htm as: 'Walking' the point of aim back and forth across the target, thus allowing for small errors in the firing solution. Often used for rapid fire and automatic weapons.

37 *CDD58-2*, p. 1.

38 The closest US Navy rating to Watanabe's would be fire controlman.

39 Watanabe, *Bali Island Sea Battle*. He noted later in his account that none of the three men who went overboard could be rescued or even reached the boat they cut loose for them. One of them did survive by swimming to Bali.

40 Ibid., pp. 4–5.

41 Unfortunately, as the name *Stewart* had been recycled, given to a destroyer escort commissioned in 1943, she was simply named USS *DD-224* for the brief time she remained in service. She was struck from the Navy List in April 1946 and sunk as a target in May of that year.

42 *DD218-2*, p. 1.

43 Morison, *Naval Operations, Vol III*, pp. 342–58; O'Hara, *U.S. Navy*, pp. 35–44.

44 The actual bore diameter of these guns was 20.32cm, which is exactly 8in.

45 *Loss of H.M.S. Exeter*, p. 1.

46 *CA30*, p. 3.

47 The force sighted northeast of Batavia was real; it was carrying the 230th Infantry Regiment to a landing site 120nm east of Batavia.

48 Hara, *Destroyer Captain*, states on p. 77: 'Some of the skippers told me later they were busy the whole time evading friendly shells and torpedoes.'

49 Japanese destroyers, at least those of the *Fubuki* or later classes, carried reload torpedoes, and crews were well trained in the rapid reloading of torpedo tubes under combat conditions.

50 The following are mostly from Gill, *Australia in the War*, pp. 619–22; *CA30*, pp. 4–9; *Senshi Sosho*; O'Hara, *U.S. Navy*, pp. 48–55.

51 A number of accounts state that *Houston* turned south after *Perth* was hit, but the location of the wrecks, which are popular dive sites, refutes this. *Houston*'s remains are 5,500yd north-northwest of *Perth*'s.

52 Gill, *Australia in the War*, p. 622 n5. Among those who died after capture, ironically, were forty-two lost when the transport on which they were being moved from one POW camp to another was torpedoed by an Allied submarine.

53 *CA30*, p. 9.

54 *CDD58-3*, p. 4.

55 *DD211*, p. 2.

56 Ibid. Interestingly, Binford, observing the same action from *Edwards*, just forward of *Alden*, stated in *CDD58-3*, p. 4: 'Enemy fire was well over and splashes no where near the formation.'

57 Ibid.

58 Ibid.

59 Unlike *Evertsen*, *Witte de With* never left Surabaya; she was damaged in an air raid in port on 1 March and scuttled by her crew the next day to prevent capture.

60 The Japanese term *Sentai* translates as 'squadron', so it can refer to a squadron of any type of warship.

61 'Val' was the Allied codename for the Aichi D3A carrier bomber Type 99.

62 'Kate' was the Allied codename for the Nakajima B5N carrier attack bomber Type 97.

63 The Japanese expended 635 20cm rounds and the same number of 12.7cm rounds to sink *Stronghold*.

CHAPTER FIVE

1 Prados, *Combined Fleet*, p. 72.

2 By pure coincidence, all three aircraft carriers assigned to the Pacific Fleet were away from Pearl Harbor on the morning of 7 December 1941.

3 Perversely, the only reason the Americans were building up any forces in western Alaska was their concern that the Japanese might consider using the Aleutians as a forward-base for moves against the rest of Alaska, western Canada and even the American Pacific Northwest.

4 All dates and times used in this chapter are those kept by the Americans, meaning they are Zone W (Z-10) and are east of the date line, even though many of the events actually occurred west of the line and therefore actually occurred a day later.

5 Paramushiro is now called Paramushir; it is an island at the northern end of the Kurile chain now under Russian control.

6 Prados, *Combined Fleet*, pp. 469–70; *Aleutians Campaign*, pp. 35–6. McMorris' nickname was a contraction of 'Socrates', stemming from his reputation as a deep thinker. *Bailey* flew the flag of ComDesRon14, Captain R S Riggs. At the beginning of the battle, Riggs only commanded *Bailey* and *Coghlan*; it was only at 1030 that McMorris officially ordered him to take command of *Dale* and *Monaghan*.

7 Much of the information in this section is from *USSBS Interrogations*, No. 205.

8 *USSBS Interrogations*, No. 102.

9 Ibid.

10 *CL9*, Enc (C), p. 1.

11 For the dates when these Japanese cruisers were equipped with radar, see Lacroix, *Japanese Cruisers*, pp. 315–21 and 371. The earliest was April 1943, when *Nachi* and *Abukuma* were being repaired.

12 *USSBS Interrogations*, No. 205. It is interesting that the Japanese were able to sight the Americans half an hour earlier and at nearly twice the range without the aid of radar. There are two main reasons for this: the southern horizon was lightening earlier than the northern, which made the masts to the south easier to see, but also the Japanese valued seamen with exceptional visual acuity and contrast discrimination because their tactical doctrine stressed night combat, and men who tested well for these abilities were used as lookouts.

13 There is disagreement among the sources as to whether *Inazuma* accompanied the two transports to the northwest or remained with the other destroyers following *Abukuma*. Commander Kuwahara in *USSBS Interrogations*, No. 205 states explicitly that *Inazuma* did not escort the two transports when they separated from Hosogaya, and, as navigator in *Asaka Maru*, he was in the best position to observe these events. He states that *Usugumo* joined the two

transports near the Komandorski Islands and was ordered to escort them back to Paramushiro.

14 *CA25*, p. 0.

15 Roscoe, *Destroyer Operations*, p. 157.

16 On American warships, Central Station was a control position located deep inside the ship from which damage control was directed and, in an emergency, from which the ship could be conned.

17 *CL9*, Enc (G), p. 2. Actually, there was minor damage from this salvo; one of *Maya*'s shells apparently cut one of the support wires between *Richmond*'s third and fourth funnels, according to *Aleutians Campaign*, p. 48.

18 *CA25*, Enc (E). This enclosure is the CIC plot of the engagement of which Rodgers was quite proud, stating: 'Enclosure (E) is the plot of the action made during the engagement in Combat Information Center. It shows own ships track as traced by the Dead Reckoning Tracer set at 1" per mile, and to the same scale the enemy is tracked and plotted using SG radar ranges and bearings. The actual plotting was done under fire, the tracks later being combined into a smooth tracing with pertinent comments added. I consider this plot one of the most interesting features of the report. As far as known, it is the first time in history an accurate picture of a long naval engagement showing movements of both forces from minute to minute has been possible.'

19 The 'Pete', a single-float, two-seat reconnaissance biplane, should not be confused with the much more famous 'Type 00' monoplane carrier fighter, the Mitsubishi A6M 'Zeke/Zero' or the Aichi E13A Type 00 'Jake' carried on *Nachi*'s port catapult. Most accounts state that *Nachi* had two aircraft on her starboard catapult, which would have been normal practice, but, according to Commander Hashimoto in *USSBS Interrogations*, No. 102, one had been left behind for overhaul.

20 *CL9*, p. 2.

21 *USSBS Interrogations*, Nos. 98 and 438. All the Japanese accounts were generated three and a half years after the event and in the aftermath of a crushing defeat, which no doubt coloured the stories being told to the former enemy. Given all this, along with the problems that always accompany eyewitness evidence, it is not difficult to explain the many discrepancies between the Japanese accounts.

22 *Battle Lesson*.

23 Many of these arguments come from Lorelli, *Komandorski Islands*, pp. 79–82.

24 *USSBS Interrogations*, No. 102. Commander Hashimoto's evidence has its own problems. The full description is of a hit 'by a 15 cm. (6 in.) blue dye loaded shell', a type that was not fired by the Americans that day. A CIC was, in early 1943, an experimental construct, a single compartment near the bridge where radar displays and tactical radio (TBS) were concentrated so that a unified tactical picture was available to the CO.

25 The origin of this story is found in *USSBS Interrogations*, No. 98. It is used by Morison, *Naval Operations, Vol. VII*, p. 26; Lorelli, *Komandorski Islands*, p. 73 and O'Hara, *Axis*, p. 155, among others.

26 Lacroix, *Japanese Cruisers*, pp. 107 and 268.

27 *USSBS Interrogations*, No. 438 and Japanese Monograph No. 89. The timelines presented in these two documents are clearly related, though it is not possible to ascertain definitively which derived from the other or whether both

drew on a third unidentified source. This author has concluded that the monograph, because the timeline is drawn in with pencil, is more likely to be the original document from which *Interrogation* No. 438, which is described as a compilation, was derived.

28 Lorelli, *Komandorski Islands*, p. 91.
29 *CA25*, p. 15. This was the chronological entry for 0910.
30 Ibid., p. 17. This was the chronological entry for 1010.
31 Ibid. 'A-302-A' and similar designations are references to hull compartments – the first letter designates the hull 'division' in which it is located ('A' division was that part of the ship's hull forward of the engineering spaces), the first number indicates the deck on which it is located and the remaining digits were assigned sequentially to compartments fore-to-aft, the last letter indicates the compartment's primary use ('A' stood for a storage space).
32 Ibid. *Salt Lake City* began making smoke at 1018.
33 *Aleutians Campaign*, p. 56.
34 Ibid., p. 58. By his calculations, McMorris placed his flagship 125nm closer to Paramushiro than Adak.
35 *CA25*, p. 18. In the USN, first lieutenant is a position rather than a rank. This officer, who, on a ship the size of *Salt Lake City*, would have held the rank of lieutenant (junior grade) or lieutenant, was in charge of the Deck Division, which made him responsible for the upkeep and appearance of all external decks, fittings and boats. On smaller ships, the first lieutenant could be a chief petty officer or even a petty officer 1st class.
36 Ibid., p. 19. This was the chronological entry for 1105.
37 *Aleutians Campaign*, p. 62.
38 Prados, *Combined Fleet*, p. 473.
39 *Aleutians Campaign*, p. 64.
40 *CA25*, p. 8.
41 *CL9*, Enc (G), p. 4; Roscoe, *Destroyer Operations*, p. 160. It is most likely that the order was *not* given by McMorris before *Salt Lake City* reported being stopped. The time discrepancy between the recording of two events was most likely caused by *Richmond*'s clock being a minute or two behind *Salt Lake City*'s.
42 All of the information on DesRon14 in this section is from *Aleutians Campaign*, pp. 66–8 and Roscoe, *Destroyer Operations*, pp. 161–2.
43 USN destroyers carried their main batteries in gun mounts rather than turrets, the difference being a technical one concerning whether or not the handling rooms under the gun house trained with the guns (as would be the case for a turret) or were fixed. The numbering system for mounts was somewhat informal, but generally was a two-digit system in which the first digit identified calibre and the second fore-to-aft order. Thus mount 54 was the fourth (and in the case of *Bailey* aftermost) 5in mount.
44 Lacroix, *Japanese Cruisers*, pp. 232–5.
45 *Aleutians Campaign*, p. 74.
46 *CA25*, p. 8.
47 Ibid., p. 15.
48 *USSBS Interrogations*, No. 98.
49 Lorelli, *Komandorski Islands*, p. 89, states that *Salt Lake City* lost the use of her FC and FD radars early in the engagement.

CHAPTER SIX

1 These were the 1st Cruiser Squadron, 10th Cruiser Squadron and 18th Cruiser Squadron, which also included three heavy cruisers and one light cruiser in dockyard hands at the beginning of March 1942.

2 Winton, *ULTRA at Sea*, p. 58.

3 Ibid., p. 59.

4 Roskill, *The War at Sea, Vol. II*, p. 121.

5 Some sources give the ship's name as *Izhora*, which may be a better transliteration from the Russian.

6 Winton, *ULTRA at Sea*, p. 60.

7 The Fairey Albacore was a carrier torpedo- and dive-bomber meant as the successor to the now-antiquated Swordfish. Also a biplane, the Albacore was only marginally faster than the Swordfish and, while more robust, was significantly less manoeuvrable, and was not very popular with FAA pilots.

8 Altenfjord is the German rendition of Altafjorden, the Norwegian name for a deep, complex inlet just west of North Cape. The largest town on this fjord is Alta. Branches of Altenfjord used as anchorages include Kaafjord (Kåfjorden) and Langfjord (Langfjorden). I use the German forms because these were used by both the Germans and English during the war.

9 Roskill, *War at Sea, Vol. II*, p. 290; Winton, *ULTRA at Sea*, p. 73.

10 Winton, *ULTRA at Sea*, p. 74. This and the following British knowledge of German activity (and knowledge) was all due to ULTRA intercepts.

11 Each day brought new settings for the German Enigma machine and a new task of breaking into the encryption scheme. Most days, at this time, GC&CS succeeded in a timely fashion, but not every day.

12 *Scheer* had made a sweep into the Kara Sea in August and September named Operation Wunderland which had netted the sinking of a Soviet icebreaker. It is curious that SKL would expect anything positive from a raid two months later when daylight would be far shorter, the weather far worse and the ice conditions far more hazardous.

13 HMS *Oribi* (G66) had suffered a gyro compass casualty and severe icing, and made her way to Murmansk independently.

14 Roskill, *The War at Sea, Vol. II*, p. 293.

15 According to O'Hara, *German Fleet at War*, p. 147, *Hipper* fired fifty-one 20.3cm and thirty-eight 10.5cm shells at *Bramble* and left her still afloat.

16 Winton, *ULTRA at Sea*, p. 76.

17 The operation was sometimes called Zitronella (Citronella).

18 At the same time as Sizilien, the Germans established a weather station on Hopen Island, the easternmost in the Svalbard Archipelago. This remained in permanent operation until the end of the war, not being captured until September 1945, reportedly the last German armed forces to surrender.

19 The Royal Navy was by no means the only navy to attempt the use of small manned underwater weapons. At one time or another during the war, the Japanese, Italians and Germans all tried their hand at these weapons. The success rate was extremely low and their use almost always led to the capture, if not the death, of the crew.

20 *Fuehrer Conferences*, p. 374.

21 Because of the poor endurance of most Royal Navy destroyers, there was a constant shuttle of destroyers between the convoy and refuelling bases, so

the number of destroyers actually escorting the convoy on any particular day might be more or less than ten.

22 Friedman, *Naval Radar*, p. 195; Brown, *Technical Imperatives*, pp. 351–2. The Type 273Q had a wavelength of 20cm and introduced continual antenna rotation and a plan position indicator (PPI) display. The Type 284M had a wavelength of 50cm and a range in excess of 48,000yd, with an accuracy at 24,000yd of 125yd.

23 Winton, *ULTRA at Sea*, p. 81; Fraser, *Sinking*, p. 3704.

24 The Beaufort Scale of wind strength defines Force 8 as 34–40kt winds, creating 'moderately high waves with breaking crests forming spindrift'. The 36th Division destroyers were selected for transfer to JW.55B because they had the greatest fuel reserves of any in RA.55A's escort.

25 Fraser, *Sinking*, p. 3704.

26 www.naval-history.net/xGM-Chrono-01BB-Duke%20of%20York.htm. This is from the entry for 25 December 1943.

27 *Battle Summary No. 24*, p. 5.

28 Ibid., p. 4.

29 Ibid., p. 6.

30 Radar detectors, the earliest form of what is now called ESM (electronic surveillance measures), were radio receivers tuned to the known wavelengths of enemy radars. They almost always could detect a radar far beyond its effective range.

31 Fraser, *Sinking*, p. 3705; *Battle Summary No. 24*, pp. 6–7.

32 *Battle Summary No. 24*, pp. 11–12. At 1027, the German destroyers were ordered by Bey to come about to 070° and then at 1135 to 030°, all in pursuit of the convoy, but well to the southeast of its actual location. At 1218, they were ordered to concentrate in a position to the northwest, and, in doing so, at 1300 they actually passed within 10nm of the convoy without seeing it. At 1418, Bey ordered the destroyers to break off operations and return to Alta, which they all did without incident, except for *Z33*, which, at 1810, sighted a straggler from the convoy and fired four torpedoes at it, all of which missed.

33 Fraser, *Sinking*, p. 3705.

34 Fraser, *Sinking*, p. 3706.

35 *Battle Summary No. 24*, p. 12.

36 Ibid., n3.

37 Ibid., p. 15 n2.

38 Roskill, *War at Sea, Vol. III, Part 1*, p. 86.

39 O'Hara, *German Fleet at War*, p. 162.

40 *Battle Summary No. 24*, p. 16; Howse, *Radar at Sea*, p. 188. *Duke of York* checked fire because the range had opened to 21,400yd. At that range, her Type 284 radar would no longer discriminate shell splashes.

41 *Battle Summary No. 24*, p. 17.

42 www.navweaps.com/Weapons/WNBR_14-45_mk7.htm. Some sources give *Scharnhorst*'s maximum armour belt thickness as 32cm.

43 *Battle Summary No. 24*, App. B(1).

44 *Battle Summary No. 24*, App. C.

45 The shot that hit *Scharnhorst* at 1824 disabling her forward fire room was fired at just over 20,000yd and thus had a significant angle of fall (c.20°), which allowed it to penetrate her armoured deck.

CHAPTER SEVEN

1 Morison, *Naval Operations, Vol. XII*, p. 7.

2 Prados, *Combined Fleet*, pp. 614–15.

3 *Campaigns*, App. 88, p. 294. This is excerpted from Imperial Headquarters Directive 435, dated 26 July 1944, 'Designation of Urgent Operations as "Sho" Operations'. This directive designated four numbered Sho operations covering areas from the Philippines (Sho-1) to Hokkaido (Sho-4).

4 This force was known in Japanese as 'Dai-Ichi Yugeki Butai', which translates most directly as 1st Striking Force. Some sources refer to it as the 1st Diversionary Attack Force.

5 Halsey and Admiral Raymond A Spruance took turns commanding the Central Pacific Force, which was designated Third Fleet when under Halsey and Fifth Fleet when under Spruance. Halsey took over command of this force in August 1944.

6 These numbers are approximate; the fire support groups were split between the northern and southern beaches, and ships rotated into and out of the firing line as necessary to replenish and refuel.

7 Prados, *Combined Fleet*, p. 604.

8 Ibid., pp. 606–10.

9 Tully, *Surigao Strait*, pp. 4–7.

10 Prados, *Combined Fleet*, pp. 653–4.

11 The 16th Sentai actually departed Brunei Bay for Manila on 21 October, the departure delayed by the need to refuel.

12 Ibid., pp. 628–30.

13 Ibid., pp. 654–5.

14 The two surviving fast battleships of the *Kongo*-class were older than *Fuso* and *Yamashiro*, but had started out life as battlecruisers, which made them significantly faster and they had also been much more extensively modernised.

15 Prados, *Combined Fleet*, p. 657; Tully, *Surigao Strait*, p. 45. The latter points out that in the few exercises in which *Fuso* participated with Kurita's fleet, she had been unable to maintain the cruising speed of 24kt.

16 Tully, *Surigao Strait*, p. 25.

17 *USSBS Interrogations*, No. 233.

18 Prados, *Combined Fleet*, p. 655. Shima had spent much of his IJN career ashore as a communications expert; he knew better than most the value of using a shore-based radio station to send his messages.

19 Ibid.

20 Tully, *Surigao Strait*, pp. 51–2.

21 The southern entrance to Surigao Strait is approximately 10nm wide, between the southern tip of Panaon Island and the northern tip of Mindanao. From there, the strait runs generally due north between Panaon and Leyte Islands on the west and Dinagat on the east, emptying into Leyte Gulf approximately 30nm from the southern entrance. The strait is more than 15nm across and easy to navigate, with no major hazards except for a strong current.

22 Prados, *Combined Fleet*, pp. 657–8; Tully, *Surigao Strait*, pp. 54–6.

23 Shima was promoted to vice-admiral on 1 May 1943 and Nishimura on 1 November 1943.

24 Tully, *Surigao Strait*, pp. 55–6.

25 *USSBS Interrogations*, No. 233.

26 Morison, *Naval Operations, Vol. XII*, pp. 184–5. Tully puts the sinking an hour later. This is most likely because *Wakaba* would have been keeping Tokyo time, which was Z+10, while the Americans were using local time, which was time zone ITEM (Z+9). I have followed American timekeeping throughout this account.

27 *USSBS Interrogations*, No. 390.

28 Tully, *Surigao Strait*, p. 71.

29 PT boats were American motor patrol-torpedo boats of approximately 54t.

30 *USSBS Interrogations*, No. 233; Tully, *Surigao Strait*, p. 81.

31 *USSBS Interrogations*, No. 233; Tully, *Surigao Strait*, p. 102.

32 Tully, *Surigao Strait*, pp. 97–8; *USSBS Interrogations*, No. 390. Tully argues that Nishimura may not have received Kurita's initial message announcing his turn to the west, but Nishino states that he did.

33 *USSBS Interrogations*, No. 390; Tully, *Surigao Strait*, p. 96.

34 Morison, *Naval Operations, Vol. XII*, pp. 290–1.

35 Ibid., pp 207–8.

36 *USSBS Interrogations*, No. 390.

37 *CA28*, Part II, p. 4.

38 Morison, *Naval Operations, Vol. XII*, pp. 209–10; Tully, *Surigao Strait*, pp. 130–1.

39 Tully, *Surigao Strait*, p. 150.

40 Ibid., p. 161.

41 *USSBS Interrogations*, No. 390. According to Tully, *Surigao Strait*, p. 171, this message was sent later, at 0331, this timing taken from Nishino's revised recollection in 1980.

42 Nishino's timekeeping was off from American reckoning by about forty minutes. The turn occurred at 0336.

43 *USSBS Interrogations*, No. 390. Nishino continued to confuse the two Japanese battleships; the ship he tried unsuccessfully to contact by telephone was *Fuso*. At this stage of the war, the Japanese had a high-frequency, short-range voice radio-telephony system similar to the American TBS.

44 Tully, *Surigao Strait*, pp. 176–8.

45 Ibid, pp. 277–8.

46 *BB38*, p. 6. This was logged at 0339 in *Pennsylvania*'s action report; it was recorded at 0332 in *CL47*, p. 7. Based on the timing of McManes' actions and Oldendorf's, it is safe to assume that *CL47* is more accurate. The clocks on the various ships reporting this action were off from each other by a few minutes, and the yeomen recording these events may well have been occasionally distracted.

47 *DD643*, p. 5.

48 *CL47*, p. 7 puts this order at 0332, as does *BB48*, Part II, p. 2; *DD643*, p. 5 has it at 0336.

49 *CL47*, p. 7.

50 *BB48*, Part II, p. 1.

51 *CA28*, Part II, p. 4.

52 *BB48*, Part II, p. 3.

53 Holloway, *Second Salvo*, pp. 59–60.

54 Czarnecki, *Performance*, p. 1.

55 *CA33*, Part II, p. 4.

56 *DD649-1*, p. 18.

57 *USSBS Interrogations*, No. 390. Remember, *Shigure*'s clock trailed American reckoning by just over forty minutes.

58 *CL47*, p. 3.

59 Gill, *Australia in the War*, Vol. 2, p. 526. The quote is from Lieutenant Commander W S Bracegirdle, RAN, gunnery officer in *Shropshire*.

60 *CL56*, Enc (B), p. 4.

61 Morison, *Naval Operations, Vol. XII*, p. 221.

62 Holloway, *Second Salvo*, p. 60.

63 At this time, the USN was in the process of replacing Mk4 fire control radars with the much-improved Mk12. However, most of DesRon56's ships, including *Bennion*, still carried the Mk4 radar.

64 Ibid. Holloway went on to achieve the rank of admiral and served as CNO from 1974 to 1978.

65 *DD649-1*, p. 18.

66 Ibid.

67 These numbers are taken from *Destroyer Report*, with some refinement based on *DD649-2*. The latter was a preliminary damage report made shortly after the battle, while the former was a postwar analysis based on shipyard data.

68 This assessment is conjecture by the author. Given the circumstances under which *Grant* was damaged, it is understandable that no attempt was made at the time to determine which source was the cause of any particular casualty.

69 *CA28*, Part II, p. 5.

70 Tully, *Surigao Strait*, p. 211.

71 Ibid., p. 19.

72 *McGarty*, DD-649, p. 173.

73 *DD649-1*, pp. 19–20.

74 Ibid, p. 21.

75 Tully, *Surigao Strait*, p. 212.

76 Ibid., p. 219.

77 Given the difference between *Shigure*'s clock and the Americans', this means Nishino claims that he sighted and communicated with Shima at approximately 0430. O'Hara, *Axis*, p. 257, puts this encounter at 0424, which is more likely. Tully, *Surigao Strait*, pp. 277–8, states this occurred at 0440 when *Nachi* was heading south, which is also plausible, except for Nishino's statement that Shima was heading north when the encounter occurred.

78 *USSBS Interrogations*, No. 390.

79 While it is difficult to be certain what Mori saw, it was most likely two patches of oil from *Fuso* burning on the surface that would be sighted and taken under fire by the Americans later in this story. *Fuso*'s stern may still have been above water at this time in one of those patches of burning oil.

80 *USSBS Interrogations*, No. 233.

81 Ibid.

82 Ibid.

83 O'Hara, *Axis*, p. 257.

84 Tully, *Surigao Strait*, pp. 234–6. This is one of the more problematic incidents of this battle; Nishino makes no mention of the encounter in *USSBS Interrogations*, No. 390.

85 *CA28*, Part IIB, p. 8.

86 Ibid., Part IV, p. 11.

87 Ibid.

88   *CL56*, Enc (B), p. 5.
89   Tully, *Surigao Strait*, p. 249.
90   *Shigure* was one class older than *Asagumo*, with a different gun layout, and displaced almost 400t less, but the distinction was not important to anyone in *Sigourney*.
91   This was because *Asagumo* was firing at *PT323* to the west and not towards the north. *Cony* was DD508.
92   *DD643*, Part II, p. 8.
93   This refers to the FH 10cm-band fire control radar.
94   The American 6in HC Mk34 shell normally had both nose and base fuses; the nose fuse could be either a standard percussion fuse or one of two anti-aircraft fuses. The substitution of a steel nose plug caused it to act more like a lightweight version of an AP shell.
95   *CL46*, p. 3.
96   Being new construction – *Columbia* was commissioned in June 1942 – she had the current Ford Range-keeper Mk8.
97   *CL56*, Enc (C), p. 1.
98   Fischer, *Ballistic Computer Design*.
99   Ibid.
100 Target ABLE was *Yamashiro*.
101 *CL56*, Enc (C), pp. 3–4.
102 Morison, *Naval Operations, Vol. XII*, p. 289.
103 Tully, *Surigao Strait*, pp. 30–3.
104 *USSBS Interrogations*, No. 390.
105 *Reading Eagle*, 29 December 1958.

Sources

It should be noted that, given the research resources available at the beginning of the twenty-first century, some sources I have used are available in cyberspace. (A small percentage of these are available only online.) In these cases, I have given the hyperlink to the source rather than the more traditional publisher information. It is characteristic of such sources that they are more ephemeral than paper-and-ink sources. When the site that serves the pages is changed or ceases to exist, the effect can be as if every copy of a particular book was instantly vaporised. All links listed here were active and available at the time this manuscript was written.

All primary sources not otherwise identified as to origin are from the US National Archives and Records Administration (NARA), which holds the US Navy's Second World War-era records at the Archives II site in College Park, MD.

Primary/Official Sources – USN Action/Damage Reports

Reports are ordered here by hull or unit number. If the listed reference is a ship's report and that ship's name is not given in the report title, I list it in parentheses at the end of the reference.

BB38 *Surigao Strait Action; Report on,* BB38/A16-3, Serial (0016), 6 November 1944. (USS *Pennsylvania*)

BB48 *Action in Battle of Surigao Straits 25 October 1944 USS West Virginia – Report of,* BB48/A16-3, Serial (0538), 1 November 1944.

CA25 *Action against Japanese Naval Surface Units – March 26, 1943 – Off Komandorskie Islands – Report on,* CA25/A16-3, Serial (001), 1 April 1943. (USS *Salt Lake City*)

CA28 *Action Report, USS Louisville (CA 28) for the Night Surface Engagement off Surigao Strait, Leyte Gulf, Philippine Islands on 25 October 1944,* CA28/A16-3, Serial (0045), 7 November 1944.

CA30 *Action Report—U.S.S. Houston CA-30 on the Battle of Sunda Strait, 28 February 1942,* no serial, 13 November 1945. (This report was compiled after the end of the war by the senior surviving officer of *Houston*'s crew, Captain Arthur L Maher, former gunnery officer.)

CA33 *Action Report – Surface Engagement in Leyte Gulf 25 October 1944,* CA33/A16-3, Serial (065), 28 October 1944. (USS *Portland*)

CDD58-1   *Report of Naval Engagement with Japanese Naval Forces During the Night of February 20, 1942*, FB58/A16-3, Serial (CF-06), 24 February 1942.

CDD58-2   *U.S.S. STEWART (DD224) – Damage in Floating Dry Dock at Sourabaya, Java – report of*, FB58/S7, Serial (CF-03), 25 February 1942.

CDD58-3   *Report of Action with Japanese on February 27, 1942. Events Before and After*, FB58/A16-3, Serial (CF-05), 4 March 1942.

CL9   *Action Report – USS Richmond – Day Action off Komandorski Islands, March 26, 1943*, CL9/A16-3, Serial (017), 28 March 1943.

CL46   *Report of Action of Surigao Straits – Philippine Islands – 25 October 1944*, CL46/A16-3/A9, Serial (091), 26 October 1944. (USS *Phoenix*)

CL47   *Action in Surigao Strait on Morning of 25 October, 1944 – Report of*, CL47/A16-3/A9-8, Serial (069), 30 October 1944. (USS *Boise*)

CL56   *U.S.S. Columbia (CL 56) – Action Report – Surigao Straits, 24–25 October 1944*, Serial (0010), 1 November 1944.

DD211   *Engagement with the Enemy: Night Action in Bali Strait, 28 February–1 March, 1942*, DD211/A16-3, no serial, 7 March 1942. (USS *Alden*)

DD218-1   *Report of Night Attack on Japanese Forces off Balik Papan, Borneo, N.E.I., on January 24, 1942*, DD218/A16-3, Serial (CF-3), 26 January 1942. (USS *Parrott*)

DD218-2   *Report of Night Attack on Japanese Forces in Badoeng Strait, Southeast Coast of Bali, N.E.I., on February 20, 1942*, DD218/A16-3/A9-8, Serial (CF-7), 21 February 1942. (USS *Parrott*)

DD225-1   *Night Destroyer Attack off Balikpapan, January 24, 1942*, DD225/A12, Serial (5), 25 January 1942. (USS *Pope*)

DD225-2   *Night Raid on Enemy Forces off Bali Island, Combined U.S. and Dutch Forces, February 19–20, 1942*, DD225/A16-3, Serial (CF-17), 20 February 1942. (USS *Pope*)

DD228   *Night Attack on Japanese Ships at Balik Papan, Morning of January 24, 1942 – Report of*, DD228/A16-3, Serial (CF-1), 25 January 1942. (USS *Ford*)

DD230-1   *Operations of this Vessel, 11–14 January, 1942*, DD230/A16(C), Serial (C-10), 14 January 1942. (USS *Paul Jones*)

DD230-2   *Report of Action off Balikpapan, Borneo, January 24, 1942*, DD230/A16. Serial (11), 24 January 1942. (USS *Paul Jones*)

DD643   *Action Report, Battle of Surigao Strait, 25 October 1944*, DD643, Serial (055), 30 October 1944. (USS *Sigourney*)

DD649-1   *Action Report – Operations Against Central Philippines, Leyte Area, and Night Surface Action of 24–25 October Against Japanese Task Force in Surigao Strait*, DD649/A16-3, Serial (006), 11 November 1944. (USS *Albert W. Grant*)

DD649-2   *War Damage Report*, DD649/A16-3, Serial (007), 14 November 1944. (USS *Albert W. Grant*)

Primary/Official Sources – Other (author/editor known)

Biagini, Antonello and Fernando Frattolillo (eds), *Diario Storico del Comando Supremo*, Vol. 1, Rome, 1986.

D'Adamo, Cristiano, *Battle of Cape Teulada*, Regia Marina Italiana, Direzione Generale del Personale Militare, Rome, www.regiamarina.net/detail_text_with_list.asp?nid=37&lid=1&cid=1.

Fraser, Admiral Sir Bruce A, 'Sinking of the German Battlecruiser Scharnhorst on the 26th December 1943, 28 January 1944', *London Gazette Supplement*, No. 38038, 5 August 1947.

Gill, G Hermon, *Australia in the War of 1939–1945, Series 2: Navy, Volume I: Royal Australian Navy, 1939–1942*, 1957, www.awm.gov.au/histories/second_world_war/AWMOHWW2/Navy/Vol1.

—— *Australia in the War of 1939–1945, Series 2: Navy, Volume 2: Royal Australian Navy, 1942–1945*, 1968, www.awm.gov.au/histories/second_world_war/AWMOHWW2/Navy/Vol2.

Holloway, Admiral James L, III, *Second Salvo at Surigao Strait*, Naval History, Vol. 24, No. 5, US Naval Institute, Annapolis, MD, 2010.

Morison, Samuel E, *History of United States Naval Operations in World War II, Vol. III: The Rising Sun in the Pacific, 1931–April 1942*, Little, Brown & Co., Boston, MA, 1948.

—— *History of United States Naval Operations in World War II, Vol. VII: Aleutians, Gilberts and Marshalls, June 1942–April 1944*, Little, Brown & Co., Boston, MA, 1951.

—— *History of United States Naval Operations in World War II, Vol. XII: Leyte, June 1944–January 1945*, Little, Brown & Co., Boston, MA, 1958.

Parker, Frederick D, *Pearl Harbor Revisited: United Staes Navy Communications Intelligence 1924–1941*, United States Cryptological History, Center for Cryptological History, National Security Agency, Ft Meade, MD, 1994.

Roskill, Captain Stephen W, RN, *The War at Sea 1939–1945, Vol. I: The Defensive*, HMSO, London, 1954.

—— *The War at Sea 1939–1945, Vol. II: The Period of Balance*, HMSO, London, 1956.

—— *The War at Sea 1939–1945, Vol. III: The Offensive – Part I*, HMSO, London, 1960.

Watanabe Daiji, *Bali Island Sea Battle by Michishio of the 8th Destroyer Division*. (Written by a former IJN chief petty officer, this was kindly supplied to me by Vincent O'Hara in a rough-translated form. In the small quoted section reproduced in Chapter 4, I have smoothed the English without, I hope, altering the meaning in any way.)

Waters, S D, *Achilles at the River Plate*, War History Branch, Department of Internal Affairs, Wellington, NZ, 1948. (This is part of *New Zealand in the Second World War – Official History* series, available online at http://nzetc.victoria.ac.nz.)

Primary/Official Sources – Other (author unknown/uncredited)

ADM 116/4351: Report on the Loss of H.M.S. Hood, www.hmshood.org.uk/reference/official/adm116/adm116-4351_POW.htm.

ADM 239/268: C.B.04039, Armour Protection, www.admirals.org.uk/records/adm/adm239/adm239-268.php#table5.

Aleutian Naval Operation, March 1942–February 1943, Military History Section, Army Forces Far East, Japanese Monograph No. 88.

Battle Lesson, Observations and Outline of Progress of Communications in the Naval Battle off ATTU Island. 5th Fleet Headquarters, 25 April 1943.

Battle Summaries, No. 2. – Mediterranean Operations – Action off Cape Spada (Crete), 19th July, 1940, ADM/234/317, The National Archives, Kew, England, 1942.

Battle Summaries, No. 9. – Action off Cape Spartivento, 27th November, 1940, ADM/234/325, The National Archives, Kew, England, 1943.

Battle Summary No. 24 – Sinking of the 'Scharnhorst', 26th December 1943, B.R. 1736 (17/50), ADM/234/343, The National Archives, Kew, England, 1950.

B.d.U. Op.'s WAR LOG, National Archives & Records Administration, Washington, DC.

Combat Narrative: The Aleutians Campaign: June 1942–August 1943, Naval Historical Center, Department of the Navy, Washington, DC, 1993. (This can be found at www.ibiblio.org/hyperwar/USN/USN-CN-Aleutians.html.)

Combat Narrative: The Java Sea Campaign, Publications Branch, Office of Naval Intelligence, US Navy, 1943. (This can be found at www.ibiblio.org/hyperwar/USN/USN-CN-Java/index.html#page1.)

Destroyer Report: Gunfire, Bomb and Kamikaze Damage, including Losses in Action – 17 October, 1941 to 15 August, 1945, War Damage Report No. 51, Preliminary Design Section, Bureau of Ships, Navy Department, Washington, DC, 25 January 1947. (A partial copy of this can be found at www.ibiblio.org/hyperwar/USN/rep/WDR/DESTROYER%20REPORT%20-%20GUNFIRE,%20BOMB%20AND%20KAMIKAZE%20%20DAMAGE%20INCLUDING%20LOSS%20IN%20ACTION%20-%20October%2017,%201942.pdf.)

Fuehrer Conferences on Naval Affairs 1939–1945, Greenhill Books, London, 1990. (This was first circulated within the Admiralty in typewritten form in 1947 and published as a supplement to *Brassey's Naval Annual* in 1948.)

Interrogations of Japanese Officials (OPNAV-P-03-100), United States Strategic Bombing Survey [Pacific], Naval Analysis Division. (Individual interrogations listed below; the first number is the USSBS number, the number in parentheses is the number assigned by the USN to those interrogations of naval interest.)

No. 98(21), Commander Miura Kintaro, *Aleutian Campaign: Seaplane Operations, the Naval Battle of the Komandorski Islands, and the Defense of the Kuriles.*

No. 102(25), Commander Hashimoto Shigefusa, *Aleutian Campaign and Defense of the Kuriles:Planning and Operations from November 1942 to August 1945.*

No. 205(51), Commander Kuwahara Tadao, *Aleutian Campaign: Transports at the Battle of the Komandorskis, 26 March 1943.*

No. 233(58), Commander Mori Kokichi, *Battle of Surigao Strait.*

No. 367(73), Vice-Admiral Omori Sentaro and Captain Arichoka Rokuji, *Aleutian Campaign: Operations of the Japanese First Destroyer Squadron.*

No. 390(79), Commander Nishino Shigeru, *Battle of Surigao Strait.*

No. 438(93), Commander Okumiya Mastake, *Aleutian Campaign: The Japanese Historical Account of the Naval Battle Fought off the Komandorski Islands, March 1943*.

'Loss of H.M. Ships *Prince of Wales* and *Repulse*', *London Gazette* supplement, pp. 1237–44, 26 February 1948. (This reproduces a report signed by Vice-Admiral Geoffrey Layton, dated 17 December 1941.)

N.E.I. – Bengal Bay Area Naval Attack Operations, Naval Operations in Southeast Area, War History Series (*Senshi Sosho*), Vol, 26, Tokyo, 1969.

Northern Area Naval Operations, February 1943–August 1945, Japanese Monograph No. 89, Office of the Chief of Military History, US Dept of the Army.

The Campaigns of the Pacific War, United States Strategic Bombing Survey (Pacific), Naval Analysis Division, 1946.

The Loss of H.M.S. Exeter: Report from the Engineering Officer, Ministry of Defence, London, 1950.

Secondary Sources (author/editor known)

Allen, Frank and Paul Bevand, *The Pursuit of Bismarck and the Sinking of H.M.S. Hood*, www.hmshood.com/history/denmarkstrait/bismarck1.htm, 2012.

Asmussen, John, *Bismarck & Tirpitz*, www.bismarck-class.dk, 2012. (This is the gateway to a series of linked sites covering the major classes of Kriegsmarine surface warships, including www.scharnhorst-class.dk.)

Bonomi, Antonio, *The Battle of the Denmark Strait, May 24th 1941*, trans. Phil Isaacs, www.hmshood.com/history/denmarkstrait/bonomi_denstrait1.htm, 2006,

Bragadin, Giorgio Dissera, *Sotto il segno di Barbara*, ed. Stamperia di Venezia, Venice, 1990.

Breyer, Siegfried, *Battleships and Battle Cruisers: 1905–1970*, Doubleday & Co, Garden City, NY, 1973.

Brooks, John, *Dreadnought Gunnery and the Battle of Jutland: The Question of Fire Control*, Routledge, Abingdon, England, 2005.

Brown, Louis, *Technical and Military Imperatives: A Radar History of World War II*, Taylor & Francis Group, Abingdon, England, 1999.

Czarnecki, Joseph, *Performance of US Battleships at Surigao Strait*, www.navweaps.com/index_tech/tech=079.htm.

DiGiulian, Tony, *Longest Gunfire Hit on an Enemy Warship*, www.navweaps.com/index_tech/tech-006.htm, 22 August 2002.

Edwards, Bernard, *Beware Raiders!: German Surface Raiders in the Second World War*, Naval Institute Press, Annapolis, MD, 2001.

Fischer, Bradley, *Overview of USN and IJN Warship Ballistic Computer Design*, www.navweaps.com/index_tech/tech-086.htm, 9 September 2003.

Friedman, Norman, *Naval Firepower: Battleship Guns and Gunnery in the Dreadnought Era*, Seaforth Publishing, Barnsley, England, 2008.

—— *Naval Radar*, Naval Institute Press, Annapolis, MD, 1981.

Garzke, William H, Jr and Robert O Dulin, Jr, 'The Bismarck's Final Battle', *Warship International*, No. 2, 1994. (This can be found at www.navweaps.com/index_inro/INRO_Bismarck_p1.htm.)

Greene, Jack and Alessandro Massignani, *The Naval War in the Mediterranean 1940–1943*, Naval Institute Press, Annapolis, MD, 2011.

Hara, Captain Tameichi, IJN, *Japanese Destroyer Captain*, Naval Institute Press, Annapolis, MD, 1967.

Howeth, Captain Linwood S, USN, *History of Communications-Electronics in the United States Navy*, US Government Printing Office, Washington, DC, 1963. (Available at http://earlyradiohistory.us/1963hw.htm.)

Howland, Captain Vernon W, RCN, *The Loss of HMS Glorious: An Analysis of the Action*, http://www.warship.org/no11994.htm.

Howse, Derek, *Radar at Sea:The Royal Navy in World War 2*, Naval Institute Press, Annapolis, MD, 1993.

Jones, Geoffrey, *Under Three Flags: The Story of Nordmark and the Armed Supply Ships of the German Navy*, William Kimber & Co., Ltd, London, 1973.

Jurens, William J, 'The Loss of HMS Hood: A Re-Examination', *Warship International*, No. 2, 1987. (This can be found at www.navweaps.com/index_inro/INRO_Hood_p1.htm.)

Kahn, David, *Seizing the Enigma: The Race to Break the German U-Boat Codes, 1939–1943*, Houghton Mifflin Co., Boston, MA, 1991.

Koop, Gerhard and Klaus-Peter Schmolke, *Heavy Cruisers of the Admiral Hipper Class*, Greenhill Books, London, 2001.

Lacroix, Eric and Linton Wells II, *Japanese Cruisers of the Pacific War*, Naval Institute Press, Annapolis, MD, 1997.

Lorelli, John A, *The Battle of the Komandorski Islands*, Naval Institute Press, Annapolis, MD, 1984.

McGarty, Terrence P and Elaine (Carlson) Dorland, *DD-649 USS Albert W Grant*, www.telmarc.com/Documents/Books/DD%20649%2010.pdf.

Millington-Drake, Sir Eugen, *The Drama of Graf Spee and the Battle of the Plate*, Peter Davies Ltd, London, 1964.

O'Hara, Vincent P, *Night Action off Cape Passero – October 12th, 1940*, http://www.regiamarina.net/engagements/capopassero/capopassero_us.htm.

—— *Struggle for the Middle Sea: The Great Navies at War in the Mediterranean Theater, 1940–1945*, Naval Institute Press, Annapolis, MD, 2009.

—— *The German Fleet at War, 1939–1945*, Naval Institute Press, Annapolis, MD, 2004.

—— *The U.S. Navy Against The Axis: Surface Combat 1941–1945*, Naval Institute Press, Annapolis, MD, 2007.

Pope, Dudley, *The Battle of the River Plate: The Hunt for the German Pocket Battleship Graf Spee*, McBooks Press, Ithaca, NY, 2005. (Originally copyrighted in 1956.)

Prados, John, *Combined Fleet Decoded: The Secret History of American Intelligence and the Japanese Navy in World War II*, Naval Institute Press, Annapolis, MD, 1995.

Roscoe, Theodore, *United States Destroyer Operations in World War II*, Naval Institute Press, Annapolis, MD, 1953.

Smith, Peter C, *Critical Conflict: The Royal Navy's Mediterranean Campaign in 1940*, Pen & Sword Maritime, Barnsley, England, 2011.

Stern, Robert C, *Destroyer Battles: Epics of Naval Close Combat*, Seaforth Publishing, Barnsley, England, 2008.

—— *The US Navy and the War in Europe*, Seaforth Publishing, Barnsley, England, 2012.

Tanaka Tsuneji, 'The Battle of the Java Sea', in Itoh Masanori et al., *Jitsuroku Taiheiyo Senso, Vol. 1*, Chuokoron, Tokyo, 1960, pp. 204–28.

Tully, Anthony P, *Battle of Surigao Strait*, Indiana University Press, Bloomington, IN, 2009.

Watson, Bruce, *Atlantic Convoys and Nazi Raiders: The Deadly Voyage of HMS Jervis Bay*, Praeger Publishers, Westport, CT, 2006.

Willmott, H P, *Empires in the Balance: Japanese and Allied Pacific Strategies to April 1942*, Naval Institute Press, Annapolis, MD, 1982.

Winslow, Captain W G, USN (Retd), *The Fleet the Gods Forgot: The U.S. Asiatic Fleet in World War II*, Naval Institute Press, Annapolis, MD, 1982.

Winton, John, *ULTRA at Sea: How Breaking the Nazi Code Affected Allied Naval Strategy during World War II*, William Morrow & Co., New York, 1988.

Woodward, Tim, *Putting Vice-Admiral Holland's Actions During the Battle of the Denmark Strait into Context*, www.hmshood.com/history/denmarkstrait/woodward.htm, 2012.

Secondary Sources (author unknown/uncredited)

'*Admiral Shima Breaks Silence* – Says He Suspected Trap in *Philippines*', *Reading Eagle*, Reading, PA, 29 December 1958. (This was an Associated Press story quoting from a letter copyrighted by the *Los Angeles Examiner*.)

Q-Ships (Anti-submarine vesels disguised as merchant vessels), www.history.navy.mil/docs/wwii/q-ships.htm.

Indispensable Sites

These are sites I referenced constantly during the writing of this and many other books.

Destroyer History Foundation, www.destroyerhistory.org/destroyers/index.html. (Comprehensive coverage of USN destroyers, particularly those that fought in the Second World War.)

Dictionary of American Naval Fighting Ships, www.history.navy.mil/danfs/index.html. (The entries in this immense effort vary considerably in detail and completeness. For the most part, though, it is an excellent first reference for any USN ship.)

H.M.S. Hood Association, www.hmshood.com. (Another useful site with much invaluable original documentation as well as well-written analysis.)

Imperial Japanese Navy, http://homepage2.nifty.com/nishidah/e/index.htm. (An invaluable resource covering the records of IJN personnel.)

Naval-History.Net, www.naval-history.net/xGM-aContents.htm. (An invaluable resource for RN ships' histories.)

NavWeaps: Naval Weapons, Naval Technology and Naval Reunions, www.navweaps.com. (This site covers, in magnificent detail, very nearly all the weapons used by the world's navies in the twentieth century, excepting aviation ordnance.)

Nihon Kaigun, www.combinedfleet.com/kaigun.htm. (This site covers the movements of most Japanese warships in great detail.)

The Second World War – A Day by Day Account, http://homepage.ntlworld.com/andrew.etherington/index.html. (This useful chronology of the war combines a number of sources.)

INDEX

Merchant ships are identified as to nationality with ISO two-letter nation codes (see www.worldatlas.com/aatlas/ctycodes.htm) in parentheses. Since that list of country codes is modern, it lacks a listing for the USSR, which is indicated in this index by the code SU. All warship and class names are followed by a navy designator and a hull type designator in parentheses.

Navy designators used below are: USN – United States of America, CSN – Confederate States of America, RN – Great Britain, RAN – Australia, RCN – Canada, KM – Germany, MN – France, IJN – Japan, RM – Italy, RNeN – Netherlands, RNZN – New Zealand and RNoN – Norway.

Type designators are US Navy standard (see www.history.navy.mil/danfs/abbreviations. htm) where possible. Naval personnel are identified as to service with the same navy designators. (Note: I have made no effort to distinguish reserve from regular naval personnel.) Page references to captions are in **bold**.

ABDA/ABDACOM/ABDAFLOAT, 99, 104, 106, **106**, 108, 110–11, **112**, 115–17, 120, 125, **128**

Abe, Captain Toshio (IJN), 110–12

Abukuma (IJN CL), 131–2, 133n11, 133n13, 137–9, 147, 189, 195, 207, 219–20

Acasta (RN DD), 32, 34–5

Achates (RN DD), 162, 164–5

Achilles (RN/RNZN CL), 6–7, **10**, 11, **15**, 16, **16**, **18**, 20–1, 26, 106

Adak Island, Aleutians, 131–3, 138, 139n34, 141, 150

Admiral Graf Spee (KM *Panzerschiff*), xvi, 3–4, **4**, 5n13, 6–7, **8**, 9, **10**, 11–17, **12**, **13**, **14**, **15**, **16**, 16n30, 17n31, **18**, **19**, 20–2, **22**, 22n35, **23**, **24**, **25**, 26, **27**, 35, 65, 69, 126, 173

Admiral Hipper (KM CA), 28, **28**, 30–1, **32**, 65–9, 67n3, **69**, 71–3, **71**, 76–7, 76n16, **79**, 152, 156–8, 162–5, 163n15, **164**

Admiral Scheer (KM *Panzerschiff*), 6, **19**, 66–7, 69, 73, 77, 152–3, 156–7, 158n12

Agria Grabusa, Crete, 50, 52–3

Ajax (RN CL), 5, 11, 15–16, **15**, 20–1, 26, **54**, 55, 55n26, 106

Akagane Maru (JP), 131

Akagi (IJN CV), 129

Akebono (IJN DD), 126, 191, 224

Akureyri, Iceland, 168

Albert W. Grant (USN DD), 211–5, 213n68, **216**, 217, **218**

Alden (USN DD), 123–4, 124n56

Alexandria, Egypt, 6, 36, 38, 39, 52–3, 55–6, 60, 63

Alfieri (RM DD), 59

Algiers, Algeria, 36, 38

Alsterufer (KM AMC), 73

Alta/Altenfjord, Norway, 152, 155–8, 156n8, 165–7, 169–70, 172n32, 173, **178**

Altmark (KM AOR), 4, 4n9, 6–7, 9, 26, **27**, 31

Amagusan Point, Leyte Island, Philippines, 200

Amchitka Island, Aleutians, 141

Amami-O-Shima, Ryukyu Islands, Japan, 189

Anson (RN BB), 157–8

Antikithera Island, Crete, 49

Antikithera Strait, 46, 48

Aoba (IJN CA), 189

Aoba-class (IJN CAs), 148

Arabistan (GB), 68

Arashi (IJN DD), 129

Arashio (IJN DD), 112, 114, 116

Ardent (RN DD), 32–4

Argus (RN CV), 68

Ark Royal (RN CV), 2, 31–2, 36, 38, 56, 58–9, 62–3, 75, 93

Artigliere (RM DD), **54**

Arunta (RAN DD), 206

Asagumo (IJN DD), 117, 192, 204–5, 207, 219–20, 223–4, 223n90, 223n91, **224**, 228

Asahi Maru (JP), 102

Asaka Maru (JP), 131–3, 133n13

Asakaze (IJN DD), 119, 121

Asashio (IJN DD), 110–14, 111n29

Asheville (USN PG), 129

Ashigara (IJN CA), 126, **127**, **128**, 189, 195, 219, 221

Atago (IJN CA), 129

Atlantis (RN AH), 31
Attu Island, Aleutians, 130–2, 134, 141, 146

Babi Island, Java, **118**, 119–20
Badung Strait, 108–9, 108n23, 111, 113, 116
Bailey (USN DD), 131–3, 131n6, 135, 138–40,
    142, 146–7, 146n43, 150–1
Balabac Strait, 194
Bali Strait, 108n23, 123–5
Balikpapan, Borneo, 96–102, 104, 108, 192
Bande Nere (RM CL), see *Giovanni delle*
    Bande Nere
Bangka Island, 108
Banten Bay, Java, 119, 122
Barentsburg, Spitsbergen, 167
Baroni, Captain Enrico (RM), 39
Bartolomeo Colleoni (RM CL), 46, 50, 50n18,
    50, **51**, 52–3, 53n23
Batavia, Java, 97, 119, 119n47, 123
battles
    Badung Strait, 106, 108–17, **108**, **110**, 112,
        112, 117
    Bali Strait, 123–4, **124**
    Balikpapan, 98, 100–4, **100**, **103**
    Barents Sea, 158–65, **159**, **160**, **161**, **166**,
        169, **175**
    Cape Passero, 54–5
    Cape Spada, 46–53, **47**, **50**, **51**, **52**, 59, 64
    Cape Teulada (Cape Spartivento), 57–64,
        57, **59**, **60**, **61**, **62**, **63**, 67, **69**, 78, 83
    Denmark Strait, 78–91, **82**, **84**, **97**
    Java Sea, 117–19, 125, **127**
    Jutland, xiii–xiv, 83
    Komandorski Islands (Sea Battle off Attu
        Island), **132**, 133–51, **143**, **144**, **145**,
        147, **149**, **150**, 188
    Leyte Gulf, 228
    Midway, 184, 192
    Narvik, xi, 56n27
    North Cape, 168–79, **169**, **179–82**, 182–3
    Pearl Harbor, 97–8, 97n3, 106, **186**, 201
    Philippine Sea, 184–5, 188
    Punta Stilo, 33, **39**, 40–5, **42**
    River Plate, 11–26, **14**, **15**, **16**, **18**, **19**, **22**,
        23, **24**, 96
    Savo Island, 189
    Sunda Strait, **118**, 119–23, **121**, 192
    Surigao Strait, **186**, **190**, 191, **193**, 202–25,
        203, **205**, **210**, **218**, **221**, **222**
    Taranto, 55–6
Bawean Island, 125
Bay of Biscay, 75, 92
Beale (USN DD), 206
Bear Island, 153, 155, 158, 169–70
Belfast (RN CL), 168, 172–6, 182–3
Bell, Captain F S (RN), 16
Benghazi, Libya, 39
Bennion (USN DD), 209, 212, 217
Bergen, Norway, 4, 7, 28, 29, 65, 78–9, **79**
Berkey, Rear-Admiral Russell S (USN), 188,
    193, 201, 207, 209, 212

Bernd von Arnim (KM DD), 30
Berwick (RN CA), 56, 58–62, **63**, 64, 67–8,
    69, 153
Bey, Captain/Rear-Admiral Erich (KM),
    169–77, 172n32
Binford, Commander Thomas H (USN),
    113–14, 113n33, 123, 124n56
Bismarck (KM BB), 76–81, **76**, 77n17, 77n18,
    78n22, **79**, 82n29, 83, **84**, 85–8, 91–3,
    92, **93**, **94**, 95, 96, 152, 155, 183, 217
Bismarck-class (KM BBs), 3
Bletchley Park, England, see GC&CS
Blinn, Lieutenant Commander W C (USN),
    126
Bohol Island, Philippines, 200, 202
Bohol Sea, 194–5, 198
Boise (USN CL), 96, 96n2, 100, **195**, **196**, 201,
    212
Bolzano (RM CA), 45, 56, 58, **60**
Bonaventure (RN CL), 68–9, 68n6
Bordeaux, France, 69, 72, 74, 74n14
Borgestad (NO), 72–3
Bracegirdle, Lieutenant Commander W S
    (RAN), 212n59
Bramble (RN MS), 158–9, 163, 163n15, **164**,
    165
Bremen, Germany, 152
Brest, France, 69, **69**, 71–3, **71**, 75, **75**, 77,
    77n19, 77n20, **94**, 152
Bretagne (MN BB), 36, 38
Briggs, Ordinary Signalman Albert E (RN),
    87
Bristol, England, 72
Brunei, Borneo, 99, 185, 189n11, 191–2, **197**,
    224
Brunsbüttel, Germany, 66
Buenos Aires, Argentina, **25**, 26
Buchanan, Commander A E (RAN), 206
Bugho Point, Leyte Island, Philippines, 201,
    206
Burnett, Rear-Admiral Robert L (RN), 157–9,
    162–6, 169, **169**, 171–7

Cabo Santa Maria, Uruguay, 11
Caio Duilio (RM BB), 55
Calcutta, India, **125**
California (USN BB), 201, 209
Calobre (PA), 165
Camaguin Island, Philippines, 200
Campioni, Vice-Admiral Inigo (RM), 40–1,
    40, **41**, **44**, 45, 56, 58–9, 61–3
Canary Islands, 67
Cape Arkona, Germany, 77
Cape Bon, Tunisia, 54, 56
Cape Busa, Crete, 50
Cape Farewell, Greenland, 5, 70, 73
Cape Finisterre, Spain, 67, 71
Cape Horn, Chile, 9
Cape of Good Hope, South Africa, 7, 36, 69,
    73
Cape Matapan, Greece, 39

Cape Passero, Italy, 53, **54**, 55
Cape Spada, Crete, 46, 49–50
Cape Spartivento, Sardinia, 56–8
Cape Teulada, Sardinia, 56–8, 67, 78
Cape Town, South Africa, 6, 7, 9, 11
Cape Verde Islands, 6, 74
Casablanca, French Morocco, 36
Casardi, Rear-Admiral Ferdinando (RM), 46,
    48–9, 52–3
Cavite, Manila, Philippines, 96, **227**
Cavour (RM BB), see *Conte di Cavour*
Cebu, Philippines, 96
Cesare (RM BB), see *Giulio Cesare*
Chatham, England, 56n27
Chikuma (IJN CA), 129
Chilean Reefer (DK), 74–5
Chömpff, Lieutenant Commander J M L I
    (RNeN), 111
Christmas Island, 128
Ciliax, Vice-Admiral Otto (KM), 153–5
City of Flint (US), 7
Clausen, Lieutenant Commander Nicolai
    (KM), 71–2
Clement (GB), 6
Coghlan (USN DD), 131–3, 131n6, 139–40,
    142, 146–7, 151
Colleoni (RM CL), see *Bartolomeo Colleoni*
Collins, Captain J A (RAN), 46, 48–50
Colombo, Ceylon, 96, 100
Columbia (USN CL), **196**, 201, 212, 214, 221,
    222, 223, 225–6, 225n96
Conte di Cavour (RM BB), **40**, 41, **41**, 43, **43**,
    45, 55
convoys
    HG.53, 71–2
    HX.84, 66–7
    HX.106, 70–1, 73
    JW.51A/B, 157–9, **159**, **164**
    JW.55A/B, 168–71, 170n24, **178**, **179**
    MW.3, 55
    No.21-RO, 131
    OB.285, 74
    OB.294, 74
    PQ.12, 153–6
    PQ.17, 156
    PQ.18, 156–7
    QP.8, 153–4, 156
    QP.13, 156
    QP.14, 156–7
    RA.51, 157
    RA.55A, 169–70, 170n24, 172
    SL.67, 74
    SLS.64, **71**, 72
    WS.5A, 68
Cony (USN DD), 223, 223n91
Cooper, Lieutenant Commander J E (USN),
    101n10, 111
Coron Bay, Philippines, 192–5, 224
Cossack (RN DD), **27**, 28
Courageous (RN CV), 2, 35n48
Courbet (MN BB), 36

Coventry (RN CL), 56, 58
Coward, Captain Jesse G (USN), 200, 204,
    220
Cumberland (USN Slp), xii
Cumberland (RN CA), 5, 11, 158
Cunningham, Admiral Sir Andrew B (RN),
    40–1, **40**, **41**, 43, 45, 53
Curteis, Vice-Admiral A T B (RN), 153
Cuyo East Passage, 195
Cuyo Islands, Philippines, 195
Cuyo West Passage, 195

Dakar, Senegal, 36
Dalanganem Islands, Philippines, 195
Dale (USN DD), 131, 131n6, 133, 140, 142,
    146, 151
Darwin, Australia, 97–8, **107**
Davao, Mindanao, Philippines, 99
Davison, Rear-Admiral Ralph E (USN), 196,
    198
Decoy (RN DD), 45
DeMeester, Captain J B (RNeN), 113
Denmark Strait, 4, 7, 66–7, 70, 73, 77–9, 95,
    157
Denver (USN CL), **196**, 201, 214, **218**, 221,
    222
De Ruyter (RNeN CL), 97, 104, 108–11,
    111n27
Deutschland (KM *Panzerschiffe*), 4n12, 5,
    5n13, 7–8, 8n18, 35n47, 65, 152,
    156–8, 163–5, **175**
Deutschland-class (KM *Panzerschiffe*), 2–3,
    2n3, 3n4
Devonshire (RN CA), 35
DeVries, Lieutenant Commander W M
    (RNeN), 122
Dinagat Island, Philippines, 187, 194n21
Ditmarschen (KM AOR), 31
Dönitz, Vice-Admiral/Admiral Karl (KM),
    71–2, 74, 152, 166–8, 170–1, 173
Doorman, Rear-Admiral Karel (RNeN), 104,
    106, 109–11, 113, 117, 125
Doric Star (GB), 9, 11
Dover Strait, 35
D'Oyly-Hughes, Captain Guy (RN), 32, 34
Dreadnought (RN BB), **xii**
Duilio (RM BB), see *Caio Duilio*
Duke of York (RN BB), 152–3, 157, 168,
    170–1, 177n40, 175–8, **177**, 182–3
Dulag, Leyte, Philippines, **189**
Dunedin (RN CL), 68
Dunkerque (MN CB), 36, 38
Dunkerque-class (MN CBs), 3, 3n6
Duquesa (GB), 67, 69
Dutch Harbor, Unalaska Island, Aleutians,
    130, **147**, **149**, **150**

Eagle (RN CV), 40, 45
Edsall (USN DD), 128–9, 189
Egersund, Norway, 28
Electra (RN DD), 91, 117

Empire Trooper (GB), 68
Encounter (RN DD), 123, 125–6
Enterprise (USN CV), 196, **199**
ESM antennas, see radars
Espero (RM DD), 39, 46
Espiritu Santo, 130, **193**
Esso Hamburg (KM AO), 73
Eurofeld (KM AO), 67, 69
Evertsen (RNeN DD), 119, 122–3, **123**, 125, 125n59
Exeter (RN CA), 5, 11–17, **12**, **18**, **19**, 20–2, **25**, 26, 96, 106, 117–19, 123, 125–6, **125**, **127**, 131

Fættenfjord, Norway, 153
Falkland Islands, 5–6, 9, 11, 21
Faroe Islands, 4, 7, 35, 78, 95
Fegen, Captain Edward S F (RN), 66–7
fire control equipment
    IJN, 225–6
    RN
        Admiralty Fire Control Clock, xv
        AFCT (Admiralty Fire Control Table), xiv, 85
        Argo Clock, xiv, xivn8
        Director Control Tower, xiv, **xv**, **18**, 20, **29**
        Dreyer Fire Control Table, xiii–xiv, xivn8, **xiv**, 82, 85–6
        Dumaresq, xiii, xiiin4
        Vickers Clock, xiii, xiin4
    USN
        Ford Range-keeper, xiv–xv, 151, 225–6, 225n96, 229
        Mk19 director, **147**, **148**
        Mk33 director, **190**
        Mk34 director, **187**, 225
        Mk37 director, **216**
        Mk38 GFCS, 225
Fisher, Sir John A 'Jacky', 3, 3n5
Fiume (RM CA), 56, 59–61
Five Power Treaty, see Washington Naval Conference
Forbes, Admiral Charles M (RN), 8, 8n19, 32
Franklin (USN CV), 196
Fraser, Admiral Sir Bruce (RN), 158, 168–73, 175–7, 182–3
Freccia (RM DD), 45
Freetown, Sierra Leone, 4–7, 9, 11, 67, 72, 74
Fremantle, Australia, 97, 123–4
Friedrich Eckoldt (KM DD), 162–3, 165
Friedrich Ihn (KM DD), 154
Frohavet Channel, Norway, 154
Fubuki (IJN DD), **118**, 119–20, 120n49
Furious (RN CV), 2, 68
Furutaka-class (IJN CAs), 148
Fuso (IJN BB), 191, 192n14, 192n15, 196, 198, 204–7, 206n43, 218n79, 221, **222**

Garibaldi (RM CL), see *Giuseppe Garibaldi*
GC&CS, xix, 65–6, 95, 153, 155, 158n11

Gibraltar, 5–6, 36, 38, 54–6, 56n27, 68, 71, 72n11, 92
Giovanni delle Bande Nere (RM CL), 46, 48–9, 52–3
Giulio Cesare (RM BB), 41, **41**, 43, **43**, **44**, 45, **46**, 56
Giuseppe Garibaldi (RM CL), 41
Glasfurd, Commander Charles (RN), 34
Glasgow (RN CL), 73
Glassford, Rear-Admiral William, Jr (USN), 99–100, 109, 123, 128
Glorious (RN CV), 2, 31–5, 32n44, **33**, **34**
Glowworm (RN DD), **28**, 29–30
Gordon, Captain O L (RN), 125–6
Gorizia (RM CA), 56, 60
Göteborg, Sweden, 78
Göteborg (SE DD), 29
Gotenhafen, Germany, 7, 77, 152, **175**
Gotland (SE CL), 78
Gneisenau (KM CB), 3, 7–8, **27**, 28, 30–1, **30**, **33**, 34, **34**, 35n47, 70, **70**, 73–5, **75**, 77, 77n20, 152
Graf Spee (KM *Panzerschiff*), see *Admiral Graf Spee*
Greenland, 3–5, 77
Guam, Marianas Islands, 97n4, 98, 184

Haguro (IJN CA), 117, 125
Halifax, Nova Scotia, 66–7, 70–1, 73
Halmahera Island, 194
Halsey, Admiral William F (USN), 186, 186n5, 188, 191, 196, 200, 228
Hancox, Lieutenant Commander P S F (RAN), 121
Hans Lüdemann (KM DD), 29–30
Hara, Rear-Admiral Kenzaburo (IJN), 119
Harstad, Norway, 31, **32**, 154
Hart, Admiral Thomas (USN), 96n2, 97–9, 104, 106
Harukaze (IJN DD), 119–21
Harwood, Commodore Henry H. (RN), 5–6, 5n16, 9, **10**, 11, **14**, 15–17, 20–1, **23**, **24**, 26
Hashimoto, Commander Shigefuso (IJN), 135n19, 136, 136n24
Hasty (RN DD), 48, 52
Hatakaze (IJN DD), 119–21
Hatsuharu (IJN DD), 191
Hatsushimo (IJN DD), 131–2, 191
Hatsuyuki (IJN DD), 119–20
Havock (RN DD), 49, 52n21, 53
Heath, Commander J B (RN), 32
Helfrich, Vice-Admiral Conrad (RNeN), 106, 108, 122
Hereward (RN DD), 45
Hermes (RN CV), 36, 73, 96
Hero (RN DD), 48, 52
Hermann Schoemann (KM DD), 154
Hibuson Island, Philippines, 201, 212
Hiei (IJN BB), 129
Hipper (KM CA), see *Admiral Hipper*

Hishi (IJN DD), see *PC37*
Hobart (RAN CL), 106, 108, 119
Hoffmann, Captain Kurt (KM), 8
Holland, Vice-Admiral Lancelot E (RN), 56, 58–60, 63, 78, 80–3, **82**, 86, 95
Holloway, Lieutenant (junior grade) James L, III (USN), 212–13, 213n64
Homonhon Island, Philippines, 187
Hong Kong, 99
Hood (RN CB), 38, 78, 82–7, 82n28, 82n29, **82**, 83n35, **84**, 84n36, **88**, **89**, 90–1, **90**, 95
Hopen Island, Svalbard Archipelago, 167n18
Hornstrandir, Iceland, 79
Hosogaya, Vice-Admiral Boshiro (IJN), 131–5, 133n13, 137–42, 146, 151, 188
Hotspur (RN DD), 56n27
Houston (USN CA), 96, 98, 104, 106, **106**, **107**, 119–22, 122n51, **121**, **123**
Hunt-class (RN DEs), 157
Hutchins (USN DD), 206–7
Hvalfjordur, Iceland, 77–8, 153, 157
Hyderabad (RN Cor), 162–3
Hyperion (RN DD), 48, 52–3

Iceland (GB), 72
Iceland–Faroes Gap, 70, 78
IJN units
 1st Protection Fleet, 100, **100**
 1st Striking Force, 185, 185n4, 189, 191–2, 192n15, 196
 2nd Air Fleet, 191
 2nd Striking Force, 192, 195
 3rd Section/'C' Force, 192–5, **197**, 198, **199**, 202, **203**, 204–6, 209, 217, 224
 5th Fleet, 131, 188–9, 191–2, **221**
 5th Sentai, 126
 16th Sentai, 189, 189n11, 191
 Battleship Division 2, 191
 Combined Fleet, 130, 189, 191–2, 194, 200
 Destroyer Division 7, 191
 Destroyer Division 18, 191
 Destroyer Division 21, 191, 194
 Destroyer Squadron 1, 131, 189
 Kido Butai, 97, 129, 130
 Main Body, 185, 188, 191
 Southwest Area Fleet, 189, 191
Ijora (SU), 154, 154n5
Ikazuchi (IJN DD), 126, 131–2, 142
Ilex (RN DD), 48, 52–3
Illustrious (RN CV), 55
Iloilo, Panay, Philippines, 96
Inazuma (IJN DD), 131–3, 133n13, 142
Indianapolis (USN CA), 131
Indomitable (RN CV), 96, 96n1
Iron Duke-class (RN BBs), xiii
Isfjorden, Spitsbergen, 167
Ishii, Captain Hisashi (IJN), 193, 195–6

Jamaica (RN CL), 157–8, 165, 168, **169**, 176, 178, 182–3

Jan Mayen Island, 77–8
Java (RNeN CL), 97, **105**, 108–12, 111n29
J.D. Edwards (USN DD), 108, 113–14, 123, 124n56
Jervis Bay (RN AMC), 66–7
Johannesson, Captain Rolf (KM), 171–2
John D. Ford (USN DD), 101–4, 101n10, 108–9, **110**, 111–12, 111n29, 117, 123
Jøssingfjord, Norway, **27**, 28
Jumna (GB), 69
Juniper (RN Tr), 31–2

Kaafjord, Norway, 156, 156n8
Kasumi (IJN DD), 191
Kataoka Bay, Paramushiro Island, Kuriles, 131
Kattegat, 77–8
Kendari, Celebes, 104, 129
Kennedy, Captain Edward C (RN), 8, 8n18
Kenya (RN CL), 153
Kiel, Germany, 31, 65, 70, 73, 77, 152
Kiel Canal, 66
Kikkawa, Commander Kiyoshi (IJN), 112
Killen (USN DD), 206
King George V (RN BB), 2n2, 77n18, 79, 91, **93**, 153
King George V-class (RN BBs), 152
King, Admiral Ernest J (USN), 185, 228
Kinkaid, Rear-Admiral/Vice-Admiral Thomas C (USN), 131, 133, 186–7, 191, 193, 200, 228
Kinloch, Lieutenant Commander D C (RN), 163–4
Kinu (IJN CL), 189
Kirishima (IJN BB), 129
Kiska Island, Aleutians, 130–1
Klüber Rear-Admiral Otto (KM), 169, 171
KM units
 4th Destroyer Flotilla, 169–70, 172
Koepang, Timor, 99
Kola Inlet, Soviet Union, 153, 157–8, 168–9
Köln (KM CL), 157
Komandorski Islands, 132, 133n13, 146
Kongo-class (IJN BBs), 192n14
Kongshavn, Faroe Islands, 78
Kormoran (KM AMC), 69
Kortenaer (RNeN DD), 109
Krancke, Captain Theodor (KM), 67, 69, 73
Kristiansand, Norway, 65
Kuantan, Malaya, 98
Kubo, Rear-Admiral Kyuji (IJN), 108, 112
Kummetz, Vice-Admiral Oskar (KM), 158–9, 162–6, 170
Kure, Japan, 117, 188
Kuretake Maru (JP), 101n8
Kurita, Vice-Admiral Takeo (IJN), 185–6, 189, 191–2, 194–6, 198, 200, 200n32, 228
Kusaka, Vice-Admiral Ryunosuke (IJN), 189, 191
KXVIII (RNeN SS), 100, 104

Lafolé (RM SS), 56n27
Lanciere (RM DD), 60–1, 63–4
Langfjord, Norway, 156n8, 170, **178**
Langley (USN AV), 128
Langsdorff, Captain Hans (KM), 4, 6–7, 9, 11–15, 17, 20–1, **22**, **24**, **25**, 26, 173
La Pallice, France, 152
La Spezia, Italy, **62**
Leach, Captain John C (RN), 81, 86–7, 90, **90**, 98
Leary (USN DD), xv, **xvi**
Lee, Vice-Admiral Willis A (USN), 187, 200
Leros Island, Greece, 46, 49
Leyte Gulf, Philippines, 184, 186–7, 189, **189**, 191–2, 194–5, 194n21, **196**, 198, 200, 219, 224, 228
Leyte Island, Philippines, 185, 187, **188**, 189, 192, 194n21, 200–1, 211
Limasawa Island, Philippines, 200
Lindemann, Captain Ernst (KM), 91
Lingayen Gulf, Philippines, 185
Lingga Roads, Singapore, 185, 191
Littorio (RM BB), 38, 55
Liverpool, England, 71, 74
Loch Cairnbawn, Scotland, 167
Loch Ewe, Scotland, 157, 168
Lofoten Islands, Norway, 31, 154
Lombok Strait, 108, 111, 116
Londonderry, Northern Ireland, 66
Lookout (RN DD), 154
Lorraine (MN BB), 36
Louisville (USN CA), **189**, 201–2, 214, 220–1, 223
Luanda, Angola, 69
Luigi di Savoia Duca degli Abruzzi (RM CL), 41
Lütjens, Vice-Admiral/Admiral Günther (KM), 28, **30**, 70–1, 73–5, 77–8, **79**, 80–3, 86, 91–2
Lützow (KM *Panzerschiff*), see *Deutschland*
Luzon Island, Philippines, 98, 185, 188–9, 191
Luzon Strait, 196

MacArthur, General Douglas (USA), 185–7
Maine (RN AH), 53
Makassar, Celebes, 108, 112, 116, 128
Makassar Strait, 99–100, 104
Mako, Pescadores Islands, 189, 191–2
Malaya (RN BB), 41, 43, 45, 74
Malta, 38–9, 45, 53–6, **54**, 56n27, 63, 153
Manchester (RN CL), 56, 58–60, 62–3
Manila, Philippines, 96–7, 96n2, 99, **99**, 185, 189, 189n11, 192–3, 195–6, **227**
Manus Island, 185–6
Marblehead (USN CL), 96, 100, 104, **105**, 106, **106**, **107**, 129, 131
Mare Island Navy Yard, California, 100, **190**
Marschall, Vice-Admiral Wilhelm (KM), 31
Maryland (USN BB), 201, 209
Matchless (RN DD), 170, 183
Matteucci, Rear-Admiral Pellegrino (RM), 56, 59, 62n38

Maya (IJN CA), 129, 131–2, 134–8, 134n17, 146–7
McCoy, Captain J A (RN), 171
McDermut (DD USN), 205
McGowan (USN DD), 204
McManes, Captain Kenmore M (USN), 206–9, 207n46, 211
McMorris, Rear-Admiral Charles 'Soc' (USN), 131–5, 131n6, 137–40, 139n34, 142, 142n41, 146, 150–1
Meisel, Captain Wilhelm (KM), 67–8, 72–3
Melvin (USN DD), 204
Menado, Celebes, 99, 104
Merrimack (USN ScFr), xiin2
Mers-el-Kébir, Algeria, 36
Messina, Italy, 45, **46**, 56
Michishio (IJN DD), 112, 114–16, 192, 204–5, 207
Midway Island, 130
Mikawa, Vice-Admiral Gunichi (IJN), 129, 189, 191–2, 194–5
Mikuma (IJN CA), 119–21
Mindanao Island, Philippines, 99, 185, 194n21, 220, 224
Mindanao Sea, see Bohol Sea
Mindoro Island, Philippines, 192, 195
Mindoro Strait, 186
Minneapolis (USN CA), **189**, 201, 223
Mississippi (USN BB), 201, 209
Miura, Commander Kintaro (IJN), 136, 151
Mogami (IJN CA), **118**, 119–21, 192, 196, 198, **199**, 200–2, 204, 206–7, 209, **210**, 211, 217, 219–21, **222**, 223–4, 228
Monaghan (USN DD), 131, 131n6, 133, 140, 142, 146, 150–1
Monitor (USN BM), xii
Monssen (USN DD), 205
Montevideo, Uruguay, 9, **16**, 21, **22**, **24**, 26, 55, 65
Mopan (GB), 66
Mori, Commander Kokichi (IJN), 192, 218n79, **221**
Mori, Rear-Admiral Tomokazu (IJN), 131
Morotai Island, 194, 198
Mozambique Channel, 7, 73
München (KM Tr), 95
Murakumo (IJN DD), 119, 122–3
Murmansk, Soviet Union, 152, 157–8, 159n13
Musketeer (RN DD), 170, 173
Myoko (IJN CA), 126, **127**, **128**

Nachi (IJN CA), 125, 131–8, 133n11, 135n19, 142, **145**, 146–7, **146**, 151, 189, 191, 194–5, 217, 217n77, 219, **227**, 228
Nagara (IJN CL), 108, 112
Nagumo, Admiral Chuichi (IJN), 129, 184
Naiad (RN CL), 70
Naka (IJN CL), 100–1, **100**, 104
Naples, Italy, 40, 56
Narvik, Norway, 28–31, **29**, **32**, 152, 155–8
Natori (IJN CL), 119–20

Negros Island, Philippines, 194–6
Nelson (RN BB), xiv, **xv**, 2, 8–9
Nelson-class (RN BBs), 2
Neptune (RN CL), 41, 45
New Caledonia, 130
Newcastle (RN CL), 9, 56, 58, 60
Newcomb (USN DD), 215
New York (USN BB), xvi
Nicolson, Commander (D) H St L (RN),
    48–9, 48n12
Nimitz, Admiral Chester W (USN), 151,
    184–6, 200
Nishimura, Rear-Admiral/Vice-Admiral
    Shoji (IJN), 100–1, **100**, **103**, 104,
    192–6, 194n23, **197**, 198, 200, 200n32,
    202, 204–9, 217, 219, 228
Nishino, Commander Shigeru (IJN), 198,
    200n32, 202, **203**, 206, 206n41,
    206n42, 206n43, 211, 217, 217n77,
    220, 220n84
Nix, Lieutenant Commander Joshua (USN),
    129
Nordmark (KM AOR), see *Westerwald*
Norfolk (RN CA), 77, 79–81, **89**, 90–1, 168,
    172–4, 176, 182
North Cape, Norway, 152–4, 156n8, 158–9, 168
North Carolina (USN BB), 77n18
Novaro, Captain Umberto (RM), 50, 52–3
Nowaki (IJN DD), 129
Nürnberg (KM CL), 157

Obedient (RN DD), 162–4
Obdurate (RN DD), 162, 164–5
Ogura, Commander Masami (IJN), 115
Oil Pioneer (GB), 31–2
Oldendorf, Rear-Admiral Jesse B (USN),
    frontispiece, 187–8, **189**, **190**, **196**,
    200–2, **205**, 207–9, 207n46, 213–15,
    220, 223–4, 226
Onslow (RN DD), 162–5, **166**, 171
Operations
    Berlin, 70, **70**, **75**
    Catapult, 36
    Collar, 55
    Gearbox, 167
    Juno, 31, **32**, **33**
    MB 9, 55
    Nordmark, **27**
    Nordseetour, 67, **69**
    Ostfront, 169–82, **179**
    R4, 29
    Regenbogen, 158
    Rheinübung, 76–7, **94**
    Rösselsprung, 156
    Sho-1, 185, 185n3, 188, 191
    Sho-4, 185, 185n3
    Sizilien/Zitronella, 166, 166n17, 167n18
    Source, 167
    Sportpalast, 154
    Weserübung, 28
    White, 56

Wilfred, 29
Wunderland, 158n12
Opportune (RN DD), 170
Orama (RN AP), 31–2, **32**
Oran, Algeria, 36
Oribi (RN DD), 159n13
Orion-class (RN BBs), 1
Orwell (RN DD), 162–4
Oshio (IJN DD), 110–14
Oslo, Norway, 28

Padgett, Chief Watertender Raymond (USN),
    117
Palawan Island, Philippines, 185, 194
Palawan Passage, 196
Palembang, Sumatra, 106
Palliser, Rear-Admiral A F E (RN), 117
Panaon Island, Philippines, 194n21, 198, 200,
    204, 220, 224
Panay Island, Philippines, 96, 194, 196
Panjang Island, Java, **118**, 119–20
Papalemos (GR), 6
Paramushiro Island, Kuriles, 131, 131n5,
    133n13, 139n34, 142
Paris (MN BB), 36
Parker, Lieutenant Commander E N (USN),
    109, 111–13, 113n33
Parrott (DD218), 101–2, 108, 113–17, 113n34
Parry, Captain W E (RN), 20
Patrol Boat No.102 (IJN PC), see *Stewart*
Paul Jones (USN DD), 101–2, 123
PC37 (IJN PC), 101n8
Pearl Harbor, Hawaii, 97, 126, 130n2, 133,
    184, **186**, 200–1
Pecos (USN AO), 128–9
Pennsylvania (USN BB), **196**, 201, **205**,
    207n46, 209
Pernambuco (Recife), Brazil, 6
Perth (RAN CL), 119–22, **121**, 122n51, **123**
Peter and Paul Rocks, 67
Philippine Sea, 186, 188
Phillips, Captain A J L (RN), **89**
Phillips, Admiral Sir Tom (RN), 97–8, 98n5
Phoenix (USN CL), **193**, **195**, **196**, 201, 225
Piet Hein (RNeN DD), 108–9, **109**, **110**,
    111–12, 111n29, 116–17
Pillau, Germany, 165
Pillsbury (USN DD), 108, 113–14, 129
Pinguin (KM AMC), 70
Plymouth, England, **25**
Pola (RM CA), 56, 60
Pope (USN DD), **99**, 101–2, **103**, 108–9, **110**,
    111, 123, 125–6, **128**
Port Antonio, Jamaica, 66
Port Arthur, Texas, 4
Portland (USN CA), **190**, 201, 211, 221
Port Stanley, Falkland Islands, 11, 11n23, **12**,
    18, **19**, **25**
Postillion Islands, 100
Pound, First Sea Lord Admiral Sir Dudley
    (RN), 98n5, 153, 156

Prince of Wales (RN BB), 78, 78n23, 79n24, 81, **82**, 83, 83n35, 85–8, **88**, 90–1, **90**, **92**, **93**, 96, 96n1, **97**, 98, **98**, 153, 155
Prinz Eugen (KM CA), 76–81, 76n16, **79**, 81n27, 82n28, 83–8, **84**, **88**, **89**, 91, 91n42, **92**, **94**, 152
Provence (MN BB), 36, 38
PT130 (USN PT), 202
PT137 (USN PT), 207
PT152 (USN PT), 202
PT321 (USN PT), 220
PT323 (USN PT), 223, 223n91
PT490 (USN PT), 204
PT491 (USN PT), 204
PT493 (USN PT), 204
Puget Sound Navy Yard, Washington, **186**, **187**

Queen Elizabeth-class (RN BBs), 1

radars/radios/ESM antennas
  IJN
    No. 21, 146
  KM
    DeTe-Gerät (FuMG 38G), xvi, 22, 22n35
    FuMB 7 Naxos, 171, 173
    FuMO 22, 67n3, 70
    FuMO 23, 80
    FuMO 26, 171
    FuMO 27, 67, 67n3, 172
  RN
    Chain Home, xvi
    Type 79, xvi
    Type 79X, xvi
    Type 273M, **174**
    Type 273Q, 168, 168n22
    Type 279, **54**, 55n26, 70, **125**
    Type 281, **174**
    Type 284, 64, 79–80, 82–3, 92, 164, **169**, **174**, 175, 177n40, 209
    Type 284M, 168, 168n22
    Type 285, **174**, **177**
    Type 286M, 79
  USN
    BK, **187**
    BL-1, **187**
    CXAM, xvi
    FC (Mk3), **147**, 151n49, 209
    FD (Mk4), **147**, **148**, 151n49, 212, 212n63, **216**
    FH (Mk8), **187**, **190**, 209, 225, 225n93
    Mk12, 212n63
    Mk28, **190**
    SC-2, **147**
    SG, 135n18, **147**, **190**, 204
    SK, **190**
    TBS, 101, 101n10, 109, 113n33, 136n24, 206n43
    XAF, xvi, **xvi**
radios, see radars
Raeder, Admiral Erich (KM), 3, 77, 166, 168

Raleigh (USN CL), **39**
Ramillies (RN BB), 56, 58, 61, 71, 73
Rantau Pandjang (NE), 73
Rasenack, Commander F W (KM), 22
Ratai Bay, Sumatra, 108n23
Rawalpindi (RN AMC), 8, 8n18, **8**, **10**
Remey (DD688), 204
Renown (RN CB), **xiv**, 29–31, **29**, **30**, **39**, 56, **57**, 58–60, **60**, 62–3, 62n38, 74n14, **98**, 153
Renown-class (RN CBs), 1
Repulse (RN CB), 91, 96, 96n1, **98**, 153
Resolution (RN BB), 38
Revenge (RN BB), **69**
Revenge-class (RN BBs), 1
Reykjavik, Iceland, 153
Rhododendron (RN Cor), 163
Richard Beitzen (KM DD), 162–3, 165
Richelieu (MN BB), 36
Richmond (USN CL), 131, 133–7, 134n17, 139–40, 142n41, 146, 151
Riggs, Captain R S (USN), 131n6, 140
Rio de Janeiro, Brazil, 11
River Plate, 9, 11, **12**, 26
Rodgers, Captain Bertram J (USN), 134, 135n18, 140, 142, 146, 148, 151
Rodney (RN BB), xiv, 2, 8–9, 75, **93**
Rooks, Captain Albert H (USN), 119, 122
Roope, Lieutenant Commander B G (RN), 29–30
Roskill, Captain Stephen W (RN), 162
Rosyth, Scotland, 35, 88
Royal Sovereign (RN BB), 41, 43, **43**
RN units
  1st Cruiser Squadron, 153n1
  2nd Battle Squadron, 153
  3rd Division, 2nd Destroyer Flotilla, 48
  7th Cruiser Squadron, 55
  10th Cruiser Squadron, 153n1
  17th Destroyer Flotilla, 158
  18th Cruiser Squadron, 95, 153n1
  36th Destroyer Division, 170, 170n24, 172–3, 175–6, 183
  Home Fleet, 6, 8, 8n19, 66, 70, 77, 80, 96, 153–7, 168
  Force '1', 168, 171–3, 175–6
  Force '2', 168–71, 173, 175–6, 178, 182
  Force 'B', 55–6, 58, 63
  Force 'D', 56, 58
  Force 'F', 55–6, 56n27, 58
  Force 'G', 6, **10**, 11, **12**, **13**, **23**, **25**
  Force 'H', 36, 38, 55, 92
  Force 'R', 158–9, **169**
  Force 'Z', 96–8, 96n1, 98n5
  Mediterranean Fleet, 6, 38–40, **40**, **54**, 55–6
Ryujo (IJN CVL), 126

Saetta (RM DD), 45
St-Nazaire, France, 92
St Nicholas Point, Java, 119, 121–2
Sakito Maru (JP), 131–2

Sakiyama, Captain Shakao (IJN), 120
Saltburn (RN AM), xvi
Salt Lake City (USN CA), 131–42, 138n32,
    139n35, **141**, 142n41, **144**, 146–8, **147**,
    148, **149**, 150–1, **150**, 151n49
Salvador (Bahia), Brazil, 6
Samanoura Maru (JP), 101n8, 104
Samar Island, Philippines, 186, 196, 200, 219,
    224
San Bernardino Strait, 186, 200, 228
San Pedro Bay, Philippines, **188**, **195**
Sandefjord (NO), 69
Sanko Maru (JP), 131–2
Sansonetti, Rear-Admiral Luigi (RM), 56,
    59–61, **59**, **60**, **61**, 62n38
Sanur Roads, Bali, 108–10, 108n23, 112
Sape Strait, 100
Sarawak, Borneo, 99
Sasago Maru (JP), 110, 112–13, 116
Satsukawa Bay, Amami-O-Shima, 189
Saumarez (RN DD), 168, 178
Savage (RN DD), 168, 178
Scapa Flow, Orkney Islands, 29, 32, 77–80,
    153, **177**
Scharnhorst (KM CB), 7–9, **8**, **27**, 28, 30–1,
    30, 33–5, 70–1, 73–4, **75**, 77, 77n19,
    152, 156, 166–78, **178**, 178n42, 182–3,
    183n45, 217
Scharnhorst-class (KM CBs), 3, 3n6
Scheer (KM *Panzerschiff*), see *Admiral Scheer*
Schewe, Lieutenant Commander Georg
    (KM), 74
Schlettstadt (KM AO), 73
Schulz, Lieutenant Commander G-W (KM),
    74
Sclater, Lieutenant Commander C E L (RN),
    162, 164–5
Scorpion (RN DD), 168, 178, 183
Seawolf (RN SS), 154
Sebuko Island, Sunda Strait, **123**
Seeadler Harbor, Manus Island, 186
Sevilla, Spain, 72
Sheffield (RN CL), xvi, 56, 58, 158, 162, **164**,
    165, 168, 172–5, **174**, **177**
Sherbrooke, Captain R St V (RN), 157, 159,
    162–3, 166
Shigure (IJN DD), 192, 196, 198, 200, 202,
    203, 204, 206–7, 209, 211–12, 211n57,
    214, 217, 217n77, 219–20, 223–4,
    223n90
Shikinami (IJN DD), 119–20
Shima, Vice-Admiral Kiyohide (IJN), 188–9,
    191–6, 192n18, 194n23, 198, 200–1,
    206–7, 209, 217–20, 217n77, **221**, 224,
    227, 228
Shirakumo (IJN DD), 119, 122–3
Shiranuhi (IJN DD), 191, 217
Shirayuki (IJN DD), 119–20
Shoji, Captain Akira (IJN), **118**
Shropshire (RAN CA), **195**, 201, 209, 212,
    212n59

Sibuyan Sea, 186, 194, 196, 198, 200
Sicilian Narrows, 56
Sigourney (USN DD), 223, 223n90
Simon's Town, South Africa, **12**
Singapore, 96–9, 97n3, **97**, **98**, 98n5, 185
Sirio (RM TB), 56, 58
Skagerrak, 7, 26
Skagerrak, 7, 26
Smoot, Captain Roland M (USN),
    frontispiece, 207–9, 211–15, 228
Somerville, Vice-Admiral Sir James F (RN),
    55–6, 58–9, 63
Sørøysund, Norway, 170
Southampton (RN CL), 56, 58, 60–1, 64
Spitsbergen, Svalbard Archipelago, 166–7
Sprague, Rear-Admiral Thomas L (USN),
    186, 188, 228
Spruance, Admiral Raymond A (USN),
    186n5
Stange, Captain Rudolf (KM), 163–6
Stark, Admiral Harold (USN), 97
Stavanger, Norway, 65–6
Stewart (USN DD), 108, 113–14, 113n34,
    116–17, **116**, 117n41
Stord (RNoN DD), 168, 178
Strasbourg (MN CB), 36, 38
Stronghold (RN DD), 129, 129n63
Suffolk (RN CA), 77–81, 92
Sulu Sea, 194–6, **199**, 224
Suluan Island, Philippines, 187–8
Sunda Strait, 119, 121, 123, 125–6, 192
Surabaya, Java, 98–9, **106**, 108n23, 116–17,
    116, 119, 123, **124**, 125, 125n59, **127**
Surigao Strait, **frontispiece**, 184, 191–4,
    194n21, **197**, 198, 200, 202, **203**, 207,
    219–20, **221**, **222**, 224, 226, 228
Svalbard Archipelago, 166, 167n18
Sydney (RAN CL), 41, 46, 48–50, **50**, 52–3, **52**
Sydney, Australia, 116

Tacoma (DE), **22**
Taefel Hoek, Bali, 108, 108n23
Takagi, Rear-Admiral Takeo (IJN), 126
Takahashi, Vice-Admiral Ibo (IJN), 126
Takao (IJN CA), 129
Takao, Formosa, 191
Takoradi, Gold Coast, 68
Talbot, Commander Paul H (USN), 100–2,
    104
Tama (IJN CL), 131–2, **132**, 138–9, **143**, **145**,
    147, 151
Tamagawa Maru (JP), 102–3
Tanjung Priok, Java, 97, 106, 119, 122, **123**
Tantalus (RN SS), 167
Tarakan, Borneo, 96, 99
Taranto, Italy, 38, 40, 55–6
Tatsugami Maru (JP), 101n8
Tennessee (USN BB), **186**, **187**, **188**, 201, 209
Thor (KM AMC), 69
Tirpitz (KM BB), 152–7, 166–7, 170
Tjilatjap, Java, 100, 106, **106**, **107**, 108n22,
    109, 117, 119, 128–9

Tobruk, Libya, 38–9, 52
Tone (IJN CA), 129
Tórshavn, Faroe Islands, 35
Toulon, France, 38
Tovey, Vice-Admiral/Admiral Sir John (RN),
    40–1, 45, 70, 77–9, 78n22, 79n24,
    81–2, 91–2, 153–5, 158
Toyoda, Admiral Soemu (IJN), 189
Trento (RM CA), 45, **46**, 56, **61**, 62n38
Tribal-class (RN DDs), **166**
Trieste (RM CA), 56, **59**, 62
Trincomalee, Ceylon, 106
Tromp (RNeN CL), 97, 104, 108, 108n23, 111,
    112, 113–14, 116
Tromsø, Norway, 35, 154, 156, 158
Trondheim, Norway, 28–30, 35, 152–7
Tsingtao, China, **99**
Tsuruga Maru (JP), 100, 102, 104
Tuscaloosa (USN CA), 156, 167

U37 (KM SS), 71–2
U105 (KM SS), 74
U124 (KM SS), 74
U354 (KM SS), 158–9
U380 (KM SS), **62**
U617 (KM SS), **62**
U716 (KM SS), 171
Ushio (IJN DD), 191, 220
USN units
    Asiatic Fleet, 96–7, 96n2, 99, **99**, 106
    BatDiv4, 208
    Central Pacific Force, 185, 186, 186n5
    CruDiv4, **189**
    DesDiv58, 113, 123, 128
    DesDiv59, 100–1, 104
    DesDiv 'X-ray', 201
    DesRon14, 131n6, 140, 142, 142n42
    DesRon24, 201, 206
    DesRon54, 200, 204, 206
    DesRon56, **frontispiece**, 201, 207, 212,
        212n63, 214–15
    Fifth Fleet, 186n5
    Left Flank Force, **190**, **196**, 201, **205**, 207,
        216, 220
    Pacific Fleet, 130n2, 186
    Right Flank Force, **193**, **195**, 201, 212
    Seventh Fleet, 186, 202
    Third Fleet, 186, 186n5, 200
    TF5, 99
    TF34, 187, 200
    TF38, 186, 188–9
    TF79, **189**
    TG16.6/TG Mike, 131, 133, 146, 150
    TG38.4, 196
    TG70.1, 202
    TG77.2 (Central Philippine Attack Force
        Bombardment and Fire Support
        Group), 187, 200
    TG77.3, 188, 201

    TG77.4, 186
    TU77.4.1, 224
Usugumo (IJN DD), 131, 133n13

Valiant (RN BB), 38
Vestfjord, Norway, 29, **29**, 30–1, **30**, 155
Veteran (RN DD), 35
Vian, Captain/Admiral Sir Philip (RN), 28
Victorious (RN CV), 79, 79n24, 91–2, 153–5
Villefranche-sur-Mer, France, **39**
Virago (RN DD), 170, 173–4
Virginia (CSN Irc), xii, xiin2
Vittorio Veneto (RM BB), 38, 56, 62–4, **62**
Vizalma (RN Tr), 159, 163

W15 (IJN MS), 101, 104
Wakaba (IJN DD), 131–2, 191, 196, 196n26
Wake Island, 98
Wake-Walker, Rear-Admiral Frederic (RN),
    77, 80–2, 91–2
Waldschmidt, Captain T M (USN), 135
Waller, Captain Hector (RAN), 119–22
Warspite (RN BB), 2, 9, 33, **39**, 40–1, 41n7,
    41, 43, **44**, 45
Washbourne, Lieutenant R E (RN), 20
Washington (USN BB), 156, 187
Washington Naval Conference, 1–2
Watanabe, CFC Daiji (IJN), 115, 115n38,
    115n39
Wattenberg, Lieutenant Commander Jürgen
    (KM), 4
Wavell, General Sir Archibald (RA), 99
Westerwald (KM AOR), 4, 4n12, 67, 69, 73
West Virginia (USN BB), **frontispiece**, **186**,
    187, **188**, **190**, 201, 208–9, **210**
Weyler, Rear-Admiral G L (USN), 201, 208–9
Whipple (USN DD), 128–9
Whitworth, Vice-Admiral W J (RN), **29**, 31
Wichita (USN CA), 156
Wiley, Captain Herbert V (USN), 208
Wilhelmshaven, Germany, 3, 4, 9, **13**, **27**, 28,
    152, 165
Witte de With (RNeN DD), 125, 125n59

Yamamoto, Adm Isoroku (IJN), 130
Yamagumo (IJN DD), 192, 204–5
Yamashiro (IJN BB), 191, 192n14, 196, **199**,
    202, 204–9, **210**, 211–13, 215, **216**,
    217, **218**, 225–6, 226n100
York (RN CA), **54**

Z11 (KM DD), see *Bernd von Arnim*
Z18 (KM DD), see *Hans Lüdemann*
Z29 (KM DD), 162, 169
Z30 (KM DD), 169
Z33 (KM DD), 169, 172n32
Z34 (KM DD), 169
Z38 (KM DD), 169
Zanzibar, 73